# PUBLIC RELATIONS WRITING

## A Planned Approach For Creating Results

***Kerry Tucker***

President
*Nuffer, Smith, Tucker Inc.*

Instructor
*Department of Journalism*
*San Diego State University*

***Doris Derelian***

President
*Health Professions Training*

Adjunct Professor
*University of California*
*Los Angeles*



PRENTICE HALL, Englewood Cliffs, New Jersey 07632

**Library of Congress Cataloging-in-Publication Data**

Tucker, Kerry.
Public relations writing: a planned approach for creating results / Kerry Tucker, Doris Derelian.
p. cm.
ISBN 0-13-738451-3
1. Public relations. 2. Public relations—Authorship.
3. Publicity. I. Derelian, Doris. II. Title.
HM263.T78 1988
659.2—dc19 88-713
CIP

Editorial/production supervision
and interior design: Douglas Ens
Cover design: Al Townsend
Manufacturing buyer: Ed O'Dougherty


A Division of Simon & Schuster
Englewood Cliffs, New Jersey 07632



Printed in the United States of America
10 9 8 7 6 5 4 3 2 1

ISBN 0-13-738451-3

Prentice-Hall International (UK) Limited, *London*
Prentice-Hall of Australia Pty. Limited, *Sydney*
Prentice-Hall Canada Inc., *Toronto*
Prentice-Hall Hispanoamericana, S.A., *Mexico*
Prentice-Hall of India Private Limited, *New Delhi*
Prentice-Hall of Japan, Inc., *Tokyo*
Simon & Schuster Asia Pte. Ltd., *Singapore*
Editora Prentice-Hall do Brasil, Ltda., *Rio de Janeiro*

To:

Linda, Brannan, and Blake Tucker

Jimmie and Stacy Sullivan

Susan Derelian

# Contents

# Part II

# Uncontrolled Media

# Foreword

In *Public Relations Writing: A Planned Approach for Creating Results*, Kerry Tucker and Doris Derelian outline the working theory that guides most public relations today. The authors make explicit what most practitioners either don't acknowledge or don't recognize—the rationale for their recommendations and actions. For some, Tucker and Derelian's model of public relations provides a conceptual framework for practicing the art and science that is public relations. For others, the book challenges commonly held views of public relations and approaches to the practice. Either way, *Public Relations Writing* expands our understanding of how public relations works and how to apply theory in the workaday tasks of producing program materials and activities.

Many choose careers in public relations because they like the creative and technical aspects of public relations work. Given the tendency to focus on communication products and activities, it is easy for practitioners to assume and to let others cast them in the role of public relations technicians. Employers and clients, however, want results. They assume that those who claim professional status will have the technical skills.

Unlike other how-to techniques books in public relations, *Public Relations Writing* explains practices without losing sight of the ends sought. Tucker and Derelian link *means* to *ends* by using their working theories of learning and motivation to achieve program objectives. By doing so, they explain public relations practices as a purposive, goal-directed management function.

This perspective has its roots in their respective professional lives: Practitioner Tucker is president of a progressive public relations firm. Educator Derelian is consultant to organizations developing education programs to change behavior. The product of this collaboration reflects their interests in both the conceptual and operational levels of public relations. The book moves nicely between these two levels as the authors illustrate abstract theory with real-world examples—thus bridging the gap between theory and practice.

But even the best working theory does not explain all situations, and therefore a great deal of work remains to be done in developing and applying a body of knowledge related to public relations. *Public Relations Writing* may signal an important turning point, however, as it goes beyond pure description and seeks to explain the reasons why things are done the way they are. Until these reasons are made explicit, they cannot be tested. Making explicit the model behind most programs may be both the greatest need in practice and the greatest contribution of *Public Relations Writing.*

From my point of view, this is a banner year in the professionalization of public relations. At the same time I received the manuscript for the book you are about to read I also was given a copy of Professor John Pavlik's *Public Relations: What Research Tells Us.* Both books discuss theory and show how it applies to public relations practice. It is beginning to look as if public relations is developing a body of knowledge—one of the hallmarks of a profession. When the practice is acutally based on that body of knowledge, it will have achieved professional status. *Public Relations Writing* moves public relations toward that goal.

*Glen M. Broom, Ph.D.*
Professor of Journalism and
Head, Public Relations Emphasis
San Diego State University

# Preface

Numerous public relations writing and usage textbooks are in the marketplace today. Most deal with satisfying the needs of the news media and other public relations communications vehicles. Some of these textbooks address the target audience and its needs, but few, if any, offer a system for satisfying the needs/concerns/interests of their audience. Others address the principles of motivation, but none provides the framework for applying those principles to public relations writing and usage skills. There are media writing and usage textbooks that also review planning, but none provides a system for linking the public relations plan to message and media decisions.

Sixty-seven media writing and usage instructors responding to a nationwide mail survey by the authors validate the importance of providing students with basic communication skills. Of equal importance to the respondents, however, is the development of messages from public relations plans. Nine of ten survey respondents rated writing print and broadcast news releases, media placements, media relations, and developing messages from public relations plans as the most critical course objectives.

Thus this textbook has its points of difference:

1. It provides students and practitioners with a system to address not only the needs of the media but the needs/concerns/interests of audiences targeted for communications.
2. It introduces an outline to apply motivational principles to messages and media.
3. It incorporates writing and media usage as part of the planning process seeking specific and measurable public relations outcomes.

By addressing the needs of both the media and targeted audiences, and by applying motivational principles and planning where it is most needed—writing and media usage—the public relations team increases its odds for successful campaigns that not only generate extensive exposure but, more importantly, motivate targeted individuals to act.

# Acknowledgments

The seeds of this book germinated during the 1970s as we watched and participated in the application of innovative motivational principles from Madeline Hunter at UCLA, and others, to education programs successfully assisting people to change their behavior.

While most industry education programs across the country were holding themselves accountable for the number of materials they could disseminate, the Dairy Council of California, under the leadership of manager Douglas Fisk, was fostering the development of education programs that were documenting actual changes in the eating habits of children.

Programs at the Dairy Council continued to expand and develop, under the tutorage of education director Rus Shortridge and consultant Fred Neidermeyer. Education programs affecting the behavior of children expanded into programs affecting the behavior of adults. The schoolteacher was soon joined by the physician, registered dietitian, and dentist as communications channels.

In the spring of 1979, Tucker and Sharon Long, now public relations director at the Dairy Council, roughed out what was later refined as the operational step of the message/media outline. Less than a year later, Tucker and Derelian, at the time a doctoral candidate at UCLA's graduate school of education, sketched the text outline. Long continued to help create and test many of the concepts presented here.

The Dairy Council of California was the laboratory for the experimentation and development of this concept, which explains why it appears in numerous examples. Without the help of the Dairy Council, the planning and motivational principles outlined here would exist only in our own heads and not on paper. Its public relations team, with full support from manager Cynthia Carson and the board of directors, has invested heavily in the application of these percolating principles. Staff who have contributed to the evolution of the message/media outline through application with the mass media include Ron Kole, Beverly McKee, Sharon Levandovich, Jennifer Myers, William Truettner, Grace Young, and Carol Dorris.

The UCLA Graduate School of Education has had tremendous influence on the development of this text. Merl Wittrock, professor and leading cognitive theorist, has provided his own brand of provocative academic stimulation, as has professor Noreen Webb, Derelian's friend and confidant. The philosophical give-and-take with colleagues Cathy Moore, Valerie Cummings, and Ann Coulston brought intellectual grounding to our gut-level intuitions.

Notable individuals early on helped develop this from an interesting concept to textbook reality. The first was Tim Wallace, a University of California agricultural economist with whom we first shared the idea in 1979. It was he who suggested developing a book, specifically with our publisher, Prentice Hall, because of his textbook relationship with the company. His enthusiasm and friendly needling were a constant motivation. We also thank Alison Reeves, our editor at Prentice Hall, for her continued vigilance and support.

When we shared the concept with Allen Center, the mentor of public relations mentors, he tactfully tried to encourage us but, at the same time, he lit the candle of reality: "You need a market," he said. Center and his colleague, Glen Broom at San Diego State University, have been of tremendous help to us in tailoring this text to the second course in the university public relations curriculum: media writing and usage. So have those who have taught the course at San Diego State, specifically, David Robinson, Tammy Smith, Sue Raney, and Melissa Johnson.

There is one particular person, however, who tops the list of mentors, our good friend and partner for thirteen years, David Nuffer. Nuffer made possible the Nuffer, Smith, Tucker commitment of significant energy, dollars, and administrative support to this seemingly never-ending project, not to mention tossing an occasional pompom our way.

The management principles presented in this text are grounded in the experience of another colleague, Robert F. Smith, who has demonstrated their effectiveness with countless chief executives representing organizations throughout the world.

Each member of the NST team has been involved at some point or another and a few have gone beyond ribbons and medals to make this text a reality: Patricia Hemphill, Shirley Rodriguez, Gretchen Griswold, Al Townsend, Bill Trumpfheller, Valerie Lemke, Larry Nuffer, and David Freeman. Griswold was particularly helpful in expanding the use of the message/media outline with other clients.

The patience of a number of public relations colleagues has been tested with our pleas for chapter inputs. These include Dale Kemery, Mike Durant, Howard Back, Roy Heatley, Duane Borovek, Jonathan Gutman, and Wally McGuire. And then there are Earl Parker, Robin Schmidt, Lou Raffel, Jean Runyon, and Rick Tucker.

Although this book is dedicated to our families, we cannot help but expand on that acknowledgment with love and appreciation. The time commitment required, above and beyond the daily toils of employment, can make life difficult for family members with other agendas. To put some perspective on the issue, when we officially started this project, Tucker's daughter Brannan, now eighteen years old and in college, was in the sixth grade and his wife, Linda, was pregnant with, now six-year-old, daughter Blake. Derelian's brother Stan still called her "the kid," and her husband's daughter Stacy, now in broadcast journalism, was a mere "cub."

It has been a long haul, but we hope that we have helped expand the profession a fraction of an inch and we are depending on at least one reader to take the concept and stretch it a bit further.

*Kerry Tucker*
*Doris Derelian*
San Diego, California

# CHAPTER 1

# Maximizing the Impact of Public Relations Campaigns

### *IN THIS CHAPTER*

The chief executives and boards of directors of corporations, not-for-profit groups, and government agencies invest in public relations campaigns for one primary reason: to generate action or support for their point of view.

The impact of the mass media on changing attitudes or behaviors is a widely disputed issue among public relations professionals. Many experts say that the mass media can be expected to set the public agenda: to make issues important enough for consumers to notice but stopping short of influencing thought and action. Thus campaign objectives promising more than message retention and acceptance may be unrealistic.

Others suggest that well-conceived, researched, and executed campaign plans can affect moderate levels of attitude and behavior when audience needs/concerns/interests are incorporated into campaign messages delivered through appropriate media. Success is enhanced when interpersonal communications are stimulated to support publicity messages.

This chapter introduces a process designed to increase the probability of success in delivering public relations messages that work the hardest to facilitate change not only for the more common objectives of message retention and acceptance but also for attitudes and/or behaviors. Public relations techniques are driven by a strategic plan; messages and media incorporate a framework for applying motivational principles. Publicity is utilized to reach targeted audience segments directly and to stimulate one-on-one discussion in support of objectives. Additional public relations techniques support publicity messages.

### *CHAPTER OBJECTIVES*

The reader will be able to

1. Explain why some public relations campaigns succeed while others fail.

2. Describe how the mass media affect the public agenda.
3. Sequence the steps of the message/media outline.
4. Track a media message from receipt to behavior change.
5. Apply ethical considerations in planning a public relations campaign.

## PUBLIC RELATIONS: SOMETIMES IT WORKS, SOMETIMES IT DOESN'T

Corporations, government agencies, public officials, consumer activists, not-for-profit groups—all invest in the dissemination of information with the hope of moving attitudes or behaviors their way. Public relations (information or communication) campaigns are an investment in getting people to appreciate a point of view or action, an opportunity to demonstrate the benefit of adopting an intended attitude or behavior. Corporations may try to sell products and points of view on issues that affect them. Government agencies may try to decrease heart disease mortality or reduce the number of forest fires. Even scientists may try to enhance the availability of research funds with public relations campaigns.

The effective utilization of mass media publicity or news is the traditional strength of the public relations practitioner. Unlike marketing personnel, who deal with "controlled" communications channels like advertising (where the practitioner buys the final say over the message that reaches the consumer), public relations people deal in the "uncontrolled" world of publicity (meaning editors have the final say over the message communicated). This means that the publicity writer is expected not only to develop communications vehicles designed to meet the needs of the client and generate a response from the target audience but also to satisfy the journalist's criteria for news.

Sometimes it works, sometimes it doesn't.

## THE OBSTACLES TO CAMPAIGN SUCCESS

### The Message Mine Fields

At the outset practitioners must realize that there are no guarantees in the public relations business. Successful campaigns must overcome a number of obstacles, starting with a few givens. First, regardless of your message, a sizable proportion of the population will have no interest in what you have to say. Second, those who are interested typically will be only mildly so. Third, most people dismiss messages that do not support their current point of view. Fourth, people perceive, absorb, and remember content differently. Finally, a person's predisposition affects the adoption of attitudes and behaviors.[1]

The common bond that all unsuccessful campaigns share is a philosophy of flooding the media with publicity without enough careful thought to audience and message: quantity above quality. Although the volume of messages transmitted increases the odds of reaching the target audience, and repetition up to a point is important for message retention, heavy message flow alone is insufficient to attract attention or stimulate learning from the mass media.[2]

### Mass Media Impact Contested

The power of the mass media cannot be taken for granted. Years ago grandiose assumptions were made about their effect on attitudes and behavior. Then the pendulum swung to the opposite pole and academicians began to question whether or not the media had any effect. Today, the debate roars on.

Scientists examining the impact of public information campaigns can be grouped into two divergent camps. On one side are the "neo-null effects" proponents, who view media as largely impotent. A closely aligned segment of the scientific community advocates a slightly moderate variation of this approach called "limited effects." On the other side are the academicians and practitioners who believe media to be potentially influential, especially if a campaign is properly designed and effects are sensitively measured and interpreted.[3]

There appears to be agreement in the academic community on at least three fronts:

1. The news media set the public agenda.
2. The news media stimulate interpersonal communication.
3. The news media influence the social milieu.

### The Public Agenda

Belief is widespread that the media most successfully generate public interest for an issue. Proponents of agenda setting believe that the editorial gatekeepers can help individuals become aware of an issue and, through day-to-day exposure, make it important. Its influence, they say, stops short of affecting how individuals think about that issue. In other words, the issue becomes important because of repeated coverage and positioning in the media, but any change in behavior resulting from that exposure is probably due to other influences (e.g., the one-on-one influence of friends, acquaintances, or family).

> In what way do you discuss news stories with others? How often has the topic of conversation been a recent news item?

### Stimulating Interpersonal Communication

How many conversations do you remember in the past few days that began with "Did you see the story in today's paper on . . ." or "I heard on the radio coming to work that . . ." or "I saw it on the news last night. . . ."?

Mass media can stimulate one-on-one discussion of an issue, particularly when messages are packaged to meet audience needs, concerns, or interests. Agenda-setting research has found that political issues stressed by the media are perceived as more important topics for interpersonal discussion, apparently because people think that what is "in the news" is interesting to others.[4] And one primary motivation for turning to the mass media in the first place is to prepare for social interaction.

"In a very real way, a principal social function of the mass media may be to facilitate interpersonal communication," says Steven Chaffee of Stanford University.[5] "The impersonality of mass communications may be socially quite functional in some situations," he says. "One can seek information via the media without exposing his ignorance on a subject; thus prepared he can enter more confidently into interpersonal communication."[6]

### The Social Milieu

There are additional social factors involved in the development of public attitudes and behaviors. Noelle-Newmann's "spiral of silence" theory contends that individuals often create attitudes and behaviors based on how they think others might view them. An individual is more inclined to conserve energy when mass media messages support the perception that others are conserving energy.[7] If mass media messages suggest that an individual will be isolated for a particular attitude or behavior, the threat of isolation can be more important than expressions of judgment.[8] A point of view, then, is strengthened when it is packaged to represent the majority view.

A point of view can also become predominant by default if voiced by the "right" spokesperson. Nelkin suggests that recent research has verified that "the effect press messages will have depends on the social context in which they are received. This context includes the educational background, personal experience and reference group of readers."[9]

### The Impact of the Mass Media

There are those in the scientific community, such as Davison, Boylan, and Yu of Columbia University, who do not believe that the full range of the societal effects of the mass media has been studied, partly because of the difficulty of examining these effects:

> One cannot put a whole society in a laboratory and in the real world there are so many variables that one scarcely knows which to measure, if indeed they can be measured at all. Furthermore, almost every imaginable type of effect is possible, and researchers are constantly stumbling on implications they did not anticipate.[10]

"In the present state of knowledge, there is a continuing flow of information and ideas through society," says Wilbur Schramm, a sage among mass communications investigators. "The mass media greatly influence—directly or indirectly—what flows through these channels. Certain individuals also influence it by sharing their special knowledge, expertise or convictions on a certain topic by being articulate or talkative," Schramm says.[11]

> Describe why you think there has been so much controversy surrounding the role of the mass media in reinforcing or changing public attitudes and/or behavior.

## IMPROVING CAMPAIGN SUCCESS ODDS

### Principles for Success

The authors contend that public relations campaigns utilizing the mass media as a primary vehicle with its mix of techniques can be designed to facilitate change more consistently not only in setting the public agenda but also in leading toward attitude and behavior change. For example, effective mass media campaigns with public service issues have been reported in the fields of mental retardation, smoking, drinking, littering,[12] and heart disease.[13]

Mendelsohn points to five principles common to successful campaigns:

1. Target audience needs, goals, and capabilities are assessed.
2. There are systematic campaign and production plans.
3. Evaluations of performance against plan are conducted continually throughout the campaign.
4. The mass media and interpersonal communication are used to complement one another.
5. The appropriate media are selected for each target audience.[14]

### Operating from a Public Relations Plan

Practitioners who hold the highest campaign batting averages are those operating from strategic public relations plans seeking end results (i.e., increased product sales, legislative victories, reduced littering). The planning process provides the practitioner with a data base to successfully launch campaigns that accelerate emerging opportunities, redirect emerging threats or obstacles, and recommend internal readjustments to adapt best to change when necessary. The last option deserves brief discussion.

### Internal Adjustments Needed at Times

Practitioners are, first and foremost, in the business of creating a positive environment for an organization to pursue its business. Communications are an important means but not the end-all. There are times when communications programs take a back seat to internal adjustments that help the organization manage environmental changes.

The ideal public relations scenario would find the practitioner charged with guiding his or her organization through the ups and downs of an ever-changing environment. Public relations plans would be in place, including systems to spot threats and opportunities as they emerge in the social, political, economic, competitive and technological environments. Planning decisions would fall into three categories:

1. Trying to change publics who can affect your organization
2. Trying to adapt your organization to the needs, concerns, and interests of those publics who can affect you
3. Trying to do both[15]

The most effective means for managing external environmental forces is to help adjust and adapt both the organization and its publics to the constantly changing environment.[16]

### Campaigns Need Measurable Objectives

Public relations techniques are most effectively utilized when they are designed to achieve specific objectives. Each news release, public service announcement, direct-mail letter, or company newspaper can be systematically executed to support public relations objectives.

Grunig and Hunt cite five impact levels of potential public relations objectives in order of achievement difficulty:

1. The act of communication itself ("I received the messages.")
2. Message retention ("I remember the message.")
3. Message acceptance ("I believe the message.")
4. Change in attitude ("I believe the message and intend to act on it.")
5. Change in behavior ("I acted on the message.") [17]

Whereas each of these objectives can be acceptable, levels 2 through 5 should be considered "end result" objectives because they are commitments to reach the mind of the audience in some quantified fashion. To evaluate objectives in levels 2 through 5 requires pre- and post-campaign research.

Level 1 communications objectives (i.e., to reach 5 million households with regional news conference message by June 15) should, at the very least, include messages packaged to affect thought and action positively even though they are not evaluated at that level of impact.

Dozier warns against setting objectives at level 1 because they represent measuring *process* rather than *end result* and have weak linkage to organizational benefit or payoff.[18] Right or wrong, it is safe to say that most organizations operate from process objectives. Mendelsohn argues against going too far on the other end with grandiose but unrealistic public relations objectives. Instead of an objective to eradicate drunk driving, for example, he recommends an objective to cut drunk driving by a small proportion.[19]

What represents a small proportion? No more than 20 percent for behavioral objectives, say Grunig and Hunt.[20] Others find that the percentage varies according to the situation.

A level 5 behavioral objective for smoking reduction might be to increase those attending smoking-cessation classes by 20 percent by December 31. Likewise, the public information staff of the forestry department might be more realistic with an objective to increase the number of park visitors adopting fire safety guidelines by 10 percent by December 31 than with a commitment to reduce the number of forest fires. (The development of public relations plans is detailed in Chapter 2.)

Levels 4 and 5 objectives are more realistic outcomes when campaigns address specific problems or situations. The identification and analysis of publics and messages by situation can enhance the effects of public relations programs.[21] A pregnant woman is more receptive to health messages because of her pregnancy. A person living in a highly urbanized area is more receptive to acting on controlled growth messages (e.g., signing a slow-growth initiative petition) because of his or her already crowded environment.

Practitioners should keep in mind that most chief executive officers *assume* that public relations investments will result in levels 4 and 5, even when objectives are established at level 1.

> **What would you say about the differences in levels of objectives to a CEO who accepts process objectives but expects behavior change?**

Although attempts to change behavior with mass media campaigns may be considered unrealistic by some, the practitioner can increase the odds of success by

1. Setting objectives as high on a behavior impact ladder as possible
2. Developing messages designed to affect the way people think (attitudes change) and act (behavior change)

### Message/Media Outline: Links Plan with Motivation Principles

Once plans are laid, public relations practitioners turn to the development of the message(s)—what to say to achieve objectives—and media—the tools used to say it. Message and media decisions are strengthened by using what we call a message/media outline.

The message/media outline applies a framework of motivational principles to public relations writing and usage skills. Although it may appear to be a vast oversimplification of the complexity of communication, such a system provides the practitioner with a tool, similar to that used by other disciplines, for the successful pursuit of reinforcing or changing thoughts and actions of target publics. Most successful public relations campaigns, in fact, are based on the implicit use of the concepts presented. The message/media outline explicates these concepts though it or they may not work in every situation.

The message/media outline (described in detail in Chapter 3) begins with six steps:

1. Identify the ultimate action you want from the reader, viewer, or listener.
2. Identify audience(s). Who are the decision makers? Who casts the votes on legislation that can impact your organization? Who makes the purchase decision for your product? Secondarily, who influences the decision makers?
3. Identify needs/concerns/interests of audience(s). What are the primary motivations that will cause action (message retention, acceptance, attitude and/or behavior change)?
4. Write message.
5. Choose channels of communications. Where do your audience members get their information?
6. Select spokesperson(s). Who is the most believable?

The most effective public relations programs use research to validate proposed target audiences (those that affect or are affected by the public relations plan), the best ways to reach them, the identification of their needs/concerns/interests, their existing attitudes toward the product, issue, or organization, and the strengths and weaknesses of the organization's point of view. "Without considering audience attributes, there is greater likelihood that receivers will ignore the message, misunderstand the content, reject applicability to self, challenge claims with counter arguments or derogate the source," says Charles Atkin of Michigan State University.[22]

The research required to make decisions for the first six steps provides a base for the final step prior to communications:

7. Package message to raise an audience need/concern/interest and offer product, issue, or organization as a means of fulfilling that need, minimizing that concern, or satisfying that interest.

This seventh and final step, prior to actual communication, houses the framework for operationalizing motivational principles in public relations writing and other techniques. A series of question clusters guides professionals in packaging and evaluating the public relations message. These clusters include

1. Does the communication raise an audience need, concern, or interest? (Can audience members easily put themselves into the situation? Can you paint a real-life scenario with words or visuals?)
2. Is your product, issue, or organization offered as a solution in a clear and concise manner? Are the benefits to the solution clearly presented? (Can the receiver jot down in one sentence "what's in it for me"?)
3. Are the consequences of leaving the need, concern, or interest unresolved clearly presented?
4. Have you helped the individual members of the target audience mentally rehearse or think through the action you would like them to take?

The seventh step applies motivational principles that initiate an internal process in the minds of receivers, increasing the likelihood that public relations techniques will cause change.

> When was the last time you took into account beforehand the benefits of acting or the consequences of not acting?

## THE MENTAL ROUTE TO BEHAVIOR CHANGE

A successful internal process in the receiver's mind takes a specific route to behavior change:

The message is transferred to personal, real-life needs/concerns/interests.

↓

The intention (to act) is triggered with an individual's own analysis of perceived benefits and consequences.

↓

The message is processed against past experience and perceived expectations of success and failure.

↓

Behavioral decisions (to act or not to act) are made.

↓

Behavior is manifested.

↓

Positive attitudes and values are formed from successful experience with the new behavior, and repetition of the cycle is encouraged.

Development of attitudes and behaviors sometimes transpose with attitude preceding behavior. Attitude alone is not an accurate indication of behavior.[23] An assumption that a positive attitude automatically leads to the desired action spells danger. However, the message/media outline advances a public relations message regardless of the order in which attitudes and behaviors form.

### Individual Motivation: Weighing the Consequences

Though the internal process described may appear similar to other sender-receiver concepts prevalent in the public relations literature, distinct points of difference can be drawn from learning theory. New knowledge about the cognitive process (how the brain utilizes information) has expanded what was once simply stimulus-response "knee-jerk" learning.

We now know more about the mental processing that occurs between the stimulus and the response. We know that when motivation is aroused, an individual has already evaluated the benefits of action against the consequences of inaction and has compared and contrasted past experience with his or her expectations for future success or failure with the behavior. Furthermore, messages that support the ultimate response—a reinforced or changed attitude and/or behavior—cite both the positive benefits of acting and the negative consequences of not acting on the message. The focus, then, is on packaging the public relations campaign message to take advantage of the benefits and avoid the consequences.

### A Case in Point

A good illustration of successfully incorporating the public relations plan with the message/media outline evolved when osteoporosis became an important health issue for women in the early 1980s. Adequate calcium intake was considered by scientists to be a primary prevention step.

When the issue caught fire and hit the public agenda, the dairy industry, whose products provide the most dietary calcium, experienced moderate increases in consumption, but sales of calcium supplements soared. The Dairy Council of California, in its annual assessment of the external environment, identified this as a priority threat to dairy foods consumption. Upon researching the issue, two important variables were uncovered that would be the basis for a national campaign to decrease consumption of calcium supplements:

1. Leading nutrition scientists shared a universal concern over the long-term health and safety consequences of a trend toward increased public use of vitamin and mineral supplements for the prevention of diseases like osteoporosis and cancer.
2. Adult women knew they needed more calcium but were unsure of the best overall source: additional dairy foods or vitamin and mineral supplements. In addition, 41 percent of adult women surveyed in California said they were consuming calcium in supplement form.

Consequently, the following objective surfaced to manage this priority threat to dairy food consumption: to decrease the use of calcium supplements by 20 percent among California women by January 31, 1987. The message/media outline looked like this:

1. *What is the ultimate action you want from the reader, viewer, or listener?*

   **To increase consumption of dairy foods.**
2. *Who are the audience decision makers?*

   **Adult women.**

   *Who influences those decision makers?*

   **Health and medical professionals and mass media.**
3. *What is a need, concern, or interest of the decision maker?*

   **Health and safety for self and household.**
4. *What is the message?*

   **Choose food instead of supplements for nutrients (i.e., dairy foods instead of calcium supplements).**
5. *What are the channels of communication?*

   **Mass media, specialty health publications, professional journals.**
6. *Who are the spokespersons?*

   **Physicians, scientists, registered dietitians, and their professional associations.**
7. *How can the message be packaged to raise an audience need/concern/interest and offer product, issue, or organization as a means of fulfilling that need, minimizing that concern, or satisfying that interest?*

CONCERN. Health and medical professionals are concerned for the long-term health and safety consequences of using vitamin and mineral supplements to prevent diseases such as osteoporosis.

SOLUTION. Consume nutrients from food instead of supplements for prevention of diseases like osteoporosis (i.e., calcium-rich foods; 75 percent of the calcium in the diet comes from dairy foods).

CONSEQUENCES OF INACTION. Potential for toxicity and changing natural balance of nutrients.

MENTAL REHEARSAL. One daily eight-ounce glass of milk, slice of cheese, or container of yogurt will increase calcium intake by one-third.

The strategy for carrying out the objective included organizing a coalition of physicians and scientists at a Los Angeles news conference, co-sponsored by the California Dietetic Association, to air their concerns about supplement use. The National Dairy Board and National Dairy Council expanded the campaign nationally with news conferences in Washington, D.C., and New York City. Local dairy councils held additional media events in Texas, Illinois, and other areas. The American Dietetic Association, American Institute of Nutrition, American Society for Clinical Nutrition, and National Council Against Health Fraud joined the campaign. The American Medical Association publicized a statement paralleling the coalition's view.

Thousands of news stories were generated in slightly less than a year questioning the safety of vitamin and mineral supplements and calling on consumers to get their nutrients from food instead of supplements.

The mass media made the issue important with publicity that eventually took on a life of its own (as most successful issues do), with reporters continuing to write their own stories throughout the year and beyond.

Research conducted prior to the campaign and one year later revealed that women who said they consumed supplements dropped by 27 percent.

> How would you summarize the results of this campaign if asked to do so by your superior?

### Some Campaigns Work, Some Don't

It is difficult to make blanket statements about the direct impact of the mass media on consumer attitudes or behavior. While we have presented evidence of campaigns positively affecting end results, there is also tremendous evidence suggesting that this is far from the norm. And we agree.

What we can say, however, is that well-conceived and orchestrated public relations campaigns utilizing the mass media can affect public attitudes and behavior both directly and indirectly. Campaigns enhance their odds for success when they are complemented by additional public relations techniques (i.e., community presentations, self-instructed educational programs, particularly face-to-face presentations and individualized instruction). While every campaign does not succeed to the attitudinal or behavioral level, successful practitioners nevertheless quietly enjoy their fair share of attitudinal or behavioral successes that remain unreported in the professional literature.

We believe the process described in this text will enhance the consistency of campaigns successfully affecting attitudes and behaviors.

## ETHICS: CRUCIAL TO YOUR INTEGRITY

With orchestrated attempts to change the way individuals act or behave come serious ethical considerations. Communications can be an all-powerful vehicle, particularly mass media publicity. A mass media campaign can both help and hurt people. Its message can lead individuals to beneficial actions, but it is also capable of misleading. The responsibility for truth and fair play falls squarely on the practitioner's shoulders.

### Mutual Benefit

Practitioners should make it their business to maintain the organizational conscience and ensure that ethical issues are aired at the planning table. Mutual benefit is a valuable ally here. By definition, an organization with a philosophy of *mutual benefit* is one whose decisions reflect a value for ensuring that organizational action equally benefits both the organization and affected constituencies.

> Describe the mutual benefit concept as it applies to a public utility engaged in a campaign to decrease energy usage?

### Ethical Decisions

Responsible organizations rarely get into trouble with black and white, right or wrong issues. The more difficult shades of debatable gray cause the most anxiety. "The difficulty of trying to pin down ethics in terms of standards or principles of conduct is that there is so little uniformity," Debra Miller of Howard University told practitioners attending a conference on ethics in public relations.

"Short of what is legal or illegal, determination of what kinds of conduct are acceptable in various circumstances, comes down to the individual or the group conscience."[24]

At that same conference, George A. Borden pointed to individual values as guides to decision making:

> When we act or say something that compromises one or more of our values, our psychological structures let us know that something isn't quite right by the feeling of dissonance that arises. If we put this in the context of communication and ethics we can say that when we compromise our values we are unethical, and being ethical means keeping our values in balance. This definition of ethics is based on the premise that all human beings are responsible for their own behaviors, whether these behaviors are part of an intimate interpersonal relationship or a corporation merger.[25]

Therefore, it is an important responsibility for the practitioners with discomforting "gut feelings" to react when plans develop a course that may negatively affect organizational constituencies.

In the end, products, issues, or organizations that do not benefit both the organization and its public will *not* be successful long-term, regardless of the public relations techniques utilized. And products, issues, or organizations that are not of mutual benefit but are positioned to be may fool target publics once or twice, but success will be short term and the consequences of diminished organizational credibility will remain long after.

The identification and promotion of the mutual benefit an organization, issue, or product shares with the target audience are the cornerstone of public relations success. No amount of bells or whistles can change this truism.

## SUMMARY


- Public relations campaigns depend on the practitioner understanding the value of the mass media, their strengths and limitations in providing access to the targeted audience.
- The mass media present an agenda for public consideration. Most researchers acknowledge that attitudes and behaviors are determined by more than simple receipt of media output.
- The public relations plan is the strategic operating device used by successful practitioners.
- The message/media outline maximizes public relations impact.
- The five-level impact ladder traces potential public relations objectives in terms of achievement difficulty.
- Public relations campaigns increase odds for success when each practitioner packages materials for audience attitude and behavior change.
- Ethics in public relations comes out of recognition that the philosophy of mutual benefit to the organization and to the audience underlies all planning and implementing decisions.


## EXERCISES

1. Explain to a fellow reader, or to yourself, why some public relations campaigns might fail at achieving their stated outcomes.
2. Define each step of the message/media outline.
3. Identify and explain how two current issues achieved significance through the mass media.
4. Write a brief explanation of the concept "mutual benefit."
5. For each of the following examples, identify the key internal processing step the receiver uses:
   a. The receiver stops working to listen to an advertisement on television.
   b. The receiver remembers what happened last time he used the product.
   c. The receiver says to herself, "I can really impress my friends with that product."
   d. The receiver feels very competent after using the product.

## REFERENCES


1. Scott M. Cutlip, Allen H. Center, and Glen M. Broom, *Effective Public Relations*, 6th ed. (Englewood Cliffs, NJ: Prentice-Hall, 1985), p. 273.

2. Charles Atkin, "Mass Media Information Campaign Effectiveness," in *Public Communications Campaigns*, ed. Ronald Rice and William Paisley (Beverly Hills, CA: Sage Publications, 1981), p. 268.
3. Ibid., p. 267.
4. Steven Chaffee, "Mass Media in Political Campaigns: An Expanding Role," in *Public Communications Campaigns*, ed. Ronald Rice and William Paisley (Beverly Hills, CA: Sage Publications, 1981), p. 194.
5. Steven Chaffee, "The Interpersonal Context of Mass Communication," in *Current Perspectives in Mass Communication Research*, ed. F. Gerald Kline and Philip J. Tichenor (Beverly Hills, CA: Sage Publications, 1972), p. 98.
6. Ibid., p. 100.
7. Barbara Farhar-Pilgrim and F. Floyd Shoemaker, "Campaigns to Affect Energy Behavior," in *Public Communications Campaigns*, ed. Ronald Rice and William Paisley (Beverly Hills, CA: Sage Publications, 1981), p. 166.
8. Elisabeth Noelle-Neumann, "The Spiral of Silence: A Theory of Public Opinion," *Journal of Communications*, 24, no. 2 (Spring 1974), 43.
9. Dorothy Nelkin, *Selling Science* (New York: W. H. Freeman, 1987), p. 74.
10. W. Phillips Davison, James Boylan, and Frederick Yu, *Mass Media Systems and Effects* (New York: Praeger, 1976), p. 184.
11. Wilbur Schramm, *Men, Messages & Media* (New York: Harper & Row, 1973), p. 124.
12. Atkin, "Mass Media Information Campaign Effectiveness," pp. 270–71.
13. Nathan McCoby and Douglas Solomon, "Heart Disease Prevention," in *Public Communications Campaigns*, ed. Ronald Rice and William Paisley (Beverly Hills, CA: Sage Publications, 1981), p. 115.
14. Rice and Paisley, *Public Communications Campaigns*, p. 7.
15. James E. Grunig and Todd Hunt, *Managing Public Relations* (New York: Holt, Rinehart & Winston, 1984), p. 94.
16. Cutlip, Center, and Broom, *Effective Public Relations*, p. 196.
17. Grunig and Hunt, *Managing Public Relations*, p. 134.
18. David Dozier, *Style Guide for Writing a Public Relations Plan*, 1983, p. 4. (San Diego State University [classroom document]).
19. Atkin, "Mass Media Information Campaign Effectiveness, " p. 272.
20. Grunig and Hunt, *Managing Public Relations*, p. 133.
21. Ibid., p. 130.
22. Atkin, "Mass Media Information Campaign Effectiveness," p. 267.
23. A. W. Wicker, "Attitudes vs. Actions: The Relationship of Verbal and Overt Behavioral Responses to Attitude Objects," *Journal of Social Issues*, 25 (1969), pp. 51–78.
24. Debra A. Miller, "Public Relations Ethics: To Teach or Not to Teach," in *Ethical Trends and Issues in Public Relations Education*, ed. Debra Miller and Barbara A. Hines (Washington, D.C.: International Association of Business Communicators, U.S. District 3, May 1986), p. 58.
25. George A. Borden, "Value and Ethics: The Communicator's Dilemma, in *Ethical Trends and Issues in Public Relations Education*, ed. Debra Miller and Barbara A. Hines (Washington, D.C.: International Association of Business Communicators, U.S. District 3, May 1986), p. 45.

# CHAPTER 2

# Planning the Public Relations Campaign

*IN THIS CHAPTER*

Strategic planning incorporates each of the four steps in the public relations process: research, planning, action, and evaluation. The process helps top management and the public relations team gather data for planning decisions both internally and externally. (Research seeks answers to the planning questions: Where are we now? How did we get here?)

With such a data base, planning decisions are made to help the organization both adjust itself and seek to adjust the outside environment toward mutually beneficial end results. (Planning seeks answers to the questions: Where do we want to be? What is the best route to take us from our current position to where we want to be?)

Plans are executed with very specific outcomes (Action), evaluated, and adjusted accordingly at regular midcourse intervals and at the completion of a public relations program or campaign. (Evaluation seeks answers to the questions: Will this action take us where we want to be? Did we get where we wanted to be?)

Strategic public relations plans, like the public relations process itself, should be viewed as a living, breathing system of environmental assessment (both internally and externally), organizational adjustment, and communications aimed at achieving goals and objectives in public harmony.

*CHAPTER OBJECTIVES*

The reader will be able to

1. Describe each element of a strategic plan, its benefit to an organization, and how it supports the four-step process of public relations.
2. Write a public relations mission statement.
3. Write public relations objectives, strategies, and action plans.
4. Prepare a situational public relations plan.

## THE PUBLIC RELATIONS PLAN

Planning, according to the American Management Associations, is the process by which an organization, or its public relations department, can become what it wants to become.[1] The charge of the public relations plan, then, is to set and achieve goals and objectives that both generate a positive environment for an organization to pursue its business and directly support marketing goals. Publics include not only customers to support the latter goal but also government officials, employees, and neighbors who can affect an organization's operational environment.

Public relations plans may include objectives to create public awareness for an emerging issue that supports an organization's mission. On the other hand, public relations might be called on to redirect an issue that poses a threat to the corporate mission. Public relations objectives may also include increasing product awareness and acceptance with customer groups. They may go a step farther to stimulate positive public attitudes and actual sales for a product or votes for a political candidate (behavior formation or change). Finally, objectives can also include public acceptance and value for an organization and its community contributions.

Of equal importance, public relations counsel may cause an organization to consider the consequences of a proposed action that does not mutually benefit the enterprise and those who are affected by its action.

Planning incorporates the four steps of the public relations process: research, planning, action, and evaluation.

### Research

Ideally, a formal, ongoing, fact-finding system is in place. One such system is an environmental scanning process whereby opinion research, periodicals, professional and trade meetings, and networks of individuals are tracked for trends that may affect an organization positively or negatively.

If such a system does not exist, the environment should be assessed at least annually for emerging threats and opportunities to the organization. That assessment is then used as a data base for annual planning.

### Planning

During the planning process, the external and internal assessments serve as a baseline for planning decisions. The key questions are: What are the most crucial threats or opportunities to an organization's mission? What is the likelihood of such a threat or opportunity occurring in a specified period of time?

Priority threats or opportunities are validated with formal research, and decisions are made either to adjust internally or set public relations plans to redirect threats or accelerate opportunities.

### Action

Once the issues are defined and plans are designed to manage them, it is time to implement the mix of public relations techniques organized to move the audience to action—be it message retention, message acceptance, or changes in attitudes and/or behavior. This text is organized to help formulate this action.

### Evaluation

The success or failure of planned objectives within the public relations plan is usually the first question asked in program evaluation. "The only effective way to evaluate anything is to establish a set of specific goals and objectives before any program is launched," says Walter K. Lindenmann of Ketchum Public Relations. "You're kidding yourself if you try to evaluate a program and start laying out the ground rules for evaluation after a project is already underway."[2]

### Link Between Planning and Activity

This text is designed to provide the necessary link between the public relations plan and public relations activity. Publicity for the sake of publicity, for example, means far less than publicity designed to support specific organizational goals and objectives. The process described in this text guards against the development of public relations materials without well-thought-out outcomes.

The long-form approach to planning describes the ideal planning situation with strategic planning being utilized to systematically anticipate change that can affect the mission of an organization with plans to best manage it. The short-form describes a method for developing a plan to manage very specific situational public relations problems or opportunities when circumstances do not provide the luxury of the ideal planning situation.

## THE STRATEGIC PLANNING PROCESS

Public relations plans ideally support the direction outlined in organization-wide planning. However, if no formal planning process exists, then public relations teams have the opportunity to demonstrate the value of planning to the rest of the organization. That value is best demonstrated by involving top management in the process. Planning is generally best addressed in two ways:

1. Developing strategic (long-term) plans
2. Developing operational (annual) plans

Operational plans constitute an organization's annual commitment to performance. In a public relations plan this could include the expected outcomes of public relations programs aimed at target audiences in a year's time.

Operational plans are most effective when designed as the first-year game plan for a long-term strategic direction. Typically, more than just a media event here and there is needed to move an audience to adopt a new attitude or behavior. The strategic planning process helps managers think beyond a year's time to where they would like to see their organization in three or five years. After charting long-term aspirations, the operational or first-year plan launches the strategic plan.

The strategic plan is just as much process as it is a written document. With annual updates management teams constantly revise their long-term direction, taking advantage of new opportunities and managing threats as they appear in the environment.

One of the biggest problems public relations counselors face is clients who often are not sure what they want from public relations besides "get our name in the paper" (under the assumption that publicity will increase business). Clients have given thought to techniques but have not thought through specifically what those techniques should accomplish for them.

The effectiveness of communication and action, according to Cutlip, Center, and Broom, depends on sound planning.

> Lack of strategic thinking and planning can lead to communications programs that reinforce controversies rather than resolve them; waste money on audiences that are not there; or add confusion, instead of clarification, to misunderstanding. In this process an organization is, in effect, making tomorrow's decisions today. Many of the difficult public relations problems presently being dealt with were born of yesterday's spur-of-the-moment decisions.[3]

The strategic planning process consists of a systematic review of four questions before establishing the annual commitments associated with an operational plan:

1. Where are we now?
2. How did we get here?
3. Where do we want to be?
4. What is the best route to take us from our current position to where we want to be?

Answers to these questions can be formulated by assessing the internal and external environments and developing action plans to manage the most critical internal strengths and weaknesses and external threats and opportunities. The assessments are necessary data-gathering steps before the definition of public relations problems or opportunities.

> How do the answers to the strategic planning process questions influence the content of the plan?

## INTERNAL ASSESSMENT

This is the "get-your-act-in-order" phase of the planning process. The steps include written clarification of the organization and/or public relations department:

- ☐ Mission
- ☐ Philosophy
- ☐ Culture
- ☐ Policies
- ☐ Organizational structure
- ☐ Performance backcast
- ☐ Strengths and weaknesses

### The Public Relations Mission

The internal assessment for public relations begins with a study of how public relations can best support an organization's mission from the perspective of managing public relationships. Public relations needs its own written mission statement or purpose. The public relations plan should evolve from such a written statement. Classic elements of a mission statement include: What needs do we meet? For whom? How? Where?[4]

To illustrate, the mission of GTE Sprint's state legislative public relations group, following deregulation of the telephone industry, was to make GTE Sprint the leading advocate for improved understanding and appreciation for a competitive telephone marketplace among targeted state legislative communities.[5]

What needs did GTE Sprint's legislative public relations group meet?

Improved understanding and appreciation for a competitive telephone marketplace

For whom? (targeted state legislative communities)

How? (not identified in mission)

Where? (targeted states)

In another example, the public relations mission of the Dairy Council of California (DCC) holds three planks:

1. To create and reinforce values for increased consumption of milk and dairy foods among targeted California audiences through mass media publicity that positions the four food groups system as a means for managing nutrition concerns.
2. To inform the California dairy industry about DCC programs and accomplishments through face-to-face communications and trade media publicity.
3. To provide public relations counsel and services to the DCC management team, other DCC divisions, and the DCC board of directors.[6]

What needs does the DCC's public relations team meet?

1. It creates and reinforces values for increased consumption of milk and dairy foods.
2. It improves dairy industry understanding and appreciation.
3. It provides internal public relations counsel and services.

For whom?

1. Target audiences
2. Dairy industry
3. DCC management team, divisions, and board

How?

1. Mass media publicity that positions the four food groups as a means for managing nutrition concerns

2. Face-to-face communications and trade media publicity
3. Not described

Where?

1. Throughout California

> **Based on the following mission statement, what needs does the Western Fairs Association meet? For whom? How? Where?**
>
> **"To promote the prosperity and unity of the fair industry, to better serve public needs in the United States and Canada by providing member fairs and associates with professional leadership, educational programs and governmental communications."[7]**

### The Organizational Philosophy

A statement of philosophy, included in an organization-wide strategic plan, is often the product of the public relations team's input to top management planning. If an organization does not have a written statement of philosophy, then public relations should take the initiative and develop one for top management's approval.

A philosophy statement, or creed, describes the values and priorities an organization holds for the way it conducts business. It is a "we believe" statement of organization values and priorities or "the heart" behind a mission statement.

A written philosophy statement, important to public relations, spells out an organization's commitments to its publics and society. It provides the practitioner with a philosophical decision-making base above and beyond personal values and integrity. The philosophy statement can be used to make or support public relations decisions.

When Johnson & Johnson was faced with the first Tylenol crisis, and specifically, the product recall decision, a *Kansas City Times* story by reporter Rick Atkinson clearly described the value of a written creed.

> J&J employees spoke almost mystically about something called The Credo, a manifesto penned by Gen. Robert Wood Johnson in 1947 and plastered throughout the headquarters.
>
> Within the family it had the force of gospel whether you were selling heart valves or pills or casket linings. It dictated that corporate behavior should be guided first by responsibility to the customer, followed in order of priority by employees, the community and stockholders.
>
> It was damnably hard to adhere to The Credo and balk at a recall.[8]

According to Thomas A. Ruddell, vice president of corporate communications at Tampa Electric, those who run organizations, work for them, patronize them, and support them should have a clear idea of what an organization stands for.

> You should ask: Does this organization have stated values? What values are only implied? If you work for a consumer products company, what are the beliefs about the price and quality of merchandise? If your employer is a hospital, what standards are set for patient care? In an investor-owned company, what values are placed on dividend payout vs earnings reinvestment? In any organization what sort of philosophy applies to the professional growth of its members or employees?[9]

> **Describe the importance of a philosophy statement to the public relations function.**

### The Organizational Culture

Whereas a written philosophy statement describes the values held by an organization, a written corporate "culture" describes the personality of an organization—that is, its system of norms.

A corporate culture describes what it is

really like to work at an enterprise versus that spelled out by top management in a philosophy statement. Cultural gaps may exist in varying degrees when actual employee behavior does not match the values described in the philosophy statement adopted by management and board of directors. Culture tells how employees operate: how they listen and talk to one another; how they behave at meetings; how they confront problems; how they reach decisions; how they are rewarded and punished.

The first step in identifying a corporate culture is to brainstorm statements that may be included in a culture statement. At Nuffer, Smith, Tucker, Inc., the management team developed its first corporate culture statement and it was scrutinized for "reality" by all staff members and revised accordingly.

Among the questions a corporate culture statement seeks to answer are: Is management formal or informal? How does communication really work within the company? Can "a little guy" rise to the top? What are the unwritten rules? What does it take to get fired? Are there "we versus they" relationships, or is it a "family" team? Are employees results-oriented? (See Figure 2–1 and 2–2.)

By identifying a corporate culture or personality, an organization best positions itself to plan action that supports rather than conflicts with that culture—plans can be developed for the more difficult task of altering that culture.

> What might be included in a culture statement about your school or work organization?

### Policy Statements/Organizational Structure

The analysis of existing or the development of new policy statements (delineation of the most important guidelines for managing) and organizational structure (including diagrams of who reports to whom) are also included in the internal assessment. (See Figures 2–3 through 2–7.)

### Backcasting

Backcasting statistics are included in the internal assessment as well. Backcasting is tracking performance history (How did we get here?) as a means for avoiding mistakes in the future and determining if operational programs still relate to an organization's long-term direction.

Charting the evolution of an organization's progress makes it possible to maintain an accurate cost-benefit data base to use when planning for the future. It tracks trends, such as changes in public relations programs impact. Backcast data become especially useful when changes in the environment call for readjustments in program priorities to manage new threats and opportunities.[10] Backcasting can help professionals formalize a process for comparing public relations programs by staff time and cost, including out-of-pocket expenses. Impact and cost are charted statistically over a three- to five-year period.

Virtually any public relations function can be tracked by backcasting. Figure 2–8 demonstrates backcast statistics for one city's regional travel writer's news conference and media tour program. The format for the annual conference in Figure 2–8 was recently revised.

> From the backcast statistics, can you speculate why a change was made?

### Internal Strengths and Weaknesses

An assessment of organizational strengths and weaknesses is the last major component of the internal assessment. A public relations team brainstorms and sets priorities for both program strengths and weaknesses as well as for priorities affecting the management of public relationships. Before launching programs to change or adapt an organization

Nuffer, Smith, Tucker, Inc.

**Corporate Culture Planks**

* Family atmosphere/attitude
* Informal communication among members
* Employee loyalty
* Sense of humor
* Value for having fun
* Attempt to innovate new PR technology
* Stable
* Supportive of professional development
* Tend not to fully rehearse for new business presentations
* We're opinionated
* Committed to client interest first; going the extra mile
* Results-oriented
* Value for research but not recommended consistently for clients
* Integrity is valued
* Genuine in our commitment to the community; tend to go overboard without considering our self interest--more so than is probably cost effective
* Tend not to think in terms of expanding current clients
* "Thinkers"
* Value planning
* Get clients from friends & client referrals
* Take the time to be educated about clients
* Timid about valuing our service for what it really costs
* There are lines of organization, but in reality decisions

**FIGURE 2–1**
**Nuffer, Smith, Tucker Planning Document 1987 (Culture)**

Nuffer, Smith, Tucker, Inc.

are made and carried out informally

* Not influence peddling
* Well known in San Diego leadership community
* Try to be up front with clients (try to educate them)
* Young folks tend to have a difficult time being taken seriously by clients
* Not 8 to 5er's
* We like each other
* Generous to employees
* Hire younger professionals
* Difficulty in making hours standards
* Willing to assume responsibility as individuals
* Clients tend to be long-term
* Top heavy
* Teams are not always clearly defined at the start of a client project/relationship
* Up to date--as individuals
* We are state and nationwide
* Rely on advisory board for outside fiscal counsel
* Feel like we're a class act; don't poach on clients
* Tendency to presume we know all of clients' needs/desires, sometimes giving their wants a back seat -- arrogant
* We do our best work when client believes in us and works as team member
* Sometimes we tend to assume client will like all we do for them
* Tend to get defensive when clients don't accept our advice, plan, approach

**FIG. 2–1 (continued)**

Dairy Council of California

Cultural Statements - General

- We develop programs that support behavior change. To just give information is not enough and can be seen as being "immoral"
- Some employees show special skills and are, therefore, given special opportunities. Some staff don't agree with the practice
- We practice the extreme of participative management which allows the organization and the individual to be stronger and causes everyone to believe they have the right to be intimately involved in every decision. This causes resistance to changes made with everyones' input.
- The informal rumor mill is a major source of information which is often based on assumptions
- We have strong support and love for team members. We often do not understand other teams; their motives or why they operate the way they do
- We expect most people to stay a fairly short period of time and then go out into the world to share our ideas. Many are staying
- Leaving Dairy Council is often a difficult thing to do
- We are almost entirely a female organization, consequently part of our staff is either thinking about, planning for, having and always talking about babies
- When there is something you want to achieve you must go after it and learn to play the game of success at Dairy Council
- Leaders at Dairy Council experience it becoming a major part of their lives, there is no 9 to 5
- We foster innovation and change for the future, to stay the same is to fail. Learning is survival.
- The people within Dairy Council are Dairy Council
- Long periods of time are offered to develop new ideas and to test to be sure they work. Things are thought through thoroughly.

**FIGURE 2–2**
**DCC Planning Document 1987 (Culture)**

DCC Cultural Statements 2

-2-

- Each employee works very independently but to a common direction

- We learn and make mistakes and triumphs in a very protective environment. It's an environment of growth and of trying out new things

- Our supported growth must be in an area or direction that has general acceptance or tracks our current ideas, otherwise we can be put in our place very quickly.

- We are very results oriented. You can often hear us ask each other, "What would the purpose be in doing that or what result would be achieved?"

- We are very skeptical and critical of most other nutrition education that occurs outside DCC

- We have a mighty pride for Dairy Council and the results we achieve

- We develop skills and expertise that stand out when placed in a group of peers

- When you are an employee of Dairy Council you are Dairy Council. At peer group meetings you are not May Smith but May Smith of Dairy Council.

- Dairy Council female employees can be picked out of a crowd. They are "clean cut", dressed in trend business clothes, nice, outgoing, ambitious, professional, and have an air of having a job that others envy or at least wonder about. You can often hear "she looks like Dairy Council".

- We operate from strongly regionalized points of view; either from program or territory basis. This is one of the sources of competition within Dairy Council

- We develop fierce ownership in what we do and products we produce

- We cherish planning and the ability it gives us to start the course of our future

- We don't really expect to work a full, full-time job. When things get busy and schedules tight, we expect some relief and to be "babied" or recognized for our efforts.

- We dislike rules and at the same time ask for them to be made

**Figure 2–2 (continued)**

DCC Cultural Statements 3

-3-

- We work at Dairy Council to learn and to be special not because there are strong income rewards.
- We are strongly focused on a mutuality concept of benefiting those who we provide services for, ourselves, and our sponsor. Our operations are surprisingly unselfish
- We believe in and worship the concept of a food grouping system
- Others seek us out when they want to know what's going on in nutrition. We are respected.
- We are dedicated to the success of ourselves, the people we work with, and Dairy Council of California.
- We are moving toward more openingly thinking about our bottom line - milk consumption.
- We can do anything we set our minds to
- We have a mighty pride in ourselves and the people we become while being at Dairy Council, we become leaders.

**Figure 2–2 (continued)**

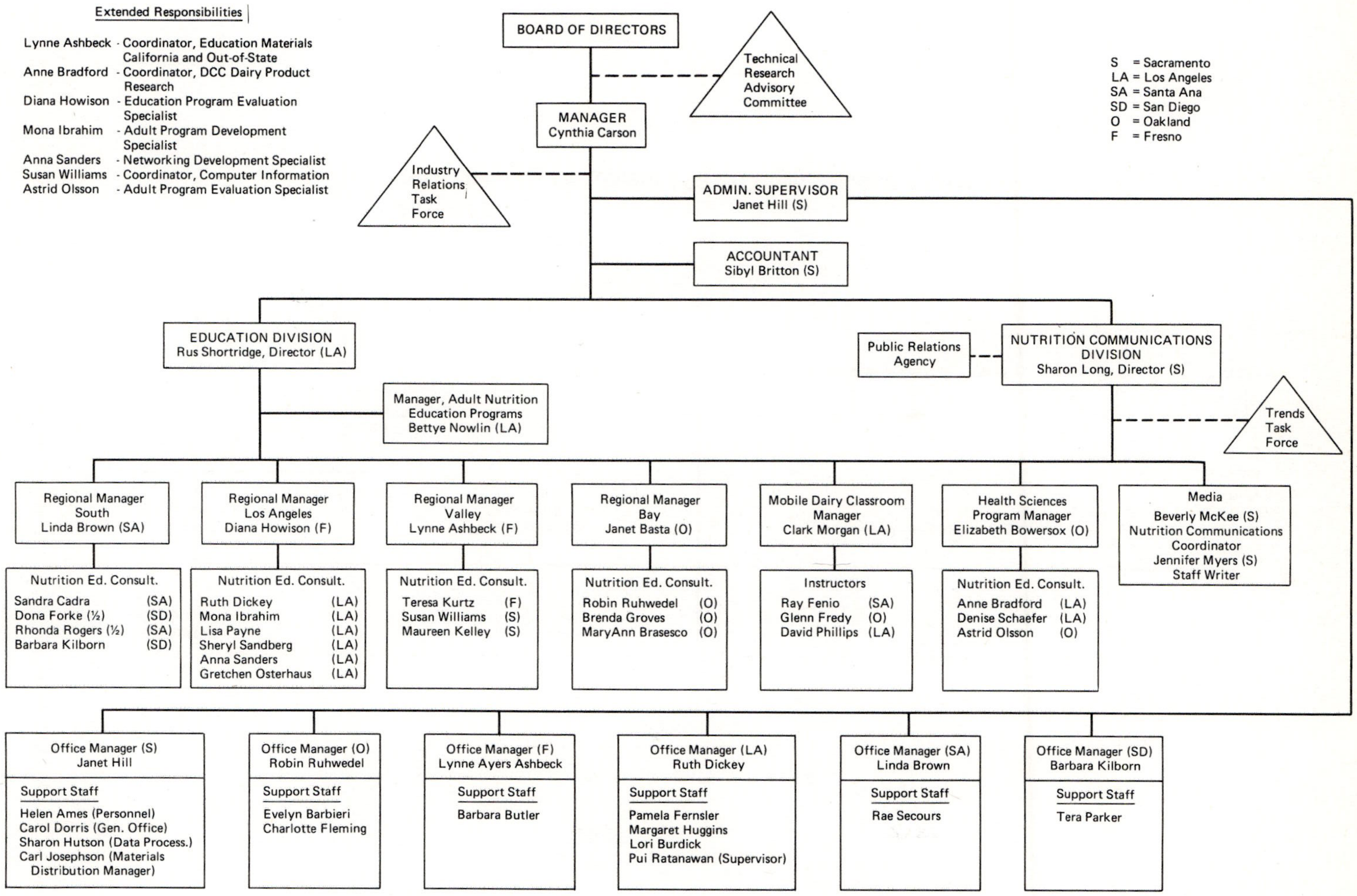

Extended Responsibilities
Lynne Ashbeck - Coordinator, Education Materials California and Out-of-State
Anne Bradford - Coordinator, DCC Dairy Product Research
Diana Howison - Education Program Evaluation Specialist
Mona Ibrahim - Adult Program Development Specialist
Anna Sanders - Networking Development Specialist
Susan Williams - Coordinator, Computer Information
Astrid Olsson - Adult Program Evaluation Specialist
BOARD OF DIRECTORS
Technical Research Advisory Committee
MANAGER
Cynthia Carson
Industry Relations Task Force
ADMIN. SUPERVISOR
Janet Hill (S)
ACCOUNTANT
Sibyl Britton (S)
S = Sacramento
LA = Los Angeles
SA = Santa Ana
SD = San Diego
O = Oakland
F = Fresno
EDUCATION DIVISION
Rus Shortridge, Director (LA)
Manager, Adult Nutrition Education Programs
Bettye Nowlin (LA)
Public Relations Agency
NUTRITION COMMUNICATIONS DIVISION
Sharon Long, Director (S)
Trends Task Force
Regional Manager
South
Linda Brown (SA)
Nutrition Ed. Consult.
Sandra Cadra (SA)
Dona Forke (½) (SD)
Rhonda Rogers (½) (SA)
Barbara Kilborn (SD)
Regional Manager
Los Angeles
Diana Howison (F)
Nutrition Ed. Consult.
Ruth Dickey (LA)
Mona Ibrahim (LA)
Lisa Payne (LA)
Sheryl Sandberg (LA)
Anna Sanders (LA)
Gretchen Osterhaus (LA)
Regional Manager
Valley
Lynne Ashbeck (F)
Nutrition Ed. Consult.
Teresa Kurtz (F)
Susan Williams (S)
Maureen Kelley (S)
Regional Manager
Bay
Janet Basta (O)
Nutrition Ed. Consult.
Robin Ruhwedel (O)
Brenda Groves (O)
MaryAnn Brasesco (O)
Mobile Dairy Classroom
Manager
Clark Morgan (LA)
Instructors
Ray Fenio (SA)
Glenn Fredy (O)
David Phillips (LA)
Health Sciences
Program Manager
Elizabeth Bowersox (O)
Nutrition Ed. Consult.
Anne Bradford (LA)
Denise Schaefer (LA)
Astrid Olsson (O)
Media
Beverly McKee (S)
Nutrition Communications Coordinator
Jennifer Myers (S)
Staff Writer
Office Manager (S)
Janet Hill
Support Staff
Helen Ames (Personnel)
Carol Dorris (Gen. Office)
Sharon Hutson (Data Process.)
Carl Josephson (Materials Distribution Manager)
Office Manager (O)
Robin Ruhwedel
Support Staff
Evelyn Barbieri
Charlotte Fleming
Office Manager (F)
Lynne Ayers Ashbeck
Support Staff
Barbara Butler
Office Manager (LA)
Ruth Dickey
Support Staff
Pamela Fernsler
Margaret Huggins
Lori Burdick
Pui Ratanawan (Supervisor)
Office Manager (SA)
Linda Brown
Support Staff
Rae Secours
Office Manager (SD)
Barbara Kilborn
Support Staff
Tera Parker

**FIGURE 2–3**
**DCC Planning Document 1987 (Organizational Chart)**

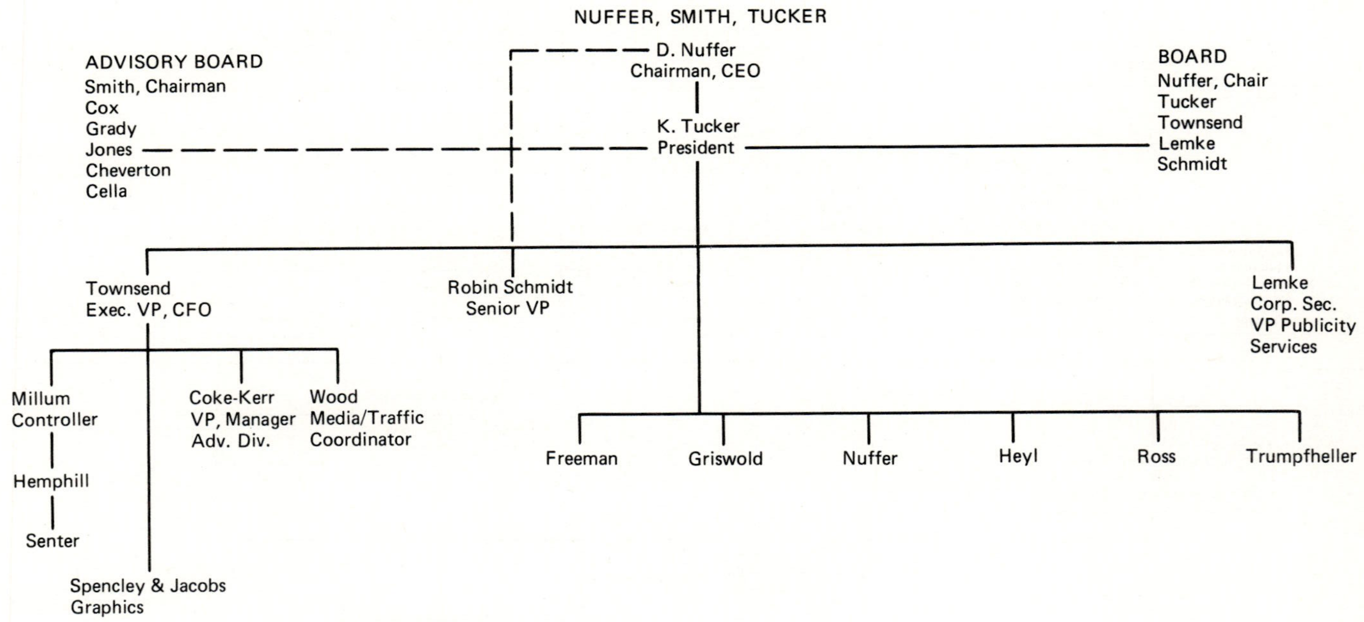


**FIGURE 2–4**
**NST Planning Document 1987 (Organizational Chart)**

Nuffer, Smith, Tucker, Inc.

**KEY POLICIES**

We will:

* Handle no business of competitive accounts.
* Accept no account brought to us by a controlling individual.
* Maintain a broad client base and prevent any single client from representing more than 20% of our business.
* Annually update a five-year economic plan and prepare annual operating plan and budget.
* Maintain an Affirmative Action Plan which provides for the hiring and promotion of women and racial minorities in all positions.
* Solicit no advertising or public relations account (ongoing) that will contribute less than $2,000 per month to gross income. The exception to this is when management agrees there is potential in a smaller account or special project.
* Keep ratio of business close to 33 1/3% business, 33 1/3% government, and 33 1/3% other not-for-profit.
* Promote company and individual achievements.
* Financially support selected political candidates where permitted by law and work for political candidates on a consultative volunteer basis only.
* Fund rather than compete for professional public relations awards; compete for advertising awards
* Annually review professionals' hourly rates.
* Maintain at least one active membership in professional organizations such as American Management Associations, Public Relations Society of America and local press clubs; take on leadership roles only with agreement of management team.
* Accept clients only after management team consultation.
* Review staff hourly standards of performance twice a year.
* Award stock to deserving employees after three years.

**FIGURE 2–5**
**NST Planning Document 1987 (Policies)**

Dairy Council of California
Management Policy Statements

1. Dairy Council of California shall operate within the specifics of the State Law under which it was created and within the regulations developed by the Department of Food and Agriculture and the policies of the Board of Directors.

2. The Manager shall be responsible for contact with the Department of Food and Agriculture, State of California.

3. Contact with the Board of Directors and the dairy industry shall be the responsibility of the Manager.

4. Program placement and pricing policies for out-of-state usage of DCC programs shall be approved by the Board of Directors using the recommendation of the Board Education Committee.

5. The Manager shall approve the hiring and termination of all program personnel. Hiring and termination of support personnel is the responsibility of the person directing each office with the approval of the Administrative Supervisor. In the Sacramento office, final approval for hiring and termination of support personnel will come from the Manager.

6. Dairy Council of California employees shall operate within the rules set forth in the DCC Employee Handbook.

7. All contact with the news media regarding food and nutrition, and subjects associated with Dairy Council or published applications with Dairy Council of California (television, radio, newspapers and magazines) shall be the responsibility of the Nutrition Communications Division.

8. Articles written about Dairy Council of California for external publication, shall be approved by the Manager and developed in consultation with the Nutrition Communications Director. Appropriate staff shall be listed as authors as designated by the Manager.

9. All outside activities like consulting and teaching regarding food/nutrition and subjects associated with Dairy Council must be approved by the Manager. Activities competitive to DCC programs are ordinarily not approved.

10. It is the employee's responsibility to bring rules or policies interpreted by an employee as hindering productivity to the attention of his/her supervisor to determine if a change is in order.

**FIGURE 2–6**
**DCC Planning Document 1987 (Policies)**

**DAIRY COUNCIL OF CALIFORNIA**
**NUTRITION COMMUNICATIONS DIVISION**

**Policy Statements**

1. The Nutrition Communications Division bases it operations on planned efforts to influence public attitudes and behaviors based on mutually beneficial two-way communications.
2. Key publics of the Nutrition Communications Division shall consist of homemakers, health professionals and dairy industry sponsors.
3. Responsibility for contact with health professionals is shared by Public Relations and Education Divisions.
4. The Division Director provides direction to outside agency to insure productivity with cost effectiveness.
5. Division staff participate in division planning.
6. Division staff and agency write and keep current position descriptions and standards of performance.
7. Division Director provides annual report of division activities as measured against division plan to Manager.
8. Division Director approves entry of DCC public relations programs in awards competition.
9. The Nutrition Communications Division, in seeking to accomplish its objectives, does so in a manner which contributes to the benefit of both Dairy Council of California and its personnel.

**FIGURE 2–7**
**DCC Planning Document 1987 (Policies)**

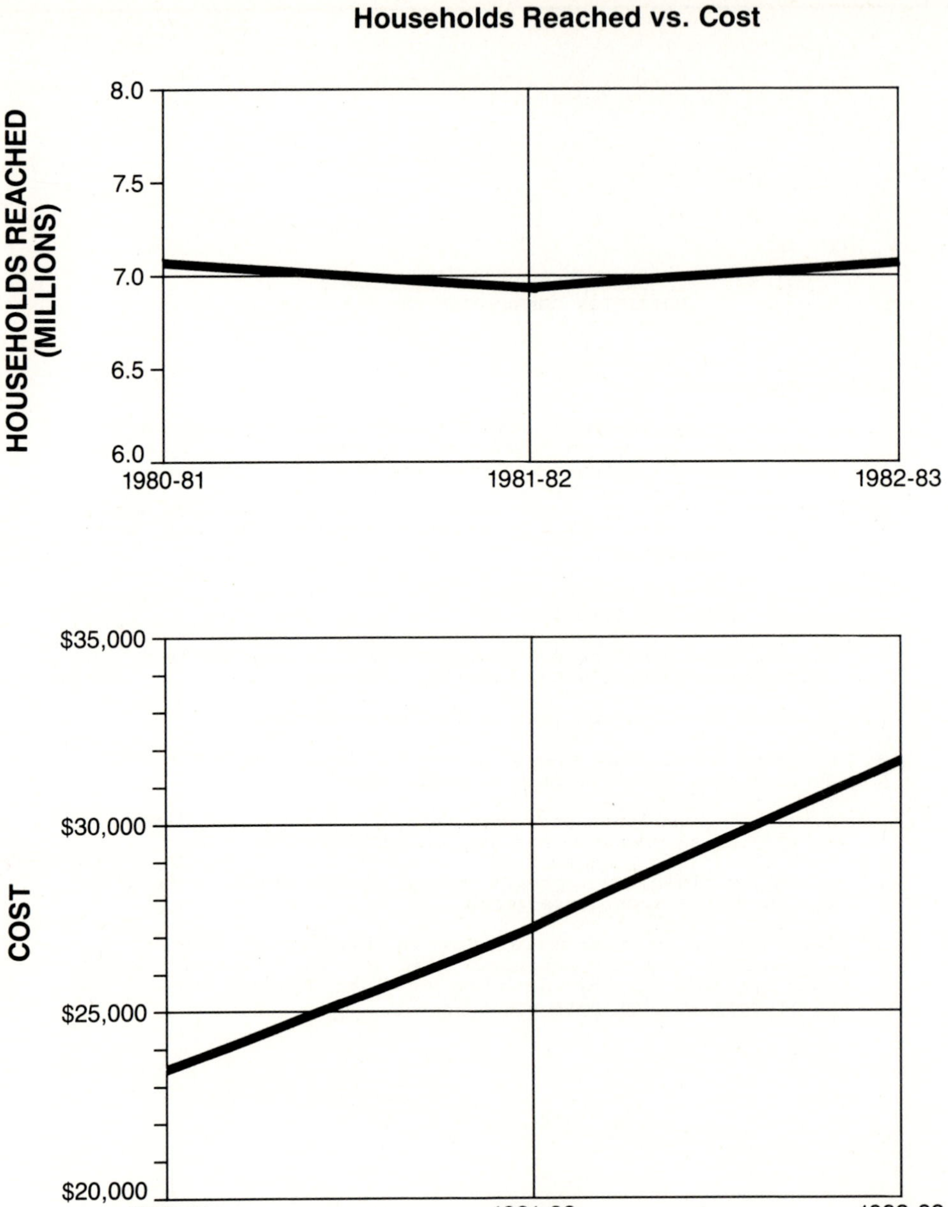


**FIGURE 2–8**
**NST Planning Document 1985 (Backcast)**

## MEDIA TOUR PLACEMENTS

**Media Placements vs. Dollars**

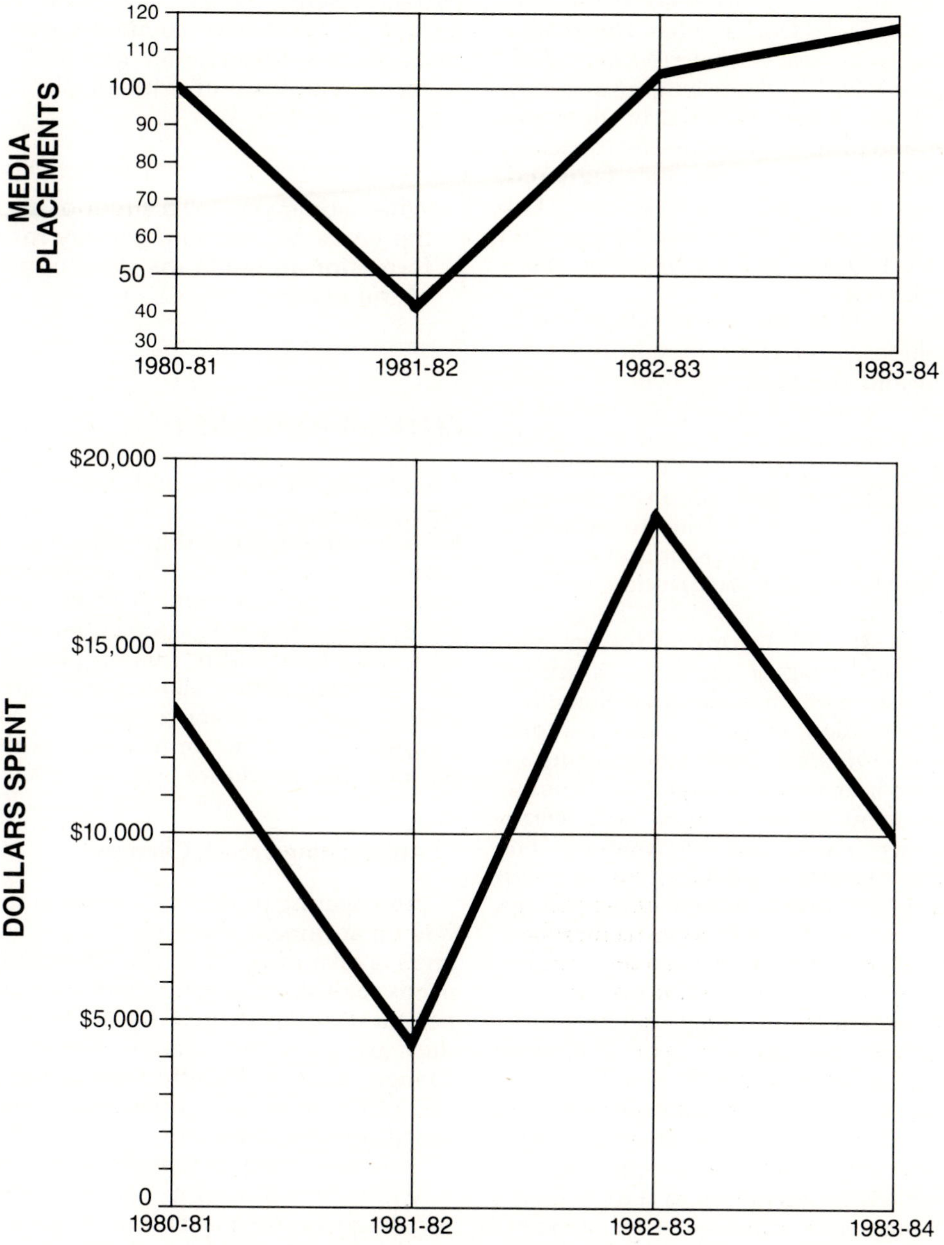


**FIGURE 2–8 (continued)**

to the outside environment, be sure your "house is in order."

"The organization's contribution to the problem must be carefully analyzed not to find fault but to attack the problem within the organization as well as outside the organization," says David Dozier of San Diego State University in his *Style Guide for Writing a Public Relations Plan*.[11] Acknowledging and writing down strengths, particularly those underused, and principal weaknesses, especially those that create major difficulties if ignored, contribute to the planning data base. Top priority strengths and weaknesses can and should be the base on which action plans are developed.

If, for example, the public relations mission includes product promotion in its description and the planning team sees it as an internal weakness, then plans should be developed and implemented to strengthen it. If, on the other hand, product promotion is considered a strength, then the planning team should plan to continue to include it in its annual operational plans and examine it from the perspective of expanding its influence.

Nothing should be taken for granted when an organization conducts its annual internal assessment. Each internal element—from the mission to public relations programs—is evaluated yearly before being incorporated into operational plans. The internal assessment is also charged with "clean-up-your-act" action plan development. The California Authority of Racing Fairs (a group of county fairs that conducts horse racing), for example, cited problems in its members' backstretch facilities, where horses, trainers, and jockeys are housed, as a major industry internal weakness. So a major portion of its first strategic plan was developed to alleviate problems in the backstretch area.[12]

Managers who hold a philosophy of open and candid communication about the internal environment complete the most successful internal assessments, from start to finish. To be completely effective, team members must be assured by their superiors that they will not be penalized for airing their opinions. The climate must foster nondefensive communication. As a result the group will produce the most useful data and the most provocative exchange of ideas. An environment only partially candid produces only partial benefits. Finally, a climate marked by uptight, defensive communication provides shallow information with little value to the development of relevant plans.[13]

> What would you tell a superior about the value of looking internally for information to guide the development of the plan?

## EXTERNAL ASSESSMENT

Attempting to analyze and understand the environment in which an organization exists keeps outside relationships functional. The assessment of the external environment consists of a written statement of assumptions about a planning team's perception of reality now and in the future. Action plans reflect how an organization plans to manage those outside forces as it moves from its current position (Where are we now?) to its desired position (Where do we want to be?).

### Anticipating Trends/Changes

Anticipating trends or changes in the outside environment three or five years ahead gives a planning team the ammunition it needs to deal with emerging threats and opportunities early in their development, when they are most manageable. Preparing for changes in areas that affect any organization can often head off undesirable trends or speed up opportunities.

Structure prognostications about the future into the following categories: economic, social, government-political, technological, and competitive. Public relations teams explore future threats and opportunities that may affect organizational relationships with key constituencies. (See Figure 2–9.)

The process can begin with something as simple as an informal brainstorm session seeking answers to such questions as: What assumptions can we make about the economic (social, government-political, technological, and competitive) environment? What changes can we project for the next three years? What trends may affect us? What special events may affect us? Which will have the most impact on the organization? How likely are they to occur during the next three (five) years?

More formal assignments for data collection and validation of assumptions can be made following such a meeting of the minds. A company task force, for example, can monitor assigned periodicals, meetings, and a network of individuals. Task force members track priority issues and spot new issues as they emerge. Quarterly meetings evaluate findings and reevaluate priorities. Systems are in place to keep top management briefed on the issues for incorporation into planning decisions.

Public relations executives can perform a special service for chief executive officers in long-range planning by monitoring changes in the outside environment and sharing such data with the rest of the top management group for use in planning. According to international management consultant Robert F. Smith:

> This way, the communications professional can become the early warning system for the whole management group. It is they who usually can, if they make the effort, have the first line on developments in government and political affairs, in social and economic change and even on certain technological and competitive fronts. They should be quick to bring that information into the enterprise for planning purposes.[14]

A public relations executive's knowledge of the strategic planning process also facilitates or leads top management through the development of an organization-wide strategic plan.

The concept of *planning for*, rather than *reacting to*, threats and opportunities as they emerge in the marketplace helped head off what could have been a national crisis for one food industry client of Nuffer, Smith, Tucker, Inc. In the annual assessment of the external environment, public relations team members uncovered a national medical association preparing a position paper warning Americans against increased consumption of an additive substance found primarily in the client's products. The position paper was scheduled to be published in the association's prestigious journal. The potential publicity fallout had all the earmarks of an industry disaster.

The problem had, in fact, surfaced a year earlier in the planning process. University research had already been funded to determine how the substance got into the food commodity. It was found to be an additive in animal feed and was used to clean processing equipment. An industry-wide campaign was launched to

- Convince feed companies to cut down on their use of the substance
- Persuade processing companies to redesign sanitation mechanisms to minimize substance residues
- Prepare a media crisis plan, including development of background papers, selection of a university scientist as the sole industry spokesperson, briefings of the industry spokesperson on potential questions from the news media, and working with the staff of the medical association to stay abreast of their activities

After the feed companies and processors were convinced to cut down on their use of the substance, university researchers were sent back into the field to test the campaign's impact. The result? The substance found in the product was reduced by half. Research findings were then placed in the right hands at the medical association. No position paper was published—and a potential crisis was averted.

Companies increasingly find that charting social change and incorporating such infor-

**FIGURE 2–9**
**Three-Year Forecast Assumptions**
**Cow Palace**
**August 1986**

| Cow Palace Planning Document 1986 (Forecast) | | | | |
|---|---|---|---|---|
| *Economic* | *Social* | *Government/Political* | *Competition* | *Technology* |
| Shows will continue to increase their costs and this will affect ticket prices.<br>Cow Palace operational costs for both shows and Grand National/Junior National will continue to increase.<br>Continued generation of corporate sponsorship will be necessary to offset the Grand National's increased per customer promotion costs.<br>Bill Graham will continue to show increases in concert business.<br>Exhibitors will continue to exhibit at the Grand National & Junior National despite tough economic times for agriculture.<br>Family shows will be forced to break the $10.00 ticket and ticket sales could be negatively affected.<br>SF will continue to be one of the leading U.S. convention centers.<br>SF-Bay Area will remain one of the most competitive U.S. entertainment markets. | Family shows will grow in popularity.<br>Increased new housing surrounding the Cow Palace may spark more complaints and the need for accelerated community relations.<br>Hispanic and Asian populations will continue to grow more dominant in the local market place.<br>The senior population will continue to grow in numbers and influence.<br>Animal rights groups will continue to be vocal.<br>State-owned facilities like the Cow Palace will be forced to justify their relevance to the community. | Governor Deukmejian will be re-elected and our board will remain stable.<br>The Daly City Council will apply taxation pressure on the Cow Palace.<br>Daly City will continue to apply pressure for use of Cow Palace land.<br>A successful Gann initiative could have negative effect on Cow Palace staff.<br>Cow Palace will need to improve and maintain relationships with the Governor and State Legislators.<br>Cow Palace relationships with state fairs and expositions will continue to grow. | The addition of seats at the Oakland Coliseum will have a major effect on the Cow Palace in the next year.<br>A decision to build a facility in San Jose or San Francisco would have major negative implications for the Cow Palace.<br>A decision to expand Moscone Center would have minimal effect on the Cow Palace.<br>New ownership of the Warriors could stir a move to another city and negatively affect the Cow Palace.<br>Shoreline will negatively affect the Cow Palace when/if phase 2 is completed.<br>ARCO Arena should not significantly affect the Cow Palace because of the distance. | The Cow Palace will not be able to take advantage of improved technology (electronic scoreboards, marquees) until new dollars are found.<br>New technology will enable customers to order tickets from their home television. |

| | | | | |
|---|---|---|---|---|
| Private and corporate sectors will increase their financial investment in fairs through sponsorships and investments.<br>It will be increasingly difficult for shows to find liability insurance and as it is, the Cow Palace will benefit.<br>If Graham puts a roof on Shoreline, he'll take the concerts away from the Cow Palace.<br>Circus will continue to play Sacramento, Oakland & Cow Palace.<br>Increased commitment of state allocation to $750,000 would allow the Cow Palace to borrow funds for major refurbishment.<br>Family entertainment will increase at the Cow Palace.<br>Sporting events will continue to drop at the Cow Palace.<br>If San Jose were to build a facility, circus will be jeopardized.<br>A coalition of San Francisco-San Mateo Area state/local legislators in agreement on the Cow Palace as their sports arena could cause a major allocation of state funds for refurbishment. | | | | |

mation into the planning process are a business necessity. "The idea of looking ahead, trying to position the direction of trends, and having a corporate mechanism that encourages anticipating societal trends, is absolutely essential for any corporation that wants to stay in business," according to Margaret A. Stroup, director of corporate responsibility at Monsanto.[15] Why? According to a comprehensive analysis of issue management by *Chemical Week*, a leading trade publication of the chemical industry:

> Catching up with today's social issues—such as concern for the environment and equal employment opportunity—has been costly, sometimes involving huge outlays for clean-up efforts, affirmative action programs and legal costs. So, forward-looking companies are trying to get ahead of the game by preparing for social change early and hoping to save money and possibly forestall a new salvo of government regulations.[16]

This kind of planning systematically attempts to avoid surprises. In the words of veteran public relations counselor Kalman Druck, "Every problem shouldn't have to be an unexpected pie in the face."[17] To a large extent, the strategic planning process helps to minimize surprises. Potential threats and opportunities should move up and down the list of forecast assumptions, but pies in the face should be few and far between.

> What assumptions might you make about the future of your county fair? Think about the potential for economic, social, government-political, technological, and competitive change during the next three years.

## CONTINGENCY PLANS

Contingency, or what-if, plans are additional insurance against surprise. Much has been written about the importance of anticipating and planning for every imaginable potential disaster and crisis, from the Tylenol tragedies to an unwanted reporter's telephone call trying to dig up trouble over industry education programs in the schools. However, company after company and organization after organization fail to plan ahead to operate or respond in times of crisis.

What-if, or crisis, planning should be a part of the public relations planning process and updated annually. Public relations members of an organization's top management team should make it their business to help other top managers think through potential what-if scenarios. Written plans should be laid out in advance outlining the basic framework on how an enterprise will operate under times of crisis.

> How would you go about helping top managers develop what-if plans?

## DEVELOPMENT OF ACTION PLANS

### Key Result Areas/Goals

From the investigation of internal strengths and weaknesses and external threats and opportunities, the most critical issues with the potential for affecting the mission of the organization are identified. While the possibility of increased local taxation may be an external threat to one organization, increased competition may pose a threat to another. Public relations can affect both. On the opportunity side, a change in the tax laws may be an external opportunity for a professional society of accountants, whereas a twenty-fifth-year anniversary celebration may be identified as an internal strength to be expanded upon as an opportunity. Both can be affected by public relations programs.

Setting priorities is a difficult but important part of the planning process. Here are some questions to ask yourself when setting priorities:

- Which internal weaknesses, if left untended, will be the biggest obstacles to carrying out our mission?
- Which strengths, if expanded upon, could make a primary difference in how we go about carrying out our mission?
- Which assumptions about the external environment pose the greatest threat or opportunity in the pursuit of our mission? Which will have the most impact on our organization?
- Which is likely to occur in the next three (five) years?

Program emphasis should not be splintered in too many directions. Public relations programs should be developed, in most cases, for the three or four most critical issues affecting relationships with priority publics.

Top priority threats and opportunities, both internal and external, are addressed with what the American Management Associations calls "Key Result Areas." Key Result Areas generally describe the direction an organization will take with the publics who are involved or affected by the outcome desired. Objectives, strategies, and action plans are developed for each Key Result Area.

Key Result Areas for The Cow Palace, an historic San Francisco entertainment facility, have included statements as simple as "refurbish facility" and "improve relationships with local public officials."[18] The former may be necessary before public relations programs can be fully effective, whereas the latter can be affected by public relations programming immediately. A Bumble Bee Seafoods, Inc., public relations Key Result Area reads "increase tuna category sales with Omega-3 fatty acids message."[19] Again, a Key Result Area should describe direction for objectives, strategies, and action plans in managing existing and potential threats and opportunities to the organization mission.

What the American Management Associations refer to as Key Result Areas, others call goals. Grunig and Hunt describe goals as ends too broad to be measurable while objectives reflect "ends in view" or outcomes that can gauge how well a public relations problem or opportunity is managed.[20] Dozier, on the other hand, believes that both goals and objectives should be measurable, with the goal being the ultimate result accomplished (increase contract securals by 20 percent) when end result objectives (message awareness, acceptance, attitude and behavioral change from priority publics) are achieved. Dozier's concern is that too often process goals (e.g., generate 2,000 news stories annually) substitute for outcomes or end states because process goals seem easier to measure. "However, such process goals generally have weak linkage to organizational benefit or payoff," he says.[21]

Semantic differences over goals should not stand in the way of one all-important point: Public relations plans must be measurable and used to evaluate performance. Practitioners can adapt to the organization's existing planning structure as long as performance can clearly be measured against plans.

This text specifies goals in a more general sense, calling them Key Result Areas. Accomplishment then lies in the development of specific and measurable objectives within each Key Result Area.

### Defining Priority Publics

According to Cutlip, Center, and Broom, researching the publics before planning program strategies is necessary to test the accuracy of assumptions about who they are, what they know and how they feel about the situation, how they are involved or affected, what information they see as important and how they see it, and even how they get their information. With that information in hand, and only then, can program objectives, strategies, and action plans be set for each public.[22]

Grunig and Hunt define publics as a loosely structured system whose members detect the same problem or issue, interact either face-to-face or through mediated channels, and behave as though they were one body.[23] Most academicians agree with Grunig and Hunt: The most effective definition of publics is situational. Individuals in the market for a car or house can share collective needs/concerns/interests. So can individuals concerned about heart disease, or parents concerned over issues that affect children, or property owners over legislation that might negatively affect property tax deductions. The categories are infinite. And a campaign can be designed to satisfy needs/concerns/interests with products or points of view presented as solutions when audiences are defined and prioritized according to

1. Decision makers
2. Those who influence decision makers

Members of the public relations planning team can begin the process of identifying and prioritizing publics informally through group brainstorming. Helpful questions include

- Who are the decision makers who can best help us achieve our Key Result Area or who are affected by it?
- Who influences these decision makers?
- How many of these audiences can we effectively influence within time and budget constraints?

In defining priority publics, practitioners should concentrate on those who can have the most effect on the success or failure of the Key Result Areas. If one Key Result Area deals with product promotion, who makes the decisions regarding the purchase of that product? Secondarily, who influences those decision makers? In a public relations campaign to sell cellular telephones, the primary purchaser may be chief executives from specific industries. Business leaders and technical experts may influence those decisions.

In a public relations campaign plan aimed at supporting specific state legislation, the decision makers may be a small number of government leaders. Those who influence those leaders may be interest groups, the news media, and hometown leaders.

Definitions of priority publics or audiences abound. Marketing organizations separate groups with similar needs and behaviors into market segments for the purpose of selling a product or service. They categorize these segments by demographics, life stage, personality, values, nationality, socioeconomics, product uses, or attitudes.

Public relations priority publics share many characteristics with marketing. However, public relations concerns often reach beyond product consumers to the many publics who may never consume organizational goods and/or services. These include suppliers, employees, neighbors, regulators, and special interest groups.

### Validating and Segmenting Priority Publics

Although public relations teams have a notion about who are the target audiences for a given issue, it is often necessary to validate those assumptions with research. Audience investigation provides the public relations practitioner with confirmation of decision makers on a given issue or product, those who influence them, and a more precise idea of what it will take to move the individual to action.

One amusement park turned around a declining attendance by studying those who make decisions regarding attendance and their motivations. The audience was then categorized by four motivational factors with messages and media developed for each. These included

1. The enthusiast who regularly attends new attractions
2. The thrill seeker who goes to attractions for the excitement
3. The animal lover who attends to see the animals
4. The passive individual who attends only when pressured by family and visitors

"Sophisticated campaign designers attempt to segment the overall audience into subgroups with similar demographics or attitudinal characteristics and then create campaigns targeted to the specialized categories or receivers," Atkin says.[24]

Research helps to segment markets when it is used to identify:

Attitudinal differences (preferences/values)
Behavioral differences (habits/traditions/lifestyles)
Demographic differences (age/gender/income/marital status)

One food industry marketing board identified the homemaker or household manager as one of its public relations priority publics. This decision was the result of ongoing research demonstrating homemaker control over most food consumed by and purchased for a household (*product use market segment*). Priority publics were further dissected and prioritized by life stage: bachelor, young married, those with children under ten years of age in the home, those with children over ten years of age in the home, empty nesters (or those whose children have left home), and retired (*situational market segment*).

Each of these homemaker life stages was prioritized according to the impact of nutrition information on food selection behavior with regard to food choices. Based on these criteria, three were selected as priority publics:

1. Homemakers with children under ten years of age
2. Homemakers with children over ten years of age
3. Young marrieds

The bachelor and empty nesters showed little interest in the subject, and seniors, although very interested in nutrition, demonstrated little willingness to change existing behavior patterns.

Health professionals, health books, and the news media were found to be of primary influence on the decisions these homemakers made with regard to feeding their households.

> In the early 1970s, the nation's legal community launched a successful campaign to stop state legislation that would allow insurance carriers to offer no-fault automobile insurance (giving up the right to trial for most injury accidents in return for lower premiums). Which publics do you think were most important in this campaign?

### Conducting Audience Research

The practitioner takes leadership in establishing research objectives and defining the audiences to be examined, but surveys should be left to professional researchers trained in the selection of representative samples, writing and administering questionnaires, and interpreting research findings.

Research is conducted with priority target audiences prior to the actual public relations campaign to identify

- ☐ Priority audiences
- ☐ Audience awareness and perceptions of the issue
- ☐ Audience needs/concerns/interests regarding the issue
- ☐ The perceived strengths/obstacles of the organization's point of view on the issue
- ☐ The validity of the issue as an organizational priority

Research can take the form of quantified telephone surveys, personal interviews (typically referred to as "intercept" surveys because respondents are recruited at shopping malls and other public places), or mail surveys.

Interviews by telephone and in person are usually preferred because researchers have the flexibility to probe for more information. The personal survey is typically used when there is something to show the prospective interviewee (e.g., a mock-up news story, direct-mail piece, or advertisement), or you want him or her to do something such as work through an educational document. The telephone survey can collect most of the data needed in the research, including responses to basic message concepts. Mail surveys are usually the least expensive, but response rates tend to be low and unpredictable without considerable follow-up staff time and effort.

Qualitative research often uses focus groups: approximately ten people assembled to examine their views on the product, issue, or organization. Focus groups are typically conducted prior to surveys to get a real-life feel for the target audience when testing a new or novel concept. This helps the practitioner who seeks appropriate vocabulary for message construction and frees the mind of preconceived notions about the people you are trying to reach.

Focus group data alone are not enough for decision making. The number of people examined is often an insufficient sample to draw valid conclusions, and group dynamics often affect the outcomes. Messages and media formats are often tested in focus group situations, but this is an expensive process. For the same or less money, you can obtain useful data and increase your sample size by one of the other research methods described, such as telephone interviews, especially if you have some history or experience about the message with which you are working.

Communications messages are also tested with priority audiences for their understanding, relevance, believability, and potential for action. Additionally, pretesting materials gives the practitioner enough data to estimate their potential effect.

Research should be conducted before a campaign begins and at midcampaign intervals to allow practitioners to make adjustments to keep messages relevant.

The practitioner must be careful not to select too many publics. Public relations objectives, strategies, and action plans are developed for each priority public. Organizations do not normally have the personnel or budget to design public relations programs for every public the organization affects. Consequently, priority setting is an important part of the planning process.

### Objectives

Specific and measurable objectives are written for each priority public. Basic questions to be answered in an objective include

1. What measurable end result is to be accomplished?
2. By when?

The American Management Associations recommends a number of guidelines to consider when writing objectives. Among them are

- □ Be definite, concise, clear, and unambiguous. They should specify results to be accomplished as well as what is to be done and when—not how.
- □ Be challenging, energizing, vitalizing, and progressive.
- □ Be results directed and aimed at significant improvement.
- □ Be realistic and attainable.
- □ Be quantifiable (measurable) and verifiable.
- □ Specify a target date for accomplishment.
- □ Be current and responsive to change.[25]

An easy formula to remember is as follows:

1. Start with the word "to" followed by an accomplishment verb.
2. Specify a single key result to be accomplished.
3. Specify a target date for accomplishment.[26]

For example an objective might be: to increase the number of women having mammography at Rusty Morris Hospital by 25 percent by December 31.

Quantifiable and time-limited objectives are developed for action plans. Such specificity should obviate meaningless objectives. Words such as "extensive," "comprehensive," "adequate," "reasonable," "as soon as possible," and "desirable" should not be used in objectives.[27]

Grunig and Hunt suggest five types of content for public relations objectives listed in order of difficulty and value:

1. **Communication**
   Example: To place 100 stories in media intended for targeted publics by January 31.
2. **Message retention**
   Example: To generate campaign message retention by 20 percent of the target audience by January 31.
3. **Message acceptance**
   Example: To generate acceptance of campaign message by 20 percent of the target audience by January 31.
4. **Attitude formation or change**
   Example: To increase those members of the target audience who (accept campaign message and) intend to change behavior by 20 percent by January 31.
5. **Overt behavior change**
   Example: To increase those members of the target audience who change or begin a new or repeated behavior (such as writing to a government official, buying a product, attending an event, or giving money to a cause) by 20 percent by January 31.[28]

For the purpose of this text, we will concentrate on the end result objectives of message retention, acceptance, attitude, and behavior formation or change—knowing full well that in practice communications or process objectives are more frequently used.

When evaluating objectives, ask yourself these six key questions:

1. Is the objective statement constructed properly? "To" (insert action or accomplishment verb) (insert single key result) by (insert target date).
2. Is it measurable and verifiable?
3. Is it obviously related to program and organizational goals, yet clearly within the province of public relations?
4. Can it be easily understood by all those who will be working to achieve the outcome indicated?
5. Is it realistic and attainable, yet representative of a significant contribution to achieving program goals?
6. Does the intended outcome justify the expenditure of time and resources required to achieve it?[29]

Describe one objective for each of the content types identified by Grunig and Hunt (except for communication) for a Western Fairs Association Key Result Area intending to increase attendance at fairs.

### Action Plans

Written action plans carry out the achievement of each objective. Included in written action plans are

- □ Strategies for achieving each objective
- □ Step-by-step tasks leading to the achievement of each strategy
- □ Individuals responsible for each task
- □ Targeted deadline dates

To illustrate, the Delta Dental Plan of California had three strategies to achieve the following objective: to secure 200 dentist participants in pilot dental plan by January 30.

The strategies were

1. Generate publicity in dental trade publications and local mass media
2. Launch direct-mail campaign
3. Make program presentations to dentists and dental groups[30]

Using strategy 1, the steps of the action plan are developed below.

Budgets are developed for action plans as they become candidates for inclusion in the operational or annual plan. Estimates of cost are made for out-of-pocket expenses and time. Out-of-pocket expenses can include such items as printing, photography,

**STRATEGY 1:** Generate Publicity in Dental Trade Publications and Local Mass Media.

| *Action Steps* | *Who Responsible* | *Completion Date* |
|---|---|---|
| 1. Write and distribute news release for use in dental trade publications. | Griswold | November 1 |
| 2. Place feature interview in at least one trade publication. | Griswold | November 15 |
| 3. Develop news angle, query business editor of metro newspaper, and secure interview agreement. | Griswold | January 5 |

graphics, postage, travel, long distance telephone—in other words, any expense incurred.

Hourly rates can be determined for professional time by adding an individual's compensation and overhead (office space, equipment, furniture, supplies) and dividing that figure by total available hours. Multiply this figure by the number of hours itemized into each specific project for cost.

With hourly rates for each employee in place, projecting cost for time can be as simple as multiplying time estimated for a project by an individual's or team of individuals hourly rates.

> Suppose you are the legislative public relations manager for The Stevahn County Trial Lawyers Association. Your objective is to defeat a specific piece of legislation that would allow no-fault automobile insurance in your state. One strategy is to secure supportive editorials from newspapers covering the hometowns of targeted lawmakers by June 30 (the close of the legislative session). Develop an action plan and budget for implementing this strategy.

## Evaluation

To reiterate Lindenmann's earlier quote: "The only effective way to evaluate anything is to establish a set of goals and objectives before any program is launched."[31] Research comes into the picture at the beginning of public relations planning (Where are we now? Where do we want to be?), in the middle of a campaign (How are we doing? Are revisions necessary?), and at the end (Did we do what we set out to do?).

Effective public relations practice in the future will necessitate a management by objectives approach to planning and programming. According to Broom and Dozier:

> They will employ objective measures to plan programs based on systematic understanding of problem situations and publics. They will use evaluation research to monitor the program, to detect changes in the situation and to make program adjustments. Programs will be evaluated against outcomes spelled out in the objectives that guided program strategy.[32]

Without such measures, Broom and Dozier suggest, public relations is nothing more than an "output function that executives systematically exclude from decision-making and strategic plans."[33] The end result for public relations should be the successful fulfillment of objectives, not just a newspaper or television story placed by company journalists-in-residence.

So how does a professional go about the evaluation of public relations?

Evaluative research at the end of a campaign allows you to determine whether or not objectives (specific message awareness, acceptance, changes in attitude or behavior) were met and provides the planning team with sound data for future planning. Backcasting statistics give public relations teams criteria for evaluating on-route operational plans to determine whether or not they constitute the best use of time and money or are still relevant to long-term direction.

Strategic planning provides public relations professionals with evaluative documentation but, just as important, it is a never-ending process of monitoring the environment for change—both internal and external—which may affect an organization's mission; setting priorities based on potential threats and opportunities; analyzing priority threats and opportunities for their impact on existing programs; setting Key Result Areas; developing objectives, strategies, and action plans—and then starting the process all over again. It is the basis for *managing* rather than *reacting* to change.

> Can you describe the value of strategic planning to a potential client, using the planning model in Figure 2–10 as a visual?

## THE SITUATIONAL PUBLIC RELATIONS PLAN

Frequently public relations plans are developed without the benefit of the strategic planning process. These plans, designed to manage specific public relations programs or situations, are actually more common than strategic plans. They operate from a similar but abbreviated data base and share common techniques for developing action plans and evaluation instruments.

The situational public relations plan consists of seven steps:

1. Statement of problem/opportunity
2. Analysis of the situation
3. Program goals
4. Priority publics
5. Objectives

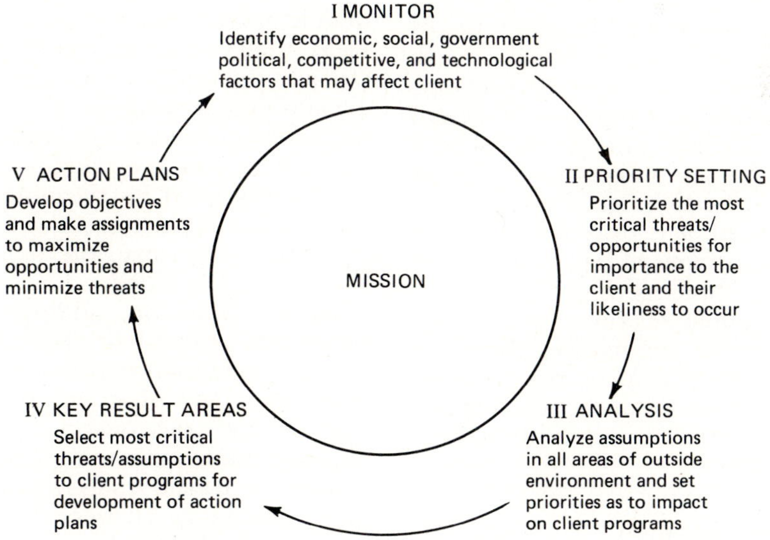


**FIGURE 2–10**
**NST Planning Document (1987)**
**The Identification of Assumptions for the Future**
**(3 Years)**
**A Model**

6. Action plan/budget
7. Evaluation/program adjustment[34]

### Statement of Problem/Opportunity

The focal point of this public relations plan identifies the problem or opportunity to be tackled by the practitioner. From this point the rest of the plan evolves, particularly the goal statement(s). This section of the plan is composed of a succinct, one-paragraph description of the problem to be resolved or opportunity to be accelerated.

A problem statement for the Center for Creative Leadership, one of the country's leading executive training organizations, is as follows: Center for Creative Leadership of Greensboro, North Carolina, a pioneer in behavioral research and its application to executive creativity, is opening its first branch training office in the Southwest. The center must become self-sufficient within two years despite limited name identity in the Southwest.[35]

Another problem statement, from the National Dairy Promotion and Research Board and the National Dairy Council, reads: American women know they need to increase their calcium intake but a significant percentage are uncertain about whether they should increase consumption of dairy foods or take vitamin/mineral supplements. Furthermore, most women think it is okay that they are consuming one serving of dairy foods daily when they need three servings.[36]

In sum, the public relations problem/opportunity statement summarizes the focus of the public relations plan, setting the scene for an analysis of the situation, the development of goals, objectives, action plans, budgets, and evaluation.

### Analysis of the Situation

The situational analysis provides the data base for the development of goals and objectives. It examines the internal and external factors that affect a specific problem or opportunity. This shortcut system assesses the internal and external environments described in strategic planning. The process examines, for example, such questions as *What do we have going for us? What do we have working against us? What internal changes could improve the situation? What external factors—threats and opportunities outside the enterprise—affect the problem, and how can they be managed?*

One systematic process for conducting a situational analysis quickly and efficiently is called Force Field Analysis. Invented in the late 1940s by Kurt Lewin, a German social scientist, Force Field Analysis effectively breaks down even the most complex situation into manageable components.

Force Field Analysis, based on Lewin's theory, states that every condition we face in life is affected by a magnetic force field. Factors continually restrain us, and factors drive us forward. Lewin theorized that performance can be increased by first weakening or removing *restraining* forces, then strengthening *driving* forces, and finally, adding new driving forces.

The natural tendency is to try to improve a situation by looking immediately to new driving forces. But the approach in Force Field Analysis tries to overcome the opposition and then to "rev up" current programs. To add only driving forces to a situation is like adding air to a tire with a hole in it. As long as you keep adding air pressure, the tire stays filled, but the minute you relieve the pressure, the tire goes flat. Why? Because the restraining force, the hole in the tire, has not been handled.

In any situation, adding new driving forces can amount to short spurts of increased performance. But once the pressure of getting a new program off the ground is gone, performance once again declines, facing those same restraining forces.[37]

The Force Field Analysis process is similar to the pursuit of answers to seven real-life questions:

Where are we now? (scale of 1 to 10)
Where do we want to be? (scale of 1 to 10)
What is holding us back?
How can it be minimized?
What is working in our favor?

How can it be strengthened?
What can we add to strengthen our position?[38]

A brief discussion of applying Force Field Analysis might be helpful to grasp its usefulness. Picture yourself leading a management or public relations team workshop and using Force Field Analysis as a process for sorting out an organization problem. The process is similar to conducting a structured brainstorm session, with one exception: The findings are used as a data base for the development of a plan to change the situation. The more *specific* the problem you want to address, the more benefit you receive from the process. The limitations of the planning group must also be considered. Addressing the planning team's general attitudes, opinions, satisfactions, and other "soft" assertions about a program with which they are familiar is useful input to the data base. But as soon as you start discussing the actual effectiveness of the program, you must have additional data collected more formally.

The results of the Force Field Analysis for the Bank of Brannan illustrated in Figure 2–11 used the process to analyze the management's satisfaction with how the bank was prepared to meet increased competition. In another instance, the condition addressed by the National Dairy Council was: readiness of Dairy Council to pursue cable television as a communications vehicle.

The process can be utilized to tackle problems as basic as rejuvenating tired publicity programs or increasing the efficiency of a community advisory board. It can also address complex issues, such as dealing more effectively with a forecasted increase in government intervention or the perceived ability of a new company to be self-sufficient in two years.

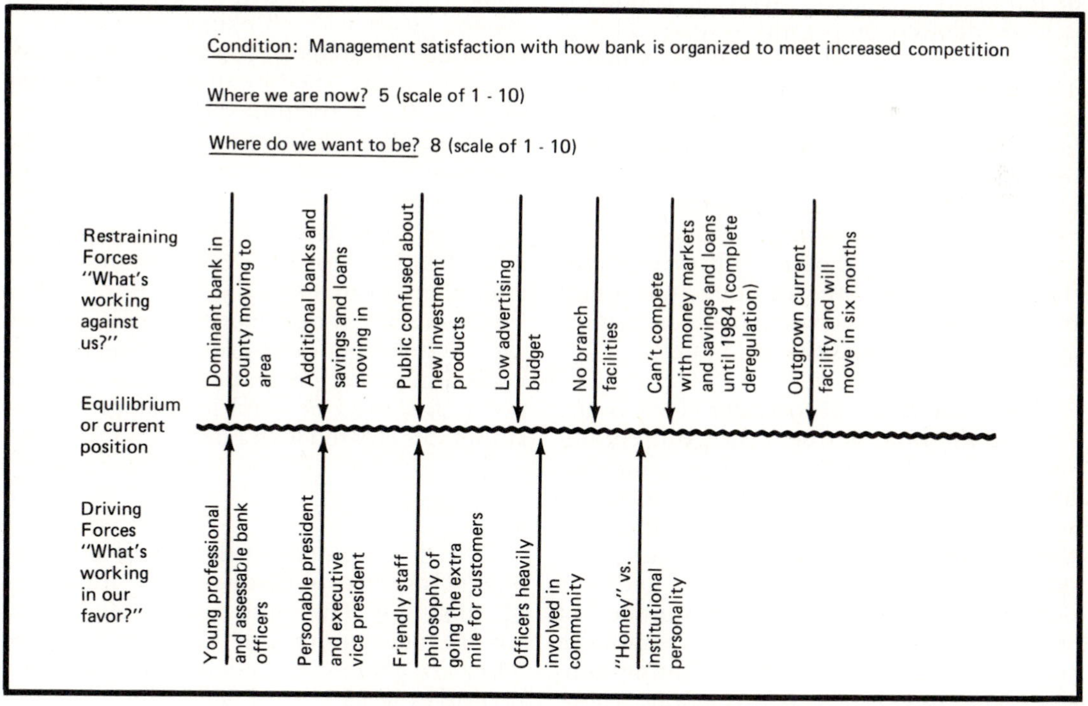


**FIGURE 2–11**
**NST Planning Document 1982**
**Force Field Analysis**
**Bank of Brannan**

***Where Are We Now?*** Once the condition is determined, make a subjective evaluation of the current situation. This is best accomplished by rating the condition on a scale of 1 to 10 (from bad to good). Although subjective at this point, research and real events can later be used to determine if we have risen on the scale after the initiation of a public relations plan.

***Where Do We Want to Be?*** The same process is initiated to determine how we would like to change the situation. How far can we increase our satisfaction with the condition or situation on the rating scale with a planned effort? If we rate our current performance at 5, can we take it to 7 or 8 with a year-long plan?

***What Is Holding Us Back?*** A group brainstorm session about those factors that may be inhibiting our success with the condition is next followed by priority setting. This is both an internal and external assessment. The Bank of Brannan, for example, cited the dominant bank in the county moving into its service area as an external restraining force; the fact that the bank had outgrown its current facility and planned to move to new quarters in six months.

Priority setting should seek to establish the most crucial three or four restraining forces to be addressed when plans are generated to manage the situation better.

***How Can It Be Minimized?*** This is the point in the process where the group brainstorms strategies for minimizing or eliminating priority restraining forces. A priority restraining force for the Bank of Brannan was the confusion about new investment products in the marketplace following industry deregulation. Consequently, a number of strategies were brainstormed to minimize confusion that later turned into comprehensive marketing and public relations plans. Strategies included touting bank officers as resources for investment decisions (versus the promotion of new products), increasing public access to bank officers, developing a column for the weekly newspaper, and the like.

***What Is Working in Our Favor?*** Organizational strengths or driving forces are brainstormed and priorities set next. Which driving forces, if fully exploited, would make the most difference in the situation? The bank cited as a strength its "homey" personality versus the institutional image of its competitors. The fact that friendly staff went the extra mile for customers was also listed.

***How Can It Be Strengthened?*** Strategies for strengthening priority driving forces are addressed here. One strategy for expanding the driving force about going the extra mile for customers included publicity and advertising aimed at helping customers set priorities on investment opportunities.

***What Can We Add to Strengthen Our Position?*** The last element of the brainstorm discussion deals with thinking through what additional strategies, yet to be discussed, might improve the situation. Here we try to get a few remaining big ideas that can make the most difference in improving the situation.

Force Field Analysis provides a preliminary data base for the development of specific plans to manage the situation. Group involvement not only motivates each participant, it helps generate group consensus and commitment to program changes. Formal research should be used to validate the assumptions created with Force Field Analysis.

### Program Goals

The development of the public relations goal(s) is similar to that described for strategic planning. The same rules apply here as for the development of Key Result Areas. They are general end result statements that objectives work toward achieving. The goal is closely linked as a solution to the problem statement. Goal statements specify end states or outcomes, not the means or process for getting you to that end state. Making the

Center for Creative Leadership's office in the Southwest self-sufficient would be a goal statement; securing a specific number of news releases would not.

### Priority Publics

Again, the same rules apply here as were put to use in strategic planning. Who can have the most effect on the goals? Secondarily, who influences those priority publics? The priority publics of the Center for Creative Leadership are vice presidents of human resources and trainers of existing and potential clients located in the Southwest.

> What additional publics might influence those two primary publics? How can your assumptions be validated?

### Objectives

As in the strategic plan, specific and measurable objectives are written for each priority public. Public relations objectives might include message awareness and acceptance and formation or changes in attitude and behavior. For example, options for objectives for the Center for Creative Leadership might be

1. To generate message retention by 20 percent of the target audience by January 31
2. To generate acceptance of campaign message by 20 percent of the target audience by January 31
3. To increase those who intend to enroll in center courses by 20 percent by January 31
4. To fill enrollment for each center course by January 31

Such objectives will look similar to those formulated in the strategic plan.

### Action Plan/Budget

As you will remember from the discussion on the strategic planning process, action plan documents spell out the strategies, tasks to accomplish in each strategy, responsibilities, and scheduled completion dates. Budget includes out-of-pocket expenses. The budget should also include expense for professional time.

### Evaluation/Program Adjustments

As in strategic planning, the public relations plan can be used to evaluate performance. Research is necessary at the beginning, at midcampaign points, and at the conclusion of the process to evaluate objectives, particularly when content includes message awareness and acceptance and formation or changes in attitude and behavior.

> Suppose you want to evaluate the Center for Creative Leadership's plan halfway through the campaign and again at the end. How would you do it? What findings would cause you to adjust the plan midway through the campaign?

Both the strategic and situational public relations planning processes are instrumental in finding consistent success in the public relations practice. A publicity story here or there has little meaning alone. However, as part of a carefully thought-out campaign plan, it can become one step in a building process to keep your organization effectively managing its environment for the good of the organization, those it affects as well as those who are affected by it.

## SUMMARY

- Planning is the initial step in public relations activities.
- Research underlies all planning and implementing of the public relations plan.
- The strategic planning process, long term and short term, prepares management and public

relations teams to move in the desired direction.

- □ The internal assessment includes mission, philosophy, culture, policies, organizational structure, performance backcast, and strengths and weaknesses.
- □ The external assessment provides economic, social, government-political, technological, and competitive data from which to prepare plans.
- □ Key Result Areas are goals in the plan that have audience specifications and actions attached in order to accomplish desired outcomes.
- □ The situational public relations plan is an abbreviated type of plan that identifies a specific problem or opportunity, assesses the environment, and identifies goals, publics, and objectives in a similar but abbreviated form than its strategic counterpart.

## EXERCISES

1. Identify problems (if there are any) with the following objectives:
   - □ To promote an understanding of corporate contributions with specially selected target publics.
   - □ Get this organization going again.
   - □ To dedicate our new $10 million research facility to the current and former employees who made it possible.
   - □ To tell the story of Lee Nuffer Corporation to the widest possible audience via the news media.
   - □ To reach all segments of the product X public.
   - □ To provide a prompt and direct means of communication to and from management.
   - □ To increase number of Key West homeowners who are aware of the three major advantages of J. Buffett swimming pools by 20 percent by May 1.
   - □ To increase seat belt usage by 25 percent of employees during the first two months of the campaign and 50 percent by August 30.
2. You have been hired by the Bank of Brannan as its first public relations director. The bank operates from an annual plan but has no long-term or strategic plan. Develop a written description of the process to persuade top management to initiate a strategic plan.
3. The Bank of Brannan is located in what is referred to as your community's "Wall Street" because of the great number of banks located in one small area. Following an external assessment, the bank projects a significant increase in new banks entering the area in the next three years, including the dominant bank in the region. Develop a situational public relations plan for preparing the bank to manage this threat using the Force Field Analysis illustrated in Figure 2–11.

## REFERENCES


1. American Management Associations International, *Strategic Planning Workbook* (New York: American Management Associations, n.d.), p. 25.
2. Walter K. Lindenmann, "Hunches No Longer Suffice," *Public Relations Journal*, 36, no. 6 (June 1980), p. 10.
3. Scott M. Cutlip, Allen H. Center, and Glen M. Broom, *Effective Public Relations*, 6th ed. (Englewood Cliffs, NJ: Prentice-Hall, 1985), p. 221.
4. Robert F. Smith and Kerry D. Tucker, "Team Up to Manage Change," *Association Management* (September 1983), p. 131.
5. Robin Schmidt, GTE Sprint, personal communication, November 10, 1984.
6. Dairy Council of California, Nutrition Communications Division Plan, June 1985.
7. Western Fairs Association, Strategic Plan, 1984.
8. Rick Atkinson, *San Diego Union*, November 12, 1982, p. A-12.
9. Thomas A. Ruddell, "Chartering the Communication Function," in *Inside Organizational Communication*, 2nd ed., ed. Carol Reuss and Donn Silvis (New York: Longman, 1985), pp. 62–63.
10. Robert F. Smith and Kerry D. Tucker, "Looking Back: 'Backcasting' Moves into the Driver's Seat," *Public Relations Journal*, 40 (December 1984), p. 29.
11. David Dozier, *Style Guide for Writing a Public*

*Relations Plan*, 1983, p. 3 (San Diego State University [classroom document]).
12. California Authority of Racing Fairs, Strategic Plan, 1985.
13. Smith and Tucker, "Team Up to Manage Change," pp. 131–133.
14. Robert F. Smith, "A Communicator's Role in Business Management," *Communicator* (June 1981), p. 34.
15. "Issues Management: Preparing for Social Change," *Chemical Week*, October 28, 1981, p. 46.
16. Ibid.
17. "The Corporate Image, PR to the Rescue," *Business Week*, January 22, 1979, p. 50.
18. Cow Palace, Strategic Plan, 1986.
19. Bumble Bee Seafoods, Inc., Public Relations Plan, 1987.
20. Grunig and Hunt, *Managing Public Relations*, (New York: Holt, Reinhart & Winston, 1984) p. 116.
21. Dozier, *Style Guide*, p. 4.
22. Cutlip, Center, and Broom, *Effective Public Relations*, p. 207.
23. Grunig and Hunt, *Managing Public Relations*, p. 144.
24. Charles Atkin, "Mass Media Information Campaign Effectiveness," in *Public Communications Campaigns*, ed. Ronald E. Rice and William J. Paisley (Beverly Hills, CA: Sage Publications, 1981), p. 273.
25. American Management Associations International, *Strategic Planning Workbook*, p. 24.
26. Glen M. Broom, "Managing for Success" (unpublished seminar, University of Texas, Austin, February 20, 1986).
27. Robert F. Smith and Kerry D. Tucker, "Measuring Individual Performance," *Public Relations Journal* (October 1982), p. 27.
28. Grunig and Hunt, *Managing Public Relations*, p. 134.
29. Broom, "Managing for Success."
30. Delta Dental Plan of California, Pacesetter Campaign Plan, 1983.
31. Walter K. Lindenmann, "Hunches No Longer Suffice," *Public Relations Journal*, 36, no. 6 (June 1980), p. 10.
32. Glen M. Broom and David Dozier, "An Overview: Evaluation Research in Public Relations," *Public Relations Quarterly* (Fall 1983), p. 7.
33. Ibid., p. 5.
34. Dozier, *Style Guide*, p. 2.
35. Center for Creative Leadership, Problem Statement, 1986.
36. National Dairy Promotion and Research Board and National Dairy Council, Pills vs. Food Campaign, 1986.
37. Kerry D. Tucker, "Force Field Analysis, New Tool for Problem Solving," *Public Relations Journal*, 35 (July 1979), 23.
38. Ibid.

## CASE STUDY

### The Problem

The city of Doraville, Brown County's second largest city, suffers from a lack of awareness among industrial site selectors. (Site selectors seek out sites for corporations to locate/relocate.) The city also suffers from a neutral to poor image among Brown County business leaders who are potential third party endorsements for a city site.

### Situational Analysis

Doraville wants to attract new business and industry to broaden its tax base. According to surveyed site selectors, Doraville has a number of valuable assets, including its labor pool, ground and air transportation, climate, cost of land, local taxes, quality of living, housing, and water. However, the city is perceived as weak in several areas considered essential to business and industry. Among those liabilities, four are considered correctable: local business climate, speed of regulatory approval, availability of land, and image. Additional research indicates that business leaders share the site selector concerns about Doraville's image.

1. Assume you have been retained as public relations counsel to the city. Develop a situational public relations plan to support the city in attracting new business and industry.

# CHAPTER 3

# Developing Message/ Media to Support the Plan

### *IN THIS CHAPTER*

The message/media outline offers a process that both links the public relations plan to day-to-day communications chores and takes advantage of human motivation principles to increase the odds of audience response to public relations messages.

Too often, public relations plans are carefully developed and filed only to be brought out again when evaluation time rolls around. The message/media outline forces the practitioner to organize communication to best carry out the plan prior to hammering out that publicity story, direct-mail piece, or presentation outline.

However, regardless of how well we plan, design, and communicate public information campaigns, there is tremendous competition for the eye and ear. Most people are not going to care about what you have to say. Consequently, your message must not only be packaged to meet the needs of your client but your audience as well. The more specific you can become about your campaign needs, the audience(s), and its needs, the better your odds for an effective campaign.

The message/media outline helps the practitioner organize communications that are specific to the needs of the client and target audience by asking a series of questions:

1. What is your end result? (communications outcome)
2. With whom do you want to communicate? (target audience)
3. What are their self-interests? (needs/concerns/interests)
4. What do you want to say? (message)
5. What means will you use to say it? (communications channel)
6. Who will you use to say it? (spokesperson)
7. How can you package it with the greatest odds for successful action? (raising an audience need/concern/interest and offering the message as a solution)

### *CHAPTER OBJECTIVES*

The reader will be able to

1. Apply the message/media outline to organize public communication.
2. Describe how each of the four question clusters, which make up step 7 of the message/media outline, benefit the public relations writer in achieving objectives.
3. Outline the process by which a receiver is motivated to act on a communication.

## CARRYING OUT THE PUBLIC RELATIONS PLAN

Once public relations plans are laid as the parameters from which to work, thought should turn to the best opportunities for applying the directives.

Our charge is to carry out the plan—be it securing and maintaining relationships between the organization and its key constituencies, gaining acceptance for products, or directing issues that may affect the mission of an organization. With Key Result Areas, measurable objectives, and action plans in hand, the practitioner has the direction necessary to *develop the messages* and *select the channels of communication* that will work the hardest to accomplish those objectives.

Successful public relations communication—as most former journalists-turned-public relations practitioners will attest—can be far more difficult to develop than a news angle or "hook." For one thing, a news hook has one basic task: to inform the reader, listener, or viewer. A publicity story must be designed to meet both the journalist's criteria for news and at the same time work toward achieving an objective of successfully communicating a message. A journalist also typically has one copy desk between his or her medium and the audience (though there are exceptions). A public relations practitioner, on the other hand, serves at least three "masters": the client (boss or enterprise), the media, and the audience targeted for influence. To be most effective, each master's interests must be mutually served. The most effective communication benefits each master or gatekeeper: a positive endorsement for your client, a usable news angle for the editor, and a message suited to the needs of the members of the target audience.

Simply put, messages describe what you will say repeatedly to achieve each objective, and media selection indicates the channels you will use to reach the intended audience. Keep in mind that with publicity the news angle is not usually considered the message but rather part of the packaging or means for communicating the message. A number of different news angles may be necessary to generate the kind of message repetition that will work the hardest to facilitate a changed attitude or behavior. If, for example, a primary message of Goodwill Industries in a Key Result Area to increase store sales is that its facilities offer quality clothing at bargain prices, then a number of news hooks would have to be created for a publicity campaign.

> Can you think of any news hooks that might be used to project that primary message?

Practitioners must consider a number of steps in designing and packaging a message for mutual benefit. This should be accomplished as part of the planning process and again each time a practitioner sits down to a word processor to develop a news angle or write a brochure. It is dangerous to assume that just because a communication is developed, members of a priority public will receive the message and follow it automatically. Because too much competes for audience attention, messages must be packaged to reflect both client and audience needs. This is not a natural tendency for the practitioner. *Too often the needs of the communications medium take precedence over the intended result of the communication.*

The written message/media outline proposed in this text can make the process of moving publics to change more deliberate, more systematic. Systematic thinking expands publicity from what our instincts tell us is a good news story to developing a news story that works the hardest to support the public relations goal.

### MESSAGE/MEDIA OUTLINE: A CHECKLIST FOR INCREASED IMPACT

#### *Step 1: Communications Outcome: What Do You Want the Reader/Viewer/Listener to Do?*

It should be painlessly clear from any communication, regardless of the objective, what action you want the motivated reader, viewer, or listener to take.

The first step in the development of a public relations communication, then, is to begin an outline with a simple statement of what the practitioner would like the audience to do with the information: vote for a particular candidate or purchase a specific product or hold a positive attitude about your company as a good corporate citizen. The communications outcome directly commands the public relations plan—more specifically, the results you want to achieve as described in Key Result Areas.

Most public relations messages are more subtle than they are direct. But the practitioner should be clear in his or her head precisely what is the end result behavior or attitude toward which the communication works. A case may be clearly built for purchasing a new Chrysler in a publicity story in the automobile section of a major newspaper without ever asking for the sale. However, when planning the communication, the practitioner should have *purchase* clearly imprinted on the brain as the action he or she would like to see the audience take. When the practitioner has a clear picture of the end result outcome, the case can be clearly built for product purchase without asking for it directly.

Such an outcome is certainly not exclusive to corporate marketing objectives. The forest service has an outcome of reducing forest fires and the Girl Scouts wants new recruits.

> In planning a communications, how do you think a practitioner benefits from clearly identifying the action he or she wants the audience to take?

#### *Step 2: Clarify Target Audience(s)*

After deciding the ultimate action you would like your communications to initiate, the next logical step is to clarify who (what audience) you want to take that intended action. Audiences are identified in the public relations plan and objectives are developed for each priority public. When applying the public relations plan, again clarify who you are trying to reach. It is too easy to slip back into the comfort of writing for the medium without giving full attention to those you want to reach.

#### *Step 3: Identify Audience Needs/Concerns/Interests*

To move an audience to action, a public relations practitioner must first know what makes that audience tick. What are the existing attitudes, values, and behavior patterns that affect your product, issue, or organization? What are the barriers to overcome in the pursuit of change? How can you minimize or eliminate those barriers? What are the benefits your product, issue, or organization offers? How can you improve those benefits? What are the consequences of not purchasing your product, siding with your issue, or valuing the contribution your organization has made? Are there any benefits/consequences you have not identified?

Public relations techniques should maximize benefits and minimize barriers. If bank customers are not investing in new opportunities because they are confused by the marketplace, then techniques should be designed to minimize confusion. If a grocery importer is being stalled by retailers because there is not enough appreciation for the profit potential of imported grocery sections, then techniques can be initiated to create better understanding of product profit potential.

Research answers these questions. The opinions of public relations staff rarely make a sufficient data base. Research helps you best position your message to maximize benefits and minimize or eliminate barriers while simultaneously meeting the needs and concerns of your audience.

A cellular telephone company whose automobile telephone product is sold primarily to service industry personnel (physicians, lawyers and chief executives) found stressing more productive use of driving time a common motivation that crossed over a number of market segments. Consequently, messages are packaged to raise audience concern for time efficiency as well as other motivations identified by research, and, in so doing, audience receptivity for the product increases.

Identifying the needs of a target audience regarding your message is a critical but often neglected step. Without such information, a practitioner may simply be disseminating materials or news stories that do not adequately maximize the impact that a product, issue, or organization can have on the lives of target audience members.

> Suppose you have been retained by your local dental society to increase the percentage of patients who visit dentists twice a year for checkups. What barriers or concerns may have to be overcome? What positive benefits may individual members of your audience have for getting checkups? What consequences may be addressed for not visiting the dentist regularly? What might motivate patients to go get a checkup? How can your organization find the answers to these questions?

### *Step 4: Choose the Message*

The key question in the development of the message is: What can be said about the product, issue, or organization that will direct the greatest change—that is, cause the desired attitude or behavior?

The first step is to assess what is working in your favor and what is working against the target audience acting on your communications outcome. The next step is to determine what you can say that will do the most to support the action you want the audience to take.

Ideally, public relations messages maximize an organization's strengths or opportunities and/or reduce weaknesses or threats regarding the Key Result Area.

Communications outcomes for the National Dairy Board and National Dairy Council invariably read: increase consumption of dairy foods. One public relations message is to increase calcium intake among women from food (75 percent of dietary calcium comes from dairy foods) rather than vitamin/mineral supplements. A secondary message is that scientists are concerned with the long-term safety consequences of taking supplements. The message derived from two driving forces identified in a Force Field Analysis workshop assessing the impact of calcium supplements on dairy food consumption:

1. Concern among scientists for the safety of supplements
2. Audience belief that food is the best source of nutrients

The city of Doraville's communications outcome is to attract business and industry. Extensive research of site selectors (those corporate executives responsible for finding new sites for companies) rated its labor pool, surface transportation, air transportation, climate, cost of land, local taxes, quality living, housing, and water as relocation assets (driving forces). Also rated were four correctable liabilities: local business climate, speed of regulatory approval, availability of land, and image (restraining forces). Message statements tout its assets, but the city also has a primary message statement to deal with its liabilities: "The city of Doraville is aggressively correcting its relocation liabilities to attract new business and industry." Public relations programs demonstrate progress toward plans to ameliorate those liabilities.

Following the deregulation of the long distance telephone industry, GTE Sprint launched a public relations campaign with a communications outcome to reduce confusion among state legislators and public utility commissioners. The long distance carrier believed that as long as legislative and regulatory decision makers were unclear on the benefits of "life after divestiture," the company's legislative and regulatory objectives would be at risk. Consequently, public relations staff designed a message to read: "GTE Sprint is an industry leader seeking to assure that the new competitive marketplace creates a more efficient telephone system at lower overall cost to the consumer."[1] All legislative and regulatory position papers, fact sheets, and publicity materials were written to support this statement. This message both minimized a primary concern public officials held for the future of long distance telephone service (primary restraining force) and promoted what was clearly the most important benefit of deregulation at the time: lower cost to the consumer (primary driving force).

Key Result Areas, or goals that support product marketing, add one additional element to the message development process: competitive strengths and weaknesses. What are the strengths and weaknesses of your competitors? How do they stack up against your product? Do you have strengths that can take advantage of their weaknesses? Do you have competitive vulnerabilities that need enhancement internally? With respect to the competition, what are your points of difference?

Such competitive restraining and driving forces should be addressed in a Force Field Analysis of the situation. By addressing your competitor's strengths and weaknesses, you have a data base from which to develop a message(s) subtly placing your strengths against your competitor's weaknesses. If, for example, you represent a local construction company and the biggest complaint potential customers (local developers) have about your competition is that they are consistently overbudget and late with job completions, then you have to make sure that your company's strengths can take advantage of these weaknesses. If they can, then the public relations message becomes: Michael Durant Corporation comes in on time and on budget with all jobs. If you are retained by the M. Robert Reider Community Bank as a client, and potential customers complain of impersonal treatment by the bank's competitors, then your public relations message is that your client provides personalized customer treatment.

You do not have to—and should not—cast negative accusations at your competitors. By promoting competitor vulnerabilities as your strengths, you accomplish the same thing.

> **How would you respond to the question, "What is the value of selecting a specific message? Can't we just tell them our name and what we do?"**

### *Step 5: Choose the Communications Channel*

Choosing the most effective media mix relies as heavily on research as each of the other outline steps. After you have identified and prioritized target audiences, it is time to identify how these decisions makers and/or those who influence them get their information. A more important series of questions could be: What is the most important media mix for reinforcing positive attitudes and behavior or facilitating change? Which media reach the broadest segment of the audience? Which are the most credible? Which media formats work the hardest for our message? What can we afford? Answers to all of these questions become criteria in the selection of communications channels.

The credibility of the medium should be your primary selection criterion, as the credibility of the medium has the greatest effect on attitude and behavior. Media can be segmented for credibility into five categories, in order of believability:

1. Individuals (one-on-one, small group, large group)
2. Personalized messages (telephone, direct mail)
3. Publications (specialty magazines, trade publications, employee media)
4. Mass media (newspapers, magazines, television, radio)
5. Advertising[2]

Media or channels of communication can be separated into two categories: controlled and uncontrolled. Controlled media suggests that the practitioner controls the final product. Examples include one-on-one communications, speeches, employee communications, direct-mail literature, advertising, and printed materials. Uncontrolled media, on the other hand, reflect media about which the practitioner does not have the final say. This includes publicity in newspapers, magazines, television, and radio. Obviously, the more control we have over the message, the more potential for effective communication. Uncontrolled media, however, expand our opportunities for impact. Both must be considered in the media mix.

Research should be conducted with your target audience to determine reading, viewing, and listening behaviors. Public relations techniques to reach physicians, for example, have traditionally focused on placing articles in medical periodicals, arranging for experts to address professional meetings, and direct mail. However, research shows that most physicians can be reached by mass media as well, particularly television news.[3] As another example, employee communications programs have traditionally focused on such techniques as employee publications and, recently, video programming, despite research that repeatedly demonstrates the superiority of one-on-one and small group communication among top management, supervisors, and employees.

Research can determine not only where an audience receives its information but those vehicles that are perceived to be the most believable and work best to achieve public relations plans.

Advertising departments provide an additional source of media usage information. Newspapers and magazines closely track the demographics of their readers. Data on radio and television stations can be collected from advertising departments and tracked in every market by commercial companies, such as Arbitron and A. C. Nielsen. Delta Dental purchases radio advertising time during commuter travel periods and baseball games because its target audience for dental insurance (specified business executives) are more likely to be listening during these times.

| |
|---|
| What else might you plan for your public relations media mix for Delta Dental? |

Though mass media cross many market segments, there can be more efficient channels of communication. The decision makers on legislation that may affect your organization, for example, may number only a handful of lawmakers. Constituent telephoning and letter writing may be the priority vehicles for such a campaign, with hometown speeches and local publicity as support. If your audiences consist of specific segments of the business community, then your campaign may include direct mail, presentations, and publicity in publications reaching those business segments as well as newspaper financial sections.

Special interest media—industry trade and professional journals, business publications—can frequently reach larger numbers of a target audience than the larger circulation mass media. Such publications cut through the wasted circulation of mass media. Specialized speaking platforms and direct-mail lists are used in the same way. Specialized media are already targeted to specific audience needs/concerns/interests and tend to reach more active information seekers. Along the same lines are the common interest magazines, such as women's, science, recreation, and city publications. There is probably at least one publication for virtually every known interest, vocation, or hobby.

Special interest sections of the newspaper have similar benefits. These sections—food, travel, business, automobile, lifestyle (formerly women's)—are also more likely to use news releases than general news sections of the newspaper.

Once we have identified how audience members get their information and which avenues offer the most potential for credibility, priorities must be set based on available time and dollars.

Media mix priorities can be established by creating criteria against which to compare cost. Such criteria can include

1. How many decision makers does the medium reach? (quantity)
2. Is the media credible with the audience? (quality)
3. How much professional time is required to be successful with the medium? Do the deadlines of the medium correspond with message timeliness? (time)

Media mix decisions can best be made by comparing potential quantity, quality, and time for each medium against cost.

**Suppose Scripps Memorial Hospitals wish to increase exposure this year in the national hospital industry as a preventive health leader. What would be included in the most cost-effective media mix?**

### *Step 6: Select Spokesperson*

Selecting the source of your message, the spokesperson who will transmit it, is just as important as creating the message itself.

Credibility is the most critical virtue of an information source. Credibility has been broken down into two elements: expertise and objectivity. Audience members are more likely to believe and be persuaded by your message if they think your spokesperson knows what he or she is talking about. But to believe the message completely, there must be an assumption that you are motivated to tell the truth. If a vested interest is perceived to be behind an issue, your objectivity may be suspect.[4]

According to Atkin, credibility has three critical dimensions:

1. Trustworthiness
2. Expertise/competence
3. Dynamism/attractiveness[5]

Selecting the most effective spokesperson varies according to the campaign situation. When the objective calls for attitude or behavior change, a trustworthy spokesperson is the most critical factor. If the objective calls for knowledge or skill development and the message is technical or complex, an expert source is preferred. The dynamic spokesperson (i.e., celebrity) is most effective with simple, straightforward messages requiring minimal audience involvement (e.g., purchase Bumble Bee Tuna).[6]

The organization you represent will often be the message source. Organizational credibility, then, is critical to public relations message acceptance.

Often an organization's advantage improves when it seeks information sources outside the company that the public would consider more unbiased than the organization itself. For example, a telephone long distance company might use university scientists as spokespersons endorsing the quality of its electronic connections. A food industry might find physicians, scientists, and registered dietitians the most believable sources. Health professionals offering advice on food selection can be far more believable than food industry officials offering that same advice.

> **Which news release lead is the most believable to you?**
>
> *Osteoporosis, an age-related, bone-thinning disease that strikes more than one-fourth of all Caucasian women above the age of 60, can be prevented if specific guidelines are followed from birth throughout life, according to the National Dairy Council.*
>
> Or:
>
> *Osteoporosis, an age-related, bone-thinning disease that strikes more than one-fourth of all Caucasian women above the age of 60, can be prevented if specific guidelines are followed from birth throughout life, according to Robert Heaney, M.D., a leading calcium researcher from Creighton University.*

For maximum believability, a source should be perceived as not only knowing the truth but being objective enough to tell the truth as he or she sees it. However, in many instances, a company's public relations goal is to engender credibility for the organization as an objective purveyor of truth. And messages that are of true mutual benefit—those that help the reader, viewer, or listener meet a need, solve a concern or problem, or satisfy an interest using the "organization" message action—can generate credibility for an organization.

A community bank positioned two of its officers, the president and executive vice president, as spokespersons. These individuals offered consumers relief from large and impersonal banks. They were positioned as a community resource to help consumers through the maze of investment confusion in the banking industry. Thus a practitioner should position the spokesperson as being knowledgeable about the subject and concerned with public needs.

The news media as a communications channel hold their own degree of credibility as third party endorsers of your message. When a medium publishes or airs your message, it takes on an implied endorsement. Publicity assumes a higher degree of credibility than other techniques because of its "objectivity" and this implied endorsement.

### *Step 7: Package Message to Raise an Audience Need/Concern/Interest and Offer Product, Issue, or Organization to Meet the Need, Minimize the Concern, or Satisfy the Interest*

Content that addresses what research identifies as a need/concern/interest of a target audience and offers a solution to manage that issue or minimize that concern is content with the best opportunity for affecting the attitudes and behaviors of the receiver.

If the primary concern of the homemaker audience with regard to nutrition is for family, then messages should be designed to meet concerns for family health. If the group purchaser of health insurance can see nothing more important than stabilizing costs, then the health insurer should position its message to manage health costs.

Identify and concentrate effort in those areas that are mutually beneficial to the company and constituency targeted for influence. Give the receiver something to do or think: an attitude, an action, or behavior to employ.

Blending the message and application, then, with needs, concerns, and interests can be designed around four clusters of questions:

1. Does the communication raise an audience need, concern, or interest? Can audience members easily put themselves into the situation? Can you paint a real-life scenario with words or visuals?
2. Is your product, issue, or organization offered as a solution in a clear and concise manner? Are the benefits to the solution clearly presented? Can the receiver jot down in one sentence, "What's in it for me?"
3. Are the consequences of leaving the need, concern, or interest unresolved clearly presented?

4. Have you helped the individual members of the target audience mentally rehearse or think through the action you would like them to take?

These questions become criteria for planning and evaluating how communications support the public relations plan. The criteria apply when writing copy for brochures, advertising, audiovisuals, speeches, news releases, and public service announcements and when preparing spokespersons for media appearances and interviews. These key questions blend message and application with needs/concerns/interests.

Such criteria support what behavioral theory demonstrates to be a common internal route to behavior change. Readers, listeners, and receivers process messages that are delivered through accessible channels. This processing is a rapid succession of mental steps leading to the end result.

**A message is first transferred to real-life needs/concerns/interests.**

Before we can react to a message, we must be able to imagine how the story will affect us in our own life situation. Connections to real-life situations cause attention to the message.

↓

**Intention (motivation) is aroused.**

This step represents the big leap between receiving a message and motivating a person to do something about it. The intention to act or to form an attitude is initiated here.

↓

**Information is processed and behavior directed.**

Once we are motivated to consider action, past experience and associations are considered and then the behaviors are selected to respond to the message stimuli.

↓

**Behavior change occurs.**

Acting on the message happens by trial at first. The first actual action is taken, thought is formed, belief is organized. Sometimes several repetitions occur during this action initiative phase while analyzing the experience from each trial action or thought.

↓

**New behavior is reinforced with experience.**

We use positive and negative consequences of our actions to measure results of the behavior. These consequences are then stored in memory and recalled when acting again.

↓

**Values/attitudes are formed.**

Positive values and attitudes toward the change encourage repetition of the cycle; negative values/attitudes discourage repetition.

Public relations messages, regardless of how well planned, designed, and communicated, are not normally met by anxiously awaiting people eager to sit down and attentively absorb the information transmitted. Nor is the public typically ready to act on the message content. The communications must contain the ingredients that will catch the attention of audience members: demonstrating the benefit of adopting a behavior (and the potential consequences of not adopting that behavior) and finally how to act on the message.

Educational psychologists tell us that receivers of a message are more likely to attend to communication that helps them transfer what is being said to their own real-life needs, concerns, and interests.[7] Consequently, then, communications content that blends the message and suggested actions with audience needs/concerns/interests can enhance the receiver's use of the information presented. We are more interested and listen more if the message meets our needs. We then process the information according to our own experiences, images, and stored verbal associations. The more the message reinforces what we believe to be a positive experience and minimizes what we believe to be negative, the greater the likelihood that we will be aroused to perform the actions desired by the message.

**Weight Watchers International minimized the negative experience of restricted food selection common to dieters when it launched a new diet program with tastier foods, more variety, and flexibility in food choices. Can you think of how you have been reached by messages that have been packaged to be associated with your needs or interests?**

Suppose a public relations message for a community bank includes information about the friendliness and accessibility of its president and other bank officers. The receiver of the message, if attending to it—that is, interested and listening—will process that message according to his or her experiences, images, and stored verbal associations about the friendliness and accessibility of bank officers. The greater the receiver's need and concern regarding bank officers' behavior, the greater the likelihood the receiver will be aroused to perform the actions desired by the message.

The transfer of the message to real life can be facilitated by wording, visuals, and format of the message itself. These techniques must be considered when preparing public relations communications.

Once a public relations message has been packaged to transfer to an audience's own real-life needs/concerns/interests, we are best positioned to help the receiver evaluate the benefits of action versus the consequences of inaction.

Suppose a practitioner has prepared a news release for a homemaker audience and the intended behavior is to prompt her to send away for tips and recipes for feeding children wearing dental braces. The message may be transferred mentally by associating it with the homemaker's need to better feed her child by using these tips and recipes. Motivation to act may depend on her answering a series of questions regarding the success of the behavior if she acts:

Will I be able to successfully follow the tips and utilize the recipes?

Will it really help my child?

Will this really be important enough to warrant sending away?

The practitioner, wary of these mental gyrations, may try to answer as many of these considerations within the story as possible so that the homemaker's ability to answer her internal thoughts comes with absorbing the communication.

The solutions to needs/concerns/interests presented in public relations messages are processed mentally by search and retrieval systems. An individual's previous experience and information about a subject make it possible for the mind to mentally file the new material, categorizing it with previous information already housed there.

Such mental search and retrieval systems rely heavily on long-term memory associations with the past. We, as receivers, utilize mental elaborations, images, and mental rehearsals (both verbal and imaginal) to transform information into conceivable behavioral responses. A message calling on fairgoers and potential fairgoers to attend the county fair may bring a number of associations to mind. One association may be an emotional recollection of attending the fair as a child. We might associate the fair with learning more about farm animals or with exhibits or entertainment. We may have positive or negative association with the carnival midway. Each association brings either greater or lesser opportunity for behavioral response.

Success, then, depends, to a great extent, on how the practitioner has sized up audience needs/concerns/interests and packaged the message accordingly. The desired communication outcome stays the same in any case: It calls for an individual to attend the county fair regardless of previous information or experience. Responsibility for behavior change lies with how the practitioner creates and packages the message.

Success hinges on focusing on the most frequently demonstrated associations (identified in audience research) and using the most common associations to package the message content, increasing the probability for behavior change. If, for example, research identifies a positive association between seeing exhibits and farm animals as a priority motivation for most potential fairgoers, then messages should be packaged to take advantage of those motivations.

Paivio suggests that images actually represent a dynamic symbol system that makes the receiver capable of making the transition from receiving information to acting on that information.[8] Image, then, is a set of symbols representing thoughts and memories in the person's head. The term "county fair" may simply be an icon for all the associations called to mind by the reader, viewer, or listener. The selection of behaviors necessary to respond to the stimuli is directed by the message and associations projected by the fair's image.

Audience members act on the message only after being motivated to process the information. The message may or may not cause replication of the intended action. The degree to which the behavior represents the intended message depends, to a large extent, on how well the public relations practitioner has

1. Helped audience members clearly put themselves into the story (transferred to real-life needs/concerns/interests)
2. Helped audience members evaluate the benefits of action and consequences of inaction (motivation)
3. Helped audience members think through or mentally rehearse the intended action (process information and direct behavior)

Success or failure of any new behavior is measured by both the positive and negative consequences we receive from it. These consequences are stored in memory and utilized the next time we are faced with the same or similar messages.

A positive experience with a new behavior produces a mental confidence that, when viewed by the receiver, makes repetition of the behavior possible, continuing to build mental confidence and satisfaction from performing the behavior. When the wool yarn industry set out to increase sales by encouraging women to reacquire the desire to knit woolen clothes, it found that it was not enough simply to design beautiful patterns and offer benefits, such as lower-cost garments. A beautiful pattern in the hands of an unskilled knitter did not reinforce the intended behavior change. It became evident that the industry also had to provide audience members with the skills necessary to produce those beautiful knits. The finished product had to produce recognizably positive feelings for the new knitter, not failure. Successful communications, then, would have to be designed to maximize positive consequences and minimize negative ones.

The Food and Drug Administration ran into similar difficulties trying to persuade physicians to begin reporting patient vitamin and mineral supplement toxicities. Despite a tremendous amount of publicity, physicians did not increase toxicity reports because they were not familiar enough or confident about the toxicity symptoms.

**Describe the reasons why the following campaign description might not ensure a successful experience for the receiver.**

**The Bank of Brannan launched a campaign to introduce new automated bank tellers to its customers. Messages stressed the convenience of 24-hour banking and the speed of transactions. The campaign was unsuccessful. Why?**

Messages, then, are more likely to be transferred, arouse motivation, direct behavior, and be reinforced for action when you can help your audience succeed at the task you encourage them to try. Few of us will attempt new behaviors when we lack mental and physical preparedness.

**Ask yourself when was the last time you were motivated to do something you did not know how to do, or were not sure you could do successfully, or were not in some way protected from personal failure.**

Public relations professionals can often assist their target audience members in overcoming this lack of preparation by helping them to think through and mentally rehearse how these new behaviors can be performed. Comfortable scenarios and how-to situations can be effective in facilitating initiation of behaviors.

Though the development of attitudes and behavior are often transposed—with attitudes being formed *before* the behavior—this process addresses the development of positive attitudes following success with a new behavior. Positive attitude encourages repetition of the cycle. The doing of the behavior successfully creates the motivation to repeat it. Forming values/attitudes can be the result of confidence created by a successful behavior attempt. It might be helpful to illustrate the complete cycle with the following scenario:

THE PRODUCT: a running shoe

THE AUDIENCE: the casual jogger

THE SITUATION: An executive who jogs daily sees a story in her local newspaper on how to prevent foot problems when running on hard surfaces (the message delivered through the newspaper channel). Because she runs on hard surfaces and has been experiencing sore feet, the executive makes an immediate transfer to her own life. Upon continued reading, she finds a description of the discomfort she is experiencing along with a type of shoe designed to minimize the problem (motivation aroused). All of these external characteristics combine with the internal associations she makes about relief from pain and callouses, access to the shoe locally, and other positive correlations (information processed, behavior directed toward purchase of the shoe). The executive purchases the shoe (behavior change). After several weeks of jogging, her feet feel better (change reinforced with experience). She begins to assign greater value to her purchase action. She now values the shoes she purchased and the sources from which she learned the information. She has a positive attitude and may even share her new attitude and behavior with others.

Successful accommodation of all aspects of the receiver's mental processing creates a value for that content/behavior that prepares the receiver for accepting the next communication from the sender. For many years, motivation alone was thought to bring about change in attitude and/or behavior. Now it is known to be more complicated than the elusive singularity of motivation. The receiver's mind processes a message in a step-by-step manner using the past, present, and future known only to the receiver. The result is observable action in response to that suggested in the message and the subsequent development of values for that successful action.

**Suppose you are the receiver of the following campaign messages. How has each been created to enhance your movement from simple receipt of message to behavioral action and positive attitude?**

**1. Exercising makes you feel better and leads to a happier life even when done in short segments.**

**2. Employees belonging to a credit union feel greater financial security and enjoy easy credit to purchase important goods and services.**

### *Step 8: Communicate Message*

The remaining step is the actual communication of the message using the medium or media mix selected. There are at least three important factors to remember in maximizing the impact of the communicated message:

1. The total volume of messages is positively related to impact. (Remember, though, that just because a message is transmitted does not mean it reaches the audience.)
2. Message repetition increases impact to a point, but after three to five successful exposures there is little additional impact. In fact, some research indicates that positive responses may reverse after a high degree of repeated exposure. Varying the packaging of the message is preferred over repeating the same message.
3. Research indicates that concentrated bursts of spot messages have more impact than the same number of messages strung out over a longer period. This kind of message pacing allows audience members to retain the message due to intensive practice while avoiding message burnout because of prolonged contact.

Placement of publicity, for example, by news release, wire service, or spokesperson interview or appearances on radio and television talk and news shows is the place at which the communication leaves the practitioner's hands. Editors judge the practitioner's ability to meet his or her journalistic needs. Those gatekeepers decide if your communication will ever have the opportunity to move your target audiences to change. The editor can minimize your message with his or her editing pencil, headlines, and to some extent, control over the broadcast interview.

A well-written news release, news hook, or talk show slant can survive the editing pencil. Regardless, at some point it leaves the hands of the public relations practitioner only to resurface again if the message is published in a newspaper or magazine or aired on television or radio.

## SUMMARY

- ☐ The message/media outline organizes the process for selecting the appropriate message and the channels of communication to accomplish the plan's Key Result Areas.
- ☐ The message/media outline consists of eight steps:
  - ☐ Clarify communications outcome
  - ☐ Clarify target audience
  - ☐ Identify audience needs/concerns/interests
  - ☐ Choose the message
  - ☐ Choose the communication channel
  - ☐ Select spokesperson
  - ☐ Package message to raise audience need/concern/interest
  - ☐ Communicate message
- ☐ Step 7 of the message/media outline utilizes four question clusters:
  - ☐ Does the communication raise an audience need, concern, or interest? Can audience members easily put themselves into the situation?
  - ☐ Is your product, issue, or organization offered as a solution in a clear and concise manner?
  - ☐ Are the benefits to the solution clearly presented? Can the receiver jot down in one sentence, "What's in it for me?"
  - ☐ Are the consequences of leaving the need, concern, or interest unresolved clearly presented?
  - ☐ Have you helped the individual members of the target audience mentally rehearse or think through the action you would like them to take?
- ☐ Behavior of the receiver in processing the message delivered through the selected channel includes
  - ☐ Transfer to real-life needs/concerns/interests is accomplished.
  - ☐ Intention (motivation) is aroused.
  - ☐ Information is processed and behavior directed.
  - ☐ Behavior change occurs.
  - ☐ New behavior is reinforced with experience.
  - ☐ Values/attitudes are formed.

## EXERCISES

1. Assume you are a public relations counselor using the message/media outline described in this chapter as a point of difference in a new business proposal. Develop a written description of the process to demonstrate its points of difference.
2. Which of the three message statements below is more likely to connect with the receiver's experiences or real life? Why?
   a. Forest fire prevention is a public responsibility.
   b. Only you can prevent forest fires.
   c. Forest fires cost taxpayers millions of dollars annually.

   Try another set of message statements. Which is the most likely to connect with the receiver's experiences or real life? Why?
   a. More investment products are available from the Bank of Brannan.
   b. We help you make investment choices at the Bank of Brannan.
   c. We have 7.5 percent interest on money market accounts at Bank of Brannan.
3. Review the Force Field Analysis assessment illustrated in Figure 3–1 for the L. Joyce Corporation. The assessed condition was plummeting employee morale following the organization's first major financial setback in many years. What are the strongest candidates for a message statement(s) to achieve a communications outcome of restoring employee morale? Develop a message statement(s) to be used as the nucleus for a Key Result Area reading: restore employee morale.
4. Suppose you have been retained by Stella Corporation to develop a publicity campaign to launch its new cellular telephone system. Develop a campaign message using the message/media outline and the Force Field Analysis document in Figure 3–2.

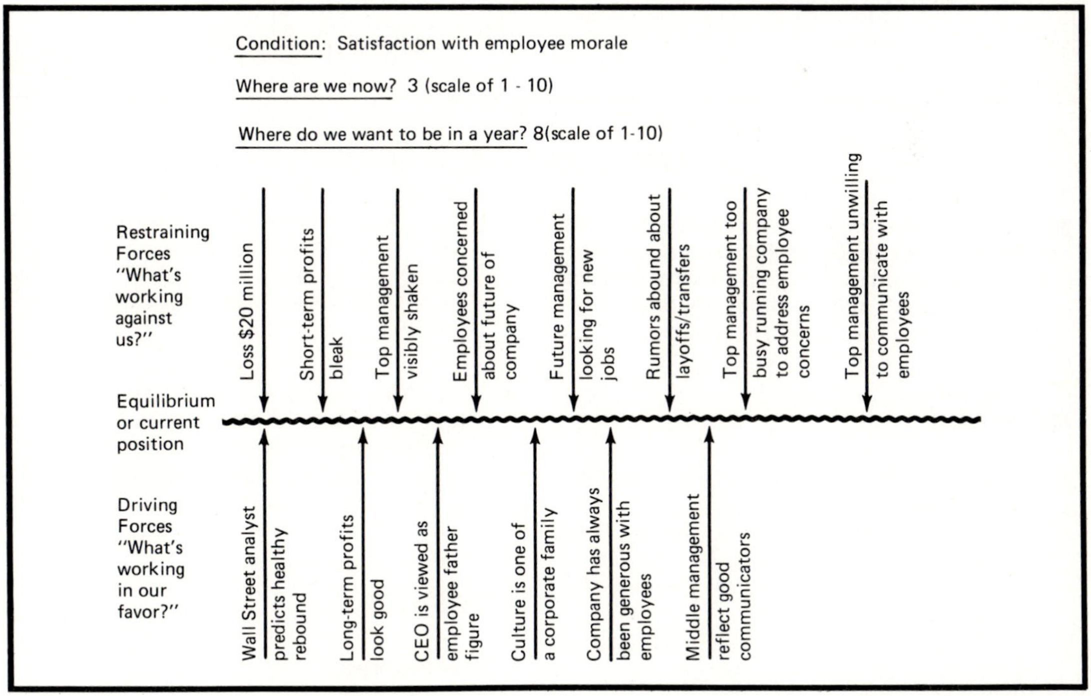


**FIGURE 3–1**
**Force Field Analysis L. Joyce Corporation**

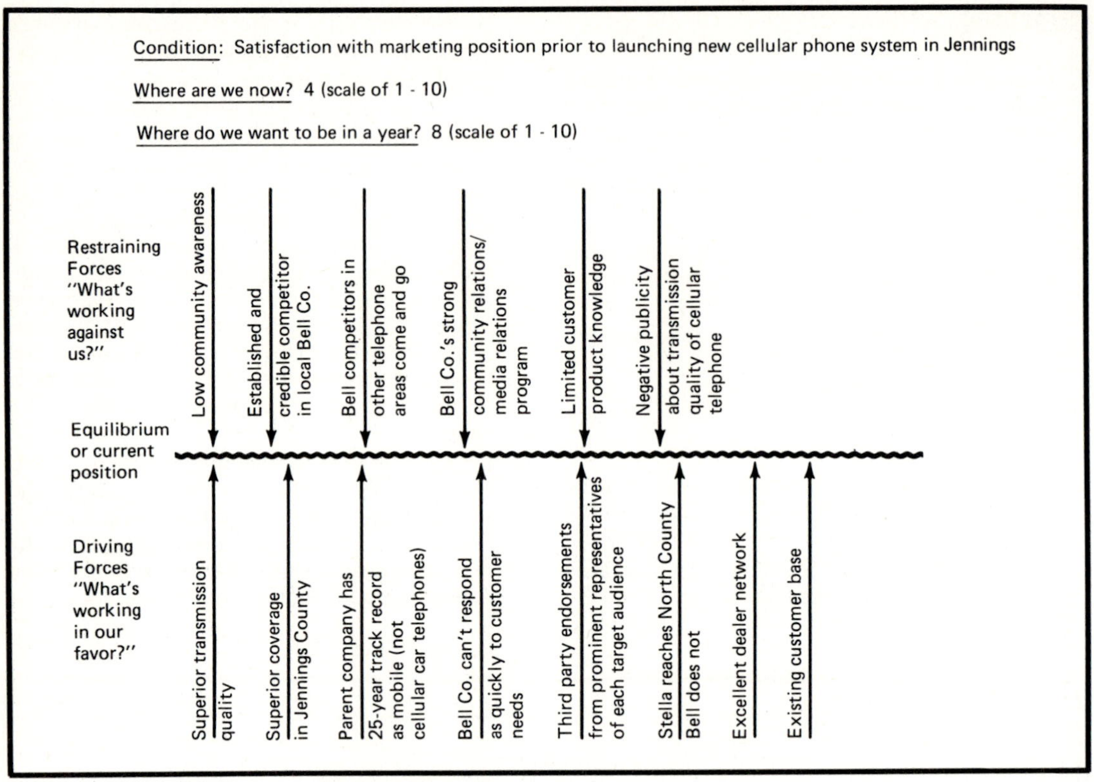


**FIGURE 3–2**
**Force Field Analysis Stella Corporation**

5. Complete the message/media outline, develop a news angle, and write a news story to be published in your community newspaper for Stella's new cellular telephone system.

## REFERENCES

1. Robin Schmidt, GTE Sprint, personal communication, November 10, 1984.
2. Allen H. Center and Frank E. Walsh, *Public Relations Practices: Managerial Case Studies and Problems* (Englewood Cliffs, NJ: Prentice-Hall, 1985), p. 17.
3. Kerry D. Tucker, "Even Doc Adams Reads the Globe," *Public Relations Journal* (December 1976), 16.
4. Doug Newsom and Tom Siegfried, *Writing in Public Relations Practice: Form and Style* (Belmont, CA: Wadsworth, 1981), p. 20.
5. Charles Atkin, "Mass Media Information Campaign Effectiveness, " in *Public Communication Campaigns*, ed. Ronald Rice and William Paisley (Beverly Hills, CA: Sage Publications, 1981), p. 275.
6. Ibid.
7. M. C. Wittrock and A. A. Lumsdaine, "Instructional Psychology," *Annual Review of Psychology*, 28 (1977), 166.
8. A. Paivio, "On the Functional Significance of Imagery," *Psychological Bulletin*, 73 (1970), 388.

## CASE STUDY

### The Problem

J. Joseph Sullivan, Inc., a commercial and industrial construction company ("They build buildings."), has opened an office in your community. Sullivan has a couple of major contracts in your town but is relatively unknown to its primary source of business: commercial and industrial developers ("They hire companies to build their buildings."). Sullivan's goal is to make its local operation self-sufficient within two years.

**Situational Analysis**

Sullivan is the largest contractor in a nearby county with a twenty-five-year track record for first-class performance. Its management team operates from a philosophy of going the extra mile to ensure the projects it builds generate a profit for its developer clients. This philosophy is carried out through what Sullivan calls "strict cost and quality control systems." Sullivan also believes that ample staffing and project supervision are necessary to carry out this philosophy.

The Sullivan management team tells you that the two primary concerns about local construction companies they hear from developers are

1. Local firms tend to take on more work than they can handle, causing delayed completion dates for existing clients.
2. Budget overruns are a common problem for local construction companies.

Many out-of-town firms have tried to break into the lucrative construction market in your town. Sullivan's well-established competitors have been able to get out-of-towners labeled as "carpetbaggers," and none has stayed in business very long.

Chief Executive Officer J. Joseph Sullivan believes that acceptance by the local business community is crucial to long-term success.

1. Develop a situational public relations plan that best supports J. Joseph Sullivan, Inc.'s, two-year goal.
2. Assume your plan has been approved and you are seated at the word processor to develop your first news release. Complete the message/media outline.

# CHAPTER 4

# Applying Motivational Principles to Publicity

### *IN THIS CHAPTER*

The application of motivational principles to the preparation of publicity significantly enhances the ability of the practitioner to achieve objectives identified in the public relations plan.

Assuming that one positive story in the newspaper will automatically move you closer to achieving a public relations objective is a mistake (with the exception of a communication-level objective).

A story about your organization or product may do wonders for internal egos, but unless you have made some effort to package that story to catch the attention of targeted individuals, the odds of it being read, let alone positively affecting public relations objectives, are remote.

In the end, the success of the public information campaign depends on how well you have caught the attention of target individuals and helped them to

1. Transfer what is being said to their own real-life situation
2. Evaluate the benefits of acting on the communications and the consequences of not acting
3. Think through or mentally rehearse the desired action

The process presented in this chapter provides the practitioner with a tool to enhance the odds of achieving public relations objectives.

### *CHAPTER OBJECTIVES*

The reader will be able to

1. Utilize the four operational question clusters of the message/media outline in news release writing.
2. Apply the use of similes, metaphors, analogies, and descriptive words in news releases to transfer communication to real-life experiences of the audience(s).
3. Incorporate behavioral techniques that help the audience think through or mentally rehearse the intended action.

## LAUNCHING THE PUBLIC RELATIONS PLAN

Once public relations plans are laid, publicity is often a means for carrying out objectives under Key Result Areas. Securing and maintaining relationships between an organization and its key constituencies, gaining acceptance for products with targeted customers, or managing issues can often be facilitated with news stories in media that effectively reach target audiences.

Chapter 2 cites five possible results for public relations objectives: communication, message retention, message acceptance, formation of or change in an attitude, and overt behavior change.[1] Programs designed to follow the process described in this text are capable of producing any one of these end products. This chapter deals with increasing the probability that written publicity messages will move up the impact ladder toward results in attitude and/or behavior change.

A new set of writing skills that builds on those learned in news writing, and reinforced in Chapters 5 and 6, can help attitude and behavior change be a more consistent objective for public relations programs.

Traditionally, good publicity writing has followed rules dictated by media stylebooks and the basic "who, what, where, when, why, and how" of news writing. These guidelines still hold true, as does a publicist's common sense regarding what is or is not a positive publicity story. What is suggested, however, are additional criteria that build on a publicist's news writing skills and instincts. These new criteria incorporate all the tools for reinforcement or change in attitude and behavior.

Consequently, the approach taken in this text expands what our instincts demonstrate is a good news story to developing a news story that best

- ☐ Supports the message necessary to carry out objectives identified in the public relations plan
- ☐ Utilizes techniques from other disciplines, primarily learning theory, to move individuals in the target public to action

Such an emphasis in the development of publicity writing works best when a public relations writer starts the development of a news story by thinking through the message/media outline steps described in Chapter 3:

1. Identify the specific action you want taken as a result of your communication.
2. Clarify target audience(s).
3. Identify audience needs/concerns/interests.
4. Choose message.
5. Choose channel of communications.
6. Select spokesperson.

Publicity guided by the message/media outline is designed to support the public relations plan while meeting the needs/concerns/interests of individual members of a specific target audience(s). Audience attention is more consistently achieved because it is packaged as a solution to the audience's needs/concerns/interests. Communications channels frequented by individual members of the target audience are utilized, and a spokesperson is selected for credibility and believability.

It is the seventh and final step prior to communication that incorporates behavioral publicity criteria. The application step of the model presented is to

7. Package message to raise an audience need/concern/interest and offer a product, issue, or organization as a means for fulfilling that need, minimizing that concern, or satisfying that interest.

The basis for this step, as cited in earlier chapters, is the development, implementation, and evaluation of content utilizing four key clusters of questions. These question clusters, which should now be familiar to you, are

1. Does the lead or first paragraphs raise an audience need/concern/interest? Can audience members easily put themselves into the story? Can you paint a real-life scenario with words or visuals?
2. Is the solution presented in a clear, concise, and believable manner? Can individual audi-

ence members jot down in one sentence, "What's in it for me?"

3. Are the consequences of leaving the need/concern/interest unresolved clearly presented?
4. Have you helped the audience members mentally rehearse or think through the action you want them to take?

A description of how to apply the four key question clusters follows.

### *1. Does the lead or first paragraph raise an audience need/concern/interest?*

The lead in a publicity release for print media consists of the first and occasionally the second paragraph of the story. With the process described in this text, the lead is used both to summarize the essential element of the story and raise an audience need/concern/interest. The latter increases our odds for generating attention by those targeted for influence. Regardless, the rules of the medium must apply here. (These rules are covered in later chapters.)

The more specific we become in identifying with whom we want to communicate—our target audience—the more specific we can become about individual needs/concerns/interests. For example, a food marketing board was targeting communications to the homemaker. It further refined its audience by life stage: bachelors, young marrieds, households with children under the age of ten years, households with children over the age of ten years, empty nesters (those whose children have left the home), and retirees. Such market segmentation enabled the public relations team to tailor programs to meet the individual needs/concerns/interests of each life stage thought to be most critical in the pursuit of the public relations mission. A young married homemaker, for example, has needs that differ from those of a retired homemaker. A homemaker with children under ten years of age has different needs from an empty nester.

The more fine-tuned the communications package, the more adept a public relations professional can be at developing communications.

If we judge three of the six life stages as top priority and we know that the chief motivation for preparing nutritious meals is concern for children and future family, then we can take just about any news angle and position it in terms of how it affects those children.

In another example, from the banking industry, if we know that there is confusion among targeted prospective bank customers over a myriad of new investment possibilities, then we can develop publicity that positions bank executives as investment resources, that is, as individuals to see regarding investment decisions.

Raising audience needs/concerns/interests is the first step in developing content designed to move members of a targeted audience to change or reinforce attitudes and behaviors. It establishes reality for the message among those individuals targeted for communication.

What is reality to the writer may not necessarily be reality to the receiver. What is reality to the working homemaker with regard to feeding her household nutritiously may not be reality to an executive without a family. Painting a realistic banking scenario for the young executive may be different from that of the retired executive. The same is true for employees, corporate neighbors, political officials, or any of the critical audiences with which an organization deals.

Identifying real-life situations for each target audience is essential in order to consistently make messages meaningful. If the working homemaker's primary obstacle is planning ahead so that her family receives nutritious meals, then messages should be designed to help minimize that obstacle. Likewise, if we know that younger, more educated employees have an entirely different reality with respect to the job than younger, less educated employees or older executives, then that reality should be identified by research. Messages can then be packaged with real-life pictures of the benefits of acting on them.

Helping an audience actually visualize themselves in the news story scenario is called *mental imagery*. Mental imagery takes into consideration the right brain/left brain theory of how people best learn information and how they subsequently act. Traditionally, communicators have concentrated on communicating with the left side of the brain, the logical side, and have paid little attention to the right side, the pictorial side. Growing evidence suggests that more attention should be paid to the brain's right side, and mental imagery is a key factor in such behavioral strategy.

Mental imagery can be incorporated into a news release through the use of similes, metaphors, and analogies.

Funk and Wagnall contrasts similes, metaphors, and analogies as follows:

> Simile is a literary device to conjure up a vivid picture; "an Alpine peak like a frosted cake" is a simile. A metaphor differs from a simile only in omitting "like" or "as," the words of comparison; "the silver pepper of the stars" is a metaphor. The purpose of analogy is to explain rather than to make vivid; it compares dynamic rather than visual aspects; "an electric current is like the flow of a river, with voltage corresponding to force, volume of water to amperage, etc." is an example of an analogy.[2]

Metaphors, similes, and analogies, then, use the principle of likeness to transfer the meaning from a familiar concept to an unfamiliar one. They relate our past experience to new concepts.

An agricultural economist used the following metaphor in an interview with a reporter from the *Los Angeles Times* to bring home the effect of tight money controls on the farming community: " 'The Federal Reserve slammed on the brakes, and much of agriculture went into the windshield,' Iowa State University economist Harl said. 'As interest rates went up, the value of land used as collateral fell.' "[3] In another example, *Fortune* magazine described internal changes at AT&T following divestiture as "a cultural train wreck."[4] The California Dietetic Association used a similar tactic in a news release quoting a registered dietitian on the value of breakfast: " 'Your body needs food in the morning the same way a cold car needs an extra tap on the accelerator to get fuel into its system,' said Long."

Most opportunities to incorporate mental imagery come in quotations used to expand on the basic who, what, where, when, why, and how of a news story. Consequently, careful thought should be given to the quotation as a means for expanding a key story point beyond factual interpretation. Try painting a picture of reality for the reader while being sensitive about being "cute." One must be wary of being too trite with descriptive language.

"Metaphors are more than an aid to explanation, they are also strategic tools," says Dorothy Nelkin, author of *Selling Science*. "A metaphor is not just a rhetorical flourish, but a basic property of language used to define experience and to evoke shared meanings," she says. "They [George Lakoff and Mark Johnson] suggest that metaphors affect the ways we perceive, think and act, for they structure our understanding of events, convey emotions and attitudes, and allow us to construct elaborate concepts about public issues and events," Nelkin says.[5]

Analogies can also be effective at painting mental pictures for the reader, viewer, or listener. President Jimmy Carter's White House papers were described in a news story as follows: "Carter's total 27-million page collection would fill a row of five-drawer filing cabinets $2\frac{1}{2}$ miles long. Among the papers released Wednesday, researchers will find documents ranging from the most trivial to issues of significant historic importance."[6] Another analogy, from a news story on the California Lottery reads: " 'In our first year, revenue collections were larger than the operating budgets of six states, two developing nations and the value of Imelda Marcos' shoe collection,' said Bill Seaton, spokesman for the California Lottery."[7] In an analogy explaining a sudden increase in mortgage interest rates, a lender was quoted as follows: "'It has been the farthest, quickest movement I've ever seen,' said John M. Teutsch, a veteran mortgage lender from Seattle. 'On the Richter (earthquake) scale,' he said, 'this has been an 8.'"[8]

Descriptive, high imagery phrases provide an opportunity for mental imagery as well, particularly when taking a feature approach to news writing. The University of Texas Health Sciences Center at Dallas used the following lead in a news release aimed at potential allergy patients:

> Dallas . . . Are your eyes red and itchy and do they burn? How about your nose? Is it runny and all stuffed up? And does this happen to you every winter, especially around Christmas time?
>
> Then, as tragic as this may seem, you may be allergic to your Christmas tree.
>
> According to Dr. Timothy Sullivan, head of the Allergy Unit at University of Texas Health Center at Dallas, there are a number of allergies associated with Christmas trees.

Although such a feature writing approach, particularly in a lead paragraph, is more the exception than the norm, it can be successful, especially with specialty sections of major metropolitan newspapers (addressed in the next chapter), weekly newspapers, and television news.

Use of examples is still another method for creating real-life scenarios. Remember that you do not have to use such terms as "for example" or "for instance" when citing examples. Such a practice only increases words that may seem correct for an English class but not necessarily for a newspaper story.

The following is an excerpt from a news release for the Center for Creative Leadership:

> "It's not enough to work hard," says Morrison. "You have to understand the rules of the corporation you're working for to get ahead. In some cases it's as trivial as not wearing white socks. In others, there is a complex hierarchy to be learned, where even the simplest faux pas may remain forever unforgiven."

The use of visuals can be extremely effective in helping individuals picture the concepts and transfer them to personal reality. Television video footage, graphic charts, and slides can help viewers of a news or talk show actually see, for example, healthy dense bones in contrast to aged, porous bones caused by insufficient intake of calcium-rich foods. Helping individuals place immediacy to such a long-term problem can be effective in increasing consumption of calcium-rich foods.

**Which of the news releases making up Figure 4–1 attempts to draw the greatest transfer to real-life experience? Why?**

Reality enables the receiver to jump from the content of the message to his or her real-life congruities. This transfer can then arouse intention that can accelerate the processing of information to direct behavior change. A successful experience from performing the behavior itself can form positive attitudes and values for the new behavior.

**How might you use mental imagery to transfer the following messages to real-life situations for the receiver?**

1. The Bank of Brannan expands hours of operation.
2. The Point Loma College enrollment deadline is next month.
3. Cubic Corporation will expand its plant and bring new jobs to your city.

Bank of Brannan
4012 Lusk Drive
Brannan Island, Florida 33160

Contact: Sharon McNurney
(305) 451-2265

BANKS, S & Ls GET GREEN LIGHT

TO OFFER MONEY MARKET ACCOUNTS

Local banks and savings and loans will soon be able to offer customers new high-interest rate accounts similar to money market funds, according to Sharon McNurney, president of the Bank of Brannan.

New legislation, effective Dec. 14, gives banks and savings and loans the green light for these federally insured accounts that will be competitive with money market funds, traditionally reserved for stock brokerage firms.

"This means that money market-type accounts set up with banks and savings and loans will be insured, like other accounts, by the FDIC up to $100,000," said McNurney.

"It also means that local investment dollars can stay here in our community in the form of loans for homes, cars and businesses rather than being shipped off to major U.S. money market centers for investments outside the local community." she added.

- more -

**FIGURE 4–1A**
**Release 1**

BANKS, S & Ls OFFER MONEY MARKET ACCOUNTS -- ADD ONE

The Bank of Brannan will offer money market checking accounts with a minimum deposit of $2,500. The new legislation stipulates that if a depositor's balance dips below $2,500, the account will earn the standard passbook interest rate.

Additionally, depositors will be permitted six transactions each month, but will have unlimited withdrawal privileges. The Bank of Brannan will honor money market account bonus coupons now being offered by all local banks.

The Bank of Brannan is offering an interim investment program which will give customers 9 percent interest until Dec. 14 when funds will be automatically transferred to the new money market checking account. Although uninsured, this interim investment program is backed by government securities.

# # #

**FIGURE 4–1A (continued)**

Dairy Council of California

601 North Market Blvd., Suite 300
Sacramento, Ca. 95834-1274/(916) 920-7691

# nutrition information

DCC-#127-84
10/19/84

Contact Beverly McKee

Call Collect (916) 920-7691

DON'T SHORTCHANGE YOUR CALCIUM INTAKE

Dieting and soft drink consumption may be shortchanging your body of calcium, the vital nutrient which plays a major role in the prevention of osteoporosis.

According to Stanford University School of Medicine Professor Robert Marcus, M.D., women who diet frequently compromise their intake of calcium.

"Unfortunately, the first thing many women eliminate on a diet is dairy products, which are the best source of calcium in the American diet. In addition, dairy products contain vitamin D, which helps in the absorption of calcium."

The recommended dietary allowance (RDA) for calcium is 800 milligrams -- the equivalent of about three glasses of milk a day. Unfortunately, most women fall short of this requirement, and many experts believe that women need even more than 800 milligrams daily.

If weight control is a concern, Marcus suggests switching to lowfat or nonfat milk and dairy products. "But don't eliminate them," he cautions.

- more -

Courtesy of Dairy Council of California

**FIGURE 4–1B**
**Release 2**

DAIRY COUNCIL OF CALIFORNIA
Page 2

Marcus is also concerned about the dramatic increase in the number of adolescents who consume soft drinks at meals or snack time.

"I become especially concerned when women regularly consume cola drinks rather than milk or other dairy products because their diet will undoubtedly be low in calcium."

Try substituting milk at meals and cheese and crackers or yogurt for afternoon soft drink breaks.

Marcus also cautions heavy coffee and tea drinkers not to consume these products in place of milk. Try substituting a milk group food for one serving of these caffeine drinks.

Try drinking your coffee and tea mixed with half-a-cup of milk, like many Europeans do. This will provide at least some calcium in the diet.

# # # #

**FIGURE 4–1B (continued)**

# NEWS

**California Dietetic Association**

Central Office: 7740 Manchester Ave., Suite 102, Playa del Rey, CA 90293
(213) 822-0177

June 22, 1987

(916) 345-1062

FOR ACCURATE PERSPECTIVE, THINK OF
SUPPLEMENTS AS OVER-THE-COUNTER DRUGS

Would you take two aspirin if you didn't have a headache, or a decongestant if you didn't have a cold?

According to the California Dietetic Association (CDA), taking single nutrient vitamin or mineral supplements in doses higher than 100 percent of the Recommended Dietary Allowance (RDA) when you don't have a nutrient deficiency risks toxicity.

More than 16 percent of the population, or 30 million Americans, consume vitamin and mineral supplements in excess of 300 percent of the Recommended Dietary Allowance (RDA).

"The overuse of vitamin and mineral supplements sets the stage for the onset of harmful side effects," said Corinne Williams, R.D., CDA president.

"Exceeding 100 percent of the RDA is unnecessary for normal, healthy people," Williams said.

(more)

**FIGURE 4–1C**
**Release 3**

PAGE TWO --- VITAMINS AS DRUGS

"Taking several times the RDA for some nutrients is the first step for vitamin or mineral toxicity, which, depending on the nutrient, can result in symptoms ranging from fatigue to permanent nerve damage. It can also upset the utilization of nutrients," she added.

Williams noted that a very small percentage of the population have physician-diagnosed nutrient deficiencies which require supplementation.

"A multi-vitamin supplement that does not exceed 100 percent RDA for any nutrient is considered safe," Williams said. "But if you feel you need extra vitamins or minerals, look to foods first to fill in the gaps."

"Foods are a better source for vitamins and minerals because the natural balance of nutrients allows optimal absorption without the risk of side effects. It also supplies needed carbohydrates, protein and fiber," she said.

If you eat a varied and balanced diet, Williams said there is little chance you need any supplementation.

"But if you suspect a serious deficiency, don't try to self-medicate. See a physician to diagnose the problem," she said.

A healthy diet from the four nutrient-based food groups includes three lowfat servings from the dairy group (two for men), two servings of lean meat or meat alternates, four servings of vegetables and fruits and four servings of whole-grain breads and cereals.

(more)

**FIGURE 4–1C (continued)**

PAGE THREE --- VITAMINS AS DRUGS

Here are some selections from each group and the nutrients they provide:

* **Dairy foods:** lowfat milk, yogurt or cheese all are rich in calcium, protein and riboflavin.

* **Lean meats:** skinless chicken, fish, turkey, fat-trimmed beef, beans and peas provide iron, vitamin B-12 and protein.

* **Fruits and vegetables:** a wide variety of fruits and vegetables can provide ample amounts of vitamins A and C and fiber.

* **Breads and cereals:** tortillas, brown rice and any whole-grain breads or cereals are good sources of fiber and B-vitamins.

# # # #

**FIGURE 4–1C (continued)**

UT News
Office of Medical Information
The University of Texas Health Science Center at Dallas
5323 Harry Hines Boulevard Dallas, Texas 75235
214/688-3404

November 21, 1985

CONTACT: Susan Rutherford
OFFICE: 214/688-3404
HOME: 214/349-7820

*****Christmas tree allergies plague the unwary.

DALLAS--Are your eyes red and itchy and do they burn? How about your nose? Is it runny and all stuffed up? And does this happen to you every winter, especially around Christmas time?

Then, as tragic as this may seem, you may be allergic to your Christmas tree.

According to Dr. Timothy Sullivan, head of the Allergy Unit at The University of Texas Health Science Center at Dallas, there are a number of allergies associated with Christmas trees.

For example, if you get into the pioneer spirit and decide to hike into the woods and chop down your own tree, you may accidently choose a male mountain cedar tree (Juniper ashei or one of its relatives) that could pollinate right in your living room. It's the mountain cedar pollen that causes allergic reactions and is second only to ragweed as the most common cause of pollen-induced allergies in this part of the country.

If you suspect you're allergic to mountain cedar, the trick is to find a female tree. "You're relatively safe if your tree has blue Juniper berries," says Sullivan.

Male trees have a pollen-producing apparatus that turns from green to brown as the pollen matures. During the time of pollen release, the male trees take on a brown hue. Sullivan points out that for use as Christmas trees, most people are attracted to the female mountain cedar, which is usually greener than the pollinating male and has blue berries. However, it is likely that a person could cut down a male tree while it's still green and therefore the tree will be primed to pollinate in his or her house.

Most people, however, wouldn't even be tempted to cut down their own trees. They prefer those found in Christmas tree lots. Unfortunately, these are often covered with mold spores that more than likely will fly off the tree into the living room, and many people are terribly allergic to mold.

**FIGURE 4–1D**
**Release 4**

If this is the case, you might opt for an artificial tree.

So, what's the answer now?

Medical science is working on it, says Sullivan.

Sullivan and a team of researchers at the health science center have purified mountain cedar pollen down to a specific molecule that causes the allergic reaction, so that physicians no longer have to use extracts of crude pollen for allergy skin testing and allergy shots for desensitization.

However, after a couple of years of use, you will probably open up the box containing your artificial tree and notice that it's covered with...you guessed it -- dust. And, as everyone knows, a lot of people are violently allergic to dust.

Now the researchers are tracking down the particular protein within the molecule that the immune system recognizes as the culprit. "We know the protein causing the allergy in considerable chemical detail," Sullivan says. "But by knowing its structure completely, we will be able to synthesize it and administer a drug containing fragments of the material to block the allergic reaction."

Sullivan also expects mountain cedar to become a model to help usher in a new era in allergy treatment -- prevention. "We're going to look at genetic factors -- who is susceptible to mountain cedar allergy and who is not. By identifying the specific gene that makes one predisposed to getting an allergy, we can, for the first time, consider strategies to keep allergies from appearing."

While allergic reactions to mountain cedar are rarely fatal, Sullivan says the discomfort can cause a lot of misery, including sleepless nights, lost days from school or work and enormous doctor bills. There are effective medications on the market today, even antihistamines that don't put the person to sleep, but he says even these may lose their effect as a pollen season progresses.

Sullivan explains that people prone to develop allergies have a "misdirected protective reaction." They begin to manufacture antibodies in the bloodstream to fight off pollen and other allergens as if they were disease-causing bacteria or parasites. Non-allergic people appear to start making these protective antibodies (called IgE antibodies) but somehow manage to suppress them. However, the immune system of the allergy-prone individual does not suppress this response, and it is here that the problem lies.

Inflammation in the eyes, nose and, sometimes, lungs is caused by the activation of the body's histamine-producing mast cells. Occasionally, the release of histamine by mast cells can be explosive enough to be fatal.

**FIGURE 4–1D (continued)**

The IgE antibodies bind to the surface of the mast cells, and signal the cells to release their histamine and other inflammatory mediators. These antibodies resemble lobsters, with long bodies and claw-like appendages that sit on the surface of the mast cells and grab onto particles the antibodies perceive as invading the body. When more than one antibody recognizes this foreign object and grabs onto it, this multiple attachment to the object (called clumping) signals the mast cell to release histamine.

By making a drug containing fragments of the allergen, the broken-up allergen would occupy the antibodies without causing the release of histamine, and the person would be temporarily free of allergy symptoms, Sullivan says.

##

DISTRIBUTION: AA,AB,AF, AG,AH,AI,AK,SL,SC

FIGURE 4–1D (continued)

### *2. Is the solution presented in a clear and concise manner? Is it believable?*

After a publicity writer has raised an issue to get the attention of individual members of the target audience, the next step is to present the company's product or message as a solution to that issue. The more concise and clear the solution, the better the opportunity for audience members to process the information. Likewise a credible spokesperson is important to message acceptance.

It would be much easier to raise issues and clearly present solutions if we were dealing with controlled media, such as employee vehicles, advertising, direct mail, audio-visual, or face-to-face communications. Publicity, however, is forced, because of its format, to meet the needs of the news media gatekeeper as well as the audience. The editor can edit a news release or a reporter can redirect an interview or both can reject the news angle out-of-hand. An editor can also make the decision to publish a news release as written or a reporter may accept the news angle and follow the logic of the course presented.

Anything other than the last alternative jeopardizes acceptance of the message. The control factor for the publicist, albeit frequently limiting, is his or her capability of packaging a message into a solid news format. A thorough knowledge of what is and what is not news and the accompanying capability to produce it are essential skills for the successful publicity writer.

What follows are examples of news release writing that raise concerns and message solutions. Though the examples are news releases, print and broadcast interviews can be planned and orchestrated similarly. Often, the spokesperson has even more control of the interview, particularly in a live broadcast.

MESSAGE: Eat from the four food groups

AUDIENCE: Young married homemakers

NEED/CONCERN/INTEREST: Future children

COMMUNICATIONS CHANNEL: Newspaper food page

SPOKESPERSON: Physician

The following is the first four paragraphs of a nine-paragraph release incorporating the above criteria:

Premature births and babies who just don't weigh enough when they are born reflect the importance of nutrition in pregnancy, according to a Blake County physician.

"A woman's body stores surplus nutrients similar to a nutritional bank account. From the moment of conception, the unborn baby begins to withdraw from that account," said Lenard Morris, M.D., of the Blake County Hospital.

"If a mother-to-be eats a well-balanced diet as part of her daily regimen, she will not have to make any drastic concessions besides eating a few more foods high in protein and calcium," says Morris.

"A key to a well balanced diet," says Morris, "is to eat a variety of foods from the four food groups—milk, meat, vegetables and fruits, and breads and cereals.

"She should also double her servings of meat and milk group foods from two to four per day to cover her increased needs for protein and calcium."

**What are the concern and message solutions in the above release?**

CONCERN. Premature babies (paragraph 1)

SOLUTION. Eat a well-balanced diet (paragraph 3)
Eat from the four food groups (paragraph 4)
Double servings of meat and milk (paragraph 5)

WHAT'S IN IT FOR ME? A healthy pregnancy and baby

Here's another example:

MESSAGE. Open an account at the Bank of Brannan

AUDIENCE. Targeted prospective bank customers

NEED/CONCERN/INTEREST. To increase savings on taxes

COMMUNICATIONS CHANNEL. A weekly newspaper

SPOKESPERSON. Bank president

Three paragraphs from a seven-paragraph release follow:

Local investors have until Dec. 31 to take advantage of a one-time tax break offered by the federal government.

According to Bank of Brannan President Sharon McNurney, the All Savers program allows individuals to earn up to $1,000 in tax-free interest with a one year certificate of deposit. If a spouse works, the couple can earn up to $2,000 tax-free.

"The advantages of this investment come into focus when you compare it with higher, yet taxable interest rates and keep in mind the income tax bracket you are in," McNurney said.

> What are the concern and message solutions in the above release?

CONCERN. Tax savings

MESSAGE SOLUTION. Open a Bank of Brannan account

WHAT'S IN IT FOR ME? $1,000 to $2,000 in tax-free income

Such a process can be applied to any subject or any audience. If prospective car purchasers are interested in fuel economy, then messages can be designed to raise the fuel economy issue and offer a specific model of Chrysler, for example, to satisfy that interest. If the prospective car purchaser is concerned about quality, then a specific model of Chrysler can be offered to minimize that concern. If the prospective car purchaser has specific dollar needs, then a specific model of Chrysler can be offered to meet those needs. Publicity, then, must focus on these needs/concerns/interests if it expects to facilitate audience behaviors and values regarding Chrysler products.

The process can work just as well with government agencies trying to prevent consumer rip-offs or heart disease or with not-for-profit associations trying to raise funds for community projects.

The closer we can come to raising issues that research shows meet audience needs/concerns/interests, and position our campaign messages as solutions to those issues, the more consistent we become in utilizing the known steps leading to behavior change.

> What are the needs, concerns, or interests raised in the news release in Figure 4–2? What are the solutions? How is the product offered to meet a need, satisfy an interest or minimize a concern?

### *3. Are the consequences of leaving the need/concern/interest unresolved clearly presented?*

Gutman says that consumers choose actions that produce desired consequences and minimize undesired consequences.[9] All actions have consequences, and consumers learn to associate particular ones with particular actions.

A desirable consequence in the example of mothers-to-be eating nutritiously is that they can enjoy a more comfortable pregnancy, a point brought out in a quote from Dr. Morris later in the release. An undesirable consequence of not acting lies in the lead paragraph concerning premature babies. A desirable consequence in the bank example is that couples can earn $2,000 in tax-free income. An undesirable conse-

*News Release*

Scripps Memorial Hospitals

9888 Genesee Avenue
Post Office Box 28
La Jolla, California 92038-0028

February 26

Contact Diane Yohe
(619) 457-6894

OBSTETRICIAN TO GIVE FREE LECTURE ON PHYSICAL AND MENTAL PREPARATION FOR PREGNANCY

Scripps Memorial Hospitals will sponsor a free lecture March 7 to help women prepare for the physical and emotional stress of pregnancy.

"Women should prepare their bodies three to six months before pregnancy to prepare for stress and eliminate potential health problems," said Richard Riggs, M.D., a La Jolla and Encinitas obstetrician and gynecologist. Riggs will conduct the lecture from 7:00 to 9:00 p.m. in the conference center at Scripps Memorial Hospital in Encinitas. Call The Well Being at 457-6945 or (North County) 753-7270 for more information.

-more-

Courtesy of Scripps Memorial Hospitals

FIGURE 4–2

PREPARATION FOR PREGNANCY
Add 1-1-1

He said couples plan for the obvious like medical bills and nursery furniture, but overlook the cost of a new washing machine or dryer.

Also, he feels consideration should be given to child care if a mother will return to work after her baby is born.

"Many women find that working full-time and caring for an infant is physically and emotionally draining," he said. "I advise women to evaluate their career situation. Can they afford to take an extended leave of absence or arrange to work part-time? If not, can they afford outside help for housework and quality child care?"

He said physical preparation should begin with a thorough physical examination to determine if there are any undiagnosed problems such as cervical infections which could cause a woman to miscarry.

Several months prior to conception, women should begin an exercise program for good muscle tone and overall fitness. He recommends they also increase their nutritional status by following a diet rich in iron and vitamins, which are necessary for a healthy pregnancy.

"We've always known the importance of good nutrition throughout pregnancy, but a recent study in England reports a two-thirds reduction of congenital malformations in babies whose mothers were given vitamins and iron before conception."

Dr. Riggs earned his medical degree at the University of Lausanne in Lausanne, Switzerland. He completed an internship at Saint Joseph's Hospital in Denver, Colorado and a residency in obstetrics and gynecology at Saint Mary's Hospital in Milwaukee, Wisconsin.

He has been in private practice in La Jolla and Encinitas since 1971. Dr. Riggs is a resident of Encinitas.

###

**FIGURE 4–2 (continued)**

quence is the loss of the tax exemption if action is not taken by December 31.

Clearly identifying the consequences of a concern left unresolved takes us another step toward consistency in behavior change. This leads to the final action question in the four clusters.

> From the three news releases making up Figure 4–3, which best describes the consequences of not acting on the message? Why?

*4. Have you helped the audience members mentally rehearse or think through the action you want them to take?*

Because most people have difficulty transferring information to behavior, providing practice to aid that transfer can be helpful. Techniques that provide practice must be incorporated into the communication after content/solutions have been presented.

Practice or rehearsal can come in a number of ways. Questions and answers can cause the receiver to think through, or mentally rehearse, the use of the new information. A question and answer news release is one approach for use in specialty pages of a newspaper or wire service. Question and answers can also be effectively used by the interviewer or the spokesperson on broadcast talk shows. News releases can also occasionally pose questions to help readers think through how they will act or the consequences of such action related to the message.

The following question was used in a news release on food labeling by a government agency: "Are there additional ways to avoid hidden excesses, such as sodium, carbohydrates or calories?"

> What do you think was the intent of this question?

A release from a not-for-profit organization concluded with the following paragraph:

> So before you reach for the vitamin or mineral supplements at the grocery store, try thinking about the foods in your basket. Can they give your child the balanced diet needed? If the answer is yes, your child probably doesn't need supplements. By passing them up, you could be avoiding a potential mishap.

> Can you speculate on the intent of this question?

An example from a dental insurance company carried this paragraph: "If nine out of 10 large U.S. businesses offer their employees dental insurance, why do only 10 percent of employers with fewer than 50 employees do the same?"

> What was the intent of this question?

News releases that include questions present a novel approach to helping an audience mentally practice or incorporate new knowledge into their memory bank. However, one should be prudent in not overusing questions in new releases. It is not something with which an editor is particularly comfortable.

Certain phrases can also help an individual think through the application of the message. Public relations writers should be particularly sensitive to "giving orders" to receivers. Although news style complements order giving, helping individuals make decisions on their own with phrases such as "think through" or "when was the last time you" support potential behaviors. Such terminology can help an audience member contemplate application of the message. Strike a balance between behavioral terminology and news style.

# NEWS

## California Dietetic Association

Central Office: 7740 Manchester Ave., Suite 102, Playa del Rey, CA 90293
(213) 822-0177

Contact: Gretchen Griswold
(619) 296-0605

MOTHERS CAUTIONED ABOUT GIVING CHEWABLE VITAMINS

Habitually rewarding your children with sweet, chewable vitamins may set the stage for accidental tragedy, according to the California Dietetic Association (CDA).

"Given as rewards or treats, it's easy to understand how taking vitamins -- even in large amounts -- can be misinterpreted as harmless by young children," said Rita Storey, president of CDA. "Unfortunately, that misunderstanding often results in accidental poisoning."

Chewable vitamins and baby aspirin are the most frequently mentioned source of accidental poisonings in children under age five, according to the Food and Drug Administration.

"You probably don't even need children's vitamins or mineral supplements around the house if you're feeding children the recommended number of servings from the four food groups -- milk, meat, vegetables and fruits, breads and cereals," says Storey.

Three daily servings from the milk group, two from the meat group and four each from the vegetable/fruit and bread/cereal groups should provide all the nutrients your children need to keep them healthy and active.

**MORE**

**FIGURE 4–3A**
**Release 1**

MOTHERS WARNED ABOUT GIVING CHEWABLE VITAMINS -- ADD ONE

So before you reach for the vitmains at the grocery store, try thinking about the foods in your basket. Can they give your child the balanced diet he needs? If the answer is yes, you child probably doesn't need vitamins. By passing them up, you could be avoiding a potential mishap.

\# # #

**FIGURE 4-3A (continued)**

**Pills vs. Food: An Emerging Controversy** **NEWS**

*American Dietetic Association*
*430 North Michigan Avenue*
*Chicago, Illinois 60611*

Sandy Morreale
(312) 280-5086
Caroline Stein
(312) 280-5012

Contact: Gretchen Griswold
(619) 296-0605
or (212) 883-1234
4/3/87-4/9/87

(April 8, 1987)

A First

NATIONAL HEALTH GROUPS JOIN FORCES

ON VITAMIN/MINERAL PILL WARNING

NEW YORK...Three national organizations of health professionals and a consumer health protection group joined forces today for the first time to warn Americans about the unsafe use of vitamin and mineral supplements.

"Evidence of widespread use of supplements, projections of further increases and professional concern that what consumers don't know may hurt them prompted the initiative," said spokesman C. Wayne Callaway, MD at a news conference here.

"Contrary to the implications of supplement promotion, there is little scientific evidence that vitamin and mineral pills will prevent cancer, osteoporosis or heart disease," Callaway said.

- more -

*Conference provided by National Dairy Board in cooperation with National Dairy Council*

Courtesy of National Dairy Board in cooperation with National Dairy Council

**FIGURE 4–3B**
**Release 2**

NATIONAL HEALTH GROUPS -- ADD ONE

The American Dietetic Association, American Institute of Nutrition, American Society for Clinical Nutrition and National Council Against Health Fraud issued the joint statement. The American Medical Association's (AMA) Council on Scientific Affairs reviewed the statement and found it consistent with its official statement on dietary supplements.

The AMA council called the joint statement a valuable synopsis for the public, according to Harold Lubin, M.D., director of AMA's Department of Personal Health and Nutrition. "All health practitioners should emphasize that properly selected diets are the primary basis of good nutrition," Lubin said.

Alice Smitherman, R.D., president of American Dietetic Association (ADA), which assembled the coalition, called on Americans to get their nutrients from food rather than pills whenever possible.

"Consuming nutrients from food doesn't put you at as much risk of overdose or toxicity as the improper use of supplements can," she said. "And the long-term ramifications of excessive doses of single nutrient supplements just aren't known."

According to the consensus statement, "meeting nutrient needs by choosing a variety of foods in moderation, rather than by supplementation, reduces the potential risk for both nutrient deficiencies and excesses."

- more -

**FIGURE 4–3B (continued)**

NATIONAL HEALTH GROUPS -- ADD TWO

A Food and Drug Administration (FDA) study reports that nearly 40 percent of adult Americans consume supplements daily. The same study showed that heavy users of supplements average 777 percent of the Recommended Dietary Allowances (RDA) -- or nearly eight times the RDA -- for nutrients they consumed in supplement form. The figure does not include nutrients from foods.

While almost half the supplement users do not exceed the RDA, 42 percent consume supplements in doses from three to eight times the RDA, not counting food.

Industry statistics show sales of supplements have more than doubled in the past 10 years and are now $2.6 billion annually. Projections from a study by SRI International indicate aupplement sales may top $10 billion by 1990.

Calcium supplements lead sales projections. Consumers will buy an estimated $200 million of calcium supplements this year compated with $47 million in 1983, making calcium the industry leader in sales growth.

The coalition warned against taking supplements in excess of the RDA but, according to Callaway, there are minimal health risks associated with a daily multi-vitamin and mineral supplement or any single nutrient supplement which doesn't exceed the RDA.

- more -

**FIGURE 4–3B (continued)**

NATIONAL HEALTH GROUPS -- ADD THREE

The statement cited five circumstances where supplements may be helpful: women who are pregnant or breastfeeding; women who have excessive menstrual bleeding; people on extremely low caloric diets; strict vegetarians and people whose nutrient needs are altered by illness or medication.

"Nutrients are toxic when ingested in sufficiently large amounts," said Callaway. "Safe intake levels vary widely from nutrient to nutrient and with the age and health of the individual."

The groups also stated that high-dose vitamin and mineral supplements can interfere with the normal metabolism of other nutrients and with the therapeutic effects of certain drugs. High doses of calcium can interfere with iron absorption. Zinc has a similar effect on copper, according to Callaway.

Overuse of vitamins A, B-6, C and D, and the minerals zinc and selenium raise the most concern because of widespread use and the severity of symptoms associated with overdose.

To address more specific needs, the ADA has developed a consumer booklet on the safe intake of nutrients. Consumers can receive a copy by mailing a self-addressed, stamped envelope and $1 to Dept. 33AS, American Dietetic Association, 430 North Michigan Avenue, Chicago, IL 60611.

# # # #

**FIGURE 4–3B (continued)**

Nuffer, Smith, Tucker, Inc.

3170 Fourth Avenue, Third Floor, San Diego, CA 92103 (619) 296-0605

News

Contact:

Kerry Tucker
(619) 296-0605

Phil George
San Diego
Unified School
District
(619) 293-8414

Hold For Release
12 noon October 3, 1985

CALIFORNIA LOTTERY DOLLARS TO PUSH EDUCATION
FUNDS TO HIGHEST LEVEL SINCE PROP 13, SAYS SD SCHOOL CHIEF

San Diego...California Lottery dollars will push expenditures for public education above the national average for the first time since the Proposition 13 tax initiative, the superintendent of San Diego City Schools predicted at a noon lottery rally today.

"We just haven't been able to keep pace with rising costs through traditional tax sources since the cutbacks brought on by Prop 13 in 1978," said Thomas Payzant, one of a handful of California school superintendents who supported the lottery initiative during last fall's election.

It's estimated that this year, not counting lottery dollars, California will spend $3,651 per kindergarten through grade 12 student in the public school system or $89 per student below the $3,740 national average. If official projections on lottery sales come through, an additional $97.32 will be added per student -- surpassing the national average.

-more-

Courtesy of the California State Lottery

**FIGURE 4–3C**
**Release 3**

Payzant said that because most school districts have tried not to eliminate student programs and services, building maintenance has been deferred, overused and outdated noninstructional equipment have not been replaced, capital improvements have been delayed and students and teachers have been short-changed on books and instructional materials.

"We can get by without replacing a leaky roof or fixing worn-out stairs and floors for only so long," said Payzant. "We have not adequately protected our investments in buildings and equipment and in San Diego that's where we'll spend the additional funds provided by the lottery.

The State Lottery Initiative Constitutional Amendment requires that at least 34 percent of total lottery revenues plus unredeemed prize money and anticipated operating savings be used for public education. Fifty percent of the revenues will be returned to the public in prizes and 16 percent is budgeted for administration costs.

Of the 34 percent slated for education, kindergarten through grade 12 will receive 81 percent of the allotment, community colleges 12 percent, California State University system 4.5 percent and the University of California system, 2.5 percent.

Noon rallies were also held simultaneously in Los Angeles, San Francisco and Sacramento prior to today's 12:30 opening of ticket sales.

# # #

**FIGURE 4–3C (continued)**

The following phrases have been used to help consumers make decisions on their own:

1. Think through your own lawn-watering practices and try developing a water conservation list.
2. Consider blending low fat with skim milk to give your taste buds an opportunity to adjust before shifting to skim milk.
3. When was the last time you prepaid property taxes to cushion the amount you will owe in April?

Providing the individual with tips is probably the widest used rehearsal strategy in publicity. Although one has to be careful with news style, particularly with questions and answers, when trying to help a person consider individual decisions, tips can be consistently used to help audience members mentally process the action you want them to take.

To increase protein and calcium, a dietetic association offered these tips in a news release: "A woman might have yogurt for a morning break and peanut butter on crackers in the afternoon." A *San Francisco Chronicle* story used tips to effectively help consumers choose a new long distance telephone company following the break-up of AT&T:

If you haven't already begun using another long-distance company, it will be wise to try one or two now to check their rates and features. First, check yourself—your billing habits, patterns and your bills. Then, advises Kelley Griffin at Telecommunications Research and Action Center, a consumer advocate group in Washington, call the toll-free numbers of the various companies operating in your region.

Caution: Call at least twice to verify the information the sales agent provides.

For an up-to-date chart that compares rates, services and features for the eight major long-distance companies, including AT&T, send a stamped, self-addressed, business-sized envelope with your request to TRAC, P.O. Box 12038, Washington, D.C. 20005.[10]

Mental rehearsal provides individuals in a target audience with a specific behavior to test their new knowledge. Given ways to improve a situation rather than simply given information about the issue people are more readily motivated to practice a behavior. Practice gives them the opportunity for a positive consequence from taking the action steps and reinforces a willingness to repeat the behavior in the future.

## SUMMARY

- ☐ A publicity story should answer appropriately the four question clusters of the message/media outline.
- ☐ Metaphors, similes, and analogies increase the transfer of the content of the publicity story to the real-life experience of audience members.
- ☐ Words and visuals increase the receptiveness of a story concept by the receiver.
- ☐ Described consequences of action or inaction improve audience members' decision-making capabilities.
- ☐ Mental rehearsals such as tips contained in the story cause audience members to interact with the message and suggested attitudes or behaviors.
- ☐ Publicity writing requires attention to behavioral techniques known to increase receiver utilization.

## EXERCISES

1. Describe the following in the news release in Figure 4–4:
   a. Audience need/concern/interest
   b. Solution
   c. Consequence of inaction
   d. Techniques for helping audience think through or mentally rehearse intended action
2. Do the same for Figure 4–5.
3. Revise one of the quotations in each of the releases in Figures 4–4 to 4–6 to include use of a simile, metaphor, example, analogy, or high imagery words to help audience members transfer the communication to real-life needs/concerns/interests.
4. Rewrite the news release in Figure 4–6 to make
   a. The need/concern/interest and solution clearer and more concise and believable
   b. The consequences of inaction clear
   c. The audience to rehearse mentally the intended action

**CONTROVERSIES IN WOMEN'S HEALTH & NUTRITION** **NEWS**

American Dietetic Association
455 Madison Avenue
New York, New York 10022

Contact: Gretchen Griswold or
Beverly McKee
(212) 888-7000/(619) 296-0605
or Ann Cole
(312) 280-5000

For Release
September 30, 1986

FIRST EVER GUIDELINES TO HELP LOWER RISK FOR CANCER, OSTEOPOROSIS, OBESITY

NEW YORK -- A panel of scientists and registered dietitians today announced a first-ever set of dietary recommendations for women who want to lower their risk for osteoporosis, cancer and other health concerns.

"There are so many single-disease dietary guidelines that consumers could very easily be confused with what appears to be conflicting information, but which really isn't," said Anita Owen, R.D., and president of The American Dietetic Association (ADA).

"These new recommendations represent a breakthrough because they unify the various nutritional recommendations made by different health organizations and consider other health concerns as well," Owen said at a news conference.

The scientists released general recommendations for overall good health and a task force of ADA dietitians issued specific food guidelines to address the specific nutritional needs of women.

- MORE -

*Forum provided by National Dairy Board in cooperation with National Dairy Council*

Courtesy of National Dairy Board in cooperation with National Dairy Council

**FIGURE 4–4**

FIRST EVER GUIDELINES -- ADD ONE

The recommendations also are aimed at helping women prevent heart disease, control weight and deal with menstrual cycle concerns.

Among the major recommendations:

* Women are encouraged to consume one-half of their daily calories from complex carbohydrates, such as whole-grain breads and cereals, and three to four servings a day of calcium-rich foods such as milk, yogurt, lowfat cheese and dark, green leafy vegetables.

* To lose weight, women should eat at least 10 calories per pound of body weight and avoid extremely low calorie diets. Studies show that a 140-pound woman consuming 1,400 calories a day will lose weight more gradually but more permanently than she will restricting herself to 1,000 calories a day or fewer.

* Fat intake should be limited to one-third of total calories per day.

* Limit alcohol to one or two drinks a day. One drink is equivalent to 12 ounces of beer, five ounces of wine or 1 1/2 ounces of distilled spirits.

"Healthy eating is important for women of all ages," Owen said. "We believe these recommendations will be extremely valuable in helping women devise a solid program that will lead them to optimum health."

- MORE -

**FIGURE 4–4 (continued)**

FIRST EVER GUIDELINES -- ADD TWO

Members of the scientific panel were C. Wayne Callaway, M.D., George Washington University Medical Center, Washington, D.C.; Bess Dawson-Hughes, M.D., USDA Human Nutrition Research Center on Aging, Tufts University, Boston; James Marshall, Ph.D., Department of Social and Preventive Medicine, State University of New York, Buffalo, and Elaine R. Monsen, Ph.D, R.D., University of Washington, Seattle.

# # # #

(Note to editors: A complete list of the general recommendations and specific food guidelines is included in the press packet)

**FIGURE 4–4 (continued)**

**NEWS** **California Dietetic Association**

Central Office: 7740 Manchester Ave., Suite 102, Playa del Rey, CA 90293
(213) 822-0177

(916) 345-1062

EASY FOOD TRADES

CUT DOWN ON FAT

Croissants are a "light" choice for breakfast. And a salad bar is a better choice for lunch than a cheeseburger, right?

Actually a croissant has five times the fat of an English muffin and a salad loaded with four tablespoons of dressing can have twice the fat of a cheeseburger.

If you're trying to cut back on fat in your diet to lose weight or help lower risk for disease, some simple food trades can painlessly help you in your low-fat endeavors, according to the California Dietetic Association (CDA).

"Begin by looking for high-fat extra foods you eat," said CDA President Joan Hudiburg, R.D. "How much salad dressing do you use? Or gravy? Sauces? How often do you eat chips or sweets? These are major sources of fat which are easily cut back."

The next step, according to Hudiburg, is categorizing the foods you eat into nutrient-based food groups: dairy, meat, vegetables and fruits, breads and cereals.

Then identify the high-fat foods you eat within those groups and substitute with moderate servings of lower fat selections.

MORE

Courtesy of California Dietetic Association

**FIGURE 4–5**

FOOD TRADES LOWER FAT -- ADD ONE

Some suggested trade-offs with grams-per-serving fat savings:

**Dairy (women should consume three daily servings, men should consume two):**

* lowfat milk (5 grams fat/cup) for whole milk (8 g/cup)
* lowfat fruit yogurt (3 g/cup) for whole yogurt (5.5 g/cup)
* lowfat yogurt (less than 1 gram/tablespoon) on fruit or pie for whipping cream (5 g/tablespoon)
* uncreamed cottage cheese (less than 1 g/one-half cup) for regular creamed (4.8 g/one-half cup)

**Meat (adults should consume two daily servings):**

* white meat chicken ( 3.8 g/3 oz.) for dark meat chicken (8.3/3 oz)
* rolled boiled ham ( 6 g/3 oz.) for hot dogs (20 g/2 average links)
* water-packed tuna (.6 g/3 oz.) for oil-packed (6 g/3 oz.)
* barbecued three-ounce lean hamburger (8.5 g/3 oz.) for 3 oz. t-bone steak (25 g/3 oz.)
* wine- or lemon-baked cod or sole (1 g/3 oz.) for batter-fried fish sticks (18 g/3 oz.)
* sliced white meat turkey (2.8 g/3 oz.) for bologna (23 g/3 oz.)

**Vegetables and Fruits (adults should consume four daily servings):**

* radishes and carrots in your salad (less than 1 g/one-fourth cup) for avocado (6.3 g/one-fourth cup)

MORE

**FIGURE 4–5 (continued)**

EASY FOOD TRADES -- ADD TWO

* lemon juice or vinegar on salads or vegetables (0 g) instead of dressing or sauces (approximately 8 g/tablespoon)

* plain, unbuttered baked potato (less than 1 g/potato) for French fries (13 g/20 pieces)

* steamed vegetables (less than 1 g) for sauteed with 1 tablespoon of oil (14 g/tablespoon of oil)

**Breads and Cereals (adults should consume four daily servings:**

* whole wheat toast (1.5 g/2 slices) for pancakes (16.4 g/2 pancakes)

* brown rice (.5 g/one-half cup) for stuffing (3.6 g/one-half cup)

* corn tortilla (.6 g/1 tortilla) for biscuits (6 g/1 biscuit)

**Extra foods (CDA suggests limiting intake to two servings a day):**

* unbuttered air-popped popcorn (.7 g/1 cup) for chips (7.4 g/10 chips)

* cocktail sauce (less than 1 g/2 tablespoon) for tartar sauce (10 g/1 tablespoon)

* graham crackers (3 g/3 crackers) for cherry pie (18 g for one-sixth pie)

# # #

**FIGURE 4–5 (continued)**

The Omega 3 Connection

# NEWS

Bumble Bee Seafoods, Inc.
P.O. Box 23508
San Diego, CA 92123
(619) 560-0404

(July 27, 1987)

contact: Valerie Lemke
(619) 296-0605

FISH OIL CAPSULES TRIPLE

BUT MDs CALL FOR FISH, NOT PILLS

Sales of fish oil capsules are projected to triple this year reaching the $100 million mark despite increasing concern among medical authorities for their long-term health consequences.

The sudden popularity of fish oil capsules stems from medical evidence linking the omega-3 fatty acids found in fish to lower risk for heart disease.

Research shows that Eskimos and other population groups consuming large amounts of fish have low rates of death from heart disease. Scientists believe that omega-3, found primarily in fish, may have a protective effect against the disease.

"However, you can't replicate a diet with pills," says Judith Ashley, M.S.P.H., R.D., research associate at the University of California - Los Angeles School of Medicine.

-more-

**FIGURE 4–6**

ADD ONE--FISH OIL SUPPLEMENTS

While medical authorities applaud increased consumption of fish to two to three servings weekly, they stop short of recommending concentrated fish oil capsules, says Ashley.

Citing research released by the Massachusetts Institute of Technology Sea Grant Program, Ashley said that canned fish such as tuna, salmon, sardines, herring and mackerel are better sources of omega-3 than fresh fish.

"A 6 1/2 ounce can of white meat tuna (albacore) has, on an average, 1850 milligrams of omega-3. A 1000-milligram fish oil supplement containing 50 percent omega-3 (currently the highest percentage available on the market) has 500 milligrams," she said.

According to Ashley, consumers should increase their consumption of fish for a variety of nutritional reasons but the scientific evidence does not justify the consumption of fish oil capsules.

A free booklet containing recipes and the latest facts on omega-3, is available by sending a self-addressed, stamped envelope to "Omega-3 Naturally," Bumble Bee Seafoods, P.O. Box 23508, San Diego CA 92123.

# # #

**FIGURE 4–6 (continued)**

## REFERENCES


1. James E. Grunig, "Basic Research Provides Knowledge That Makes Evaluation Possible," *Public Relations Quarterly* (Fall 1983), 30–31.
2. *Funk and Wagnall's Standard College Dictionary* (New York: Harcourt, Brace & World, 1963), p. 1251.
3. *Los Angeles Times*, February 25, 1985, p. 11.
4. Jeremy Main, "Waking Up AT&T: There's Life After Culture Shock," *Fortune*, December 24, 1984, pp. 66–74.
5. Dorothy Nelkin, *Selling Science* (New York: W. H. Freeman, 1987), p. 10.
6. *Los Angeles Times*, January 29, 1987, p. 4.
7. *Orlando Sentinel*, January 17, 1987, p. B-1.
8. *Los Angeles Times*, April 29, 1987, p. 1.
9. Jonathon Gutman, "A Means-End Chain Model Based on Consumer Categorization Processes," *Journal of Marketing*, 46 (Spring 1982), 61.
10. Sylvia Porter, "Long Distance Revolution Is Coming," *San Francisco Chronicle*, September 8, 1984. p. 51.


## CASE STUDY

### The Problem

Local business leaders founded First National Bank three years ago as the largest capitalized bank in U.S. history. Although First National Bank has shown spectacular growth in its early years, management is concerned because bank awareness is limited to a small, close-knit circle of business leaders. The future, as perceived by bank officers, lies in the bank's ability to reach beyond its primary concentric circle of founders, supporters, and clients to other business people.

### Situational Analysis

The First National Bank symbolizes what a local business bank should be. It was founded by those who comprise the leadership of the business community. Its board reflects a "who's who" in local business. Its chairperson and board members are among the community's most influential and respected business leaders.

The bank's primary point of difference is in its emphasis on custom service for the middle-sized enterprise and its executives. The bank exists, according to the officers, because of time-delayed loan decisions caused because most banking decisions are made in larger cities outside the area. Not only are transactions slower and less flexible but turnover is a problem with these large banks and there is no assurance that the individual you are dealing with today will be there tomorrow. First National Bank, on the other hand, is the model of executive stability. Not only is officer turnover virtually nonexistent but the experience average per lending officer is eighteen years.

Assume that a survey of the business community demonstrates a legitimate audience concern for quick, efficient, and flexible bank transactions; research also shows this as a perceived vulnerability for competitors. Assume as well that turnover among young bank officers employed by the competition is a major concern for those the bank is targeting as clients.

You are sitting down at your word processor to write a news release announcing a business symposium the bank is sponsoring at the local university on how banks will operate in the future. The faculty you have assembled at the symposium will draw assumptions that include the audience concerns your research has identified. Develop a message/media outline to reflect a need, concern, or interest of the business community. Develop an idea for a news angle to support the outline.

# CHAPTER 5

# Writing News Releases for Print Media

### *IN THIS CHAPTER*

The public relations plan and utilization of motivational principles are the basic premises of this text. Equally important, however, is a working knowledge of the needs of the medium selected for communication.

The most effective news releases are those written by publicists who have grasped basic news writing skills, utilize news style (Associated Press or United Press International), and present the release in a professional format.

Unfortunately, not all public relations writers put their writing skills through serious scrutiny. Editors love to boast of the hundreds of news releases that end up in the daily "round file." Many enjoy maintaining files of the "worst-of-the-worst," bringing them out with glee when asked or surveyed.

Generating the respect of reporters and editors is a critical element in the publicity success quotient. Respect is an easier commodity to muster when a journalist thinks you know his or her business. Well-written news releases demonstrate this knowledge.

### *CHAPTER OBJECTIVES*

The reader will be able to

1. Discuss the basic criteria for a news angle.
2. Delineate the ways in which a news release is used by the print media.
3. Write and edit a news release from the message/media outline that meets the needs of client, media, and target audience.
4. Write a photo caption from the message/media outline that meets the needs of client, media, and target audience.

## KNOWING THE PRINT MEDIA

Public relations writers should be at least as good as a journalist in

1. Knowing the needs of the medium for which they are writing

2. Spotting a good news opportunity
3. Writing a basic news story

The ability to generate publicity is typically the "bread and butter" skill for practitioners. Bosses and clients alike expect the practitioner to produce publicity results. Getting that first job without mastery of news-generating skills is very difficult, and, until mastery, management consulting opportunities are usually few and far between. In short, practitioners earn their stars on their ability to generate "ink". Publicity normally pays the freight as you gain the experience necessary to maximize your professional contribution.

Most practitioners cut their teeth on the print media. With the news release, the practitioner learns to apply basic news writing skills.

## WHAT IS NEWS?

The basic premise of news release writing is developing what journalists call news judgment. News judgment takes years of experience to develop and even then veteran journalists seek input from colleagues and editors on the value of a news "angle" or "hook." This is because there are few absolutes in news writing, few black and white decisions. Subjectivity varies with and by an editor's experience and talent, based solely on professional opinion. In a very practical sense, then, such subjectivity makes news whatever the decision-making editor determines it to be.

There are some guidelines to consider when making decisions on whether or not a publicity opportunity has news value. Try asking yourself these questions:

1. Is it new, different, or unusual (or can it be packaged as such)?
2. Does it have a sense of immediacy? Is it timely?
3. Does it affect great numbers of people?
4. Is it controversial?
5. Does it involve a prominent individual or organization?
6. Is it local?

> Study the three news releases making up Figure 5–1. Using the above criteria, which is the most newsworthy? Why? Which is second, third?

University journalism classes can provide public relations students with basic training in news judgment and writing. Working on a college or community newspaper helps to fine-tune news judgment and writing skills. Studying the way news is presented in a variety of newspapers and magazines provides another opportunity for skill development. Consider clipping a variety of stories from the print media and practice writing stories on any subject using the styles collected. Remember that subjectivity makes it important to get to know the reporters and editors with whom you must deal. Study their medium and their work and get to know their interests.

## NEWS FORMAT

The most consistent and safest style for a public relations writer to use in news release writing is that of Associated Press or United Press International. Although the styles of major newspapers vary—you should study the media with which you deal most—AP and UPI are respected by most gatekeepers. The *AP Stylebook*, for example, is organized like a dictionary. It provides guidelines on acceptable word abbreviations, capitalization, numerals, word usage (such as *lay* versus *lie*), standard acronyms, forming and using plural words, punctuation—virtually every grammatical and syntactical question you may face.[1] Journalistic style is frequently different from what you may have learned in college English courses. Get an *AP Stylebook*; use it and, through use, put its guidelines to memory. Copies may be obtained for a nominal cost from the Associated Press, AP Newsfeatures Department, 50 Rockefeller Plaza, New York, New York 10020.

# News

PENNSTATE

Telephone: 814-865-7517

Department of
Public Information

312 Old Main
The Pennsylvania State University
University Park, Pennsylvania 16802

4-18-85

Contact: Marcus Schneck
(814) 865-7517 (office)
(814) 237-9107 (home) or
Bill Mahon: (814) 865-7517
(814) 237-5625 (home)

For Immediate Release

University Park, Pa. --- A human powered vehicle, which the student designers hope will be the first to cross the United States, took its maiden voyage today at Penn State's pavement test track.

After an initial delay, as the mechanical engineering students worked out a few last-minute bugs, the three-wheeled recumbent vehicle moved out for its first one-mile run around the track.

About midway through the lap a small piece of wood intended to hold a steering cable in place snapped, forcing driver Robert Kershner, project leader and a senior from Plymouth Meeting, to finish the run by steering with a grip on the rear axle.

The students, who have spent many sleepless nights with their 62-pound vehicle since they started construction in January, descended on the problem and within minutes the vehicle was ready for its second run.

"Look at that thing," said Gerhard Pawelka, a junior from Allentown, almost in disbelief, as the vehicle rounded the far turn for the second time. "We built it."

The human powered vehicle is 11 feet long, 19 inches wide and 31 inches tall. It has front-wheel drive and rear-wheel steering that combines with leaning capability for superior handling.

The ultralight shell of graphite and Kevlar incorporates computer-aided design with wind tunnel-tested aerodynamics. The vehicle has no frame.

Kershner said the team of 10 students will make several refinements on the vehicle before they take it to the National Collegiate Human Powered Vehicle Championship in Santa Barbara, Calif., May 3-5 for competition with entries from 22 other colleges and universities.

- more -

Courtesy of Pennsylvania State University

**FIGURE 5–1A**
**Release 1**

--2--

After the competition, at 5 a.m. May 7, a team of six of the students will begin a six-day cross-country ride with the vehicle from the Santa Monica Pier to the Empire State Building in New York City.

This trip will set a world record as the first human powered vehicle to cross the country. The trip has been made by bicycle riders, but not by human powered vehicle.

"That will be the absolute toughest endurance race imaginable," Kershner pointed out.

*ms*

**FIGURE 5–1A (continued)**

**News Release**

For further information contact

550 Madison Ave., New York, N.Y. 10022

Esther Novak, AT&T Foundation
(212) 605-6695

Angela Duryea, N.W. Ayer
(212) 708-5664

For Release: Wednesday, September 11, 1985

AT&T ANNOUNCES 1985-86 TOURING GRANTS
TO THREE MAJOR AMERICAN DANCE COMPANIES

AT&T Touring Grants Called Unprecedented

New York, N.Y. -- AT&T today announced 1985-86 touring grants totaling $205,000 to three of America's finest dance companies: the American Ballet Theatre, the Dance Theatre of Harlem and the Paul Taylor Dance Company.

The grants - the largest touring grants ever presented by a corporation to these companies - were presented by the AT&T Foundation, the principal source of philanthropy for AT&T and its subsidiaries.

According to Nigel Redden, Director, Dance Program, of the National Endowment for the Arts, touring grants by corporations are rare, and touring grants to three companies simultaneously are unprecedented.

"Today's announcement is in AT&T's long tradition of supporting the fine arts," said Reynold Levy, President, AT&T Foundation. "Dance is an important, 20th-century art form which must be seen live to be completely appreciated, and there is nothing more exciting than going to a wonderful live performance."

Levy said AT&T chose these particular companies because they offer a diverse look at dance in America today.

Courtesy of NW Ayer

**FIGURE 5–1B**
**Release 2**

- 2 -

The American Ballet Theatre offers lush, extravagant productions of a magnitude that many other dance companies cannot match. The Dance Theatre of Harlem is electric, with a wide range of dance from classical and contemporary ballet to modern dance; and Paul Taylor is acknowledged as one of the leading choreographers of modern dance of our time...a creative genius.

According to the NEA, the audience for dance has grown to about 20 times what it was in 1965. Now, at the very time audiences across the country are clamoring for live dance events, the NEA has had to phase out its dance touring program.

Says Nigel Redden, "The appetite for dance was growing faster than our budget, so it is essential that national corporations recognize this national art form. It is important and wonderful that AT&T has stepped in to fill this niche. The federal government is just not large enough to fill every niche."

The AT&T grant to the American Ballet Theatre, under its artistic director Mikhail Baryshnikov, covers its domestic performances, beginning in New York at the Metropolitan Opera House September 2, through Philadelphia to the Mann Music Center next August. One of the highlights of its domestic tour will be the world premiere performance of "Requiem" (music by Andrew Lloyd Webber) choreographed by Sir Kenneth MacMillan in Chicago in February. Another highlight will be a new work choreographed by John Taras, which premiers in Miami in January, set to music from Tchaikovsky's "Francesca da Rimini."

The grant to the Dance Theatre of Harlem, founded by Arthur Mitchell, covers coast-to-coast performances from January through April. Highlighting the season will be four new ballets: Lady of the Camellias, choreographed by Domy Reiter-Soffer: Concerto in F, choreographed by Billy Wilson; and two new works choreographed by Garth Fagan and John McFall.

**FIGURE 5–1B (continued)**

- 3 -

The grant to the Paul Taylor Company, established by Paul Taylor 30 years ago, covers the company's domestic performances beginning in Dallas in October, through its City Center engagement in April and May. This tour includes the company's debut performance in the Kennedy Center Opera House this November, and features two of Paul Taylor's newest dances, Roses and Last Look, which premiered to raves at City Center in New York this past Spring.

# # #

**FIGURE 5–1B (continued)**

**TREE TOP** ® INC.

Second & Railroad Avenue, Selah, WA 98942
MA: P.O. Box 248, Selah, WA 98942
Phone (509) 697-7251 Telex: 15-2867TT CORP SELH

FROM: Jay Rockey Public Relations June 10, 1985
2121 Fifth Avenue, Seattle, WA 98121
(206) 728-1100 (Contact: Sherry Hartman or Melinda McCorkle)

FOR: TREE TOP INC
(509) 697-7251 (Contact: John McAlister or Pat Moss)

RELEASE FOR GENERAL PUBLICATIONS

FOR IMMEDIATE RELEASE

ATLANTA -- Tree Top Inc. has developed the world's first concentrated low-moisture pure apple fiber, the company announced at a food industry convention here today.

The Selah, Wash.-based company hopes its new product will move along side of bran as a fiber ingredient for processed foods aimed at health-minded consumers, one of the fastest growing segments of the food industry.

The announcement was made at the Institute of Food Technologists' convention, where food processors -- potential customers for Tree Top's fiber -- gather to view the industry's latest developments.

Tree Top, the largest U.S. processor of pure apple juice, spent more than three years developing its low-moisture apple fiber and the new apple juice processing technology that makes it possible. "Low moisture" is an industry term meaning the product contains less than four percent moisture, which makes it shelf stable and free-flowing.

(more)

TREE TOP 25 ANNIVERSARY 25

Courtesy of Jay Rockey Public Relations

**FIGURE 5–1C**
**Release 3**

Tree Top Inc. - 2
June 10, 1985

The grower-owned fruit processing cooperative also is developing a similar product made from pears. In addition to processed foods, both fibers have potential application in laxatives and other pharmaceuticals.

"We needed to find new uses for our growers' fruit and a new source of profit in an increasingly competitive marketplace," said Sherman A. Carlson, vice president for industrial sales. "This fiber product helps fill that need. It also meets the processed food industry's need for new sources of high-dietary fiber. We think it's a product whose time has come."

As a cooperative, Tree Top is charged with processing and marketing all processor-quality apples from its more than 3,500 grower-owners. Profits on apple juice, Tree Top's basic business, are under intense competition from brands made entirely from foreign concentrates, Carlson said. Tree Top's apple fiber is the newest in a line of value-added products the company has begun producing in the last several years to maintain its financial strength.

"This is an entirely new product for the food processing industry, one that offers an appealing new option in the fast-growing category of fiber-oriented, health-oriented foods," Carlson said. "It offers the healthful appeal of the apple, along with the marketing momentum of fiber. That's a powerful marketing message."

The apple fiber is made from apple solids separated from the juice during processing.

(more)

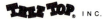

TREE TOP® INC.

**FIGURE 5–1C (continued)**

Tree Top Inc. - 3
June 10, 1985

According to Dr. H. Wallace Ewart, Tree Top's director of research and development, traditional apple juice processing requires the use of "press aids" such as rice hulls and paper, to be crushed with the apple to extract the juice. The addition of press aids renders the remaining apple solids suitable only for use as cattle feed or land fill.

Tree Top's new technology eliminates the need for press aids, so the apple solids remaining after juicing can be dehydrated, granulated and used as a food ingredient. The low-moisture fiber contains no preservatives.

Other attempts at producing an apple fiber product have been made in Italy, Ireland and the United States, according to Ewart. But Tree Top's is the first to be made only from the "interior," or "flesh" of the apple, free of seeds, peel and stems. Tree Top also reduces sugars and acids to lower levels, making a more concentrated fiber source and a better, lower-calorie ingredient for food manufacturers, he said.

"Our apple fiber is one of the highest commercial sources of dietary fiber -- and it's competitively priced," Ewart said. "Because we've engineered it from the start for ease of use as an ingredient, we expect it to be very popular with food manufacturers."

To add appeal to food manufacturers, Tree Top is supporting a research study at Washington State University to explore the apple fiber's qualities and function as an ingredient in processed foods, Ewart said.

(more)

TREE TOP, INC.

**FIGURE 5–1C (continued)**

Tree Top Inc. - 4
June 10, 1985

"The information from the WSU study will make it that much simpler for our customers' research and development people to formulate products with our fiber," Ewart said.

Ewart also noted a possible nutritional advantage of Tree Top apple fiber over more traditional fiber ingredients such as wheat bran. Tree Top apple fiber contains no phytates, substances that prevents the body from absorbing minerals. Wheat bran and most popular fiber ingredients contain at least some phytates.

"The specific health benefits of all types of fiber are still being researched," Ewart said. "But in general we know that fiber is necessary to good health, and that most Americans don't get enough of it. Food and pharmaceutical manufacturers are creating products with a mixture of fiber sources, and we're giving them a new option that's bound to have marketing appeal."

Tree Top Inc. is a grower-owned cooperative and one of the nation's largest fruit processors. Based in Selah in Central Washington, the company has more than 3,500 grower-owners in Washington, Oregon and Idaho. Tree Top is the largest U.S. processor of 100 percent pure apple juice, with major markets in juice blends. It also produces "industrial" fruit products for the processed food industry, including evaporated, low-moisture, frozen and pureed apples and pears. Total sales topped $167 million in fiscal 1984.

###

TREE TOP® INC.

**FIGURE 51C (continued)**

## PRINT MEDIA OPTIONS

Generally speaking, the print media include daily newspapers, community newspapers, general news magazines, specialty publications, and industry trade publications. Each has its own advantages and disadvantages.

### Daily Newspapers

There are approximately 1,500 daily newspapers in the United States with combined circulations reaching more than 62 million households. The daily newspaper sets the public agenda, making consumers aware of public issues and through day-to-day exposure increasing their importance. Although radio news directors and television assignment editors contribute to the public agenda, much of what they broadcast they see first in the daily newspaper. There is an old joke among network television reporters that if they truly want to see their segments receive "proper" treatment on the evening news, they had best leak the story to the *New York Times* where their bosses will see it.

General news items occurring within city limits are assigned to reporters by metropolitan or city editors. Frequently a county editor is responsible for events outside the city. Major metropolitan newspapers also maintain reporters in bureaus in the suburbs and outlying areas.

Specialty sections of the daily newspaper have their own editors as well. They include, but are not limited to, business, lifestyle (formerly women's), real estate, food, health, outdoor, travel, automobile, sports, and entertainment. These specialty sections are categorized by audience needs/concerns/interests. Members of the business community, for example, are more likely to read the business section of the local newspaper. Commercial developers and real estate consumers more likely read the real estate section. Campers more likely read outdoor sections.

The primary disadvantage of the daily newspaper is that not all those who pay to receive it, read it. Studies indicate that only about one-fourth of the newspaper is read daily. Opinion leaders are more likely to read more of the daily paper than others. It is dangerous to assume that just because a news release is published in your local newspaper that it will, in fact, be read by your target audience.

### Community Newspapers

Besides the daily newspaper, most communities or neighborhoods have at least one "weekly" newspaper (published once, twice, or three times weekly). There are about 7,000 weekly newspapers in the United States covering community or neighborhood news. The obvious disadvantage of the weekly newspaper is its small circulation, but these publications are read more consistently and more thoroughly than the daily newspaper. Therefore, a news release appearing in the weekly newspaper can have more impact per capita than the daily (and the weeklies print more news releases verbatim).

> Which type of newspaper do you most frequently read? Why? Do you read a community newspaper? Why?

### Magazines

More than 11,000 magazines are published in the United States, with the average circulation of the top 400 reaching more than 360 million readers.

General interest and specialty magazines generally attract younger, more affluent readers. Whereas newspapers are generally discarded in a day or two, magazines tend to enjoy an average life of three to five weeks. General interest magazines are not likely to use news releases, but they do track newspaper and wire service coverage and frequently assign reporters to follow up on stories appearing in daily newspapers.

### Specialty Publications

Specialty newspapers, magazines, and newsletters—business, labor, cultural—and industry trade publications (virtually every industry has at least one and frequently several) provide a more direct route to the target audience. Like specialty sections of newspapers, they are prescreened for the target audience and already address the needs/concerns/interests of readers. They often carry more credibility with the reader than the mass media because of the in-depth way in which they cover their subject. Their readers also tend to be more active seekers of information than mass media readers and, as such, more receptive to attitudinal and behavioral objectives.

> To which of the print media do you subscribe and/or read most often?

### Wire Services

Wire services, such as the Associated Press and United Press International, provide the public relations practitioner with opportunities for reaching large numbers of print and broadcast media regionally, nationally, and internationally.

Newspapers and radio and television stations depend on the wire services to cover stories that they cannot; they provide an extension to local news staffs and enable local media to provide worldwide coverage. Normally a wire service story in your local newspaper is preceded by the initials AP (Associated Press) or UPI (United Press International). While the larger media subscribe to both services, AP is the more prominent of the two.

Most major cities have AP and UPI bureaus, and smaller towns have local reporters, called "stringers," who provide the wires with coverage. The wire services provide news to the media in two ways: (1) coverage of events by wire service reporters and (2) rewrites of stories appearing in local media. The latter provides most of the material for media outside the local area. Hence, a local story with regional, national, or international interest may expand beyond the local area by wire service coverage on regional, national, or international wires.

Some cities also have local wire services that provide news to local media and the major wire services. Wire services include Reuters, covering international news, and Dow-Jones, covering financial news.

In addition to coverage, wire services also produce a daily listing of events for media coverage considerations. A news conference or special event must be listed on the daily budget of the major and local wire services if you expect reporters to attend.

Placement of a news release or news angle on a wire service offers immediate widespread coverage. It also makes the public relations news angle "legitimate." In other words, your angle is no longer a public relations source but a news source. The wire services provide the media with a tremendous number of stories daily. A story on the wires does not necessarily guarantee widespread coverage, but your odds increase significantly.

There are also public relations wire services, such as Business Wire and PR Newswire, that transmit publicity, for a fee, directly into the computers of publications—the same way a wire service does. They too provide a daily budget of events to which editors refer (like they do the major wire services) when making daily reporting assignments. While these "for hire" services do not have the credibility of the major services, news releases nonetheless have met some quality standards, and are convenient for journalists, as they do not have to retype the printed release into their computer.

> What advantages can you describe about having a wire service pick up one of your stories or releases?

## HOW THE MEDIA USE THE NEWS RELEASE

Each medium uses news releases in a variety of ways. A general interest magazine (all media, for that matter) might use a release as an idea for a story and assign a reporter to expand it. A wire service might edit a release and put it on the local, regional, or national wire for pickup by both print and broadcast media. A newspaper might run a release verbatim, particularly in specialty sections, which tend to use more "as is" releases than other sections. A trade publication might take a more lengthy release on a subject of interest to the industry it serves.

Because trade publications often desire author bylines, such releases provide an opportunity to improve the credibility of the story with a byline from a third party expert, without a perceived point of view.

## THE ELEMENTS OF GOOD WRITING

The traditional who, what, where, when, why, and how of news writing are critically important to the development of the news release. But so is a clear, concise, and crisp writing style. The well-thought-out news hook provides direction to the rest of the release. Paragraphs following the lead should demonstrate a sense of flow, one sentence building to the next.

Brevity is a valued trait. Paragraphs are best kept short, primarily one sentence with some multisentence paragraphs deep within the release, as are punchy, one-thought sentences, fifteen to twenty words, with a few longer ones thrown in for greater readability. Too many short sentences are boring. The best words are also the shortest and the most common to the lay reader.

Many unseasoned writers make the mistake of trying to include more than one thought in a sentence. Evaluate what is necessary to paint a complete and accurate picture and cut out what is not.

Space is a valuable commodity in the print media. Each sentence must hold its own. Thoughts and information that might be nice for the reader to know but not essential to telling the story, as established by the lead paragraph, should be omitted. Redundancy and unnecessary words are simply unacceptable. More to the point, shorter releases stand a better chance of being printed.

The classic journalistic style is characterized by short, simple paragraphs and sentences and a notable absence of superlatives, qualifiers, or an abundance of adjectives. Poor news release writing can run to the opposite extreme with long, convoluted sentences, hackneyed or trite phrases, and flowery prose.

Although grammar and punctuation can take a backseat to a clearly expressed thought (i.e., one-word sentences), one should generally strive for literacy. And under no circumstances are spelling or typing errors tolerated.

In public relations writing some of the traditional rules of expository writing may be sacrificed for the sake of impact, but the rules of clear English may not. Some rules frequently broken for stronger writing include

- Ending a sentence with a preposition
  "The woman was invited in."
- Splitting an infinitive
  "To boldly go where no man has gone before."
- Beginning a sentence with a conjunction
  "And patients who have gone through the center share their experiences at weekly meetings."

Rules that may not be broken are

- Agreement of subject and verb
- Agreement of tense
- Prohibition of double negative (except in dialectic quotes)

The following are some techniques that can strengthen news release writing:

***Active Voice.*** "Don't tell me, show me" is a criticism often sighed by journalism instructors and public relations managers. Using the active voice demonstrates, rather than tells, what a person is doing. This makes a release more interesting.

Instead of "His vote was influenced by the candidate's remarks," a sentence might read, "The candidate's remarks influenced his vote." Employing the active voice also helps to keep sentences shorter.

***Simple Words.*** If you do not use a particular word in every-day conversation, it probably does not belong in a news release.

***Sentence Length.*** Sentences should average fifteen to twenty words. Sentences much shorter than that may not convey a thought effectively. Sentences much longer than that run the risk of losing the message they aim to convey.

***Punctuation.*** Ambitious writers tend to overpunctuate. Here are some simple punctuation rules to keep in mind:

- Use commas judiciously. There is a tendency to incorrectly put a comma anywhere a conversational pause occurs. If you have a doubt about whether the comma belongs, it probably does not belong.
- If you want to be taken seriously by editors, do not use exclamation points.
- If you ask a question, do not forget the question mark.
- Keep punctuation inside quotation marks except when the quote is included in a question.

## DEVELOPING THE NEWS RELEASE

Too often generating publicity means setting a public relations writer loose to scurry around an organization in pursuit of potential news hooks to put the organization in a favorable light—any favorable light. This text, however, emphasizes the importance of starting first with the public relations plan—what the organization wants to accomplish through public relations—and using the message/media outline as a base for brainstorming potential story ideas to support the plan. With the message/media outline in hand, the practitioner can dig into an organization or an issue in a more directed manner with more specificity about what change he or she would like to see occur in the minds of the target audience as a result of the potential news hook.

The message/media outline, emanating from the public relations plan, should be the base for each communication. The message and media are identified through a series of steps, which, as you will remember, include

1. Determine the specific action you want taken as a result of your communication.
2. Identify the target audience(s).
3. Identify the needs/concerns/interests of the target audience(s).
4. Choose message.
5. Choose channels of communication.
6. Select the most believable spokesperson.
7. Package message to raise an audience need/concern/interest and offer the product, issue, or organization as a means of fulfilling that need, minimizing that concern, or satisfying that interest.

To illustrate, assume you have been retained to help a symphony organization in a medium-sized town increase attendance at its ten yearly performances. The community has increased its population base significantly, but symphony attendance does not reflect that growth.

1. What is the communications outcome? What action do you want taken?

   Increased season tickets purchases
2. Who are the target audience(s)?

   Community newcomers who have attended at least one symphony performance in the last three years
3. What are the needs/concerns/interests of the target audience?

   To see a series of concerts comparable to a "big city" symphony
4. What is the message?

   The quality of big city symphony has come to our community.
5. What is a channel of communication?

   Newspaper arts section
6. Who are the most believable spokespersons?

Renowned symphony leader and/or president of local arts group

7. What communication will raise an audience need/concern/interest and offer the product, issue, or organization as a means of fulfilling that need, minimizing that concern, or satisfying that interest?

   That which increases awareness for the concert series as comparable in quality to those enjoyed in the big city and offers the season ticket as a means of enjoying those performances

> How would you summarize the necessity of preparing the symphony's release in this way if asked by your client?

**Finding the Content**

Content for news releases can vary from product, staff, or special event announcements to ongoing product marketing feature releases to what your client said in a speech about quarterly financial results. Community or market surveys provide good content for news releases, as do reports from conventions or professional meetings. An article presented in an industry or professional periodical can be the subject of a news release. And do not forget the brief human interest items for the local newspaper columnist.

Content begins with the message/media outline. One might begin the process of generating ideas for the content of news releases by brainstorming potential news ideas that support the identified message(s).

The public relations writer then gathers the facts. Content for news releases for a regional construction company that has recently opened an office in your community might include the hiring of local people, new local contract securals, and construction progress releases—project start-up, midway, and completion. Look for ways to quote not only the local manager of the company but also local clients. Each release should utilize the message/media outline.

**Setting Up the Interview**

Writing a news release frequently requires interviewing those who have the information you need. Preparation is necessary prior to the call or personal interview. There are at least five helpful preparation steps:

*1. Define the purpose of the interview*

You should know in your own mind what you want to accomplish with this interview—the story angle which best supports the message/media outline.

*2. Obtain the interview*

For releases requiring information from within the company, such as personnel, product, or financial announcements, find and talk to the most knowledgeable individuals in the company—either in person or by telephone. There are also experts outside the company who can offer a more believable third party view of your company's new product. Talk to them as well. Although it is easy to be intimidated and talk yourself out of calling a leading expert on a given subject, overcome your reluctance. Most people are willing to share their areas of expertise, particularly when the conversation can result in publicity. Publicity is usually considered a mutually beneficial outcome.

*3. Research the individual and the topic*

Come prepared with knowledge about the individual and his or her area of expertise. You must know enough about the person and the subject to ask the questions that will lead you to the story you want. One caution: You can waste a lot of time trying to become an expert yourself. That is not your job. You are the reporter and need only enough knowledge to ask the right questions.

*4. Determine questions and interview strategy*

Direct the interview to your intended result. Some individuals are easily interviewed whereas others are not. Prepare yourself for the tough interview. Develop an interview outline with more questions than you will need to garner the information you want. Think through a number of ways to approach the same question, or you may find yourself at the end of your list within a short time with nothing on paper.

Try to avoid "closed" questions. When you receive brief responses (i.e., yes and no answers), probe for more information with statements like, "What do you mean by that?" or "Can you explain that further?".

Be alert and flexible to new thinking that can strengthen your news angle or communications outcome. Ask the expert his or her opinion on how best to build a case for your communications outcome.

Hold sensitive questions to the end of your list. If you put the expert on the spot immediately, there may be discomfort, and you run the risk of obtaining less information.

*5. Establish rapport and conduct interview*

Use some information about the individual to break the ice and get to know the expert. The first few minutes of an interview are usually spent getting to know one another and establishing a level of confidence. Each interview should be considered an opportunity for additional sources. Seek them out.

Take accurate notes, or better yet, tape-record the interview and check back with any resource you use in the news release to be sure you have accurately interpreted what you have been told.[2]

> How would you organize the questions for an interview on a highly sensitive issue like environmental pollution or an impending employee strike?

## WRITING THE NEWS RELEASE

### The Lead

The most critical stage of a news release is its beginning. Journalists call it *the lead.* Without an effective lead, the editor, like the reader, will read no further. A lead is usually considered the first paragraph of a news story, although it is not unusual for the lead to include the first couple of paragraphs. A good lead sells your story, piques an editor's need/concern/interest in the news angle, and gets him or her into the second paragraph and then the third, fourth, fifth, and so on.

Veteran public relations academician Raymond Simon has this to say about the importance of the lead:

> Why the stress on the lead of the press release?
>
> The answer is that you are a guest in the medium's house, and the lead is your calling card. You are also an uninvited guest, and the average daily newspaper and radio-television station receives scores of uninvited guests every day. Your release competes with many other releases for an editor's attention. The average editor has neither the time nor the inclination to read through scores of press releases. A quick glance through the lead tells the experienced editor if the release will be of any use to him.[3]

The lead should represent the most important and most interesting point in a story, focusing the attention of the reader on the need, concern, or interest with the most potential for drawing that reader into the story.

The lead is typically one thought, one sentence. In fact, as a general rule most paragraphs should stick to one thought contained in one or two sentences. Exceptions to this rule may occur in paragraphs lower in the story. The rest of the story elaborates on and substantiates the claim made in the lead.

The lead or news hook draws the attention of the editorial gatekeeper. This may or may not represent the most important point in your publicity message. The lead is the practitioner's opportunity both to raise an audience need/concern/interest and demonstrate to the editor that he or she knows how to write a news story.

One should try not to exceed twenty to thirty action-packed words in the lead (or three typewritten lines), and normally the source of the information is identified.

The best leads have simple sentence structure, and most begin with the subject, followed by the action verb and concluded with the object of the verb. To illustrate:

The local drive to rebuild Balboa Stadium got a shot of school spirit from San Diego High School today when students donated half their treasury to the project.

Rudolf Nureyev and the Stars of the Paris Opera Ballet will perform here Jan. 15–16 at the Civic Theater.

**Does the sentence structure in the following news release lead comply with the above recommendation?**

**Sawyer's Gas and Electric Co. customers are beginning to receive refunds totaling approximately $75 million because of lower natural gas costs, the utility announced today.**

The importance of localizing a lead for a community or metropolitan newspaper cannot be overestimated. A release featuring the promotion of a company executive is far more significant to the *Roseville Press-Tribune* if

1. Your organization is located in Roseville.
2. The executive promoted is a Roseville resident.
3. The executive promoted is a Roseville native.

**Review the news release in Figure 5–2. How is the lead localized?**

Likewise, a release on tourism takes on more importance when local statistics are cited. Word processors allow practitioners to localize releases easily. At one time, localization of a news release for a state tourism bureau would mean retyping the entire release for each locality. Today, word processors can automatically plug in localized leads to statewide stories.

Strong news leads that complement the criteria mentioned earlier can occasionally result in verbatim or essentially verbatim pickup from the wire services. News events emanating from conventions, professional meetings, or news conferences have the most potential for wire service coverage—if they are positioned as timely, new (or freshly packaged), controversial, or involving a prominent individual/organization or affecting a large number of people.

The Rockey Company, Inc., scored two slightly edited wire service placements for Tree Top, Inc., the apple juice company, with the lead in Figure 5–1C.

Tree Top Inc. has announced it will introduce the world's first concentrated low-moisture apple fiber at a food industry convention in Atlanta.

Simon/McGarry Public Relations, Inc., scored a verbatim wire release with this lead:

Miniscribe Corp. today announced a $20 million equity financing agreement with a venture capital group led by Hambrecht and Quist, Inc.

A verbatim or slightly edited news release picked up on the wires and distributed to newspapers, magazines, and radio and television stations can be more effective than an interview by a wire service reporter. Why? Because the message remains intact as the practitioner wrote it.

NEWS BUREAU
Akron, Ohio 44316-0001 • (216) 796-2490
Houston (713) 475-5430 New York (212) 582-3939
Washington (202) 638-4054

GOODYEAR

#17668-185 FOR IMMEDIATE RELEASE

AKRON, Ohio -- Buckling up seat belts and rejecting that one last "belt" at the bar are life-saving reminders being stressed by Goodyear in an intensive company-wide safety campaign.

The facts are sobering and the reduction of injury and death is a goal worth striving for, said Tom Barrett, Goodyear president, as the Akron headquarters campaign kicked off recently.

"Two basic philosophies of the program are -- drive soberly and wear seat belts," he said. "The use of seat belts cuts traffic accident injuries in half and reduces fatalities 40 to 60 percent. These facts alone justify an all-out campaign to get more belts buckled."

Employee awareness of sober driving and seat belts is encouraged by a slogan search that will earn the winner and guests a three-day trip to Disney World. The phrase will be made into car window decals and distributed throughout the Goodyear organization, and it will become the focal point for an ongoing motoring safety campaign extending to Goodyear's global operations.

Also, employees who submit first-hand accounts of lives saved by seat belt use are eligible to win a $100 U.S. Savings Bond.

Weekly articles appear in company publications, including a recent one describing a Canadian government-backed campaign at Goodyear's Collingwood, Ontario plant, where employee seat belt use soared from 35 to 84 percent in a 10-day period.

(more)

Courtesy of Goodyear Tire & Rubber Company

**FIGURE 5–2**

#17668-185 -2-

Closer to Akron, employees also learned from an analysis of medical records of 52 auto accident victims at Akron City Hospital during one week, that only eight (or 15 percent) wore seat belts, which roughly is the U.S. average. Of the non-users, one died and all the others had facial and chest injuries -- and a hospital physician said seat belts would have spared most victims from injury.

In the state of Ohio, of the 296 traffic deaths in the first three months of 1984, 105 (35 percent) were alcohol-related and 220 occurred when seat belts were not used, according to statistics.

Other facets of the seat belt program extend outside Goodyear. The three U.S.-based blimps are flashing public service messages across the nation, while readers of major business and financial magazines are receiving the seat belt and drunk driving messages through a Goodyear corporate ad campaign.

The company plans to buckle up its official Akron-based campaign about mid-February after a winning slogan is adopted.

-0-

**FIGURE 5–2 (continued)**

> Which of the two news releases making up Figure 5–3 do you think was carried on a national wire service? Why? Of the one that wasn't, why not?

Although it is far more unusual to score a verbatim placement on one of the major wire services, the intended result is to clearly deliver your message. Consequently, an edited version with your message left intact is a more reasonable expectation.

The National Dairy Board and National Dairy Council used both controversy and significance when launching a campaign to counter the increased use of calcium supplements to lower the risk of osteoporosis. Their target audience was the adult woman. Their spokespersons were a prominent panel of scientists and the American Dietetic Association. Their message was twofold:

1. Consumers should get their nutrients from food before turning to vitamin/mineral supplements.
2. Scientists are concerned with the long-term safety consequences of the growing use of vitamin and mineral supplements to lower the risk of diseases, such as cancer and osteoporosis.

The following news release lead was provided to reporters attending a news conference and planted with the major wire services:

Washington . . . A panel of leading scientists today expressed alarm at the growing use in America of vitamin and mineral supplements, especially those taken to prevent such diseases as cancer and osteoporosis.

One of the leads used by Associated Press strengthened the concept:

Thousands of Americans, attempting to become healthier, may be poisoning their bodies with huge doses of vitamin supplements that can be dangerous in large quantities, a group of scientists said Monday.[4]

The Associated Press lead raised an audience concern (supplements may be dangerous) and the third and fourth paragraphs delivered the second part of the message verbatim from the news release:

"We in the scientific community are concerned with the increasing notion that supplements can be used to prevent serious diseases, such as cancer and osteoporosis," said Dr. David Heber, chief of clinical nutrition at the UCLA School of Medicine.

"Americans should get their nutrients from food instead of pills," Heber said. "Large supplement doses of single nutrients won't prevent diseases, but instead will upset absorption of other nutrients."[5]

> How would you rewrite the lead in Figure 5–4 to increase its likelihood of being picked up by a major wire service?

### The Body Copy

After the lead is written, the public relations writer should consciously think about questions raised by the lead and organize the release in order of their importance to the story and to build a case for the message. In other words, subsequent paragraphs expand on the lead or most crucial element of the news hook. The story should flow naturally from point to point, from the most important to the least important points. Journalists call this the inverted pyramid style of writing.

If one were to adapt the process described in earlier chapters, the lead would raise the need/concern/interest while offering the product, issue, or organization as a solution. This is followed by a description of the benefits of acting on the message and the consequences of inaction. A mental rehearsal of the intended action concludes the release. At the same time, the story describes and develops the who, what, where, when, why, and how of the news story. A release developed in this way has the most potential for meeting both the needs of the editorial gatekeeper and the target audience.

*News Release*

**Scripps Memorial Hospitals**

9888 Genesee Avenue
Post Office Box 28
La Jolla, California 92038-0028

(For Immediate Release)

September 21

Contact Mike Bardin
(619) 457-6891

ALCOHOLISM MAY BE GENETIC DISEASE

La Jolla, California...Children born of alcoholic parents are four times more likely to fall prey to alcoholism than children of non-alcoholic couples, a Scripps Memorial Hospitals symposium revealed today.

"Children of alcoholic parents are a 20 percent risk for alcoholism by their early 30s, even if they are separated from their parents near birth," said Dr. Marc Schuckit, psychiatry professor at University of California, San Diego.

"By comparison," Schuckit continued, "adopted children of non-alcoholic parents are only a five percent alcoholism risk."

Schuckit said that although these studies could not be considered conclusive, they are impressive enough to justify speculations that alcoholism can be passed on genetically.

MORE

**FIGURE 5–3A**
**Release 1** Courtesy of Scripps Memorial Hospitals

SCRIPPS MEMORIAL HOSPITALS page 2

Claims that alcoholism is tied to genetics appear to be further substantiated by studies conducted on identical and fraternal twins.

"Because twins are born at the same time and exposed to the same environment, it was suggested that alcoholism, if genetically influenced, would be more prevalent in identical twins than in same-sex fraternal twins," the professor said.

Studies showed that when one member of an identical twin pair is alcoholic, the other also will be struck by the disease in 55 percent of the cases. When one fraternal twin is alcoholic the other will show alcoholism 28 percent of the time, Schuckit said.

Alcoholism also runs very high among family relatives. Schuckit said the chance a man will become alcoholic during his life increases with the number of close relatives who are alcoholic as well as with the severity of problems in those relatives.

"The lifetime risk for the development of alcoholism in sons or brothers of a severely alcoholic man ranges from 25 to 50 percent," he said.

**FIGURE 5–3A (continued)**

NEWS BUREAU
Akron, Ohio 44316-0001 • (216) 796-2490
Houston (713) 475-5430 New York (212) 582-3939
Washington (202) 638-4054

GOODYEAR

FOR IMMEDIATE RELEASE

#17790-785

HOUSTON -- A large grain exporting company recently celebrated its 19th anniversary in Houston by handling its two billionth bushel of grain, and Goodyear conveyor belting, a partner from the beginning, dished up the goodies.

Union Equity Cooperative Exchange of Enid, Okla., installed in excess of 14,000 feet of Goodyear grain conveyor belting at its Houston site in 1966.

"We specified Goodyear belting for the project," said Wayne Slovacek, vice president of the Houston exporting group. "We have not regretted the decision, either. We have been very satisfied with the Goodyear belts."

The original 46-inch wide, 7-ply rayon belting has been replaced in the 19 years, but Pathfinder 330, Goodyear's premium grain conveyor belting, transported the two billionth bushel.

The two billionth bushel of grain was loaded onto the Greek flagship Mount Taygetos in early spring bound for the Mediterranean with two million bushels of Hard Red winter wheat.

The Union Equity Houston facility is one of the largest export elevator operations in the U.S. The entire company handles over 200 million bushels of grain a year for 340 local co-ops in eight Midwestern states.

Besides wheat, the Goodyear Pathfinder grain belt on Union Equity conveyors has handled corn, soybeans, sorghum and rice. Pathfinder is a low-stretch, high-strength and low-static grain handling belt which is manufactured at Goodyear's Marysville, Ohio, facility.

In addition to grain and elevator conveyor belting, Goodyear produces belting for mining, food handling, package conveying and industrial elevators.

Courtesy of Goodyear Tire & Rubber Company

**FIGURE 5–3B**
**Release 2**

Nann Miller Enterprises, Inc. APR
Public Relations / Advertising / Show Promotions
Bunker Hill Towers
800 West First Street, Suite 1710
Los Angeles, California 90012
(213) 620-1215

FOR IMMEDIATE RELEASE — CONTACT: NANN MILLER

JULY 19, 1985 — (213) 482-4740

14 TONS OF ICE CREAM & TOPPINGS TO BE

CONSTRUCTED INTO WORLD'S LARGEST SUNDAE --ON SUNDAY, JULY 28

Will Beat Guinness Record by 1,000 pounds

LOS ANGELES, CA -- When 7,000 pounds of fudge, caramel, strawberry and other toppings are poured from high ladders onto 3,500 gallons of ice cream, smothered with whipped cream and topped with a giant cherry, Knudsen Corporation and Smucker's will have created the World's Largest Ice Cream Sundae.

The 10-foot tall, 14-ton, 30-million-calorie sundae is being engineered to highlight the "All About Ice Cream Consumer Expo" at the Disneyland Hotel and Convention Center July 27-28. This sundae will beat the current world record, set in 1983, by 1,000 pounds. Those attending the show, open to the public, are invited to indulge themselves to their stomach's content at no extra charge.

A group in Olympia, Washington will be creating the World's Biggest Banana Split on the same day.

Construction of the sundae will involve nearly 50 people overall and take about 7 hours. Work will begin at 5:30 a.m. when 1500 pounds of dry ice (-110 degrees) will be placed in the bottom of a specially constructed pool.

-more-

Courtesy of Nann Miller Enterprise, Inc. APR

FIGURE 5–4

Sundae/2-2-2

The ice cream will arrive in 375 pound blocks with special tear-away coverings for easy transportation and cleanliness. About 25 people will be scurrying up and down ladders, opening cases and cans, stacking, sculpting, pouring and spraying. The sundae will be completed with the ceremonial placing of the final cherry on top about noon on July 28.

Servers will use boat oars to dish out samples of this ice-cream marvel. This sundae will be 47,000 times larger than the average six-ounce sundae.

Spokespersons Martha McNair and Tom Fulcher of Knudsen will be on hand to discuss all the behind-the-scenes planning going into the creation.

Proceeds from the "All About Ice Cream Consumer Expo" will go to the Boy Scouts of America to celebrate their "75th Diamond Jubilee." Discount opportunities for the Expo are available on the side panel of Knudsen milk cartons.

Broadcast-sized tape, shot of the event from the 5:30 a.m. beginning to completion, will be available to the news media.

####

**FIGURE 5–4 (continued)**

Nann Miller Enterprises, Inc. APR
Public Relations / Advertising / Show Promotions
Bunker Hill Towers
800 West First Street, Suite 1710
Los Angeles, California 90012
(213) 620-1215

CONTACT: NANN MILLER
(213) 482-4740

EASY DESSERT TO PLEASE 47,000 FRIENDS

"RECIPE" FOR WORLD'S LARGEST ICE CREAM SUNDAE

Ingredients needed:

1. 21,000 pounds (3,500 gallons) of Knudsen vanilla and chocolate ice cream, formed into specially wrapped, 375 pound blocks

2. 7,000 pounds (1800 cans) Smucker's toppings in assorted flavors

3. 10 cases (3 quart cans) whipped cream

4. 1 giant maraschino "cherry"

5. 1500 pounds dry ice (-110 degrees) for cooling

Equipment needed:

1. Specially designed, sanitary pool to hold sundae

2. Forklifts and other mechanical equipment to help transport and stack ice cream blocks

3. Several can openers

4. Several ladders

5. About 50 people to aid in the engineering and construction of the sundae

Directions:

Begin construction on "Ice Cream" Sunday, July 28 at 5:30 a.m. Line your special pool with dry ice blocks to keep sundae frozen during construction. Stack blocks of ice cream and remove protective coverings. Place 44 blocks on bottom layer, 12 in second layer and 2 on top. Pour various flavors of topping over sundae from high ladders. Smother entire ice cream marvel generously with whipped cream. Top completed sundae with giant maraschino "cherry."

Preparation time is approximately 7 hours. World's Largest Sundae should be complete around noon.

Serve with boat oars. Makes about 47,000 six-ounce servings.

A demonstration of this recipe will be given on July 28 at the "All About Ice Cream Consumer Expo" at the Disneyland Convention Center on Sunday, July 28.

**FIGURE 5–4 (continued)**

**Identify the following elements in the release in Figure 5–5: audience need, concern, or interest; solution; benefits of action; consequences of inaction; mental rehearsal steps; who, what, where, when, why, and how.**

The body of the news release should be designed to build the case for the public relations message. If a news release lead has raised the interest of corporate executives in automobile telephones, then the rest of the news release should build the case for the benefits of owning a car phone—adding more working hours to the day, the potential consequences of not owning a car phone such as wasted freeway commute hours and lost business contacts. Descriptions should help the executive reader think through how he or she can benefit from having a car telephone and avoid the consequences of not purchasing the new equipment.

Frequently, behavior is not the communications outcome. When GTE Sprint restored the historic Union Railway Station in Phoenix, Arizona, as its switching station, its outcome was to demonstrate the company's long-term community commitment to city leaders. The benefits and consequences of the Sprint investment are inherent in the restoration need raised by the release in Figure 5–6. The description of the need for the restoration should help the reader think through why a positive attitude about this Sprint action is warranted.

**How would you strengthen the way the news release in Figure 5–6 raises the need, offers Sprint as the solution, handles the benefits and consequences of inaction, and helps the reader think through why a positive attitude toward the company is warranted?**

Mental imagery, or creating a sharp picture in the mind of the reader, is important to message retention. We are not talking about flowery lead paragraphs oozing with adjectives. We are talking about the intelligent use of language (metaphors, similes, analogies, examples, comparisons, and good, crisp writing) to help individuals transfer the public relations message to their own real-life needs/concerns/interests. Concrete words that bring a picture to mind are recalled two to four times better than abstract words.[6]

Describing Lockheed's C-130/L-100 Hercules transport as a "flying truck" gives real-life interpretation to a transport airliner. When the University of Illinois at Champaign-Urbana describes a new mechanism for killing weeds as causing them to "literally commit suicide," it gives the reader a description he or she can easily remember. When Aerojet-General Corporation describes a research instrument that will be carried into space as a three-inch, three-pound "mini-planet" that "will spin just like earth and come complete with an atmosphere and gravity," it paints a mental picture that transfers what would probably be perceived as just another technological advancement into something readers can more clearly visualize.

The following lead from a University of Texas Health Science Center at Dallas release on heart attacks among young athletes is a prime example of concrete words that bring the reader into the story:

> Dallas—On a warm July evening in 1979, J. V. Cain went out for a pass during a practice game for the St. Louis Cardinals and never made it back to the huddle. At age 28, he was dead of a heart attack.
>
> It doesn't happen often, but every year young athletes drop dead during or after training or competition. Like Cain, most of them have heart abnormalities. And while the risk of sudden death is low in any athlete, even one with cardiovascular disease, these tragedies have a great effect on public thinking as well as attitudes in the medical profession.

A story about a cheese plant that appeared in *Dairyman* magazine, a trade publication

# NEWS

**CALIFORNIA DIETETIC ASSOCIATION**
Central Office, 1609 Westwood Blvd., Suite 101, Los Angeles, Calif. 90024
(213) 479-8228

SUMMERTIME NUTRITION BLUES
EASILY CURED SAYS CDA

Contact: Venesa Strong
(805) 937-4520

Hot weather decreases the appetite and makes getting nutrients more difficult, warns the California Dietetic Association (CDA).

"When summer temperatures climb above 85 degrees, your body burns extra calories and nutrients to keep cool," says Sharon Long, R.D., president of CDA.

"To replace lost nutrients and keep your body feeling light, eat light summer meals making sure each of the four food groups -- milk, meat, vegetables and fruits, breads and cereals -- is fully represented," Long says.

The CDA recommends California's homegrown foods for light meals that will impress out-of-state guests. Try stuffing an artichoke heart with California baby shrimp on a bed of lettuce. With a tangy vinegrette dressing and slice of San Francisco sourdough bread you get three of the four food groups necessary to good health and well being.

"To complete the picture, serve fresh California strawberries and grapes with mellow Monterey Jack cheese for dessert and you have a healthy sample of the four food groups to get you lightly through a warm summer evening.

# # #

Courtesy of California Dietetic Association

FIGURE 5–5

GTE SPRINT

GTE Sprint Communications Corporation
2201 E. Camelback, Suite 600
Phoenix, Arizona 85016
602 956-6200

Contact: Larry Nuffer
(602) 956-6200
or
(619) 296-0605

FOR APRIL 3 RELEASE:

CITY, GTE SPRINT ACCORD PAVES WAY

FOR UNION STATION RESTORATION

Phoenix's Union Station will receive a $300,000 facelift next fall as a result of an agreement approved yesterday between the city council and GTE Sprint Communications Corp.

The agreement -- which still requires the council's formal approval today--was approved in policy session Tuesday in the form of a resolution allowing the city to relinquish rights-of-way across southern portions of both Fourth and Fifth avenues.

In return for the property rights-of-way, valued at $26,000, the long-distance telephone company will restore the aging Union Station to its original appearance and provide new parking, curbing and landscaping. The station was originally built in 1923.

In addition, GTE Sprint will maintain the 62-year-old station for 15 years and cooperate in nominating the building to the National Registry of Historic Places April 16.

GTE Sprint has leased a portion of the station since 1974 from Southern Pacific Transportation Co. and Santa Fe Railroad Co., using it as a switching center to connect Sprint's long-distance telephone customers in Phoenix, Prescott and Albuquerque with the rest of the country.

(MORE)

A part of GTE Corporation

Courtesy of GTE Sprint

**FIGURE 5–6**

CITY, GTE SPRINT ACCORD PAVES WAY FOR RESTORATION -- PAGE TWO

Sprint plans to buy the land and station from Southern Pacific and continue a leasing arrangement with Amtrak, which operates a ticketing office there.

"This is the kind of mutally beneficial, creative partnership that public and private sectors across the country are aggressively seeking," Mayor Terry Goddard said.

"The city wants to restore one of downtown's most historic buildings and GTE Sprint wants to make a long-term commitment to maintaining facilities in Phoenix," Goddard said.

David C. Niklaus, director of corporate relations for GTE Sprint, said: "We're very pleased to help preserve an important part of Phoenix's past and at the same time be able to further strengthen our cooperative relationship with the city."

Donna Schober, a state historic preservation officer for the Arizona State Parks Board, said the agreement between the city and GTE Sprint is further proof of the growing interest in preserving Phoenix's historical landmarks.

"Sprint is setting a precedent in Phoenix for sensitive restoration of an historic building," she said. "Everything done to the rotunda will be historically accurate."

Assisting GTE Sprint in the restoration process will be Architectural Planning & Managers, Inc. (APMI) of Phoenix.

GTE Sprint Communications Corp. is a subsidiary of GTE Corp. and is based in Burlingame, California. Sprint is a leading supplier of long-distance telephone service, provided through its network extending more than 100 million circuit miles. Sprint has more than 370 U.S. cities and surrounding communities on its network. Sprint now provides service to Australia, United Kingdom and major regions of Canada.

# # #

**FIGURE 5–6 (continued)**

for the dairy industry, also paints a vivid picture for its dairy farmer readers:

> More than $42 million worth of equipment and facilities are already in place. And an army of construction crews is running better than a week ahead of schedule at what will be the world's largest cheese factory.
>
> As impressive an undertaking as it was on paper, the new plant seems even bigger now that the walls are up. The tall silos, which look so ho-hum in the accompanying photograph, are actually 60,000 gallons each. The dry product storage areas look like they could hold several 747 jets. And after touring the various processing rooms inside the plant, you begin to wonder if maybe this one job isn't causing a worldwide shortage of stainless steel.[7]

**How can the news release in Figure 5–7 paint a better real-life picture for the reader?**

Direct quotations from your spokesperson provide an opportunity to interpret the benefits of the intended action or consequences of inaction. A note of caution: Do not be too cute or blatantly self-serving. If you are, the release will probably never get past the editor's desk. Review quotations in your daily newspaper as a guide for acceptability and seek out those that use vivid language to paint a picture for the reader.

Quotations should make your spokesperson sound like people talk contractions and all, not like a formal memo from a chief executive officer. One advantage the public relations practitioner has over the journalist is that he or she has the freedom to compose a quotation to best support the message/media outline. So do not be afraid to create quotes to support communication outcomes as long as you get them approved by the spokesperson. The quotation is also an opportunity to paint real-life scenarios for your audience using similes, metaphors, analogies, examples, and vivid language.

**The first quotation in Figure 5–8 was received by a public relations department and rewritten as shown. How would you make the second quotation more conversational?**

The body of the news release should clearly describe the benefits of the action you want the target audience members to take. The consequences of inaction should be described to help the reader reflect on how he or she can take advantage of the benefits and avoid the consequences of inaction.

**What are the benefits, consequences, and action tips presented in the release from the dental association in Figure 5–9?**

News releases, like news stories, do not often end with conclusions. News space is a precious commodity. The inverted pyramid style of news writing purposely begins and expands paragraphs by their importance to the story. The body of the news release then amplifies the lead and builds the case for the story. The release, like the news story, should be written so it can easily be cut anywhere after the product is introduced as the solution to the need/concern/interest.

Once the case is adequately made—preferably one page but no more than two to three pages—the release is completed.

## CHECKING FOR ACCURACY

Once a release is completed, check the finished product carefully for accuracy. If you interviewed an expert, make sure he or she sees or has read a copy for accuracy as opposed to writing style, which remains the expertise of the writer. Some practitioners

Nuffer, Smith, Tucker, Inc.

3170 Fourth Avenue, Third Floor, San Diego, CA 92103 (619) 296-0605

News

Contact: Gretchen Griswold
or David Freeman
(619) 296-0605

FOR WESTERN FAIRS ASSOCIATION

For Immediate Release

(January 19, 1987)

FAIRS ARE URBANITES'
CLOSEST LINK TO AGRICULTURE

There's nothing special about a calf being born. But last summer, a single calf brought 2,000 people together at 1 o'clock in the morning.

"These were city people who rarely, if ever, have contact with livestock and agriculture," said Bob Dunlap, manager of the Kern County Fair.

His livestock birthing center, which last year welcomed 46 calves during the fair's 12-day run, is just one way fairs bring agriculture to the public.

"When you lay out all of our competition for the entertainment dollar, the fair industry's number one point of difference is the focus on agriculture," said Dunlap.

Other parks offer fun food, games, rides and entertainment, but he says fairs educate as well as entertain.

According to Norb Bartosik, president of Western Fairs Association (WFA), a trade organization for fairs in 27 western states and five Canadian provinces, focusing on agriculture is a return to the roots of fairs.

MORE

Courtesy of Western Fairs Association

**FIGURE 5–7**

Nuffer, Smith, Tucker, Inc.

FAIRS LINK URBANITES TO AGRICULTURE -- ADD ONE

"Fairs began as open markets for agricultural products and livestock," he said.

Both Dunlap and Bartosik are in San Diego this week to attend WFA's 64th Annual Fairman's Fair. Dunlap will lead a panel session exploring innovative ways of bringing agriculture to the public.

The Orange County Fair, which is headed up by Bartosik, centers its fair theme around a different farm animal each year. Educational exhibits and hands-on displays teach fairgoers everything about the lifecycle of the animal.

Last year, a dairy cow was featured as the fair's mascot. Exhibits on a year in the life of a cow, butter churning and ice cream making competitions, a milking parlor and dairy product cooking demonstrations highlighted fair activities.

In addition to agriculture, Bartosik sees the community-focus of fairs as a major point of difference.

"The opportunity to display your own handiwork or admire your neighbor's is a service only fairs offer to their community."

\# # #

**FIGURE 5–7 (continued)**

Quote #1

"I require all students seeking graduation to meet the same basic skill standards on high school competency tests. Vocational educators should examine and redesign their curriculum to include a range and level of instruction in the same essential skills as required of academic track students," said the school administrator.

Revision for news release:

"High school graduates require basic skills," the administrator said.

Quote #2

"It is probable that job selection by gender is at least as much a broad cultural tradition as a specific school influence. Although there is some evidence of diminished discrimination in at least wages, it would be naive to consider discrimination a problem solved by legal remedies that are directed toward geniune equality."

Your revision?

**FIGURE 5–8**

Ravenswood Dental Society
304 Main Street
Ravenswood, CO 81612

Contact: Earl Parker
(303) 238-1445

GOOD-FOR-YOUR-TEETH FOODS:

EVERYDAY FARE TO BUILD STRONG BITE

Grabbing the wrong kind of snack for a family on the run can harm teeth, while the right kind of snack may actually promote stronger teeth, according to the Ravenswood Dental Society (RDS).

"Food can be broken down into three groups when it comes to dental health: helpful, harmful and innocuous," said Scott Wallace, D.D.S., chariman of RDS's Council on Dental Health.

"Getting into the habit of choosing good-for-your-teeth snacks along with daily brushing and flossing, and regular visits to your dentist will help prevent tooth decay," he said.

Snacks such as candy bars, chewy candy, cookies, cake -- nearly any sweets -- can damage teeth if the plaque-causing residue isn't brushed away after eating between meals.

However, according to Wallace, there are some snacks which actually have a protective effect against tooth decay.

"Monterey Jack cheese, cheddar cheese, milk and other non-sweetened dairy products may inhibit or neutralize the formation of acids that cause cavities," he said. And dairy products are rich in calcium, necessary to keep teeth and bones strong and

- more -

**FIGURE 5–9**

GOOD FOR YOUR TEETH FOODS -- ADD ONE

healthy. Unsweetened snacks, such as popcorn, peanuts, sunflower seeds, corn chips or corn nuts are neither harmful, nor helpful toward teeth.

"If you want to eat for the best dental health, as well as good health in general, select a variety of foods from the four food groups: dairy, meat, vegetables and fruits, breads and cereals," he said.

Children should consume three daily servings from the dairy group, two meat group servings and four servings from both the vegetables and fruits and breads and cereals groups, said Wallace.

Some four food group snacks to choose instead of sweet or starchy snacks are:

* cubed cheese (dairy group)
* string cheese (dairy group)
* plain yogurt (dairy group)
* cheese and ham roll-ups (dairy and meat groups)
* peanuts, soynuts (meat alternates)
* hard boiled eggs (meat group)
* raw carrots, celery, jicima or radishes (vegetables and fruits group)
* whole wheat crackers (bread and cereals group)
* rice cakes (breads and cereals group)
* breadsticks (breads and cereals group)

"And if your child must have sweets, try serving them with a glass of milk to wash the food particles away," said Wallace. "And just one glass of milk will boost your child's recommended daily intake of calcium by one-third."

# # #

**FIGURE 5–9 (continued)**

take the added precaution of having the expert initial his or her approval at the top of each release. Each fact should be carefully reviewed for accuracy before the release is sent to management for approval or distributed to the media. The credibility of the public relations writer depends on accuracy. Put simply: The practitioner cannot afford to be incorrect—either within or outside the organization.

## EDITING THE RELEASE

Upon completing the release, it is time for a final edit. Ask yourself a number of questions:

1. Have you clearly raised an audience need/concern/interest and positioned the product, issue, or organization as the solution? Are the benefits of action and the consequences of inaction clearly presented? Have you helped the reader think through how he or she will carry out the intended action?
2. Have you answered the who, what, where, when, why, and how?
3. Are all editorial comments removed except when used as a quotation by a spokesperson?
4. Have you removed all unnecessary adjectives?
5. Have you corrected any typographical or spelling errors? When in doubt, consult a dictionary.
6. Have you followed news style as defined by Associated Press, United Press International, or the targeted medium?
7. Are your words clear and familiar? Avoid jargon and words that need a dictionary for interpretation. Use the shortest, most common words in the English language.
8. Have you written in a conversational tone? Have you used an active versus passive voice? Read the release aloud. Is it written as one would speak? If not, rewrite it.
9. Are there words that can be eliminated? If so, delete them.
10. Are most of your sentences short? Approximately twenty to thirty words per sentence should be your standard, with forty words the absolute maximum. Short sentences interspersed with an occasional longer sentence to break up the monotony improves readability.
11. Are your paragraphs short? Three to five lines should be your standard; seven lines your maximum. Shorter paragraphs also improve readability.
12. Is it one to two pages in length? If not, why not? Three pages should be the maximum. Be tough on yourself. Cut out those points that are not necessary to support the lead and the message.

**Would you send the news release in Figure 5–10? Why or why not? If you would not send it, how might you change the release to make it acceptable?**

## HEADLINES

The use of headlines in news releases is controversial. There are those who say that to put a headline on a news release is too presumptuous. The headline is the journalist's responsibility, these critics argue. In the authors' opinion, however, headlines help sell both the story and your news angle to the fast-reading gatekeeper. It emphasizes the local angle. The outcome of the headline and lead should be to generate enough interest from the gatekeeper to read the release.

Headlines should provide the reader (the gatekeeper) with a brief, direct, and descriptive statement of the release content. The emphasis should be on the news angle—for example, "Exxon Declares Dividend" or "Exxon Announces New President, Directors." Some additional examples:

Sealants Help Keep Health Care Costs Down

U.S. Elevator Acquires Austin Elevator Co.

Local Mothers Cautioned Against Chewable Vitamins

BRIGHAM YOUNG UNIVERSITY
Public Communications
Provo, UT 84602
Phone: (801) 378-4511

April 25, 1985

Book by BYU Professors Explores Who Commits Fraud and Why

Robbers steal millions from banks each year, but their heists amount to only one-sixth of what bank workers themselves steal from their employers.

That growing problem--internal employee fraud--and why it occurs is the focus of a book by W. Steve Albrecht, Keith R. Howe and Marshall B. Romney, all accounting professors at Brigham Young University.

"Deterring Fraud: The Internal Auditor's Perspective," published by the Institute of Internal Auditors Research Foundation, is a report on a study conducted by the authors to test which factors commonly believed to make fraud likely actually are relevant. The professors relied on analysis of 212 frauds for their conclusions, which they hope will help auditors deter and detect the crime.

The authors begin with a well-established assumption that perpetrators of fraud cannot be profiled readily because just about anyone is capable of the act given three prerequisites: enough financial pressure, a tempting opportunity and the ability to rationalize or justify the fraud.

"All employees are potential perpetrators," the authors say. "As soon as the combination of pressures, perceived opportunities and rationalizations become strong enough, dishonest acts are committed."

-more-

Courtesy of Brigham Young University

**FIGURE 5–10**

FRAUD 2-2-2-2

The authors tested the predictive power of 50 "red flags" which signal whether a company or person is ripe for fraud. Red flags on the list include an employee with unusually high debts or alcohol or drug problems, a department that lacks good records and documents, and an employer who places too much trust in key employees.

They found that the major cause of fraud was a company's failure to enforce established controls. Lack of internal company controls was also a significant cause, while overriding established controls was not a significant cause.

The study did not turn up any one or two personality characteristics that seemed pervasive among fraud perpetrators, but the top three red flag traits were living beyond means, overwhelming desire for personal gain and high personal debt.

Findings also indicated that 74 percent of the perpetrators were between the ages of 26 and 45 and only two percent were over 55; 59 percent of the frauds were committed by men and 41 percent by women; 29 percent of the cases involved collusion; in 57 percent of the cases less than $40,000 was stolen while in 22 percent more than $100,000 was taken; and only 51 percent of accused perpetrators were prosecuted.

The data indicate most perpetrators spent fraud monies on expensive automobiles, homes, extramarital relationships, vacations and wardrobes.

-###-

**FIGURE 5–10 (continued)**

> Can you identify a recent story that you chose to read based on the headline or lead?

## RELEASE FORMAT

News releases written for the print media have some standard specifications. They include the following:

- Double-space and type on $8\frac{1}{2}''$ by $11''$ paper.
- Set left- and right-hand margins at $1\frac{1}{2}''$ for easy editing by gatekeeper.
- List an organization's name, address, and telephone number at the upper left-hand corner or on the first page of the release, if not on letterhead. On subsequent pages, describe the release contact in a word or two at the upper left-hand corner and indicate the page number with "add one," "add two"—in other words, "School Boards—Add One" (for page 2). Journalists call this a slug line.
- Type the date when the release may be used or "For Immediate Release" on the left-hand side above the headline.
- List contact name on the upper right-hand corner with business and home telephone numbers.
- Try not to exceed two pages; feature releases may be an exception.
- Use only one side of a page.
- Use a headline to localize the release (if possible) and clearly illustrate the news hook (and need/concern/interest you are raising).
- Indent paragraphs five spaces.
- If the release is more than one page, center the word "more" at the bottom of the page; center the number "30" or the symbols "###" at the bottom of the final page.

## WHEN TO USE THE NEWS RELEASE

A news release should accompany virtually every effort to generate publicity. It influences how the editor or reporter interprets and writes the story. If he or she likes your news hook, it could be adopted by the reporter. News conferences, special events, speeches, and media tours should include a news release as a starting point or backup for the less than ambitious reporter who may very well use your material intact.

The news release sets the scene, along with preparation of participants and creation of graphics, for generating campaign messages with the most potential for

1. Transfering to the real-life needs/concerns interests of the target audience
2. Arousing motivation for action
3. Processing information and directing behavior
4. Actually changing behavior
5. Setting the audience up to reinforce that behavior change with positive experience
6. Forming positive values/attitudes toward the message, leading to repetition of the behavior

The news release is frequently the most cost-effective publicity technique. Typically, out-of-pocket expenses are minimal, but a public relations writer's time should not be overlooked when budgeting news releases. Time can range from \$40 to \$200 per hour, depending on the market.

## WHEN TO USE A PHOTOGRAPH OR ARTWORK WITH YOUR RELEASE

Nothing catches the eye more effectively than a good photograph. This is especially true for photographs in newspapers and magazines.

One can write story after story about the way osteoporosis, a bone-thinning disease, gradually erodes the bones in older American women to the point of fracture. But until one sees a photograph contrasting paper-thin osteoporotic bone with healthy bone, it is very difficult to paint a mental picture of the consequences for women who do not consume adequate amounts of dietary calcium. Painting mental pictures for your target audiences—helping them picture themselves in the situation you are presenting—

can be effectively accomplished with good photography.

The most common use of photographs with news releases is in the announcement release: newly hired executives, elected association officers, the opening of a new construction site. Although publicity photographs are more likely to be used by community newspapers and specialty and industry publications, be on the lookout for unusual photo possibilities to expand the message with larger newspapers. Specialty sections, such as food, fashion, real estate, automobile, entertainment, and travel, are more receptive to photographs than other sections.

Wire services have photo departments and can be queried for publicity placements. Western Fairs Association provides wire service photo editors with an annual "unusual events" calendar specifying photo opportunities at member fairs each month.

Studies of media use of photographs indicate five important points to consider:

1. Less than 5 percent of the photographs that newspapers publish are released from public relations offices.
2. Providing a photograph with a news story does not necessarily increase use.
3. Photos with people in them have better chance of use.
4. Photos are less likely to be used if they are posed than those that demonstrate spontaneous action.
5. The number of items or persons in a photo should be limited.[8]

Many public relations professionals, budget permitting, rely on the expertise of professional photographers, trained in photojournalism as opposed to portrait or commercial photography. Most newspaper photographers also do freelance work for public relations professionals. Although some practitioners shoot their own photographs, it is, in the authors' view, a questionable use of professional time.

Have specific outcomes when deciding to use a photograph in publicity. Will a photograph expand the impact of the message identified in the message/media outline? Will the message be clearer? Will it raise an audience need/concern/interest? Can it both raise an issue and offer your product as a solution?

Choosing a photograph just because it is different, interesting, or artistic does not justify its use. Does it expand the impact of the action you want the audience to take? Does it have the potential for making a difference in message retention or acceptance? Does it have potential for supporting attitude and behavior objectives?

What you want in a photo should be communicated clearly to the photographer. One common mistake made in working with photographers is assuming that they do not need instructions. They may know how to shoot photographs, but never assume that because of this, photographers will know what you want to accomplish with the photo.

> Suppose you created a news release about the opening of a new branch of the Bank of Brannan. What photos might accompany the release?

## PHOTO CAPTIONS

Photographs that jump off the page have an advantage because the reader is immediately drawn to both the photo itself and the caption, making captions a critical communications tool for the publicist. In fact, research repeatedly demonstrates that photographs with captions are more effective at increasing readership and understanding than news stories standing alone. Studies also show that news stories are more effective than photographs without a caption.[9]

Captions should briefly describe the photograph and correctly name each of those pictured from left to right. Captions should briefly raise the audience need/concern/interest and, if possible, suggest the product, issue, or organization as the solution. For

**FIGURE 5–11**

**Vitamin and mineral supplements should carry warning labels, a panel of scientists said today in New York.** Pictured are, from left to right, Victor Herbert, M.D., Robert Heaney, M.D., and David Heber, M.D.

example, the caption for the photograph in Figure 5–11 reads: "Vitamin and mineral supplements should carry warning labels, a panel of scientists said today in New York. Pictured are, from left to right, Victor Herbert, M.D., Robert Heaney, M.D., and David Heber, M.D." The caption for the photograph in Figure 5–12 could read: "Timmy, a 26-year-old gorilla from Metroparks Zoo in Cleveland, Ohio, shows his muscle with a new Goodyear extra-strength hose named Gorilla."

Associated Press cites the Ten Tests of a Good Caption:

1. Is it complete?
2. Does it identify, fully and clearly?
3. Does it tell when?
4. Does it tell where?
5. Does it tell what's in the picture?

GOODYEAR

NEWS BUREAU
Akron, Ohio 44316-0001 · (216) 796-2490
Houston (713) 230-5131 New York (212) 582-3939
Washington (202) 638-4054

FOR IMMEDIATE RELEASE

#17730-485

GOING APE -- "Timmy," the Cleveland Metroparks Zoo's 26-year-old gorilla, borrowed this Goodyear multi-purpose hose from his caretaker, and obviously wanted to play with it rather than give it back. Named Gorilla for its strength, the new hose was designed primarily for the agriculture, mining and construction industries in addition to washing down zoo exhibits. But no one will argue with Timmy's new application.

-0-

G 409

**FIGURE 5–12**

Courtesy of Goodyear Tire & Rubber Company

6. Does it have the names spelled correctly, with the proper name on the right person?
7. Is it specific?
8. Is it easy to read?
9. Have as many adjectives as possible been removed?
10. Does it suggest another picture?

Captions should reflect news release format. They should be typewritten and double-spaced, with the organization's name, address, and telephone number in the upper left-hand corner. The contact name, that is, the person to be contacted for more information, should be listed in the upper right-hand corner. The caption should be attached to the back of the photo with tape or glue and the written description folded and covering a portion of the front of the photograph.

## PHOTO DOS AND DON'TS

Some tips on publicity photographs:

1. Identify communications outcome before deciding to use a photograph.
2. Discourage group photos of more than four people.
3. Encourage natural-appearing group photos.
4. Be sure to get written consent agreements from each of those individuals photographed.
5. Attach captions to all photographs.
6. Check each medium for its size requirements. As a general rule, most publications want only 8″ × 10″ or 5″ × 7″ glossy black and white photos. Color photos should only be used when special arrangements have been made with the editor.
7. Mail in manila envelopes with cardboard support.

> Which of the two photographs making up Figure 5–13 has the best opportunity for publication in your local newspaper? Why?

## GRAPHICS

Graphic illustration can also be used to expand the message. A professional artist can

FIGURE 5–13A

FIGURE 5–13B

tailor artwork to the needs of specific publications. Trade publications are often receptive to graphic illustration, not only on the inside pages but also on the cover. Like photography, graphic illustration should be used only to expand the message. Beautiful artwork that does not expand a message has little value, even if it is on the cover of the leading industry trade publication. With the exception of cover art, a caption is needed for artwork too.

## DISTRIBUTION OF THE RELEASE

Distribution decisions, when and when not to send a release, depend to a great extent on the public relations writer's creativity and ability to meet the needs of the media. Put yourself in the editor's chair and ask yourself if what you have to offer is legitimate news. Is it new, or can it be packaged with a new slant? Is it timely? Is it different or unusual? Does it affect a lot of people? Is it controversial? Does it involve a prominent individual or organization? Is it local (for newspapers)?

Updated mailing lists or use of a publicity distribution service or even Business Wire or PR Newswire which sends the release directly into media computers is critical to proper distribution. Editors move from job to job frequently. Releases addressed to those departed are usually not appreciated.

Releases should be addressed to the editor appropriate to the release content. For example, an announcement of a corporate promotion should go to the business editor of a major daily newspaper and probably the editor of the weekly in the community in which the individual or company resides. General local release slants should go to the city editor, food stories should go to the food editor, and so on. Know who the appropriate gatekeepers are at each medium and address releases accordingly.

Decide whether or not to personalize envelopes with the names of those you are intending to reach. Editors and reporters receive enormous amounts of mail daily. Harry Nelson, the eminent *Los Angeles Times* science writer, once said that he separated his mail into two stacks: The first stack was addressed to Harry Nelson, the second stack was addressed to Science Writer. Can you guess which one he opened first? Which one would you?

Hand-delivering a news release may give you an opportunity to further sell the gatekeeper on the importance of the release. While the release must stand on its own, there are times when personal delivery matters. You have an opportunity to make contact with an important gatekeeper. A word of caution: Be judicious in your decision to hand-plant a release. Editors often view it as an imposition, particularly if the release is just a standard announcement.

There are numerous media guides that catalogue names and addresses of the major print media and their editors. But even then, prudent public relations writers telephone targeted media at least annually to confirm names and avoid errors.

## TRACKING COVERAGE

Commercial clipping services are essential elements in determining and evaluating coverage of regional and national releases and locally if you cannot track every publication on the distribution list. Clipping services, such as Burrelle's or Allen's, have readers who review newspapers and magazines for key words, supplied by you. When a key word appears in a story, the article is clipped and sent to you. The name of the publication and its circulation are attached to each clip. Clipping services are helpful in tracking coverage about your organization, its people, and issues that affect it.

## SUMMARY

- Writing the news release for the print media requires utilization of the message/media outline.
- News stories and releases must be newsworthy to pass the critical eye of the gatekeeper.

- Good writing means concisely addressing the main style guidelines, such as use of the active voice, simple words, controlling sentence length, punctuation, and requirements stated in either the AP or UPI style manual.
- The lead encapsulates the message typically as one thought and one sentence, while the body expands on each element in the lead.
- Photography or graphic illustration should expand the public relations message visually.
- Distribution of newsworthy releases demands attention to maintaining accurate contact lists, including who and where gatekeepers are and their correct names, titles, and addresses.
- Well-written and -distributed news releases demonstrate respect from the reporters and editors who decide if and when to publish your "news."

## EXERCISES

1. Review the *AP Stylebook* and review the release in Figure 5–14. What style errors can you find? What news release format errors can you find?
2. Develop a message/media outline from the Conlee Jeans/YWCA fact sheet in Figure 5–15. Make some thoughtful assumptions concerning target audience needs/concerns/interests.
3. Write an advance news release and include a headline from the fact sheet in Figure 5–15. Be sure you offer the product as a solution to the need/concern/interest raised; describe the benefits of the action you want the reader to take; describe the consequences of not acting; and help the reader think through how he or she will benefit from the action taken.
4. Write a photo caption for the winner of the Conlee Jeans/YWCA race using the message/media outline you developed.
5. Develop a message/media outline and write a news release from the brief news conference speech in Figure 5–16. The client (product) is the Regional Employment and Training Consortium.

## REFERENCES


1. *The Associated Press Stylebook and Libel Manual* (New York: Associated Press, 1980), p. 269.
2. G. Paul Smeyak, *Broadcast News Writing*, 2nd ed. (Columbus, OH: Grid Publishing, 1983), p. 98.
3. Raymond Simon, *Publicity and Public Relations Worktext* (Columbus, OH: Grid Publishing, 1983), p. 7.
4. Associated Press, *Arizona Daily Star*, May 6, 1986, p. 1.
5. Ibid.
6. Chris John Amorosino, "The Throat You Save May Be Your Own," *Journal of Communications Management* (1982/4), 13.
7. Dennis Halladay, "Corona Cheese Plant Ahead of Schedule for October Start-up," *The Dairyman* (May 1985), 10.
8. Linda P. Morton, "Use of Photos in Public Relations Message," *Public Relations Review* (Winter 1984), 18.
9. Ibid., pp. 17–18.


## CASE STUDY

### The Problem

U.S. Elevator, a $100-million subsidiary of Cubic Corporation, is a pioneer in the high technology revolution of the elevator industry. The only trouble is that no one outside the elevator industry knows about it, and U.S. Elevator wants to promote its technology as a competitive point of difference.

### Situation Analysis

U.S. Elevator was the first company to incorporate microprocessing controls that shorten waiting times from several minutes to less than thirty seconds. Computerization virtually eliminated the threat of being stranded between floors and offered troubleshooting devices to provide maintenance personnel with advance warning of potential mechanical failures. Such technological advances reduced maintenance and energy costs by as much as 25 percent.

Priority target audiences are small-to-mid-range building owners and property

Nuffer, Smith, Tucker, Inc.

3170 Fourth Avenue, Third Floor, San Diego, CA 92103 (619) 296-0605

News

FOR WESTERN FAIRS ASSOCIATION

Contact: Gretchen Griswold
or David Freeman
(619) 296-0605

For Immediate Release

(January 19, 1987)

**A One-Stop Supermarket for Fair Managers**

FAIRMEN'S FAIR OPENS THIS
WEEK IN SAN DIEGO

SAN DIEGO...One shopping list includes corn dogs, a Ferris Wheel, pennants, some picnic tables, hand writing analysis, a rodeo holding pen and Jimmy Buffett.

Another seeks several jugglers, a demolition derby, stuffed animals and security guards.

This week, fair managers are checking off their shopping lists at the 64th annual Western Fairs Association (WFA) Fairman's Fair, a convention in the form of a fair.

"We come together each year to accomplish two things," said Norb Bartosik, WFA president and manager of the Orange County Fair. "We exchange information with other fair managers and directors about trends in the industry, and our successes and failures and we shop for the things we need to make our fairs successful."

"Hosting the annual meeting gives us a chance to show off San Diego," said Roger Vitaich, manager of the Southern California Exposition. "For the past three months, staff and board time has been devoted to making this event a success."

MORE

**FIGURE 5–14**

Nuffer, Smith, Tucker, Inc.

A ONE-STOP SUPERMARKET FOR FAIRS -- ADD ONE

A mini-midway has been set up in the parking lot of the convention hotel which offers the latest in fair food such as Cajun black beans and a German-come-Californian dish called Stuffies.

And inside, the ballroom has been turned into a supermarket for fair managers.

"There's Talent Row with all of the top agencies where we can book nearly any big-name entertainer," said Bartosik.

Clowns, puppeteers and jugglers stroll about demonstrating their talents, hoping to become part of a few fair's schedules.

Mounds of day-glo stuffed animals loom in the booth next to the amazing robot that, in a split-second, can tell you what happened the day you were born.

In the hall next door, rising stars and established entertainers pay an audition fee to entertain fair managers for a half hour each in anticipation of putting together a circuit of fair dates.

During the day, fair managers and directors can also take advantage of nuts and bolts workshops on insurance, racing regulations and maintainance.

"Just as county fairs are the mirrors of the communities they serve, this fair is a mirror of the fair industry," said Bartosik.

MORE

**FIGURE 5–14 (continued)**

Nuffer, Smith, Tucker, Inc.

A ONE-STOP SUPERMARKET FOR FAIR MANAGERS -- ADD TWO

"Fairs in their earliest forms, dating back 2,000 years, were large temporary markets where merchants and tradesmen would gather to show and sell their wares," he said. "That's occuring here, but so is professional development for fair managers. And we can't get away from the fun of a fair. That's what we're all about."

# # #

**FIGURE 5–14 (continued)**

Becky Russell Heil
Becky Russell Heil Public Relations
4233 Scott Drive
Freeman Park, GA 30327
(404) 296-0605

Conlee Jeans/YWCA 10K and 2 Mile Fun Run

Preliminary Fact Sheet

WHAT: Ninth annual Conlee Jeans/YWCA 10K (6.2 miles) and 2 Mile Fun Run for Women. 1,000 runners expected. $8 entry fee ($10 if paid after Feb. 15) with all proceeds going to the local YWCA. A souvenir T-shirt given to each starter in the run, with a medal to each 10K finisher.

Also: For the first time, corporate teams are invited to compete in the 10K. Teams will consist of three women from the same company with each runner being scored individually. The average of the three times will be the team score and prizes will be awarded to the top three teams.

And: Little Conlee Jeans 1/4 Mile-Fun Run for girls age 7 and under. No entry fee, however, registration and parental or guardian permission is required. T-shirts given to all entrants.

A pre-race clinic will be offered to help 10K race participants prepare for Saturday's race. The clinic will be conducted by Cristy Morris, spokeswoman for Conlee Jeans national running circuit. Morris holds a national record in 50K cross country.

- more -

FIGURE 5–15

ADD ONE -- CONLEE JEANS FACTS

| | |
|---|---|
| | The clinic will be Thursday, Feb. 20 from 6:00 to 7:00 p.m. at the local YWCA. |
| WHERE: | David A. Freeman Memorial Park, (the start of all three races will be near the Organ Pavilion and the 10K finish is in the Pan Am Plaza parking lot. |
| WHEN: | Saturday, February 20<br>7:45 a.m. Little Conlee Jeans Run<br>8:00 a.m. Conlee Jeans/YWCA 10K Run<br>8:05 a.m. Two Mile Fun Run |
| WHO: | 10K and Two Mile Fun Run are open to women of all ages.<br>Little Conlee Jeans 1/4-Mile Fun Run is open to girls 7 and under. |
| AWARDS: | 10K Run: Every finisher will receive a medal. Overall winner receives an all-expenses-paid trip to New York City to compete in the Conlee Jeans Mini-Marathon, May 31. Special corporate team award to winning three-woman team.<br><br>2 Mile Fun Run and Little Conlee Jeans Run: Flowers and ribbons to all 2 Mile Fun Run finishers. |

# # #

FIGURE 5–15 (continued)

MAYOR O'CONNOR'S REMARKS
HIRE-A-YOUTH NEWS CONFERENCE
MAY 26, 1987

WHEN I WAS ASKED TO HELP KICK OFF THE 1987 HIRE-A-YOUTH CAMPAIGN, IT BROUGHT BACK MEMORIES OF MY OWN FIRST JOB WHEN I WAS GROWING UP. THE MORE I THOUGHT ABOUT IT, THE MORE I REALIZED JUST HOW IMPORTANT THAT JOB WAS TO ME.

I SUSPECT THAT MANY OF YOU FEEL MUCH THE SAME WAY ABOUT YOUR FIRST JOB. IN MANY WAYS, IT WAS A BRIDGE TO THE FUTURE.

FOR TODAY'S YOUTH, THOSE FIRST JOBS ARE EVEN MORE CRITICAL, FOR THE BRIDGE GROWS EVER HARDER TO CROSS.

ALL ACROSS THE UNITED STATES OUR YOUTH FACE A CRISIS OF MOUNTING PROPORTIONS. THE SCHOOL DROPOUT RATE IS SOARING, ESPECIALLY AMONG MINORITIES. IN SOME AREAS INCLUDING SAN DIEGO, THE DROPOUT RATE FOR MINORITIES IS A STAGGERING 40% OR MORE.

AT THE SAME TIME, YOUTH UNEMPLOYMENT REMAINS TRAGICALLY HIGH. OVERALL, 15% OF YOUTH IN SAN DIEGO CAN'T FIND JOBS, AND IN MINORITY AREAS IT RANGES FROM 30 TO 40%.

IT IS CLEAR THAT FINDING JOBS FOR YOUTH IS SERIOUS BUSINESS.

Courtesy of Private Industry Council

**FIGURE 5–16**

O'CONNOR REMARKS -- PAGE 2

TODAY I AM HAPPY TO REPORT THAT WE WILL MAKE THIS SEARCH A LOT EASIER. THE HIRE-A-YOUTH CAMPAIGN WE'RE LAUNCHING TODAY HAS BEEN AND WILL CONTINUE TO REPRESENT A MAJOR EFFORT TO ASSIST OUR YOUTH. GLEN WILL GIVE YOU THE PROGRAM DETAILS IN A MOMENT.

BUT HIRE-A-YOUTH IS NOT ENOUGH. WE'VE GOT TO ATTACK THE PROBLEM IN EVERY AREA WHERE YOUTH ARE AFFECTED. THAT IS WHY I AND THE MAJOR BUSINESS, EDUCATION AND GOVERNMENT LEADERS OF SAN DIEGO HAVE JOINED FORCES AND SIGNED THE SAN DIEGO COMPACT AGREEMENT.

THIS EFFORT WILL POOL THE ENERGY, RESOURCES AND VISION OF OUR OWN LOCAL LEADERS TO INSURE THAT OUR YOUTH HAVE THE BEST POSSIBLE ACADEMIC PREPARATION LINKED WITH SOLID JOB OPPORTUNITIES.

WE BELIEVE THE COMPACT WILL RESULT IN A LOWER DROPOUT RATE, REDUCE YOUTH UNEMPLOYMENT AND, ULTIMATELY, A WORKFORCE BETTER ADAPTED TO THE RAPIDLY CHANGING NEEDS OF SAN DIEGO'S LABOR MARKET.

THROUGH THE PRIVATE INDUSTRY COUNCIL, SAN DIEGO IS ALSO PARTICIPATING IN THE U.S. DEPARTMENT OF LABOR'S YOUTH 2000 INITIATIVE, WHICH HAS AS ITS GOAL THE FOCUSING OF NATIONAL ATTENTION ON THE ISSUE OF YOUTH UNEMPLOYMENT.

**FIGURE 5–16 (continued)**

O'CONNOR REMARKS -- PAGE 3

IN RECENT YEARS, SAN DIEGO HAS MOVED TO THE FOREFRONT NATIONALLY IN JOB TRAINING AND EMPLOYMENT, WHETHER FOR ADULTS OR YOUTH. WE NOW HAVE THE OPPORTUNITY TO BE A PIONEERING ROLE MODEL FOR THE REST OF THE COUNTRY IN HOW WE SOLVE OUR YOUTH PROBLEMS.

I WOULD JUST LIKE TO CONCLUDE WITH A MESSAGE TO OUR SAN DIEGO EMPLOYERS -- YOU ARE THE KEY TO THE SUCCESS OF HIRE-A-YOUTH AND ALL OF OUR YOUTH EFFORTS BECAUSE YOU HAVE THE JOBS.

I URGE YOU TO BECOME INVOLVED WITH HIRE-A-YOUTH, AND TO LOOK AT THE PROGRAM AS MORE THAN JUST A WAY OF GETTING TEMPORARY, INEXPENSIVE SUMMER HELP. LOOK ON IT AS AN INVESTMENT. FOR THEM, FOR YOUR COMPANY AND FOR YOUR COMMUNITY.

WHEN YOU HIRE A YOUTH, YOU HAVE IN YOUR HANDS OUR MOST VALUABLE RESOURCE. TEACH THEM. ENCOURAGE THEM. MOTIVATE THEM. HELP THEM EXPAND THEIR HORIZONS AND PREPARE FOR A PRODUCTIVE FUTURE.

YOU HAVE AN INCREDIBLE POWER TO SHAPE THEIR YOUNG LIVES FOR THE BETTER. USE IT! I THINK YOU'LL FIND IT ONE OF THE MOST REWARDING THINGS YOU'LL EVER DO. AN INVESTMENT IN OUR YOUTH IS AN INVESTMENT IN OURSELVES, OUR COMMUNITY AND OUR SOCIETY.

I'LL TURN THE PROGRAM BACK OVER TO GLEN, WHO WILL FILL YOU IN ON THE SPECIFICS OF HIRE-A-YOUTH.

**FIGURE 5–16 (continued)**

U.S. ELEVATOR PRODUCES INDUSTRY'S
FIRST PRE-ENGINEERED GLASS CAB

The elevator industry's first pre-engineered glass cab designed for cost savings and reduced delivery times, were announced today by U.S. Elevator.

"The demand for glass-cab elevators has doubled in the past few years because more hotels, office buildings and shopping centers around the country are being designed with interior atriums that can be accentuated by these types of elevators," said Richard Lucas, general manager of U.S. Elevator, a wholly-owned subsidiary of Cubic Corporation in San Diego.

Because the new glass cabs are pre-engineered, they can be assembled and delivered in 12 weeks, or about half the time required for delivery of most glass cabs. In addition, it's estimated the new cab will cost building owners about half that of glass cabs that are not pre-engineered.

The U.S. Elevator glass cabs will be installed with hydraulic systems in buildings up to six stories high and with geared systems in structures up to 15 stories.

The cabs will be assembled in three sizes with weight capacities ranging from 3,000 to 3,500 pounds. Four types of interior decor, three different ceiling types and a variety of fixtures will be available.

U.S. Elevator is the fifth largest elevator company in the United States, specializing in the manufacture and service of microprocessor-controlled elevator systems.

# # # #

Courtesy of Cubic Corporation

**FIGURE 5–17**

managers. Research has identified three common priority audience needs:

1. Decreased maintenance and energy costs
2. Increased response time and speed of delivery
3. Increased tenant satisfaction

The U.S. Elevator public relations plan includes a Key Result Area that reads: Position U.S. Elevator as the high technology pioneer.

Develop a message/media outline for one of the above audiences and audience needs. Rewrite the news release in Figure 5–17 to reflect the message/media outline for a leading trade publication reaching your audience.

# CHAPTER 6

# Writing for Broadcast Media

*IN THIS CHAPTER*

Most radio and television publicity opportunities come from interview placements on talk and news shows. Consequently, public relations professionals have not traditionally mastered broadcast writing skills.

Success with broadcast publicity has come from mastering the needs of the broadcast journalist: knowing a good news story, providing articulate and accessible experts, packaging the public relations message to fit the time limitations, and, in the case of television, creating visuals to bring news stories alive. Success has also emanated from knowing that a primary source of broadcast news is newspapers, and a well-played print story enhances radio and television news opportunities.

Although most video news release scripts are prepared by commercial producers, practitioners are still responsible for initiating the news and visual concept and evaluating effective interaction between voice and visual. Practitioners must also know how to spot a good broadcast news opportunity, package a message to fit it in less than 30 seconds for radio, and frequently television, and prepare the spokesperson to successfully deliver it.

Furthermore, there are few practitioners who have not been called on to write public service announcements. Quality, time-intensive but conversational writing can be the difference for successful public service announcements.

Successful practitioners incorporate the needs of broadcast media and those who guard its gates with those of the target audience. A knowledge and appreciation for solid broadcast writing enhance the practitioner's ability to generate publicity that mutually benefits journalists, clients and target audiences.

### CHAPTER OBJECTIVES

The reader will be able to

1. Differentiate between writing for broadcast and print media.
2. Define the strengths and limitations of radio and television as communications media.
3. Explain techniques for generating television and radio news placements.
4. Write public service announcements for both radio and television that meet the needs of client, media, and audience.
5. Identify techniques for placing public service announcements with radio and television stations.

## BROADCAST VERSUS PRINT: THE DIFFERENCES

Broadcast writing means communicating as you talk, say two former television newsmen-turned-public relations counselors, Roy Heatly and Duane Borovec. "It's more informal than print. Clarity is the key. Finding the right concept to make people respond to your message is another." Edward Bliss, Jr., in *Writing News for Broadcast*, says that copy should be written to be read aloud, to be heard once, and, with only one hearing, be understood.[1]

"Print reporters could find a dose of broadcast writing skills to be good medicine for the ills of run-on writing," says Dale Kemery of the Kemery Media Group. Kemery, who has written extensively for both broadcast and print media, does not view the need for concise writing skills to be exclusive to the broadcast media. Too often, print writers get woefully carried away with obtuse, convoluted sentences that are so complex they require careful analysis to understand. Short words and simple sentences are the backbone of good writing skills. And, with certain adjustments, good writing can fit any medium.

According to Howard Back, president of National Television News, the best broadcast style is no style at all. Simple declarative sentences are usually the best. Back, a long-time producer of broadcast material for public relations practitioners, echoes the sentiments of David Belasco, the American theatrical producer: "If you can't write your idea on the back of a calling card you don't have a clear idea."

Some basic characteristics differentiate broadcast writing from print writing:

1. A radio listener or television viewer sees or hears each story as it unfolds; a print reader learns of the event after the fact through the eyes and ears of a reporter.
2. A radio-television message is here one minute and gone the next. You cannot go back and reread it as you can a newspaper or magazine story.
3. The television medium relies on the use of visuals to make its stories come alive.
4. In broadcast, news and information are brought to you by voices and faces that can become familiar. Familiarity can inspire trust.
5. Radio and television are headline services. The average radio news story is under 30 seconds; most television segments average 60 to 90 seconds. An in-depth interview may last only 5 to 6 minutes.
6. Radio and television are accessible 24 hours a day. Virtually every home has a television, and every home and car have at least one radio.[2]

Writing for broadcast requires the same thought process as writing for print. There is one primary difference between the two media of broadcast: With radio you write for the ear; with television you add the eye.

Writing for television follows the rules of radio. However, visuals or "pictures" as they are known in the trade, not words, are the driving force of the television story. Writing a script to be matched with pictures is called a voice-over. The visual concept should lead the story, and the narration should reinforce those visuals. Words should be used to fill in what the visual picture cannot tell. Writers should be sensitive to the interplay between words and visuals. Narration should reinforce and explain visuals but leave pauses for places where the visual needs no words.[3] "Writing a silence is as important as writing words, particularly when you have film that carries (the story)," says NBC news correspondent John Hart. "I personally don't think we rely on that enough."[4]

Necessarily, for the strongest impact, visual ideas and copy should be developed together.

As with the print story, the lead is the most crucial point of the story. Ideally, a broadcast lead raises an audience need/concern/interest. From the lead, the story expands to answer questions raised by the lead. One of the questions raised by the lead should be your opportunity to present the public relations message or solution to the need/concern/interest raised.

The listener must be given time to tune into the story. Raising audience needs/concerns/interests in the lead should do the most efficient job of getting the attention of the listener. The message then should be delivered a few seconds into the story as the solution to the need/concern/interest identified. If the message is presented in the lead, there is the chance that it may not be heard.

Broadcast leads seldom are as detailed or explicit as newspaper leads. Broadcast leads emphasize the who, what, when, and where. The how and why of the news event will probably be found in the body of the news story.[5]

A suggested lead for a video news release from the American College of Radiology reads:

> Multiple sclerosis. They call it MS. Some 250 thousand Americans have it. Today a report from Nashville, Tennessee, where new technology is helping doctors get clearer pictures of MS, pictures that may help unravel the mysteries of the often-crippling disease. (See Figure 6–1A, Release 1.)

One way to think about a broadcast lead is to consider how you talk to a friend over dinner—"Hey, you know what happened?"—with the story flowing naturally from one thought to another.[6]

A video news release lead, from American Honda Motor Company, reads:

> You may have noticed them—they're called A-T-Vs, all terrain vehicles. A report today from California on the booming sales that are making three- and four-wheeled off-road vehicles one of the fastest growing segments of the transportation industry in the United States . . ." (See Figure 6–1B, Release 2.)

Reading copy aloud is the best way to find out whether or not your release is written for the ear as opposed to the eye.

Writing for radio and television has far greater time restraints than writing for the print media. For instance, radio news spots should be written for 30-second time slots; television news items are 60 to 90 seconds. Broadcast writing, particularly radio, is perhaps the most demanding and disciplined writing form because it forces the writer to be parsimonious with words. Because each word has to count, there is little room for flabby writing. A 5-minute newscast may have $3\frac{1}{2}$ minutes of news. If eight stories are told, each must be communicated in fewer than 30 seconds. Most radio news directors try to include between eight and ten stories in each 5-minute newscast.[7]

It may be unrealistic to expect any more from a radio news story than raising an audience need/concern/interest and offering your product, issue, or organization as a solution. Frequently, however, story ideas can be developed to combine the concern with consequence.

When popular recording artist Karen Carpenter died from the eating disorder anorexia nervosa, the California Dietetic Association expanded the concern to parents of teenagers (with potential of death as a concern/consequence) and offered the registered dietitian as part of the solution. Parents who may have faced similar difficulties with their own children were offered tips through broadcast and print media on spotting symptoms of anorexia nervosa. The guidelines were designed to help determine whether

National Television News

13691 West Eleven Mile Road • Oak Park, Michigan 48237 • (313) 541-1440
23480 Park Sorrento • Calabasas Park, California 91302 • (818) 883-6121

NTN

EDITED STORY + B-ROLL AND EXTRA BITES
TRACK 1 - VOICE-OVER ONLY ** TRACK 2 - NATURAL SOUND ONLY

MAGNETIC IMAGER GETS SHARP PICTURES OF MULTIPLE SCLEROSIS DAMAGE IN BRAIN

(Suggested introduction before tape)

Multiple sclerosis. They call it MS. Some 250 thousand Americans have it. Today a report from Nashville, Tennessee, where new technology is helping doctors get clearer pictures of MS, pictures that may help unravel the mysteries of the often-crippling disease.

| (SCENES) | (SUGGESTED VOICE-OVER) |
| --- | --- |
| LS LEVINSON AT MAILBOX<br>CU WALKING<br>(8 seconds) | The cause of multiple sclerosis is unknown; there is no cure. Until now, even diagnosis of MS has been very difficult. |
| LS LEVINSON WALKING<br>CU LEVINSON SPEAKS<br>(Suggested Super: Joan Levinson)<br>(22 seconds) | (SOUND-ON, JOAN LEVINSON)<br>"I had the first symptoms in 1969 when I lost the feeling from my waist down. I had many spinal taps, and I had many examinations by various doctors and they still didn't come to a positive conclusion until I thought a lot of these symptoms were imaginary." |
| | (SUGGESTED VOICE-OVER) |
| LS PATIENT INTO IMAGER<br>MS CONSOLE<br>LS IMAGES<br>CU ONE PICTURE<br>(26 seconds) | But now, at the Vanderbilt Medical Center in Nashville, a new tool, the magnetic resonance imager, is being used for brain scans. The patient gets no x-rays, no injection of dye, and can be tested on an out-patient basis. Radiologists say it lets them see tissues and organs in great detail. About 400 persons have been given magnetic brain scans at Vanderbilt; for about 200, the diagnosis has been firm: multiple sclerosis. |

Courtesy of National Television News

**FIGURE 6–1A**
**Release 1**

| | |
|---|---|
| CU DR. RUNGE SPEAKS<br>(Suggested Super:<br>Val Runge, M.D.<br>Radiologist)<br>(20 seconds) | (SOUND-ON, DR. VAL RUNGE)<br>"Now we have a scanner that will detect the disease with much better sensitivity than any other test, and we can say to the patient, you have this disease--multiple sclerosis. Your symptoms are due to this disease and you don't have to worry that you have a tumor or that you have some sort of psychological problem." |
| CU LEVINSON<br>CU LEGS<br>MS LEVINSON<br>CU LEVINSON<br>(20 seconds) | (SOUND-ON, JOAN LEVINSON)<br>"The scanner finally showed lesions on my brain which gave a definite diagnosis. And I know that they can't do anything for multiple sclerosis, but just knowing that this is what I have, and that I'm not imagining these symptoms, I'm able to be more of a mother and more of a wife." |
| LS CONSOLE, IMAGER<br>CU VIDEO TUBE<br>(11 seconds) | (SUGGESTED VOICE-OVER)<br>For now, there are just a handful of magnetic scanners in use at hospitals, but from them may come clues that will one day lead to the cause or a cure for multiple sclerosis. |

(Total running time: One minute, 47 seconds)

AMERICAN COLLEGE OF RADIOLOGY
20 N. Wacker Drive
Chicago, IL 60606
Contact: Richard Cantrall
(312) 236-4963

c2020
485

FIGURE 6–1A (continued)

National Television News

13691 West Eleven Mile Road • Oak Park, Michigan 48237 • (313) 541-1440
23480 Park Sorrento • Calabasas Park, California 91302 • (818) 883-6121

NTN

MAGNETIC RESONANCE IMAGER - ADDITIONAL B-ROLL AND EXTRA BITES

| | |
|---|---|
| MS PATIENT INTO MAGNETIC RESONANCE IMAGER | (18 seconds) |
| CU PATIENT INTO MR | (31 seconds) |
| CU MR CONTROL PANEL | ( 5 seconds) |
| LS REMOVING PATIENT FROM MR | (10 seconds) |
| LS TWO DOCTORS LOOKING AT IMAGES | (11 seconds) |
| MS FOUR IMAGES | (11 seconds) |

The following four sequences are file footage showing multiple sclerosis patients.

| | |
|---|---|
| MS ENTERING MS CLINIC | ( 8 seconds) |
| MS WOMAN IN MOTORIZED WHEELCHAIR | (15 seconds) |
| MS SWIMMING POOL THERAPY | (13 seconds) |
| LS MS PATIENTS IN RECREATIONAL HALL | (11 seconds) |

EXTRA BITE

MS DR. VAL RUNGE: "In the past, patients with multiple sclerosis have had to have a number of painful tests. These have included many spinal taps, blood tests, cat scans, and now we can offer for these patients a simple test which is non-invasive, a magnetic resonance scan, and be able to tell these patients if they have multiple sclerosis or if they don't."
(22 seconds)

AMERICAN COLLEGE OF RADIOLOGY
20 N. Wacker Drive
Chicago, IL 60606
Contact: Richard Cantrall
(312) 236-4963

**FIGURE 6–1A (continued)**

National Television News
NTN
13691 West Eleven Mile Road • Oak Park, Michigan 48237 • (313) 541-1440
23480 Park Sorrento • Calabasas Park, California 91302 • (818) 883-6121

EDITED STORY + B-ROLL AND EXTRA BITES
TRACK 1 - VOICE-OVER ** TRACK 2 - NATURAL SOUND ONLY

A-T-Vs GROW IN LEAPS AND BOUNDS

(Suggested introduction)

You may have noticed them -- they're called A-T-Vs, all terrain vehicles. A report today from California on the booming sales that are making three and four-wheeled off-road vehicles one of the fastest growing segments of the transportation industry in the United States...

| (SCENES) | (SUGGESTED VOICE-OVER) |
|---|---|
| LS ATV TOWARD CAMERA<br>MS ATV WHEELS<br>LS ATVs, FAMILY<br>(17 seconds) | It started back in 1971; the three-wheeler was developed by Honda for recreational use. Just 10 thousand were sold that first year; but in the last five years A-T-V sales have increased by 600 percent. According to Alan Isley, president of the Specialty Vehicle Institute of America: |
| CU ALAN ISLEY<br>(14 seconds) | (SOUND-ON, ALAN ISLEY)<br>"It may have begun with the recreation rider but those riders through word of mouth, through application on their farms or in their businesses found a great variety of utility use for the machine". |
| | (SUGGESTED VOICE-OVER) |
| MS ATV AND CATTLE<br>MS ATV, OIL FIELD<br>CU ATV, LOG<br>MS PULLING LOG<br>LS ATV DEALERSHIP<br>CU CUSTOMER ON ATV<br>MS CUSTOMER, SALESMAN<br>(20 seconds) | A-T-Vs are being used on farms, in oil fields, and at construction sites. National Park officials are finding them invaluable, and law enforcement agencies are using them too. Industry officials predict that sales will jump 40 percent this year to over 700 thousand units. Thirty-six different A-T-V models are currently available. |

Courtesy of National Television News

**FIGURE 6–1B**
**Release 2**

| | |
|---|---|
| | (SUGGESTED VOICE-OVER) |
| LS INSTRUCTOR TRAINING<br>CU INSTRUCTOR'S GUIDE<br>(11 seconds) | With consumer demand at an all-time high, the industry's association -- the Specialty Vehicle Institute of America -- will soon be offering a series of national rider education seminars. |
| CU ALAN ISLEY<br>(Suggested Super:<br>Alan Isley, President<br>Specialty Vehicle Institute of America)<br>MS ATV ON HILL<br>LS ATVs TURNING<br>CU ALAN ISLEY<br>(24 seconds) | (SOUND-ON, ALAN ISLEY)<br>"Our course involves a 4 1/2 to 6 hour riding experience, and it starts from the very very beginning of how to operate the machines. It goes all the way through the different types of terrain, turning, braking and the heaviest emphasis is on personal judgment, not riding over your head, not riding beyond your skills." |
| | (SUGGESTED VOICE-OVER) |
| MS INSTRUCTOR, ATVs PASS<br>MS ATVs AROUND TURN<br>(27 seconds) | To accomplish that, the institute's goal is to train one thousand instructors by August of this year...and to give driving instruction to 40 thousand ATV riders by the end of 1985. About a million and a half A-T-Vs are in use around the country now. And industry officials are optimistic about the future. They say that new uses for recreation and business will make A-T-Vs one of the biggest business success stories of the '80s. |

(Total running time: one minute, 53 seconds)

AMERICAN HONDA MOTOR COMPANY
Contact: Kurt Antonius
P.O. Box 50 - 100 W. Alondra Blvd.
Gardena, CA 90247
(213) 327-8280

485

**FIGURE 6–1B (continued)**

National Television News
NTN
13691 West Eleven Mile Road • Oak Park, Michigan 48237 • (313) 541-1440
23480 Park Sorrento • Calabasas Park, California 91302 • (818) 883-6121

A-T-Vs - ADDITIONAL B-ROLL AND EXTRA BITES

(SCENES)

| | | |
|---|---|---|
| MS | ATVs DRIVE OFF | (12 seconds) |
| MS | INSTRUCTOR, ATV INTO PATTERN | (13 seconds) |
| MS | ATV COMES TO STOP | (12 seconds) |
| CU | INSTRUCTOR | (13 seconds) |
| MS | ALAN ISLEY AT DESK | ( 5 seconds) |

EXTRA BITES

MS ALAN ISLEY: "My advice to a new buyer of an ATV is to go slow and to take the time it takes to learn the machine's capabilities, take the time that is needed to personally investigate your own riding skills. Probably do not assume if you can ride a motorcycle, or a snow mobile or a jet ski that you can automatically climb onto an ATV and ride it off immediately. Take time and learn your skills and learn the machine's capabilities. They're great. It'll do a lot of things but taking the time to experience those things slowly is my most important piece of advice." (48 seconds)

MS ALAN ISLEY: "They're essentially very simple machines right now, and as you add better suspension, as you add more powerful engines, as you add instrumentation, as you add accessories that will help the utility of these machines you're going to see this market continue to grow for many many years." (21 seconds)

AMERICAN HONDA MOTOR COMPANY
Contact: Kurt Antonius
P.O. Box 50 - 100 W. Alondra Blvd.
Gardena, CA 90247
(213) 327-8280

485

**FIGURE 6–1B (continued)**

or not the counsel of a registered dietitian was warranted. (See Figure 6–2.)[8]

## RADIO: ITS STRENGTHS AND LIMITATIONS

### Radio Reaches Large Numbers

There are some 450 million radios in the United States and radio listening averages three hours a day. A typical household has five or six radios.[9]

### Radio Is Local

A local news or public service message is as important to radio as to the community newspaper. Whereas the television networks battle for a share of time, radio reaches more people on a daily basis than any other information medium.[10]

### Radio Provides Instant Access

Radio is a medium with instant access. Spokespersons can be on the air almost instantly to announce the results of a fund-raising drive or to inform the community about a crisis at a local manufacturing plant. Radio also makes possible a local twist to a national news story. The local chapter of the cancer society, for example, can telephone news directors and offer a spokesperson over the telephone to localize a major story emanating from a national cancer symposium.

> If you represented the dietetic association, what would you do to get the guidelines for anorexia nervosa on your local radio news show?

### Time Is Radio's Limitation

Radio's primary limitation to the public relations practitioner is the time available for both news and public service messages.

### Radio Can Generate Visuals Too

Some say radio can do a better job than television in creating the mental pictures necessary to transfer a message to an individual's own real life.

"Sounds evoke pictures in the mind of things as they are and as we want them to be," says William Stakelin, chief executive officer of the Radio Advertising Bureau. "When you think of radio, don't think of lack of pictures but the opportunity to create countless pictures. Where a TV spot plants one image in a million heads, radio can evoke a million images—each listener developing a personal picture associated with your product," Stakelin says.[11]

> Can you think of how you might use a radio news hook to help listeners picture the importance of not letting friends drive an automobile while intoxicated?

## TELEVISION: ITS STRENGTHS AND LIMITATIONS

Public relations professionals tend to get very excited about a placement on a national news show or a national talk show. Television is typically a priority medium on media tours. And you can sense the guarded excitement of management or spokesperson when a camera crew walks into a news conference or special event. Television is the glamour medium. News reporters and anchorpersons are more like celebrities than journalists. They are regular guests in great numbers of American homes. Nearly every home has at least one television set, and more people watch television than any other activity aside from working or sleeping.[12]

### Visuals: The Strength of Television

There is tremendous potential for transferring messages to real-life audience scenar-

# Anorexia nervosa victims avoid permanent damage by early diagnosis

LOS ANGELES (AP) —Starvation-prone victims of anorexia nervosa, the eating disorder linked to the recent death of singer Karen Carpenter, have a better chance of avoiding permanent damage if warning signs are spotted early, medical experts say.

The *California Dietician Association* released six warning signs of the disorder on Friday, as Miss Carpenter's death a week before focused increased attention on the rare affliction, which most often hits young, goal-oriented American women.

Miss Carpenter, 32, had struggled against anorexia nervosa—compulsive dieting that amounts to starvation—and doctors said it may have contributed to her death from cardiac arrest. Starvation weakens the muscles of the heart.

"Early diagnosis can definitely boost the cure rate," said Cheryl Rock, a UCLA clinical nutritionist and dietician who works with the medical school's Eating Disorders Clinic. "It's easier to prevent very low body weight than it is to rehabilitate someone who's already lost it."

She noted that anorexia nervosa is "an extremely complex disorder," and that effective treatment must combine the skills of physical, phychologists or psychiatrists and dieticians.

Ms. Rock said parents' attention to early warnings can be vital since "with young people who start developing anorexia nervosa, there is a strong denial of illness. They would rather be left alone, especially in the early stages."

The dietician association warning signs are:

—Dramatic weight loss that continues even after an ideal weight is reached. Ms. Rock said a girl may begin dieting when she's overweight then find herself unable to stop.

—Denial of hunger in which the victim insists she feels full, even after eating minute amounts for days on end.

—Marathon exercise and hyperactivity, even without enough food to maintain a sedate lifestyle. "They often have incredibly high energy when it comes to exercise until they reach the point where they faint," Ms. Rock said.

—Increased social isolation. "It becomes so all-encompassing. It takes all of one's energy to starve oneself in a society where almost everyone is overweight," she said.

—Bizarre rituals surrounding eating and food handling. Ms. Rock said one common ritual, seen in people who are starved for any reason, is to literally stretch meals for hours to get maximum enjoyment from minimum quantity. Also, "they get more and more picky about what foods they will eat and may eat only one or two items all day long." Those can be extreme, she said, citing patients who choose tablespoons of mustard on a lettuce leaf or five dill pickles with hot cocoa.

—Establishment of rigid schedules that are maintained with excessive zeal. "They do exact things at exact times," Ms. Rock said. "They have a very tight schedule to incorporate all their exercise regimens and all their food regimens."

Driven by an obsessive fear of being fat and a wildly distorted image of their own bodies, victims may even resort to self-induced vomiting or abuse of laxatives. "I had a patient who weighed 76 pounds and considered herself fat," Ms. Rock said. As many as 5 percent may die and others may suffer permanent damage such as heart or intestinal problems.

Victims are overwhelmingly female, probably because "our society's ideal female is so far removed from the reality of the female body. . . . Women are supposed to maintain this ideal (of thinness). And women in our society are still judged very much by their body," Ms. Rock said.

The disorder, she said, "is extremely rare in lower socioeconomic groups. In the higher socioeconomic levels, I've heard figures as high as one in every 200 women" with varying degrees of the problem.

She said it most often strikes in adolescence, "although I've had a patient who was 45," and frequently follows a sudden stress on the family or individual, as when a woman leaves for college or enters the job market.

Source: *Anaheim Bulletin*, Anaheim, CA. Feb. 15, 1983.

Courtesy of the Associated Press

**FIGURE 6–2**

ios, arousing intention, and directing behavior with dramatic visuals. Attitudes and behaviors expressed against the Vietnam War are a primary example of the impact of television. Television brought the tragedy of war home to Americans like no other situation in history. Night after night, distant Vietnam was brought into American living rooms.

Who of us who saw the gun-to-the-head killing of a weeping Vietcong soldier will ever forget that picture as a symbol of the horrors of war? Likewise, who of us who saw police dogs snapping at black women and children during civil rights demonstrations in Alabama or the explosion of the *Challenger* spacecraft before our very eyes will forget those mental pictures?

Television visuals that raise identified audience needs/concerns/interests and offer a product, issue, or organization as a solution can evoke emotions like no other medium. The key is finding the right need/concern/interest, the right emotion.

> What other television visuals have affected you? How?

The message/media outline described in this text will help the professional identify these issues in a logical way and develop messages accordingly. When developing visuals for television, you should ask yourself some questions:

What picture will best demonstrate what action you want the audience to take?

What picture will best help the viewer to

- ☐ Raise a need/concern/interest?
- ☐ Recognize your product, issue, or organization as a solution?
- ☐ Identify the consequences of inaction?
- ☐ Help think through or mentally rehearse the action you want him or her to take?

### Impact of Television Can Be Overestimated

Overestimating the impact of television is easy. Though communicating with large numbers of Americans is without question the strength of television, message retention from television requires repetition to ensure an impact.

"Television news introduces issues to the public agenda," say James Grunig and Todd Hunt in *Managing Public Relations*. "But television news stays with the issues for a shorter time than the print media—usually not long enough to *fix* the issues on the public agenda. Television commercials, similarly, must be repeated many times before people remember them," say the two authors.[13] Television news typically sets *its* agenda by what appears in the daily newspaper.

> How would you compare the strengths and limitations of radio with those of television?

## TECHNIQUES FOR GENERATING PUBLICITY AND PUBLIC SERVICE TIME

At least five modes are available to the public relations practitioner seeking publicity and public service time on radio and television:

1. Spokesperson interviews
2. Public service announcements
3. Station tie-in promotions
4. Public affairs programs
5. Community calendars

### Radio

### Spokesperson Interviews

Although securing interviews for spokespersons is covered extensively for radio-television talk and news shows as well as print media in the next chapter, we discuss here some techniques specific to broadcast that can help generate interviews.

Spokesperson interviews telephoned into the radio news director offer the best means of generating publicity for public relations messages on radio news shows. This technique can be used to localize a national story or expand the reach of a news release, news conference, or special event. The California Dietetic Association reacted virtually overnight with its guidelines for parents of anorexic children, following singer Karen Carpenter's death.

Some professionals generate radio publicity by distributing interviews recorded on tape to stations by telephone or mail. These are called actualities or audio feeds. Still others establish telephone systems to provide radio news directors with daily taped interviews. In such cases, all the reporter has to do is call a certain telephone number and record the interview over the telephone. These types of programs require constant promotion to get reporters to use the system.

> Assume you are the public relations director for the drug treatment center in your town. You hear on the early morning radio news that a professional athlete with a history of drug problems did not show up for last night's game. Sources are speculating drug relapse. How might you turn this unfortunate situation into a radio publicity opportunity supporting the facility's message/media outline and helping other individuals with health problems?

### Television

Providing visuals is the best way to improve your odds for success with television interviews: background videotape, video news releases, directions to television stations on where to find supportive visual sites, and props to expand the message visually.

Interviews and real-life visuals, both for news and talk shows, are probably the most cost-effective means of getting on the air. Whereas the video news release can cost tens of thousands of dollars, interview placement costs are primarily for the professionals' time and out-of-pocket expenses.

When the American Society for Bone and Mineral Research held a news conference in 1981 to launch its osteoporosis awareness campaign, human bones (both healthy and osteoporotic) were framed and displayed at the news conference, as well as enlarged easel-sized color prints contrasting healthy with unhealthy bone. Prevention guidelines were also outlined on easel boards. These graphic depictions expanded the message visually via television news coverage.

When Scripps Memorial Hospitals opened its diabetes research center, diabetic children dropped syringes, diet sheets, and all of the disease paraphernalia into a time capsule. The capsule was then sealed inside the walls to symbolize a future for diabetic children without the burdens of their disease. Again, this made excellent visual impact needed for television news publicity.

When the National Dairy Promotion and Research Board and National Dairy Council launched a campaign to convince women to use dairy foods instead of vitamin/mineral supplements to get added calcium, they held a news conference in Washington, D.C. An aquarium-sized jar filled with a four-year supply of supplements needed to balance the diet was placed in front of the podium and cameras. At the appointed time, a scientist poured an additional one-year supply from packages representing each of the four basic food groups (milk, meat, vegetables/fruits, breads/cereals) into the jar, asking viewers, "Do you really want to put all of these pills in your body?" It proved to be an effective visual for demonstrating scientists' concern for replacing food with supplements in hope of reducing the risk for diseases like cancer and osteoporosis.

In another example, Western Fairs Association turned its annual convention exhibit area into a simulated midway, complete with food stands, games, and carnival rides, to create a fairlike atmosphere for the media (and conventioneers).

> Assume you are retained by Old Town Mexican Cafe. Its owners plan to open a new restaurant on Cinco de Mayo (May 5), Mexico's independence day. What visuals could be used to help you get a spokesperson on a local television talk show to demonstrate one of its public relations message statements: quality food in a fun environment?

### Working with Assignment Editors

Knowing the needs of your local television assignment editors is another way to create television news opportunities.

Decisions on which stories will be covered by camera crews for the evening news are made at early morning meetings. Late coverage assignments are typically decided at a second meeting a couple of hours before the early evening newscast.

Most broadcast stories come from the daily newspaper. A story prominently placed in the local newspaper is covered by local television and radio stations. Likewise, the best way to get on network television and radio is to get good coverage in the *New York Times* or *Wall Street Journal* because of their prominence in New York City, where network news decision makers reside.

Some additional tips for working with local television news:

- Remember visuals. A hard news story without visuals gets 20 seconds of time; a "softer" news angle with visuals can get 90 seconds.
- Telephone assignment editors with a local expert available to respond to breaking national stories appearing in the morning newspaper.
- Inform assignment editors of inaccuracies of major newspaper stories if you want to guard against these errors being repeated on the evening news.
- Do not call during deadline (typically two hours before newscast).
- Organize a list of experts from within your organization or clientele and offer a source list to assignment editors and reporters.
- Work with specialty reporters when possible, as they can help sell the story.
- Try to offer interviews with those affected by a story, for instance, a teenager who gets a job through a government youth work program instead of the mayor.
- Schedule events as early in the day as possible (after film crews are on the job).
- Send weekend stories to weekend assignment editors on Friday.
- Do not forget that stations have holiday crews.
- Get direct line telephone numbers of assignment editors for weekend/holiday opportunities (i.e., local angle to national story appearing in the morning newspaper).
- Do not send press kits to assignment editors. Most keep annual day files with room for one-page memos only. Media memos are filed until the day they are used.
- Offer news ideas occasionally that do not necessarily benefit you. Assignment editors remember favors.

### Providing Background Videotape

Providing background videotape to talk and news show producers does two things. First, the station may use the footage. Smaller stations are more apt to use tape from outside sources, but do not rule out the larger stations even though gatekeepers may tell you they have policies against such use. Second, outside videotape can be used to influence the way a station shoots its own version of the story.

Roy Heatly organized the Californians for Better Transportation campaign to convince state lawmakers to repair neglected highways. The visual concept he wanted to project was not just potholes in the road but rather the effect of those potholes on public safety. Public safety was the concern raised. Specific legislation was offered as the solution. The consequences of inaction centered around injury to human life. Writing a lawmaker was the behavior the campaign wanted to initiate.[14]

Background videotape used to support spokespersons placed on talk shows depicted a school bus stopping in front of a dilapidated bridge. Viewers saw the children get out to walk across the bridge. The driver followed in the bus when the children were safely on the other side.

The school bus visual transferred the message to a universal concern (child safety), aroused audience intention (creating an important issue), directed behavior (write your lawmaker), and was part of an extensive educational campaign that successfully resulted in the only tax increase measure signed in 1981 by then Governor Edmund G. Brown, Jr.

During the legislative public relations campaign to improve roads, Heatly offered both footage and site selections for camera crews. "News and talk show decision makers would frequently reject our video footage initially but by the day of the interview we would get requests for our visuals," said Heatly.

> Suppose you participated in a brainstorming session with Heatly and his staff to generate visual ideas for the Californians for Better Transportation campaign. What additional visual ideas would you generate to raise a concern for the effect of shoddy roads on public safety while suggesting support of state legislation as a solution?

### The Video News Release

The video news release often runs into the same kind of reaction from television stations as background videotape. Smaller stations are more apt to use the release, but they occasionally show up on the major stations as well.

Every effort is made to create a release just like a local station would do if it had access to the same inputs.

The successful video news release is one with a strong news hook. This is no place to get overly commercial with repeated mention of the product or company name. Success is in the strength of the news angle and the subtlety of the message. Television news directors are extremely sensitive about using material from public relations sources. Most news directors from metropolitan network affiliates claim they do not use video news releases at all. Use does come most frequently from news directors in small to mid-sized markets and independent stations in the larger markets. However, use is also recorded, albeit less frequently, from those who say they never use handouts.

The key to getting a video news release on the air is to offer the stations newsworthy material that they cannot duplicate themselves, says George Glazer, president of Hill and Knowlton's broadcast division.[15] A number of television news directors welcome footage of press conferences and teleconferences because they represent "events" where bona fide reporters ask questions so news directors can pick and choose which segments of the sound track to use.[16]

A sensitive point is whether or not the video news release sponsor is identified as having provided the footage. Some stations use segments of the free material as part of their own reports. Some use the stories exactly as they were put together without disclosing that they came from a public relations source. A growing number of stations briefly flash a sponsor across the screen while the tape is rolling.

The video news release is generally produced by specialists, like Back, Heatly, and Kemery, who employ reporters and camera crews. The result is a three-quarter-inch videocassette, one and a half to three minutes in length. It often contains additional tape footage for use by the station. A written release, including introductions and conclusions for the anchorperson and descriptions of each scene, accompanies the videotape. There are two audio channels on the tape—one completely packaged with announcer, interviewees, and all appropriate sound; the second, without a reporter's voice, which allows stations to insert the local commentator's voice. These are customizing approaches that provide local stations with maximum choice and flexibility. The latter provides stations with visuals and a written release to do the story with their own narration. Videocassettes are mailed and hand-planted with television stations. Usage reply cards are included in the package, and those stations not returning reply cards are surveyed by telephone to determine usage.

Some producers, like Back, are also supplying "Video News Backgrounders," which include a visual press kit, especially designed for TV, covering a broad news area for use now or later by the station.[17]

Video monitoring services can also be retained to monitor news shows throughout the country and provide videotapes of actual use.

Increasingly, video news releases are being distributed by satellite. Satellite time is purchased, stations are alerted when the videotape will be sent across the airwaves, and interested news directors can take the news spot from the satellite.

Encyclopaedia Britannica distributed a two-minute, five-and-a-half-second historical video news release to introduce a new edition of its line of encyclopedias. (See Figure 6–3.) The written release, or script, included the following lead to be read by an anchorperson before airing tape: "Keeping track of all the world's knowledge . . . that's been the task of encyclopaedias for hundreds of years; today, a report on a major new revision of the world's oldest continuously published reference books."

The second paragraph contained a suggested narrative for an anchorperson to read as a voice-over while tape and sound captured the printing of encyclopedias at a printing plant: "At a large publishing house near Lexington, Kentucky, a new printing of Encyclopaedia Britannica is pouring off the presses. The numbers are big: each set includes more than 30 thousand pages, 24 thousand illustrations."

The video news release then added an interpretation, in the form of an audio-video quotation from Encyclopaedia Britannica President Charles Swanson. The quote was followed by more suggested voice-overs for the anchorperson with two additional quotes from Swanson.

On the same tape, additional footage and sound of the printing plant, production scenes from the first edition of the company's encyclopedias, as well as scenes from the most recent production were included. There were also three additional interview segments.

Encyclopaedia Britannica used history to raise an interest in encyclopedias and offered its brand as a means of satisfying that interest.

In another example, Mercedes-Benz of North America produced a three-minute video news release as part of a campaign to caution Americans about the pitfalls of purchasing luxury cars directly from Europe. (See Figure 6–4.)

Its suggested lead, to be read by the anchorperson: "It started out as a trickle . . . Americans buying luxury cars in Europe at prices below those in the United States. A strong American dollar makes them seem cheap. Now, it's turned into a flood: thousands of fancy European cars pouring into the United States. For the buyer, though, these cars may not be the bargains they seem."

The script's suggested voice-over film and sound had the anchorperson saying: "Almost every day, BMWs, Mercedes, Ferraris and other European cars arrive in American ports. . . ."

The rest of the videotape outlined the consequences of purchasing those cars that do not meet U.S. standards, including sound-on quotes from U.S. custom inspectors and an automotive engineer. Videotape captured advertisements promoting the sale of these

National Television News
13691 West Eleven Mile Road • Oak Park, Michigan 48237 • (313) 541-1440
23480 Park Sorrento • Calabasas Park, California 91302 • (818) 883-6121
NTN

EDITED STORY + B-ROLL AND EXTRA BITES
TRACK 1 - VOICE-OVER ** TRACK 2 - NATURAL SOUND ONLY

NEW . . . AND OLD . . . ENCYCLOPAEDIA

(Suggested introduction)

Keeping track of all the world's knowledge . . . that's been the task of encyclopaedias for hundreds of years; today, a report on a major new revision of the world's oldest continuously published reference books.

| (SCENES) | (SUGGESTED VOICE-OVER) |
|---|---|
| LS PRINTING<br>MS BOOKS<br>CU BOOKS<br>MS CHARLES SWANSON<br>(15½ Seconds) | At a large publishing house near Lexington, Kentucky a new printing of Encyclopaedia Britannica is pouring off the presses. The numbers are big: each set includes more than 30 thousand pages, 24 thousand illustrations. Encyclopaedia Britannica President Charles Swanson explains: |
| MS SWANSON SPEAKS<br>(10 Seconds) | (SOUND-ON, CHARLES SWANSON)<br>"Well, there's been a tremendous explosion of knowledge since the first edition was published in 1768, when we had three volumes, and today we have 32 volumes." |
| | (SUGGESTED VOICE-OVER) |
| CU THREE BOOKS<br>CU TITLE PAGE<br>CU SMELLIE, PAN TO BELL<br>CU CROCODILE<br>CU "ANATOMY", SKELETON<br>CU "WOMAN" DEFINED<br>CU "SEX" DEFINED<br>(29 Seconds) | That first edition was published in Edinboro, Scotland by a self-styled Society of Gentlemen. The first editor, William Smellie, had to agree to stay sober to complete the job; Andrew Bell, an engraver with a huge nose, did the illustrations. The first edition documented much of nature . . there were many animals . . . And the anatomy of man . . in great detail. As for woman, she was dismissed in a few words, as the female of man. Sex was quickly passed over too, in a single phrase.<br>(more) |

Courtesy of National Television News

**FIGURE 6–3**

- 2 -

| | |
|---|---|
| CU MIDWIFERY<br>MS SHIPS<br>CU YACHT<br>CU MAP<br>CU SHORTHAND PAGES<br>(23 Seconds) | But midwifery was the subject of a major article in the first Britannica -- 40 pages, with illustrations that so offended the British crown that citizens were ordered to rip the pages from their books. Transportation was important in the 18th century. Geography, too; even though no one was sure just where the American northwest ended. And those early editors thought shorthand important enough to expound about it for six pages. |
| CU SWANSON SPEAKING<br>(Suggested Super:<br>Charles Swanson, President<br>Encyclopaedia Britannica)<br>(10½ Seconds) | (SOUND-ON, CHARLES SWANSON)<br>"The editors of the first Britannica, which was in three volumes, would probably be startled to look at the size and the scope of Britannica today." |
| CU OPEN BOOK<br>CU FERRARO<br>CU HITCHCOCK<br>CU SPACE ARTICLE<br>CU FULL SET<br>CU INDEX BOOKS<br>ZOOM TO SHORTHAND SECTION<br>CU ANATOMY OVERLAYS<br>CU AEROTRAIN<br>CU CONCORDE<br>(26 Seconds) | (SUGGESTED VOICE-OVER)<br>The 1985 printing is simply organized: 12 volumes of short articles for ready reference, 17 volumes with longer, in-depth articles, for the serious student. The index to the new encyclopaedia alone fills two more volumes. Shorthand is just a small section in the new encyclopaedia; human anatomy is still a big section, and it's well illustrated. Old sailing ships have been replaced by more exotic forms of transportation.<br>(more) |

**FIGURE 6–3 (continued)**

- 3 -

| | | |
|---|---|---|
| MS | SWANSON SPEAKING<br>(5½ Seconds) | (SOUND-ON, CHARLES SWANSON)<br>"At 43 million words, it's the largest data base available in the English language world." |
| | | (SUGGESTED VOICE-OVER) |
| MS | BOOKS OFF LINE<br>(6 Seconds) | There are five thousand contributors to the new Britannica, from 131 countries around the world. |
| | | (TOTAL RUNNING TIME: 2 Minutes, 5½ Seconds) |

ENCYCLOPAEDIA BRITANNICA, INC.
310 S. Michigan Avenue
Chicago, IL 60604
Contact: Norman L. Braun
(312) 347-7230

385
C2043

**FIGURE 6–3 (continued)**

National Television News
13691 West Eleven Mile Road • Oak Park, Michigan 48237 • (313) 541-1440
23480 Park Sorrento • Calabasas Park, California 91302 • (818) 883-6121
NTN

ENCYCLOPAEDIA - ADDITIONAL B-ROLL AND EXTRA BITES

(SCENES AT PUBLISHING PLANT)

| | | |
|---|---|---|
| LS | Stripping operation, preparing visuals for printing | (5 seconds) |
| CU | Stripping operation | (5 seconds) |
| CU | Book covers falling | (7 seconds) |
| MS | Covers on machine | (9 seconds) |
| LS | Man checking books | (10 seconds) |

(SCENES FROM FIRST EDITION)

| | | |
|---|---|---|
| CU | Astronomy title on page | (4 seconds) |
| CU | Illustration of Sun in astronomy article | (4 seconds) |
| CU | Electrical apparatus, machine, battery | (8 seconds) |
| CU | Elephant | (3 seconds) |
| CU | Snake | (4 seconds) |

(SCENES OF 1985 EDITION)

| | | |
|---|---|---|
| CU | Pan full set of books | (8 seconds) |
| CU | Books - 1 to 4, Micropaedia (12 volumes of ready reference) | (3 seconds) |
| CU | Books - 1 and 2, Micropaedia | (3 seconds) |
| CU | Books - 13 and 14, Macropaedia (17 volumes of longer articles) | (3 seconds) |
| CU | Propaedia (single volume - outline of knowledge and study guide) | (3 seconds) |
| LS | Full set of books | (4 seconds) |

EXTRA BITES

MS CHARLES SWANSON: "The 1985 edition is a major revision in that we have a brand new two volume index. We have a completely revised outline of knowledge and the ready reference section has been completely redone, which means 15 out of the 32 volumes have been revised." (19 Seconds)

CU CHARLES SWANSON: "Well, we believe that encyclopaedias in the form they're in today, books, will be here for many, many decades ahead. We suspect that there may be uses of new technology to access information but the book will still be the principal means of providing that information." (20 Seconds)

CU CHARLES SWANSON: "The editors of the first Britannica, which was in three volumes, would probably be startled to look at the size and the scope of Britannica today. I'm sure they'd also be amazed at the budget that's required to produce the Encyclopaedia Britannica and probably would have been delighted had they had a similar budget. They had a problem in the sense they started out with their first volume being A to B, the second volume was C to L, and then they were quickly running out of money and had to put M thru Z in the last volume." (33 Seconds)

ENCYCLOPAEDIA BRITANNICA, INC.
310 S. Michigan Avenue
Chicago, IL 60604
Contact: Norman L. Braun
(312) 347-7230

385

FIGURE 6–3 (continued)

National Television News

NTN

13691 West Eleven Mile Road • Oak Park, Michigan 48237 • (313) 541-1440
23480 Park Sorrento • Calabasas Park, California 91302 • (818) 883-6121

EDITED STORY + B-ROLL AND EXTRA BITES
TRACK 1 - VOICE-OVER ONLY ** TRACK 2 - NATURAL SOUND ONLY

GRAY MARKET CARS - "BUYER BEWARE"

(Suggested introduction)

It started out as a trickle...Americans buying luxury cars in Europe at prices below those in the United States. A strong American dollar makes them seem cheap. Now, it's turned into a flood: thousands of fancy European cars pouring into the United States. For the buyer, though, these cars may not be the bargains they seem.

| (SCENES) | (SUGGESTED VOICE-OVER) |
|---|---|
| MS CARS<br>LS CARS<br>CU NEWSPAPER AD<br>CU NEWSPAPER AD<br>LS CAR OFF BOAT<br>(25 seconds) | Almost every day, BMWs, Mercedes, Ferraris and other European cars arrive in American ports. Most, designated for authorized dealers, have been built to meet U.S. standards. But among them are more and more European models, imported by individuals or small companies, which don't meet U.S. safety and pollution standards. More than 35 thousand of these so-called gray market cars entered the United States this year. |
| CU SHORT SPEAKING<br>(Suggested Super:<br>Leroy Short<br>U.S. Customs Inspector)<br>(14 seconds) | (SOUND-ON, LEROY SHORT)<br>"There's bad apples in all businesses. In the automobile used car market it has its fair share of bad apples. If you're going to buy a car from an ad in the newspaper, the buyer beware is a good thing to remember." |
| | (SUGGESTED VOICE-OVER) |
| MS INSPECTING CARS<br>(9 seconds) | After inspection, the importer can post a bond and Customs will release a gray market car for 90 days to see if it can be modified to meet U.S. standards. |

Courtesy of National Television News

**FIGURE 6–4**

| | |
|---|---|
| | (SOUND-ON, LEROY SHORT) |
| CU SHORT SPEAKING<br>LS INSPECTION<br>CU HEADLAMPS<br>CU SHORT SPEAKING<br>(16 seconds) | "The actual conversion cost of the automobile... of course there's things like door beams and there's upholstery and there's ignition, warning buzzers, there's glass, there's bumpers, there's headlamps. There's a variety of things which cost money to convert." |
| | (SUGGESTED VOICE-OVER) |
| CU NEWSPAPER AD<br>CU ANOTHER AD<br>LS CAR IN TEST LAB<br>(14 seconds) | Conversion can cost many thousands of dollars. So modifying gray market cars is getting to be a big business. After conversion a car must go to an independent laboratory for tests, to see if it meets federal emission standards. |
| | (SOUND-ON, DON OLSON) |
| CU OLSON SPEAKING<br>(Suggested Super:<br>Don Olson<br>Olson Engineering Inc.)<br><br>CU ENGINE<br>LS CAR BEING TESTED<br>CU OLSON SPEAKING<br>LS TEST<br>CU EXHAUST<br>CU EXHAUST BAGS<br>CU MARKING GRAPH<br>MS COMPUTER<br>CU READ-OUT<br>(49 seconds) | "It's a very complicated process frankly, It involves, in the case of pollution requirements, maybe as many as 75 to 100 components that have to be added to the vehicle. There are poor jobs done and some bad work still exists. In fact, quite a lot of it. Like any business there are some people that are of course doing the best they can to make money at it without too much regard for how good their work is. There are in the past, difficult vehicles have failed this test in our laboratory maybe as many as 10, 15, 20 times for a vehicle to meet the pollution requirements. So there are those kinds of horror stories in this business." |
| | (SUGGESTED VOICE-OVER) |
| MS EMISSIONS TEST<br>MS INSPECTING CAR<br>(9 seconds) | Each emissions test can cost seven or eight hundred dollars. And there can be other problems for buyers of gray market cars: parts and service can be hard to get. |

**FIGURE 6–4 (continued)**

| | |
|---|---|
| CU SHORT SPEAKING<br>LS MANY CARS<br>CU SHORT SPEAKING<br>(11 seconds) | (SOUND-ON, LEROY SHORT)<br>"There's no warranty of course. The vehicle is not purchased through an American distributorship, and the American distributorship is the one that grants the warranty, so if your car breaks down on the road, its your problem." |
| | (SUGGESTED VOICE-OVER) |
| LS INSPECTING CAR<br>(9 seconds) | Resale value of gray market cars is much lower than for cars built for the U.S. market. And in some cases the origin of a gray market car can be suspect: |
| CU SHORT SPEAKING<br>(Suggested super:<br>Leroy Short<br>U.S. Customs Inspector)<br>(11 seconds) | (SOUND-ON, LEROY SHORT)<br>"You have to be sure that the car when you obtain it overseas, has a clear title, and that you are actually buying a car that is not stolen." |
| | (SUGGESTED VOICE-OVER) |
| LS CARS OFF BOAT<br>(14 seconds) | More federal and state agencies are expressing concern about these cars. And legislation to ban them entirely has been introduced in Congress. But for now, gray market cars continue to arrive in American ports in ever-growing numbers. |

(Total running time: three minutes and one second)

MERCEDES-BENZ OF NORTH AMERICA
One Mercedes Drive
Montvale, NJ 07645
Contact: Leo Levine
(201) 573-2238

**FIGURE 6–4 (continued)**

National Television News

13691 West Eleven Mile Road • Oak Park, Michigan 48237 • (313) 541-1440
23480 Park Sorrento • Calabasas Park, California 91302 • (818) 883-6121

NTN

GRAY MARKET CARS - ADDITIONAL SCENES AND EXTRA BITES

(SCENES)

| | |
|---|---|
| Four shots, European cars unloading at Port of Los Angeles | (62 seconds) |
| CU Customs patch, badge, face of Inspector | (12 seconds) |
| Three shots, Customs Inspector checking cars on dock | (38 seconds) |
| Four shots, masses of European cars on dock, with Inspector checking in final scene | (47 seconds) |
| Seven shots, emmission testing of gray market car, at Olson Engineering Inc., Huntington Beach, California. This is one of a small number of independent laboratories around the country, recognized by E.P.A. to perform testing for E.P.A. certification | (49 seconds) |

EXTRA BITES

DON OLSON, PRESIDENT, OLSON ENGINEERING INC.: "Well, the gray market cars are a bargain in the sense that they can be bought for less money and when you look at that alone, that's a large amount of money. For example in a Mercedes 500, you can save 10,000 dollars compared to buying a car, maybe more, compared to buying a similar car here in the United States. But naturally a bargain is what a person thinks he has, so we could certainly conclude that many people haven't been as satisfied as they thought they were going to be when they entered into this price bargain that they got."

LEROY SHORT, U.S. CUSTOMS INSPECTOR: "I would agree that it is possible to get certain savings on this type of automobile, this type of purchase. But there are pitfalls. He'd have to be aware of course that there were the cost of conversions. Some vehicles are much more difficult to convert than others, and there would be the cost of the bonding, and there would be the possibility that the conversion that would be performed would not be adequate to meet the criteria of D.O.T. and E.P.A. Some people go through several times their environmental protection agency testing for instance before they're able to get the car complied out. This can be a very expensive process."

MERCEDES-BENZ OF NORTH AMERICA
One Mercedes Drive
Montvale, NJ 07645
Contact: Leo Levine
(201) 573-2238

185

**FIGURE 6–4 (continued)**

automobiles, cars landing at U.S. ports, and government inspection teams testing the automobiles. The tape included additional footage and interview segments from the two sources.

The Mercedes-Benz of North America video news release raised a concern and consequence about purchasing a car in Europe and offered domestic purchase as a means of minimizing that concern.

> **From the description of these two examples, what do you think the video news release is designed to do?**

### Script Format for Video News Releases/ Radio Actualities

News releases written for broadcast are normally included with audio "feeds" sent to radio news departments and video news releases for television.

Radio and television news release formats differ primarily because of television's visual needs. Whereas the radio news release looks more like a print release, a television release is divided in half, with the audio portion on the right-hand side of the page and the visual descriptions (videotape, slides) on the left-hand side of the page.

For radio, set typewriter margins for a 60-space line.[18] When writing for television, set the margins between 35 and 80 and type the audio portion on the right-hand side of the page. The visual suggestions are typed on the left-hand side.[19]

Broadcast releases are triple-spaced, sometimes double-spaced, with "slug" lines—story identification, time, date, name of organization, name of contact, and phone numbers—in the upper right-hand corner of the first page, similar to print news releases. Additional pages need only the slug line, page number, and organization name. Do not forget to type "30" or the symbols "# # #" at the end of the story and "more" on the pages leading to the end as in the print news releases. Leave plenty of margin room at top, bottom, and sides for editing.[20]

Here are some additional tips:

- □ Do not split words between lines or sentences between pages.
- □ If a word is difficult to pronounce, insert in parentheses the pronunciation in phonetics after the word. For example, Rajiv Ghandi (Rah-Jeeve Gahn′-dee).
- □ Avoid tongue twisters.
- □ Do not use colons, semicolons, percentage signs, dollar signs, fractions, or ampersands.
- □ Do use commas, periods, question marks, quotation marks, and dots/dashes (for pauses).
- □ Use quotation marks only when exact wording is essential and to add special vocal emphasis. Avoid long quotes. Lead directly into quotes with such phrases as "In his words" or "As she put it."
- □ Use hyphens only when you want the letters spelled out.
- □ Avoid using numbers when possible; round them off and spell them out.
- □ For times of day use "this morning," "this afternoon," or "this evening" rather than A.M. or P.M.
- □ Put the date beside the reference (Friday, June 6).
- □ Do not begin sentences with a name; do not use middle initials (or anything else you do not have to use).
- □ Be careful about pronouns; listeners have trouble following references.[21]
- □ Use dependent clauses only to vary the pace or for ornamentation.[22]

### Public Service Announcements

Public service announcements (PSAs) constitute advertising time provided by radio and television stations for messages in the public interest. The Federal Communications Commission (FCC) requires that radio and television stations operate in the public interest. Airing such announcements is one way of complying with this requirement. However, federal deregulation of broadcasting has led to dwindling opportunities for PSAs, particularly on radio. Specifically, the

Federal Communications Commission defines a public service announcement as

> any announcement for which no charge is made and which promotes programs, activities or services of federal, state or local governments or the programs, activities or service of nonprofit organizations and other announcements regarded as serving community interests, excluding time signals, routine weather announcements and promotional announcements.[23]

Television PSAs range from low-cost announcer-read scripts provided to stations to spots produced by station production personnel to elaborate productions comparable to any quality advertisement. Radio PSAs are now limited largely to short announcer-read spots.

Groups seeking help with national public service campaigns often turn to the Advertising Council for help. Funded by the business and advertising communities, the Advertising Council annually generates approximately $600 million in public service time and space for the organizations it supports. The council receives about 200 requests for assistance per year. In 1987, it handled thirty-six campaigns, including two of its oldest, Smokey the Bear and U.S. Savings Bonds.[24]

Once a campaign is approved by the council, the American Association of Advertising Agencies provides a volunteer advertising agency to produce everything from radio and television spots to magazine and newspaper advertising and collateral promotion materials. Agencies donate all creative work and charge only for out-of-pocket expenses.

Sponsorship of public service announcements comes most often from not-for-profit organizations, such as the Boy Scouts of America, a local museum, college, or hospital. Public service messages must be of mutual benefit. The Boy Scouts want members, parents want their children taught Boy Scout values; a local museum wants visitors or funding, it provides a community forum for appreciation of the arts; a community college wants students, it offers low cost education and opportunities for financial aid; a local hospital wants patients, it can offer the community health prevention tips.

Orthopaedic Hospital used public service announcements to promote both patient services and raise funds. While television spots, like those making up Figure 6–5, promoted the benefits of the hospital, a line calling for donations was extremely hard-hitting: "They'll treat young patients even if the family can't afford to pay. That's why they need contributions."

A National Association of Broadcasters survey found most stations give priority to health-related issues. Public safety issues rank second, social issues third, and fourth government and economic issues.[25]

Companies occasionally produce public service spots when the message is clearly in the public interest. PSAs were used to promote a community cleanup using Glad trashbags, and 9-Lives Catfood produced PSAs promoting Adopt-a-Cat month using the company's product symbol, Morris the cat.[26] By investing in community projects, these companies gained credible avenues for generating product awareness.

Business and industry can also produce public service spots jointly with not-for-profit groups, government agencies, and even colleges or universities that share common needs, concerns, or interests.

However, many public service directors shy away from corporate-sponsored public service announcements. "If a corporation wants to help a not-for-profit group then it should do so for that reason and not expect free air time for public service material," says Fred Norfleet, longtime public service director for KGTV, an ABC affiliate and McGraw-Hill–owned television station. "There are times when we'll use one but they are infrequent and only when the sponsor's name is buried."[27]

One additional option for taking advantage of public service time is through trade and professional associations, which are also not-for-profit. To illustrate, the American Optometric Association produced radio public service spots offering tips to prevent eye damage from computer screens; one of the

National Television News

13691 West Eleven Mile Road • Oak Park, Michigan 48237 • (313) 541-1440
23480 Park Sorrento • Calabasas Park, California 91302 • (818) 883-6121

Public Service Announcement
60 Seconds

ARTHRITIS

(SCENES)

MS ROCKING CHAIR
CU GIRL OUT OF CHAIR
LS GIRL, GRANDMOTHER
MS GIRL, GRANDMOTHER
CU GRANDMOTHER
CU HANDS AND GIRL
CU HANDS IN HOSPITAL, PULL BACK
MS MAN ON CYCLE, TILT
CU LITTLE BOY
MS THROWING BALL
MS GIRL, THERAPIST
CU ARM

(NARRATION)

Arthritis is painful. And it doesn't always wait for you to grow old. Rheumatoid arthritis strikes children. Its causes are different from adult arthritis, but the pain and physical disability can be the same. Children with arthritis, like adults, require individualized treatment to manage that pain and disability. Orthopaedic Hospital in downtown Los Angeles is a specialized treatment center. It provides help for both children and adults with arthritis and other problems of the joints, bones, and muscles. It's especially committed to caring for children whose parents can't afford to pay. Orthopaedic Hospital depends upon community support. You can help. Give today. Because arthritis doesn't always wait for tomorrow.

ORTHOPAEDIC HOSPITAL
P.O. Box 60132/TA
Los Angeles, CA 90060
Contact: Anita Bennett
213/742-1515

**FIGURE 6–5A**

National Television News

13691 West Eleven Mile Road • Oak Park, Michigan 48237 • (313) 541-1440
23480 Park Sorrento • Calabasas Park, California 91302 • (818) 883-6121

NTN

Public Service Announcement
60 Seconds

TOMBOY

| (SCENES) | (NARRATION) |
|---|---|
| LS GIRL THRU DOOR<br>CU CAT<br>CU GIRL<br>LS GIRL DOWN STEPS<br>MS GIRL IN TREE<br>MS CLIMBING FENCE<br>CU X-RAY, PULL BACK<br>CU GIRL<br>CU MAN, PAN DOWN<br>CU BANDAGE, TILT UP<br>CU GIRL<br>CU MAN<br>CU GIRL<br>CU MAN<br>LS GIRL PLAYING<br>CU KICKING BALL<br>MS PLAYING | I worry about her...not a lot, you know...not every minute of the day. But I think about what could happen. She's twice as active as any little boy! And just as mischievous too. What would I do if anything happened to her? Well, I guess that depends on what happens. When she broke her arm, I took her to Orthopaedic Hospital. They're specialized, and they have a clinic for children with broken bones. They'll treat young patients even if the family can't afford to pay. That's why they need contributions. I send money when I can. You should help too. Give to Orthopaedic Hospital, Los Angeles. I know they'll be there if I need them again--someday you might need them, too. |

ORTHOPAEDIC HOSPITAL
P.O. Box 60132/TA
Los Angeles, CA 90060
Contact: Anita Bennett
213/742-1515

884

FIGURE 6–5B

tips was to visit the optometrist for checkups. (See Figure 6–6.)

Bar associations can offer legal tips, certified public accountant associations tax tips, dietetic associations nutrition tips. Inevitably, one of these tips can legitimately be to see your lawyer, accountant, or dietitian when in need.

The National Science Foundation encourages teenagers to consider careers in science and engineering in a series of public service spots. (See Figure 6–7.) The Motor Vehicle Manufacturers Association addresses its industry's concern for drinking and driving with a public service campaign aimed at raising concern among social drinkers for allowing drunk friends to drive. (See Figure 6–8, A, B, C & D.)

Public service messages are not hard-sell commercials. As in all public relations techniques, mutual benefit—to the listener or viewer and the sponsor—is essential for success.

One clear strength of the public service announcement lies in the free air time provided by radio and television stations for messages in the public interest. A weakness, equally important, however, is the difficulty of measuring impact on target audiences. PSAs are typically aired in time periods when paid advertising is not sold, and that often means the wee hours of the morning.

The inconsistency of when a PSA is aired makes evaluations difficult. Evaluations usually consist of how many times the station used the announcement. Public service directors are asked to complete and return a self-addressed, stamped card, and those not returning cards are often surveyed by telephone.

A public service announcement can be aired in prime time. Animated spots aimed at children, for example, often end up at prime viewing times for children. But this is more the exception than the rule.

Good relationships with radio and television public service directors can occasionally pay off in effective negotiations for air time during time periods when target audiences are listening or watching. However, success varies from practitioner to practitioner and public service director to public service director.

As in all media programs, a good up-to-date mailing list of public service directors is essential. It should be updated at least twice a year.

Estimates of audience demographics—who listens/watches what and when—can be provided, for a fee, by demographic tracking services, such as Arbitron and A. C. Nielsen. Station advertising departments also have this kind of information.

> Which of the issues below is likely as a local radio PSA topic? Why or why not?
>
> Opening a new branch of a supermarket
> Children's Day Parade information
> Mayoral campaign calendar
> Visit by a movie crew to film downtown
> Girl Scouts annual bake-off and car wash
> Best ways to conserve water during peak summer days
> Merger of two competing department stores

***Writing the PSA.*** Broadcast writing skills can be the difference between success and failure with a public service spot. "Many PSAs attempt to do too much," says Dale Kemery. "They race from point to point in a limited word count like a frantic shopper during a 10-minute sale. As a result, these spots are either not remembered by audience members if broadcast or else not broadcast at all," he says.[28]

When writing PSAs, *keep it simple.* Ask yourself:

What is the one single concept I want to project?
Is it of mutual benefit or too self-serving?
What is the one audience need/concern/interest

National Radio News

13691 West Eleven Mile Road • Oak Park, Michigan 48237 • (313) 541-1440
23480 Park Sorrento • Calabasas Park, California 91302 • (818) 883-6121

Radio Public Service Announcements
7.5 i.p.s.

LIFE IS WORTH SEEING

VDT OPERATOR. . . 60 seconds

(MUSIC -- WITH VOCAL)-- "The world is a beautiful place to be, so many things to do and see. Every day a new surprise, happening before your eyes. Life is worth seeing . . . " (MUSIC FADES UNDER VOICE OF VDT OPERATOR) I'm an airline reservation agent . . . and I love my job. Helping people get where they want to go . . . taking good care of them. And of course I take care of myself, too. I work all day at a video display terminal . . . a computer screen. And I make sure I rest my eyes periodically and maintain the proper posture and distance from the VDT screen. That's a good way to help avoid eye strain. And I take the advice of my optometrist by having regular vision exams. After all, vision problems can occur at any age. And there's a lot of the world I still want to see! (MUSIC UP -- WITH VOCAL) "Life is worth seeing . . ." (ANNOUNCER) A public service from the American Optometric Association.

VDT OPERATOR . . . 30 seconds

(MUSIC -- WITH VOCAL) -- "The world is a beautiful place to be, so many things to do and see . . . " (MUSIC FADES UNDER VOICE OF VDT OPERATOR) As an airline reservation agent, I like taking care of people. And I take care of myself too. Working at a video display terminal, requires that I keep my vision at peak efficiency; and I take the advice of my optometrist by having regular vision exams. There's a lot of the world I still want to see! (MUSIC UP -- WITH VOCAL) "Life is worth seeing . . . " (ANNOUNCER) A public service from the American Optometric Association.

Courtesy of National Radio News

**FIGURE 6–6**

FASHION MODEL . . . 30 seconds
(MUSIC -- WITH VOCAL) "The world is a beautiful place to be, so many things to do and see . . . " (MUSIC FADES UNDER VOICE OF FASHION MODEL) I'm a fashion model. To look and feel my best, I watch my diet, get exercise and take care of my eyes too, especially since I wear contact lenses. Wearing contacts takes care . . . and professional help. So I take my optometrist's advice, and have regular vision exams, to keep me looking good! (MUSIC UP -- WITH VOCAL) "Life is worth seeing . . . " (ANNOUNCER) A public service from the American Optometric Association.

TENNIS PLAYER . . . 30 seconds
(MUSIC __ WITH VOCAL) "The world is a beautiful place to be, so many things to do and see . . ." (MUSIC FADES UNDER VOICE OF TENNIS PLAYER) I'm getting older; but I still play tennis every week. And I take care of myself in other ways too. You know, vision problems can occur at any age, but eyes over 50 need special attention. So I take my optometrist's advice, I get regular vision exams. That helps me keep my eye right "on the ball." (MUSIC UP -- WITH VOCAL) "Life is worth seeing . . . (ANNOUNCER) A public service from the American Optometric Association.

CHILDHOOD VISION . . . 30 seconds
(MUSIC -- WITH VOCAL) "The world is a beautiful place to be, so many things to do and see . . . " (MUSIC FADES UNDER VOICE OF MOTHER) My children are very special to me; I try to keep them happy and healthy. And I take my optometrist's advice -- regular vision exams. We started when they were each a year old. Early detection of eye problems is possible, even in pre-schoolers, and that can make a life time of difference. (MUSIC UP -- WITH VOCAL) "Life is worth seeing. . . " (ANNOUNCER) A public service from the American Optometric Association.

**AMERICAN OPTOMETRIC ASSOCIATION**
243 N. Lindbergh Blvd.
St. Louis, MO 63141
Contact: Reynold Malmer
(314) 991-4100

C-2019
285

**FIGURE 6–6 (continued)**

National Radio News 13691 West Eleven Mile Road • Oak Park, Michigan 48237 • (313) 541-1440
23480 Park Sorrento • Calabasas Park, California 91302 • (818) 883-6121

Radio Public Service Announcements 7.5 i.p.s.

BILL COSBY

**Explorers And Pioneers . . . 60 seconds**

(Bill Cosby:) This is Bill Cosby. A long time ago when I was a teenager my father used to say, "William, it's time to begin thinking about your future -- someday you'll make a fine doctor." Well, why think about the future if he says I'm going to be a doctor. I mean, he didn't know about my blood allergy - the fact that I pass out whenever I see blood. I wanted to be an explorer or a pioneer . . . but then I didn't dare say that out loud. Your friends would laugh at you 'cause everybody knows that there are no more explorers or pioneers around, right? I mean man, if you're a teenager who thinks like I did, you couldn't be more wrong. Do you know that a whole flock of pioneers, right now, are exploring everything from the center of the earth to the edge of our universe. They're searching for new worlds - and new energy sources for this one. If you want to make things happen instead of watching them happen, consider a career in science or engineering. It can be one of life's great adventures! And dear old dad might be sooo proud! (Announcer:) A public service from this station and the National Science Foundation.

**Engineers Of Another Kind . . . 60 seconds**

(Bill Cosby:) This is Bill Cosby. Most kids have dreams about what they'd like to be when they grow up. I remember when I was a little kid . . . grown-ups would say, "William, what do you want to be when you grow up?" And I'd say, (childish falsetto), I wanna be an engineer! In those days, an engineer was a guy who drove a train . . . one of the most important jobs in the world. And I could just see myself sittin' up there in the cab with my head out the window . . . layin' on the horn . . . doin' ninety miles an hour (here, Bill does a vocal doppler-effect sound effect into microphone). And I still get excited thinking about it! There aren't as many of those train-jockey-type engineers around anymore. But today, the other kind are doing more exciting things. They're working with scientists exploring new frontiers under the earth, at the bottom of the seas and in space; developing ways to send messages that will make today's system old hat. And that's just the beginning. If you're a teenager who wants to make things happen instead of watching them happen, consider a career in science or engineering. It could be one of life's great adventures! (Announcer:) A public service from this station and the National Science Foundation.

**How To Get Un-Bored . . . 60 seconds**

(Bill Cosby:) This is Bill Cosby. I'd like to talk to you teenagers about your future. Now right away, a lot of you are saying, "Wow . . . this is gonna be boring!" Well that's cool . . . 'cause y'know only smart people get bored . . . dumb people never get bored. Well, it's true . . . some of the smartest people in history were bored. Columbus sat around with his friends, one day he stood up and said, "This is boring . . . I think I'll go discover America!" And if Tom Edison hadn't been bored, then we might all be watching TV by candlelight! So what does this mean to you? Well, if you're bored and you want to be un-bored, then you should know that today there are more opportunities for discovery and adventure than Chris Columbus and Tom Edison ever dreamed of. Today's explorers, inventors and pioneers are called scientists and engineers. They're learning how life began . . . searching for new energy sources . . . even new worlds . . . and I have yet to meet one who's bored. If you want to make things happen instead of watching them happen, consider a career in science or engineering. It can be one of life's great adventures! (Announcer:) A public service from this station and the National Science Foundation.

Courtesy of National Radio News

FIGURE 6–7

-2-

**How To Get Un-Bored . . . 30 seconds**

(Bill Cosby:) This is Bill Cosby. If you're a bored teenager, then you should know that today there are more opportunities for discovery and adventure than Chris Columbus and Tom Edison ever dreamed of. Today's explorers, inventors and pioneers are called scientists and engineers. They're searching for new energy sources . . . even new worlds. And I have yet to meet one who's bored. If you want to make things happen consider a career in science or engineering. Because it can be one of life's great adventures! (Announcer:) A public service from this station and the National Science Foundation.

**Explorers And Pioneers . . . 30 seconds**

(Bill Cosby:) This is Bill Cosby. If you're a teenager who thinks that there are no more explorers or pioneers you couldn't be more wrong. Do you know that some explorers, right now, are learning how the brain works . . . not necessarily mine . . . and a whole flock of pioneers are searching for new worlds -- and new energy sources for this one. Now, if you want to make things happen, consider a career in science or engineering. It can be one of life's greatest adventures! (Announcer:) A public service from this station and the National Science Foundation.

**Engineers Of Another Kind . . . 30 seconds**

(Bill Cosby:) This is Bill Cosby. Did you ever think of engineers doing exciting things . . . like designing buildings that will still be there even after an earthquake? That's just the beginning. If you're a teenager who wants to make things happen instead of watching them happen, consider a career in science or engineering. It can be on of life's greatest adventures! I love it! I love it! (Announcer:) A public service from this station and the National Science Foundation.

**NATIONAL SCIENCE FOUNDATION**
1800 "G" Street, N.W.
Public Affairs Office, Room 533
Washington, D.C. 20550
Contact: Susan Bartlett
Phone: (202) 357-9498

2589
0185

**FIGURE 6–7 (continued)**

National Radio News 13691 West Eleven Mile Road • Oak Park, Michigan 48237 • (313) 541-1440
23480 Park Sorrento • Calabasas Park, California 91302 • (818) 883-6121

Radio Public Service Announcements

7.5 i.p.s.

DRUNK DRIVING -- "EMERGENCY PHYSICIAN"

Emergency Physician . . . . 60 seconds
**(Narrator:)** "Each year, drunk drivers cause half of all highway fatalities and they seriously injure or cripple three quarters of a million people. Emergency room doctors deal with this tragedy every day." **(Doctor:)** "One of the most difficult situations of all for me as an emergency physician to deal with is when I have to face up to the family of an innocent victim. And when I have to tell them that, 'm'am, I'm sorry to tell you your son is dead because of being hit by a car driven by a drunk driver. I can't understand why people drink and then drive. It would seem to me if they could see the injury that's caused by this, they would not do that. But tests have shown that the person who drinks socially is the one who causes the accidents for the most part." **(Narrator:)** "Every twenty minutes of every day, someone drunk is involved in a fatal accident because someone sober didn't get involved. If you have friends who've had too much to drink . . . be a true friend, don't let them drive. A public service from the Motor Vehicle Manufacturers Association."

**Emergency Physician . . . . 30 seconds**
**(Narrator:)** "If you think social drinkers aren't dangerous behind the wheel, ask an emergency room doctor." **(Doctor:)** "The person who is, in my opinion, the most dangerous is not the one who is smashed . . . it's the person who's done some social drinking. He may not be drinking a lot and not feel drunk, but tests have shown that the person who drinks socially is the one who causes the accidents, for the most part." **(Narrator:)** "If you have friends who've had too much to drink . . . be a true friend, don't let them drive. A public service from the Motor Vehicle Manufacturers Association."

**MOTOR VEHICLE MANUFACTURERS ASSOCIATION**
300 New Center Building
Detroit, Michigan 48202
Contact: Gene McKinney
Phone: (313) 872-4311

2581
1284

Courtesy of National Radio News

**FIGURE 6–8A**

National Radio News

13691 West Eleven Mile Road • Oak Park, Michigan 48237 • (313) 541-1440
23480 Park Sorrento • Calabasas Park, California 91302 • (818) 883-6121

Radio Public Service Announcements

7.5 i.p.s.

**DRUNK DRIVING -- "MOTHER OF VICTIM"**

**Mother of Victim . . . . 60 seconds**
**(Narrator:)** "Each year drunk drivers cause half of all highway fatalities. The mother of an innocent victim whose life was snuffed out by a drunk driver talks about her feelings." **(Mother:)** "I think at first you're angry at everybody that you think ever hurt your kid, but your anger really centers around the person that caused the death. You go into court -- people are afraid of the drunk's constitutional rights. It angers you to see the people in the jury and I know they sit back a lot of times and they think, boy, I've gone to a going away party or I've stopped for a couple of beers and boy this poor fool got caught. How can I prove him guilty and say yes, he's guilty when I've done the same thing myself. But they don't realize maybe the next year it could be one of their kids." **(Narrator:)** "What can you do to prevent tragedies like these? Well, if you have friends who've had too much to drink . . . be a true friend, don't let them drive. A public service from the Motor Vehicle Manufacturers Association."

**Mother of Victim . . . . 30 seconds**
**(Narrator:)** "David was killed by a drunk driver. His mother's life will never be the same." **(Mother:)** "I think at first you're angry at everybody that you think ever hurt your kid and the only thing that helps is that you figure for every life that's saved, that's in their memory. And for every drunk that's taken off the road, that's in tribute to them." **(Narrator:)** "How can you pay tribute to victims like David? If you have friends who've had too much to drink . . . be a true friend, don't let them drive. A public service from the Motor Vehicle Manufacturers Association."

**MOTOR VEHICLE MANUFACTURERS ASSOCIATION**
300 New Center Building
Detroit, Michigan 48202
Contact: Gene McKinney
Phone: (313) 872-4311

2581
1284

Courtesy of National Radio News

**FIGURE 6–8B**

National Radio News 13691 West Eleven Mile Road • Oak Park, Michigan 48237 • (313) 541-1440
23480 Park Sorrento • Calabasas Park, California 91302 • (818) 883-6121

Radio Public Service Announcements

7.5 i.p.s.

DRUNK DRIVING -- "POLICE OFFICER"

**Police Officer . . . . 60 seconds**
**(Narrator:)** "Each year, drunk drivers cause half of all highway fatalities and they seriously injure or cripple three quarters of a million people. A police officer who sees the tragedy every day has some ideas on how to deal with this problem." **(Police Officer:)** "I think the best general solution to the drunk driver problem in the United States today is, we have to educate people to prevent other people from driving intoxicated. And I think those people that are friends or that are acquaintances of the potential drunk driver have a big responsibility in making sure that they don't get on the road. And we have to have stronger laws that we are willing to enforce. If it's driver's license suspensions or jail sentences or community work . . . have a drunk driver ride in an ambulance for awhile . . . have him see what some of the victims look like. Maybe that'll help. It's a tough problem and it gets worse and worse!" **(Narrator:)** " If you have friends who've had too much to drink . . . be a true friend, don't let them drive. A public service from the Motor Vehicle Manufacturers Association."

**Police Officer . . . . 30 seconds**
**(Narrator:)** "Each year drunk drivers cause half of all highway fatalities. One angry police officer who sees the tragedy every day has some ideas on how to deal with this problem." **(Police Officer:)** "We have to have stronger laws that we are willing to enforce. Have a drunk driver ride in an ambulance for awhile . . . have him see what some of the victims look like. Maybe that'll help. It's a tough problem and it gets worse and worse!" **(Narrator:)** "If you have friends who've had too much to drink . . . be a true friend, don't let them drive. A public service from the Motor Vehicle Manufacturers Association."

**MOTOR VEHICLE MANUFACTURERS ASSOCIATION**
300 New Center Building
Detroit, Michigan 48202
Contact: Gene McKinney
Phone: (313) 872-4311

2581
1284

Courtesy of National Radio News

**FIGURE 6–8C**

National Radio News 13691 West Eleven Mile Road • Oak Park, Michigan 48237 • (313) 541-1440
23480 Park Sorrento • Calabasas Park, California 91302 • (818) 883-6121

Radio Public Service Announcement
7.5 i.p.s.

**DRUNK DRIVING -- A DEADLY WEAPON . . . 30 SECONDS**

**NARRATOR:**

"Do you know what the deadliest weapons in America are? They're not weapons of war, yet they've killed more Americans than have died in all our wars. What are these terrible weapons? They're steering wheels in the hands of drunks! How do we stop these killers? Well, if they're friends, talk them out of driving . . . or, if they won't listen, call the police. But for god's sake, stop them, because each year drunk drivers cause more than half of all traffic fatalities! A public service from the Motor Vehicle Manufacturers Association."

**MOTOR VEHICLE MANUFACTURERS ASSOCIATION**
300 New Center Building
Detroit, Michigan 48202
Contact: Gene McKinney
Phone: (313) 872-4311

2581
1284

Courtesy of National Radio News

**FIGURE 6–8D**

I can raise that best positions the public relations message as a solution?

What picture do I want to paint for the listener or viewer?

Radio narrative or television visual/narrative should work together to progressively unveil your idea. By the end of the spot, your single message should be clearly understood. This can be validated beforehand by assembling representative groups of your target audience in focus groups (see Chapter 2) to see what message(s) they received from the PSA.

Radio PSAs are timed to run 10, 20, 30, or occasionally 60 seconds. Most however are 10s and 30s. Television PSAs should also be 10 or 30 seconds in length. While the 20-second spots are rarely used, 60-second spots are typically aired after midnight. Offer stations the same spot in each time length; and offer stations several different PSAs so they are not repeating the same one day after day.

While some practitioners are offering 15-second public service spots (following the lead of the advertising community), 15-second public service time availability is virtually nonexistent and, as such, is not worth the effort.

Remember to set your typewriter margins for 60 spaces. That means 16 lines of copy per minute (eight for 30 seconds, five for 20 seconds, and two-and-a-half to three for 10 seconds).[29]

Radio PSAs are usually read live on the air. Television PSAs can also be read live on the air or videotaped. If you opt for production, hire a production specialist. Quality production can be the difference between getting on and not getting on the air.

Whereas a message in the public interest and quality production are two criteria for getting on the air, localizing the message and the sponsor is another. Local organizations have no trouble with this criterion and often have an edge on the state and national groups sending PSAs to community radio and television stations. Localize a spot to a specific market. Tag the end of the spot with the name of your local office: "This message has been brought to you by the Key West Chapter of the American Cancer Society."

Five questions to ask yourself regarding public service announcements:

1. Is it top production quality?
2. Is it not-for-profit?
3. Is it a true community service?
4. Do a lot of people need to know?
5. Is it local?

***Format.*** Television PSAs utilize $\frac{3}{4}$-, 1-, and 2-inch videotapes, 16 millimeter film, or 35 millimeter slides. When not scripted, radio spots should be recorded on high-quality audiocassettes. The high-quality taped television spot is far and away the best but most expensive option, costing as much as $50,000 to $75,000 for a set of three taped PSAs..

A package of television PSAs will normally include videotape, written script, and evaluation reply card. A radio PSA will include script and evaluation card, although sometimes it will include a recorded spot on reel-to-reel tape, cassette, or disk.

Smaller, not-for-profit organizations should work with local stations to produce PSAs. Stations will often actually produce spots for such groups. To get production help from local stations, write the station public service director describing your organization and why it is in the community's interest to air your message. Include a rough script. The station will clean it up. The public service director sells your idea to management, so sell your idea to him or her.

### Station Tie-Ins

Radio and television stations frequently cosponsor promotions with community groups. This means a tremendous amount of exposure, including public service, paid advertising, on location broadcasts, and news coverage. A television station might sponsor a month-long cholesterol check promotion with a local hospital. A talk radio station might commit a similar amount of time to public service, paid advertising, and talk show appearances to a teacher's credit union honoring high school graduates. The cost to the community group is minimal. Station tie-ins can be generated by writing to the station manager, describing why the promotion is in the public interest and how the station can help.

### Public Affairs Programs

With deregulation in broadcasting, the number of public affairs programs has steadily declined. The FCC no longer requires a station to air as many public service hours as it once did and many stations are acting accordingly.

Programming in the larger cities is usually only about local issues such as upcoming local elections, policy changes before the voters, local education happenings, local health issues, and interviews with local authors, politicians, educators, civic leaders, and health professionals. The smaller towns, however, schedule more variety and are more eager to interview out-of-town guests than the larger city stations.

Public affairs programs get your message to your audience clearly and comprehensively due to the time allotted the interview. These shows range from one-half hour to two hours in length. One interview can last for the entire hour.

Public affairs programs are usually aired in early mornings, late evenings, or on weekends. Consequently, although you receive a quality time allotment, the number of people reached is limited.

The hosts or hostesses of public affairs programs are typically not as experienced as those during prime time. Provide the interviewer with ample material, including potential interview questions and visuals designed to support your message.

### Community Calendars

Radio and television stations frequently air community calendars to help listeners and viewers keep abreast of local events.

Not-for-profit groups can receive free air time for car washes, auctions, art shows, and other fund-raising events. Pertinent information, including date, time, and location, should go to the public affairs or program director at radio or television stations two weeks prior to the event. Practitioners should follow up with a telephone call a week or so after mailing the notice. Successful calendar events generally cover topics of broad appeal to the station's listeners or viewers.

Some stations also provide a telephone line for viewers and listeners to call for information about community events.

## SUMMARY

- □ Conversational style and limited time are the primary differences between writing for broadcast and print media.
- □ Newspapers set the agenda for the news appearing on radio and television.
- □ Instant access and localization of national stories are the publicity strengths of radio.
- □ Providing effective visuals with news hooks are the best entree to television news and talk shows.
- □ The video news release is used primarily by small to medium-sized stations.
- □ Public service announcement messages for not-for-profit groups and government agencies are aired in the public interest when advertising space is not sold. As such, they appear at varying times, making audience evaluation difficult.
- □ Joint tie-in promotions with radio or television stations can accelerate an issue on the public agenda locally.

## EXERCISES

1. Assume you are the public relations director for the Motor Vehicle Manufacturers Association and your organization has launched a campaign to discourage drunk driving. The key message is: "If you have friends who have had too much to drink, be a true friend and don't let them drive." Write 10- and 30-second public service announcements raising a need/concern/interest and offering

D R A F T

**SOUTH BAY TRAINING CENTER PUBLIC SERVICE ANNOUNCEMENT**

:30 sec. television

| VIDEO | AUDIO |
| --- | --- |
| fade up to out-of-focus shot of badge | NOW YOU HAVE A CHANCE TO GO GOLD. |
| slowly pull into focus | THE PRIVATE INDUSTRY COUNCIL AND THE STATE DEPARTMENT OF CORRECTIONS ARE LOOKING FOR MORE THAN 300 MEN AND WOMEN TO BE TRAINED AS CORRECTIONAL OFFICERS FOR THE RICHARD J. DONOVAN CORRECTIONAL FACILITY IN OTAY MESA. |
| | START A REWARDING CAREER IN LAW ENFORCEMENT. CALL THE SOUTH BAY TRAINING CENTER AT 429-3881. OR STOP BY ANY WEEKDAY FROM 9 TO 5 AT 1664 INDUSTRIAL BOULEVARD IN CHULA VISTA.....AND GO GOLD. |

Courtesy of Private Industry Council

**FIGURE 6–9**

your message as a solution. Do the same for television and include ideas for visuals to share with production specialists.

2. Edit the 30-second television public service announcement from the Private Industry Council (Figure 6–9) to strengthen the need/concern/interest and the Private Industry Council as a solution.
3. Rewrite the Associated Press story in Figure 6–2 as a 30-second public service announcement for radio using the message/media outline. Now edit it to 10 seconds without losing the need/concern/interest and message solution.
4. Write a 30-second message from the Associated Press article (Figure 6–2) for dietitian media representatives to call into local radio stations. Be sure to raise a need/concern/interest among parents and offer the registered dietitian as a solution.
5. How would you go about generating a local placement for a registered dietitian on an evening television news show? What visual suggestions would you offer to expand your message?
6. Sketch out a rough video news release script with both audio and visual to share with a commercial video producer.

## REFERENCES


1. Edward Bliss, Jr., and John M. Patterson, *Writing News for Broadcast*, 2nd ed. (New York: Columbia University Press, 1978), p. 5.
2. Michael Klepper, *Getting Your Message Out* (Englewood Cliffs, NJ: Prentice-Hall, 1984), pp. 5–18.
3. Bliss and Patterson, *Writing News for Broadcast*, p. 52.
4. Ibid., p. 149.
5. G. Paul Smeyak, *Broadcast News Writing*, 2nd ed. (Columbus, OH: Grid Publishing, 1983), p. 67.
6. Bliss and Patterson, *Writing News for Broadcast*, p. 138.
7. Klepper, *Getting Your Message Out*, pp. 68–69.
8. *Anaheim Bulletin*, February 15, 1983, p. 4.
9. Scott M. Cutlip, Allen H. Center, and Glen M. Broom, *Effective Public Relations*, 6th ed. (Englewood Cliffs, NJ: Prentice-Hall, 1985), p. 384.
10. Klepper, *Getting Your Message Out*, p. 20.
11. William Stakelin, *Advertising Age*, January 28, 1985, p. 16.
12. Lawrence E. Nolte and Dennis L. Wilcox, *Effective Publicity: How to Reach the Public* (New York: John Wiley, 1984), p. 237.
13. James E. Grunig and Todd Hunt, *Managing Public Relations* (New York: Holt, Rinehart & Winston, 1984), p. 425.
14. Roy Heatly, personal communication, April 1984.
15. Alissa Rubin, *Public Relations Journal* (October 1985), 20.
16. Ibid, pp. 22–23.
17. Howard Back, written communication, July 1987.
18. Nolte and Wilcox, *Effective Publicity*, p. 166.
19. Doug Newsom and Tom Siegfried, *Writing in Public Relations Practice: Form and Style* (Belmont, CA: Wadsworth, 1981), p. 137.
20. Ibid, p. 143.
21. Ibid, pp. 143–145.
22. Bliss and Patterson, *Writing News for Broadcast*, p. 2.
23. Federal Communications Commission, Form 303, Statement of TV Program Service, sec. IV, p. iii.
24. Ronald E. Rice and William J. Paisley, *Public Communication Campaigns* (Beverly Hills, CA: Sage Publications, 1981), pp. 155–56.
25. Joe Mandese, *Adweek*, May 18, 1987, p. 56.
26. *Publicity Craft* (New York: PR Aids, 1981), p. 4.
27. Frederick Norfleet, personal communication, Feb. 1987.
28. Dale Kemery, personal communication, May 1987.
29. Nolte and Wilcox, *Effective Publicity*, p. 166.


## CASE STUDY

### The Problem

The Bloomington Metabolic Foundation funds research and treatment for diabetic children. The foundation has become frustrated by the limited number of families who have applied for financial aid to take advantage of a revolutionary new treatment called the insulin pump. Consequently, a Key Result Area in its strategic plan calls for increased usage of the insulin pump among diabetic children.

### Situational Analysis

The insulin pump is a remarkable new advance in the treatment of diabetes. Instead of the diabetic administering daily injections of insulin, a small mechanical device pumps insulin regularly into the system, mimicking the human pancreas. The new device reduces diabetic symptoms such as hypoglycemia, headaches, nausea, and blackouts. Unfortunately, few families of diabetic children have taken advantage of the new device, largely because of ignorance about cost and the foundation as a source of financial aid. As part of an awareness objective in the public relations plan, you, as foundation public relations director, have received agreement from several medical professionals to appear in the media. The communications outcome is to generate applications for financial aid. Since you have selected radio and television as part of your media mix:

1. Develop a message/media outline.
2. How will you get on radio news programming?
3. Write a video news release script, including visual concepts to be used as part of a video news release that is being funded as a public service by the National Diabetes Association. How will you distribute it to local sta tions?
4. Write 10- and 30-second public service announcements for both radio and television.
5. Describe how you will evaluate the effectiveness of your broadcast publicity effort.
6. Describe how you will evaluate the effectiveness of your broadcast publicity effort.

# CHAPTER 7

# Generating Media Interviews

### *IN THIS CHAPTER*

Placing an interview or multiple media tour interviews with a newspaper, magazine, or television/radio news or talk show is the keystone of publicity success. Interviews provide opportunities for major news stories carrying reporter bylines. Guest interviews can provide more than a fleeting mention of the product, issue, or organization. The major stories work the hardest to set the public agenda and position issues as important.

The successful generation of interviews can be a particularly exhilarating experience, but the rejection ratio can humble even the most successful practitioners. The subjectivity of gatekeeper decisions and the contempt some gatekeepers demonstrate to public relations inquiries make it a challenging task.

Interview placements require the same kind of thinking as the development of the news release. In fact, a good news release idea frequently makes a salable interview. As with all public relations techniques, the thought process should begin with brainstorming and setting priority news angles with the most potential for carrying out the message/media outline.

Although media friends are not necessary to sell a good news angle or interview idea (and will not sell a bad one), they cushion the success/failure ratio. It is somehow easier to call someone you know well, accept his or her acceptance or rejection, without negative connotations.

The process starts with the written query letter to the appropriate gatekeeper and telephone follow-up. Spokespersons are engaged to help formulate the message/media outline. Involvement in the outline generates spokesperson ownership in the message, thus taking steps to ensure proper delivery.

### *CHAPTER OBJECTIVES*

The reader will be able to

1. Describe how to initiate a media relations program.

2. Write an interview query letter utilizing the message/media outline.
3. Describe how to conduct a pre-interview briefing.
4. Construct the steps necessary to set up a media tour.
5. Illustrate how to place an editorial in a local medium.

## ESTABLISHING MEDIA RELATIONS

Generating interviews can be accomplished through news conferences, special events, and one-on-one queries to the decision makers who guard the media gates. This chapter will devote itself primarily to one-on-one queries; special events and news conferences are detailed in the next chapter.

We will explore some common techniques in initiating a communication with a reporter, producer, editor, or editorial board (senior editors who make decisions regarding editorials).

### Study Medium First

Public relations practitioners should carefully study the medium or media targeted for placement of interviews before ever sitting down to the word processor or typewriter or making that initial telephone call. You should seek answers to such questions as the following:

Which sections or programs reach your target audience? Which sections of the publication or broadcast shows are most appropriate for the subjects you are addressing? Then, which section or program is most likely to cover your subject content? For example, do you find your subject covered in the newspaper front section? metropolitan section? business section? living section? sports section? food section? health section? travel section? If you have selected television and/or radio as media targeted to reach your audience, are there appropriate talk shows? What about the news? What about the specialty segments of the news?

After you have made your media selection decisions, find out who has the say of whether or not you are granted an interview. Who are the decision makers? Is it the editor or beat reporter (or both) who covers your subject area? Is it a specific talk show producer? Is it a radio news director? Is it a television assignment editor, responsible for assigning camera crews for news stories?

After you have determined the media and their decision makers, then launch your personal media relations campaign. In other words, now that you have targeted the players, get to know them. What are their needs/concerns/interests? What is their definition of a good news story or interview? When are their deadlines? What kind of lead time is comfortable for interview queries? When is the best time to reach them? Do they want to be queried by letter or telephone?

### Get to Know Editors and Reporters

How do you answer these questions? Seek out opportunities and listen well. There are no hard and fast rules. Opportunities for contact with representatives of the media depend to a great extent on the ingenuity of the practitioner. One can, however, make some general recommendations:

#### *1. Get Involved with Media Organizations*

Though reporters are not generally known as joiners of community groups, they do have their own media clubs. Most communities have a local press club and many have a chapter of the Society of Professional Journalists, Sigma Delta Chi. The Society of Professional Journalists restricts membership to journalists and journalism students. Thus public relations practitioner members joined when they were journalists or students. Local press clubs normally welcome public relations members. Attend meetings of these groups but, more importantly, get involved in committees, become an officer, and work side by side with reporters. Make sure your organization is generous about funding press club events. Another specific opportunity for contact comes with fund-raising drives for public television. Reporters and broadcasters tend to work annual telethons.

*2. Become a Resource.*

Once a gatekeeper's needs/concerns/interests are identified, be on the lookout for items of interest even when they have nothing to do with your own interests. Attach your card to reprints of periodicals, jot a brief message on it like "for your information" or "thought this might interest you," and mail to journalists. Share potential story ideas, even when you seemingly have nothing to gain.

*3. Look for Social Opportunities.*

Lunching with reporters is only one way to get to know gatekeepers. Some reporters may shy away from lunches, while others will be receptive. However, there are other avenues. If you know that a reporter is an avid fan of the local college football team, offer to take her to a game. When you attend press club functions, develop "hit lists" of individuals with whom you want to make contact and make sure you sit next to at least one of them at the meal.

*4. Organize a Company Softball Team.*

In most major cities there are co-ed media softball leagues. Organize a team and get involved. Bring after-game refreshments for both teams and get to know the journalists.

*5. Provide Speaking Opportunities.*

Invite key reporters to speak to community or professional groups with which you are affiliated. Use the speaking engagement as a means for getting to know the reporter. Offer to provide transportation to and from the event. Make sure you introduce the speaker and are seated next to him or her.

*6. Invite a Reporter to Brief Your Staff.*

Invite key editors to your office for a brown bag lunch briefing on the needs of his or her medium. More often than not, editors are surprisingly willing to brief public relations staffs on their needs. Write the editor or reporter(s) with whom you have to deal. Outline what you have in mind and follow up by telephone three or four days after you send the letter. Send a confirmation letter with potential questions.

*7. Provide Solid News Angles.*

The most important factor in generating good professional relationships is consistently providing good stories. If you can give the reporter good news stories, demonstrate your knowledge of what is and is not news, be candid about what you can and cannot say, and demonstrate your willingness to go the "extra mile" to help him or her do the job, you will generate the kind of respect that will make day-to-day dealings with the media the most effective for your organization.

Nothing is wrong with an introductory telephone call as long as it does not conflict with a deadline. Write down questions ahead of time and then pick up the telephone and call the gatekeeper. Tell him or her that you are new on the job and would like a few minutes of time. When would be the best time to talk? If necessary, schedule a designated time to call back. Such dialogue can progress into a mutually beneficial professional relationship.

> Which of the media relations activities listed above are ones you might consider using to further friendships with media representatives?

### Identify Gatekeepers' Outside Interests

Occasionally story angles can be generated around the outside interests of your gatekeeper. If the food editor is a gourmet cook, remember it for opportunities to design an appropriate story, supporting your message, around gourmet cooking. The best of all worlds is when the reporter's outside interests coincide directly with those of your client or employer.

To illustrate, Western Fairs Association found journalists either had no interest in fairs or were head-over-heels crazy about them. The trick, of course, was to find the interested reporters who covered beats reaching the appropriate target audiences. Once that was accomplished, interested reporters from major metropolitan area newspapers were spending a full day, with photographer, attending a Western Fairs Association annual convention. Unusual, but this is an excellent example of uncovering a reporter's outside interest and facilitating it for the mutual benefit of the client (message exposure) and the reporter (interest in fairs).

The underlying point in media relations is that interviews are more comfortable to initiate when you know the gatekeepers to whom you must sell your news angle or talk show idea. Although this is not always possible, *nor is it necessary for selling a good interview*, it just makes it easier when you know their needs/concerns/interests.

The business gatekeepers interviewed in a Simon/McGarry survey offered the following media relations do's and don't's, which can be considered a generic gatekeeper laundry list:

### Do

1. Know your industry, company, and the needs of the publications inside and out.

   In other words know your subject, anticipate questions, and have answers. Be able to describe why the story is right for the reporter and fits the format of the medium.
2. Make fewer, but better quality, contacts.

   Do not be a pest.
3. Include all pertinent information in releases.

   Who, what, where, when, why and how.
4. Do not waste an editor's time.

   Have a mutually beneficial purpose for your contact.
5. Know your client or employer inside and out.

   See interpretation under item 1.

### Don't

1. Stonewall, mislead, or lie to an editor. It is "a fatal mistake."

   If you want to stay in the public relations business, it is just a matter of common sense to stay candid and honest. There is absolutely no other way. If you cannot give an inquiring reporter an answer to a question, tell him or her and explain why.
2. Try to place the same story in several publications.

   Placing the same interview in competing publications or broadcast media shows is risky, although this is a common result of news conferences, special events, and frequently with news releases. Normally, when querying for one-on-one placements, it is prudent to assume that competition exists until you learn differently. If you are successful with an interview placement with the financial section of one newspaper, do not seek a placement with the financial section of its competitor. Or if you have one morning television talk show, do not go after another morning television talk show with the same angle. Hit one medium with one angle and the competition with another. And, for long-term relationships, do not play favorites.
3. Telephone at deadline.

   Know the medium; know the gatekeeper.
4. Confuse consumer news with business news.

   This goes back to knowing the needs of the gatekeepers and their sections regardless of their specialty.
5. Bury the news hook in deference to the client's name: "Joe Blow, president of XYZ, announces . . ."

   Use Associated Press or United Press International as your style guide.
6. Oversell the idea.

   You have to know when to quit: Trying to overcome one negative response is persistence, trying to overcome two negatives is being a pest. Remember, you are in it for the long term, and generally speaking, no single interview is worth jeopardizing a professional relationship. Be courteous and await a new opportunity.
7. Interpose yourself between the editor and your spokesperson, an act editors call "the absolute worst."

The spokesperson should know the subject, believe the message, and be able to articulate it clearly and enthusiastically. These should be the criteria for selecting the spokesperson. A well-prepared spokesperson is your best defense against this "no-no."

8. Propose inappropriate stories.[1]

   Know your medium; know your gatekeeper. Seeking publicity is not an easy task, even with a good slant. Many reporters, editors, or producers are antagonistic toward public relations people. They can demonstrate the ultimate rudeness and disrespect. Do not take it personally or give in to rejection. Even though you may go through ten rejections for one seed of interest, that one seed of interest—from the right journalist—can make the entire process worthwhile. Rejection comes with the publicity-seeking territory. It occurs for a wide variety of reasons, many of which have nothing to do with the validity of your idea. Rejection is a fact of life, a truism, even for the world's best publicity seekers.

> Describe ways you can examine and correct each *"Don't"* error before it reaches the gatekeeper. What happens to your chances of obtaining publicity when such errors are committed?

## THE INTERVIEW QUERY

Media interview queries can be made in person, by telephone or by mail. The decision regarding whether one should mail an interview query letter or simply pick up the telephone and call the editorial gatekeeper is a controversial one.

If the practitioner has a hot, breaking news story, the telephone is, without question, the first option. Radio interviews, taken over the telephone from your spokesperson, for example, can be on the air instantly or within a matter of minutes. Some practitioners swear by telephoning first regardless of the urgency of the news angle. Their rationale is that editors and reporters receive so much mail that letters are frequently overlooked. In fact, some reporters prefer telephone contact, particularly from long-valued sources.

However, the experience of the authors demonstrates that, as a general rule, it is better to write a brief query letter, mail it to the appropriate gatekeeper, and follow up by telephone within three days to a week later. Such advice is validated by a Simon/McGarry Public Relations, Inc., survey showing that seven of ten business press editors preferred written queries. Fifty-seven percent approved the practice of following up a query letter with a telephone call. There are those, though, who indicate a call could hurt consideration. A Forbes bureau chief offered what has become a standard reply from those not wishing to be bothered by phone: "Let the editor respond if he or she is interested."[2]

The decision of whether to call or write first should be made on a case-by-case basis. But as a general rule the public relations practitioner cannot afford *not* to make a follow-up telephone call. Media placements are often the bread and butter of his or her livelihood, and the risk of the written communication never making it to the gatekeeper is normally greater than the risk of offending a busy news reporter, editor or producer.

> What response can you give to an editor upset with your follow-up call?

### The Query Letter

The query letter is usually a one-page description of the news angle. It provides at least three valuable benefits. First, the query letter forces the practitioner to organize his or her thoughts, to crystallize the most salient news angle. Second, it permits a discreet choreography of how you would like the interview to go. Third, the query letter serves as a vehicle for piquing the interest of the reporter in a story idea. It lays the groundwork if it is read for the practitioner to "close the sale" with additional reasons why it is a legitimate story and worth the interview.

Planning interview placements should begin with the message/media outline. Content should be designed to support the public relations plan. Media should be selected based on their credibility and efficiency at reaching the broadest segment of the target audience. As in news releases, start with brainstorming of ideas supporting the message/media outline. When dealing in television, however, there is the added element: the need for visual ideas.

The query letter to television news assignment editors or talk show producers must provide suggestions for bringing the story alive for the eye. Providing videotape, suggesting where to shoot visuals, or actually bringing props to the interview help the gatekeeper and yourself bring the story to life visually. Remember, however, that just any "interesting" visual is not maximizing the opportunity you have for effectively communicating with your audience. The visual-seeking thought process begins by asking questions like *What action do we want the audience to take? How can we expand the message with visuals? What visual best demonstrates our message? How can we best transfer the message to the viewer's own real-life experiences?*

Sending a videotape of your spokesperson in action is an effective tool when querying television talk shows. A good query letter can pique gatekeeper interest; a good videotape can further sell the gatekeeper; a telephone call can close the sale.

As for timing, if possible send your query letter a few weeks prior to when you want the interview to occur and stay flexible to the gatekeeper's timing needs. Some broadcast talk shows in major metropolitan areas work four to six weeks ahead on interview placements and some national shows even longer.

***First Paragraph: The Key.*** The first paragraph of the query letter is as important as the lead in a news release. It must grab the reader's interest. To illustrate, the following query letter from Nann Miller Enterprises, Inc., to television consumer reporters reads: "There are boats, cars and planes seized by law enforcement agencies in the Bay Area every day, and on any given day there are hundreds of these items in government lots waiting to be sold for pennies on the dollar." Another, from US WEST's mobile communications subsidiary, US WEST NewVector Group, to local newspapers." The stage is set. The gloves are off. The battle lines drawn. To the victor goes dominance in Seattle's growing cellular telephone service."

Still another, to national magazine editors from Nuffer, Smith, Tucker, Inc., reads: "Millions of Americans and their children are taking vitamin and mineral supplements past the point of safety, making them among the most abused drugs in the country." A Dairy Council of California query letter lead reads: "Polyunsaturated Thanksgiving? Low cholesterol Christmas?" N.W. Ayer sent the following query to print editors for Steuben Glass of New York City: "Did you ever wonder how a sea serpent celebrates Christmas? Has a wide-eyed five-year-old ever asked you how an elephant goes sledding?"

***The Body: Tightly Written.*** The lead paragraph should be followed up with a series of tightly written, brief paragraphs or bulleted facts describing the news angle, its importance (i.e., supports or backs an emerging trend), and, for broadcast, how the format fits the targeted show. Localizing the pitch also strengthens it (e.g., "One of three Bostonians are rapidly becoming 'grazers' rather than traditional eaters"). Supporting paragraphs also describe the expertise of the individual spokesperson.

> Which of the three query letters making up Figure 7–1 do you like best? Why?

Nuffer, Smith, Tucker, Inc.

3170 Fourth Avenue, Third Floor, San Diego, CA 92103 (619) 296-0605

January 25, 1988

Bill Ritter
Business Editor
KCST-TV
8330 Engineer Road
San Diego, CA 92111

Dear Bill:

How do you build a staff without hiring employees? Sounds impossible, but it can and is being done via "employee leasing," a concept well known in other parts of the country, but relatively new to San Diego.

Simply, employee leasing involves allowing a personnel administration (employee leasing) firm to recruit, screen and hire primarily full-time employees -- or hire current staff -- for a company.

The employee leasing firm handles all the burdens of personnel administration, including quarterly tax deposits, payroll processing, and workman's compensation and medical claims. Plus, economies of scale enable the leasing firm to offer more affordable and often better quality health benefits than the contract company. The end result: management enjoys fewer hassles and has more time to devote to improving profitability.

Primo Team, Inc. is a local company specializing in employee leasing. We can set up interviews with the general manager and some of her current clients. You can visit their worksites to help illustrate the process.

This one's got broad appeal, Bill. It most certainly will interest employers. And employees should be interested from the better benefits perspective.

I'll give you a ring in a day or so to check your interest.

Cordially,

Larry Nuffer

Larry Nuffer
Account Executive

**FIGURE 7–1A**

# Nuffer, Smith, Tucker, Inc.

3170 Fourth Avenue, Third Floor, San Diego, CA 92103 (619) 296-0605

June 12, 1987

Herb Lockwood
The Daily Transcript
P.O. Box 85469
San Diego CA 92138

Dear Herb:

The worksite gender issue has climbed out of the typing pool and into the office of the chief executive officer.

A newly released three-year study has exposed an invisible barrier keeping women from top level jobs. Not managerial positions, or even vice presidencies.

According to Ann M. Morrison, there is a glass ceiling between women and the position of CEO in Fortune 100 companies, which no woman has been able to penetrate.

In her new book, **Breaking the Glass Ceiling: Can Women Make it to the Top of America's Largest Corporations?** Morrison draws profound profiles of what it takes to be a successful woman, in any business environment, and what can derail her off the track of success.

She and her colleagues, Randall P. White and Ellen Van Velsor, conducted and analyzed extensive interviews with Fortune 100 executives which uncovered specific steps to take to reach often elusive top level jobs.

Morrison, director of the Center for Creative Leadership-San Diego, an executive training institute founded in 1970, is available to talk about her research and her new book, due to hit the stands June 26.

She can provide your readers with salient points to help them, male or female, climb the corporate ladder successfully. This is information your audience can use.

I'll call in a few days to see if you agree.

Sincerely,

Gretchen Griswold
Account Executive

**FIGURE 7–1B**

Nuffer, Smith, Tucker, Inc.

3170 Fourth Avenue, Third Floor San Diego, CA 92103 (619) 296-0605

July 22, 1986

Dean Elwood
SUNUP
KFMB TV
7677 Engineer Road
San Diego, CA 92111

Dear Dean:

Photojournalism--a firmly established profession today-- had its roots in the work of one man, an established photographer of more than 100 years ago.

Scotsman John Thomson sowed the seeds with his haunting photographs of the peoples and the countries of China, Siam, Laos, Cambodia, Vietnam--of a time now gone forever.

He was the first in a spate of photographers during those days when the camera was new, to capture the individuality of each of his subjects--nobility and commoner alike--and the photographic world hasn't been the same since.

165 of Thomson's photographs will be on display at the Museum of Photographic Arts August 19 through October 12--the only exhibit of his work on the west coast--and we think your viewers would appreciate being apprised of the show as well as the man.

The persons to do this--Arthur Ollman, director of the Museum of Photographic Arts and Jim Sterrett, a partner with Lillick McHose & Charles, the law firm sponsoring this powerful show--are articulate and available (with a supply of Thomson photos) at your convenience.

I'll be giving you a call, or call me at 296-0605.

Sincerely,

Valerie A. Lemke

Valerie Lemke
Vice President/Publicity

**FIGURE 7–1C**

### Query Letter Tips

Michael Klepper, a public relations broadcast specialist, makes the following recommendations for writing query letters:

1. Get the reader's attention immediately.
   - □ What's your subject.
   - □ What are you trying to convey?
   - □ Find that one word or phrase that best describes the very essence of your idea and start there.
2. Write sparingly.
   - □ Pare your letter down to the briefest, most meaningful elements.
   - □ Don't tell them, sell them.
3. Keep it short.
   - □ Never write more than one page.
   - □ Tell the story in the first two paragraphs.
4. Use a conversational tone.
   - □ Short words; simple sentences.
   - □ No technical jargon or statistics.
5. Demonstrate familiarity with show (publication) format.
   - □ Tell why your idea will fit.
6. Send your letter to the right person.
   - □ Call and confirm the decision maker's name and correct spelling before sending query letter.[3]

Novel media queries can also be effective. Imagination is your only limitation. Media queries have been written and delivered in running shoes, on tortillas, even on footballs. However, you have to be careful. Some reporters take offense to novel approaches. Know your gatekeeper before employing novelty.

> If you were to review a query letter written by one of your subordinates, what would you look for in evaluating it according to Klepper?

### Magazine Placements Are Often Indirect

Well-written query letters provide the most direct route to placements on talk and news shows and print interviews. Magazines, however, frequently select stories by additional means.

"Placing material in news magazines should first be directed to building material up in syndicates like wire services, feature services, photographic services," says Herbert Baus, a long-time public relations practitioner. According to Baus, the next important source of information for these publications are the field regional editors and the stringers, or freelance writers, they rely on for material. Third in importance are stories appearing in daily newspapers and trade magazines. And last is the direct approach to the appropriate editor on the news magazine.[4]

The experience of the authors suggest that Baus is right. Magazine gatekeepers monitor media for story ideas. A news conference may not be attended by a magazine reporter, but could result in a more in-depth story or new approach to the news story. However, one cannot afford to sit back and wait for a phone call.

Planning to know and utilize freelancers frequently published in the targeted publication is sound advice. After all, they already have the credibility and entree necessary for success. Listen to them for tips on each magazine. Even if you decide not to work with them, they are a source of useful inside information.

Try giving an interested freelancer a first attempt at a story placement. But keep a short time line. If the angle does not work with the freelancer, find out why and adjust accordingly. Seek advice on the next move, but do not give up.

> How would you determine whether to work through a magazine stringer, regional editor, or the lead editor of the section for a story placement?

If the query is the most appropriate avenue, send it to both a regional editor and the appropriate specialty editor indicating that you have written to both. Follow up by telephone a week later with the regional editor first and, if unsuccessful, call the specialty editor.

## PREPARING YOUR SPOKESPERSON

The public relations practitioner should take leadership in training organizational spokespersons. Training is a burgeoning industry within the public relations community. Corporate and not-for-profit executives, as well as lawyers and physicians, shell out many dollars learning how to handle themselves effectively during media interviews. The training usually focuses on television interviews. The following lead, which appeared in a *Los Angeles Times* story on media training for physicians, describes the phenomenon:

> In true Mike Wallace fashion, the "TV interviewer" fixed his gaze on the nervous-looking doctor and demanded in a cool baritone voice whether physicians are "pushing pills in collusion with the pharmaceutical industry" and "experimenting with human beings."
>
> The scene could have been every interviewee's nightmare, but it was only simulation.
>
> Eager to improve the medical community's declining credibility, about 120 doctors from across the United States—including some prominent Southern California physicians—are honing their media skills this weekend at a $410-a-person course at the Sheraton Harbor Island East offered by the politically powerful American Medical Association.[5]

Virtually any spokesperson, regardless of his or her media experience, can benefit from interview training. Formal training, as described in the above example, usually consists of one or two days of instruction, videotaped interview simulation, and evaluation. Trainees learn the dos and don'ts of getting messages across in a believable manner. The television interview is emphasized but the principles apply to all interview situations. Such training should provide spokespersons with new or polished interview skills, experience with the worst of situations and, with hard work, increased self-confidence.

All spokespersons should get this kind of training. When this is not possible, for whatever reason, public relations professionals should provide spokesperson briefings on media needs and interview expectations.

Reporter interviews, thanks to Watergate and generally negative attitudes held by the business community, can intimidate even the best of spokespersons. Education and training are ways of minimizing this anxiety. Along with briefing the spokesperson, consider asking a reporter friend to help in the education process. Reporters, like most of us, receive some ego satisfaction from sharing their expertise with others. An hour or two with a friendly reporter can help the spokesperson feel more comfortable with the interview situation.

> What training might you need if you were asked to be an expert spokesperson on radio television talk shows?

### Planning Message Delivery

Being comfortable in an interview is only part of the interview success quotient. Planning the message delivery is crucial. Reaching through the interviewer to members of the target audience presents a formidable challenge.

The spokesperson is selected because of his or her knowledge, belief in the message, and ability to articulate it clearly and enthusiastically. Then we plan message delivery to increase our odds of bringing about change—message retention, acceptance, and attitude or behavior change. A spokesperson should position an interview in a way similar to the practitioner organizing a news release:

1. Raise audience need/concern/interest.
2. Offer the client product/issue/organization as a solution.

3. Describe the benefits of the intended action.
4. Describe the consequences of inaction.
5. Help the reader, viewer, or listener think through how to incorporate the solution into his or her own life.

Setting up a spokesperson with a presentation outline is a far easier process when the spokesperson already believes the message, understands it thoroughly, and presents it well. Involve the spokesperson in completing the message/media outline. Decide with the public relations professional on the need/concern/interest to be raised, how the solution is presented, the benefits of action, the consequences of inaction, and helping the consumer think through how he or she will take the action in the real world.

This process should generate agreements from the spokesperson on how best to communicate certain points most likely to bring about behavioral results. Such agreements are best negotiated and rehearsed before the stress of the interview. A pre-interview briefing should be scheduled, if possible, a day or two prior to the interview.

A pre-interview session makes possible an opportunity to work with the message/media outline, beginning with a clarification of agreements already received prior to your spokesperson selection. The public relations practitioner provides the behavioral outline, the spokesperson fills in content with which he or she is comfortable. Together, the practitioner and the spokesperson develop the two or three key message points that build the case they want the viewer, listener, or reader to obtain from the broadcast interview or printed story.

To illustrate, the president of the Bank of Brannan knows the banking business inside and out. She needs help in reasoning out how she can best position the Bank of Brannan message as a solution to identified audience needs/concerns/interests. Therefore, a pre-interview briefing is scheduled to discuss the outline and how the case can best be built to support it.

With agreements about the outcome, the spokesperson can follow the message/media outline based on his or her own expertise. The spokesperson can think about how to raise an audience need/concern/interest, offer the product, issue, or organization as a solution, offer the benefits of action and consequences of inaction, and steps to help the individual apply the message—in words familiar to that spokesperson.

### Executing the Message

Common guidelines can be shared with the spokesperson about the interview process for television. Most of them can be easily transferred to other media. They are:

1. Don't be passive.

   It takes planning to manage—rather than react to—an interview. You cannot just wait for the right question to be asked; plans must be laid ahead of time for how the message will be interjected.

2. Don't be defensive.

   Interviews are one-sided. The interviewer asks a question; the guest answers it. If you just sit back and wait for the questions, you will remain on the defensive and never wrest the advantage away from the interviewer. Questions are the opportunity to present the message.

3. Show enthusiasm.

   Enthusiasm sells the message as being important. Do not just offer facts and opinions; explain why they matter.

4. Bridge from negative to positive.

   This is also the opportunity to bridge from subject to message as well as to emphasize audience behavior as contained or implied in the message.

5. End on a positive note.

   Broadcasters do not like to edit statements in midsentence. When asked to respond to a negative question or one that does not relate to the message, answer directly without repeating the negative and flow into the positive, or the message. Complete every negative comment with a statement that is positive to you. That way, your negative reply will be balanced by a positive conclusion and more than likely will be aired intact just as you said it.[6]

Klepper offers a three-step technique for bridging from the negative to the positive in 40 to 45 seconds:

1. Respond directly to the question; yes or no in 15 seconds.
2. Offer a brief transition statement to your message in 5 to 10 seconds.
3. Introduce message in 15 seconds.[7]

> How would you prepare a spokesperson to respond to the following negative question: "Why has your company failed to follow industry safety regulations?"

### Some Additional Tips

Some general tips to help prepare the spokesperson include the following:

- ☐ Never say "no comment." If you cannot answer a question, tell the reporter why.
- ☐ Never answer a question to which you do not know the answer. You cannot know everything and it is very risky to enter areas beyond your expertise.
- ☐ Never go "off the record" and assume that you are. Always picture anything you say appearing in the *New York Times*.
- ☐ Practice every possible answer to every potential question. Operate under the assumption that the question you fear most will be asked. Do not answer hypothetical questions.
- ☐ Plan on leaving no more than three key points with your target audience and seek out opportunities to go back and reinforce those points.
- ☐ Remember that the interviewer is not the target audience and that his or her agenda may differ from yours.
- ☐ Be brief and to the point. Do not be concerned with dead air. The interviewer must keep the interview going.

After each interview, the practitioner should evaluate the interview using step 7 of the message/media outline as success criteria. Most spokespersons appreciate a post-interview discussion and frequently message delivery is improved with each subsequent interview.

### Facing the Camera

Much has been written about how to dress for the television interview. In preparing spokespersons, recommend avoiding clothing or accessories that distract the viewers' attention from the message. Spokespersons should dress conservatively and stay away from too much red or white clothing.

Books have been written on and workshops designed to cover the how-to of facing the camera. A few general points need elaboration. One deals with demonstrating confidence. Fidgeting, swiveling in a movable chair, looking anywhere but straight into the eyes of the interviewer all give the viewer a negative impression. Sitting slightly forward in a chair creates a feeling of alertness and involvement in an interview. Using, but not overusing, hand gestures, a smile, the first name of the interviewer, anecdotes meaningful to the audience, and anything else that comes naturally makes you more human and believable. The spokesperson should work from his or her communications strengths—the same ones used in any one-on-one conversation with a neighbor or friend. Do not forget the law of the broadcasting world: short words, simple sentences.

## MEDIA TOURS

Multiple interview placements in print and broadcast media are often scheduled at one time in various cities. This type of multiple interview scheduling is called a *media tour*. From four to six interviews are scheduled daily with print reporters and broadcast talk and news shows. A spokesperson normally travels from city to city accompanied by a public relations professional.

Food companies put home economists on television and radio talk and news shows to demonstrate how to cook with their products. Authors hit the media trail to promote their books. Scientists and physicians travel the circuit as spokespersons to address issues for professional societies and corporate clients.

Bumble Bee Seafoods used a media tour to begin a campaign to squelch an unfounded rumor that canned tuna did not retain its omega-3 fatty acid content following canning. Research linked the omega-3 fat found in fish to the prevention of heart disease. A UCLA scientist and a representative of the Massachusetts Institute of Technology (MIT) Sea Grant Program were assigned interviews in New York City, Boston, Washington, D.C.–Baltimore, and Hartford–New Haven (key tuna markets).

The American Dietetic Association conducts its media tours differently. It provides a corps of registered dietitian members in major metropolitan areas and outlying rural areas with media training. Public relations staff develop news angles, query the media in writing, make telephone follow-ups, and coordinate appearances. At the appointed time and place journalists meet the dietetic association representatives for an interview.

### Media Tour Logistics

Query letters for media tours are typically sent out to gatekeepers in all cities simultaneously and followed up in a few days with telephone contact. The query letter basically pitches the story and informs the gatekeeper the day(s) your spokesperson will be in the area. As with one-on-one interviews, practitioners send the query letter two to three weeks prior to the week the tour is scheduled. The exception is those shows that demand greater lead time. Placements are scheduled before the tour is initiated. Usually logistics and the physical strain of the day limit effective on-site interviews to four per day. Telephone interviews, generally for radio, are not as taxing and can be added to the daily agenda of the four interviews. Telephone interviews can also be offered as a contingency when reporters are unavailable during the alloted time periods. Contingency telephone interviews can be used for both broadcast and print media.

One organization separates its media tours by major and minor market classifications. The major markets are determined by the potential number of people reached. Major markets include greater Chicago, Indianapolis, St. Louis, Kansas City, Milwaukee, and Detroit. The minor markets are determined by regional criteria. They include Springfield, Topeka, greater Rockford, Des Moines, Madison, and Grand Rapids.

In each scheduled city, a major market media tour should result in at least one to two television placements, one newspaper interview, and two to three radio appearances. Minor market tours, because of limited competition for interviews, can result in significantly more interview placements.

### Media Tour Evaluation

Media tours can result in comprehensive coverage for a given product or issue. One way of evaluating their result and effect on behavior is to precede an advertising campaign with a media tour. One baking soda manufacturer wanted to launch a campaign to get backyard swimming pool owners to use baking soda as a water purifier. In five cities, the firm mounted a media tour before launching its advertising campaign. In another five cities, the firm conducted advertising without the media tour. Sales improved in all ten cities, but the five cities covered by the media tour sold significantly more product than those without.[8]

The practitioner will definitely want to track coverage by obtaining a print clipping service and a video monitoring.

### Added Benefits

One additional benefit of the media tour is in the relationships generated between media gatekeepers and good spokespersons. A successful interview can result in a spokesperson being called on to respond to emerging stories and as a source for reporter-generated stories. Establishing the spokesperson as a reputable source for reporters and talk show producers is a good secondary goal for media tour programs.

> Suppose you have been retained by Tony Roma's Restaurant, famous for barbequed ribs, to conduct a media tour in cities where the restaurant will open soon. One of those cities is Miami. Describe the steps you would take in arranging a media tour for Tony Roma's.

## PLACING EDITORIALS

An editorial in a newspaper, magazine, specialty publication, or television or radio station is generated like an interview. First, you must know the medium. Placing editorials requires a knowledge of the editorial policies of a medium. These policies reflect publishers' and senior editors' opinions. Most newspapers, for example, can be labeled conservative or liberal, Republican or Democrat. It would be highly unusual for the *Chicago Tribune* to support a conservative candidate; likewise, the *Chicago Sun-Times* would rarely support a liberal party candidate.

With a little study, it is not difficult to determine the editorial position of a newspaper. With partisan issues, such as politics or business philosophy, it wastes time to attempt to place editorials in those publications philosophically opposed to your point of view. However, still important for those who develop editorial positions is to understand clearly both sides of an issue.

Laudatory editorials are also written about nonpartisan subjects worthy of community recognition and praise: A new research facility opens in a community, a business restores an historic monument, a sports team wins a championship.

Though occasionally a small newspaper or trade publication might accept editorials written by public relations practitioners, most gatekeepers write their own editorials. A major metropolitan newspaper, for example, normally has a staff of editorial specialist writers; editorials for a smaller newspaper or trade publication are written by editors and publishers.

### Meet with Editorial Board

The best opportunity for all is a meeting with the editor of the editorial page or editorial board (a number of senior editors). At these meetings, spokespersons are given the opportunity to make their case, answer questions, and leave materials. With nonpartisan issues, supportive materials and a follow-up telephone call may be enough to generate a supportive editorial.

Nolte and Wilcox offer the following success story:

> A publicist who felt strongly about a public issue arranged a meeting with the publisher of the *San Francisco Examiner*. He asked for five minutes, presented the reasons why the *Examiner* should take a position on the issue and wound up with a front page editorial in every Hearst newspaper in the United States. The success was attained because the publicist had prepared a strong and well organized case which was in agreement with the basic editorial policies of the Hearst papers.[9]

### Seek Help from Beat Reporters

The best place to begin your investigation of editorial opportunities is to seek the counsel of the appropriate beat reporter. Ask such questions as, *Would the editorial board be receptive to such a position? What is the best way to approach them? Whom should we approach?* Sometimes a reporter is willing to approach the appropriate editor for you. If not, he or she can lead you to the right person.

### Write Query Letter

The query letter is the most appropriate way of beginning dialogue with a printed publication, television or radio station. The letter should be addressed to the editorial page editor, in major newspapers and magazines, or in smaller publications, the editor. Radio and television stations also take editorial positions but less frequently than the print media. A practitioner should find out which stations take these positions and which do not. Query letters should be addressed to the station general manager. Background materials that support your case are appropriate enclosures.

### Additional Editorial Page Opportunities

Many major newspapers provide a forum for opinion and observation from outside experts opposite the editorial page. An "Op-Ed" article is typically written by an outside expert on topical issues, current events, even holidays and humor. These newspapers frequently want exclusive rights for their area. Some require local authors. A national association, for example, can develop an Op-Ed article on an issue that concerns it and recruit local by-lines from members. A listing of newspapers carrying Op-Ed articles and their requirements can be found in the National Survey of Newspaper Op Ed Pages, Box 213, Saguache, Colorado 81149.

Letters to the editor round out editorial page opportunities. Organizations use these to set the record straight about a story or editorial that may have appeared. Letters to the editor can call attention to a particular issue or concern.

> Suppose you are the public relations director for St. Anne Community Hospital and want to place an editorial with your local newspaper and television station as part of a plan to launch a new chemical dependency center. What steps will you take to secure the editorial?

## SUMMARY

- ☐ Effective media relations begin with the identification of priority media and editors most appropriate to your audience and an assessment of their needs/concerns/interests.
- ☐ Generating a media interview should be initiated with a query letter, followed by a telephone call to the appropriate editor. Telephone first when the spokesperson has a breaking news story.
- ☐ The query letter should be a one-page, tightly written description of the news angle and spokesperson qualifications. The lead should be hard-hitting to pique the interest of the gatekeeper.
- ☐ The query letter should be sent a week or two prior to the interview. The exception is with broadcast shows requiring four to six week (or longer) lead times.
- ☐ The public relations practitioner should take leadership in providing organizational spokespersons with interview training.
- ☐ The spokesperson should clearly understand and agree with the communications outcome and assist in development of step 7 of the message/media outline.
- ☐ The media tour is a string of city-to-city media interviews for organizational spokespersons.
- ☐ The best way of initiating an editorial to present your case in a major newspaper is by written query to the editor of the editorial page and soliciting an appearance before the editorial board (composed of senior editors).

## EXERCISES

1 Assume you are the public relations director for Twinings of London, a major tea company. One Key Result Area in your public relations plan is to establish afternoon tea as a new meeting opportunity for American business people. Using the information in the news release in Figure 7–2, develop a message/media outline.

2. Assume television has been selected as part of your media mix. You have provided Samuel H. G. Twining with media training; he has helped you develop the message/media outline. You are impressed with his test market television appearances you have arranged. Develop an action plan and

TWININGS OF LONDON
*Established 1706*

Contact: Joan Magnuson
Bruce Friedman
(212) 213-9200

For Immediate Release

THE POWER TEA:

A REFRESHING ALTERNATIVE TO THE BUSINESS LUNCH

Tea, once the mainstay beverage of the leisured class in Britain, has captured the afternoon palate of American business people. More and more, as executives seek alternative ways to entertain business associates and clients, business meetings are being conducted in mid-afternoon over the subtle, yet brisk aroma and taste of tea.

Pleasantly removed from harried lunch crowds and comfortably free from the over-indulgence of rich dinners, business men and women structure mergers and acquisitions, review cases, publish novels, finalize advertising campaigns and take a moment to relax.

Mr. Claus Mennekes, Director of Food and Beverage at New York's Pierre Hotel, attributes this fashionable new business trend to greater culinary and beverage sophistication in the United States.

"Our afternoon tea clientele are not only those accustomed to the tradition, but also business executives who have found afternoon tea an interesting and productive time to conduct meetings," he noted.

Grossich & Bond, Inc./Public Relations
38 East 29th Street, New York, N.Y. 10016 (212) 213-9200

Courtesy of Grossich & Bond Inc./Public Relations

**FIGURE 7–2**

-2-

Other hotels such as the Mayfair Regent in Chicago, the Colonnade in Boston, the Adolphus in Dallas and the Westwood Marquis in Los Angeles, are reporting that a substantial proportion of their afternoon tea clientele is made up of business men and women conducting afternoon meetings.

According to Samuel H.G. Twining, ninth generation of the world-famous tea family and leading authority on tea, there are a number of reasons for the popularity of afternoon tea among the business community.

"Lifestyles today are more active," he says. "Many people are trying to stay away from heavy meals and, because they often have plans for after work, don't want to spend large amounts of time at lunch or dinner meetings."

"Afternoon tea is the perfect alternative for these executives," he continues. "A few finger sandwiches and a biscuit or two are just enough to take the edge off your appetite without adding too many calories. And, since most hotels set definite tea-time hours --usually 3:30 to 5:30-- it's easy to keep meetings to a reasonable length."

The custom of afternoon tea is usually credited to Anna, seventh Duchess of Bedford, who found she needed something to soothe her hunger pangs in the long interval between lunch and dinner. She had her cook prepare tea and thin slices of bread and butter around mid-afternoon to tide her over. Soon, her friends began dropping by

**FIGURE 7–2 (continued)**

-3-

and small cakes and biscuits were added to the menu. The idea caught on and all of fashionable London began taking afternoon tea before their daily promenade in Hyde Park.

Similarly, many modern executives find that afternoon tea is ideally timed to carry them through after-work tennis, running or exercise class. "Tea can pick you up after a long day," says Sam Twining.

Malcolm Forbes, publisher of Forbes Magazine agrees. "Whether for leisure or business, there is nothing quite as refreshing in the afternoon as piping hot pot of tea," Mr. Forbes commented.

While afternoon tea will probably never totally replace the business lunch, it is becoming a viable alternative meeting time for many business people. And as more hotels and restaurants begin offering tea-time, executives all across the country will be able to experience this rejuvenating pause.

# # #

**FIGURE 7–2 (continued)**

HOTELS SERVING AFTERNOON TEA

Atlanta - Ritz Carlton

Boston - Colonnade, Ritz Carlton, Parker House

Chicago - Mayfair Regent, The Whitehall

Dallas - The Adolphus, The Mansion on Turtle Creek,
Plaza of the Americas, Four Seasons

Denver - The Oxford

Detroit - The St. Regis

Houston - Inn on the Park, The Remington, Four Seasons

Los Angeles - Westwood Marquis, Sheraton Grand

New Orleans - The Royal Orleans

New York - Berkshire Place, Carlyle, Inter-Continental,
Pierre, Mayfair Regent, Plaza

Philadelphia - Four Seasons

San Antonio - Four Seasons

San Francisco - The St. Francis, Four Seasons Clift

Washington , DC - Four Seasons, Ritz-Carlton

**FIGURE 7–2 (continued)**

materials for a broadcast media tour of the top ten U.S. markets: New York, Los Angeles, Chicago, San Francisco, Philadelphia, Detroit, Boston, Washington D.C., Houston, and Dallas. Materials should include
   a. Query letter to stations
   b. Written suggestions for in-studio television visuals
   c. Rehearsal outline for spokesperson.
3. After reading an editorial about overconsumption of caffeine-containing beverages such as tea, Samuel H. G. Twining tells you to do something. How would you respond?

## REFERENCES

1. *PR Reporter*, November 9, 1982, p. 4.
2. Ibid.
3. Michael Klepper, *Getting Your Message Out* (Englewood Cliffs, NJ: Prentice-Hall, 1984), pp. 76–78.
4. Herbert Baus, "Publicity in Magazines," in *Lesly's Public Relations Handbook*, 3rd ed., ed. Philip Lesly (Englewood Cliffs, NJ: Prentice-Hall, 1983), p. 492.
5. Keay Davidson, *Los Angles Times*, May 5, 1985, pt. II, p. 1.
6. Klepper, *Getting Your Message Out*, pp. 126–135.
7. Ibid.
8. Ibid., pp. 91–92.
9. Lawrence E. Nolte and Dennis L. Wilcox, *Effective Publicity: How to Reach the Public* (New York: John Wiley, 1984), p. 214.

## CASE STUDY

### The Problem

Registered dietitians suffer from low public awareness of their roles as the nutrition expert on the health care team. The dietitian, in the traditional sense, counsels physicians' patients in a hospital setting on the modification of diet to manage disease. He or she also manages hospital food service. Increasingly, registered dietitians are opening private nutrition counseling practices and are dealing directly with consumers. Your state dietetic association wants to establish a higher profile for dietitians.

### Situational Analysis

The professional society of registered dietitians, which number 5,000 in your state, wants to increase public awareness for the registered dietitian as a provider of nutrition counseling. Its targer audience is the adult woman because she makes most health care, food preparation, and food purchase decisions for the household. A quantified personal interview survey, followed by focus group interviews of adult women, reveals a neutral to negative perception of registered dietitians. Too often respondents think of the registered dietitian as one who recommends salt-free, fat-free, taste-free menus to sick people. The dietetic association would like to use the current "wellness" trend to change the perception of the dietitian to one of a progressive health professional who can work with consumers to help prevent disease by dietary interaction.

Working on a shoe string budget, the association is mounting a public relations plan to try to do just that. One Key Result Area reads: To get women to contact a registered dietitian for answers to questions about diet and nutrition.

After assessing the situation, you recommend a media tour program whereby a cadre of articulate dietitians is trained to appear before the media to support the Key Result Area.

Assuming that research has shown that the primary motivation women have with regard to nutrition is a concern for the welfare of household members, complete a message/media outline to be used in the dietetic association campaign.

Next, complete an action plan, including objective(s), strategies, and action plan documents, for placing the dietetic association's spokesperson on radio and television talk and news shows and with newspaper interviews.

# CHAPTER 8

# Generating Publicity from Special Events and News Conferences

*IN THIS CHAPTER*

Special events and news conferences launch new ideas. Product introductions, positions on issues, political candidates, and organizational events are packaged to create public attention. The route to shifts in attitude and behavior frequently begins with the publicity generated from a special event or news conference. Such publicity places issues on the public agenda.

While the Olympic Torch Run or a news conference at Washington, D.C.'s, National Press Club may generate widespread attention, local ground breakings or introducing a new business to a community are more frequent occurrences.

Logistical details can make or break a special event or news conference. The event relies on the public relations plan to break down what sometimes appears to be awesome undertakings into manageable components. The message/media outline does the same for message and media considerations.

The message/media outline provides the framework for event packaging. Each element of the event should support the outline. Publicity is normally generated using a media memo that is designed to attract the attention of journalists (while preserving the integrity of the message); the press kit packages the message as news and provides materials to support its case.

*CHAPTER OBJECTIVES*

The reader will be able to

1. Describe how a special event or news conference utilizes the message/media outline.
2. Relate the logistical steps necessary to implement a special event or news conference.
3. Compare and contrast the impact of a special event or news conference with a single news release or publicity placement.
4. Write a media memo.
5. Define a contingency plan and how to use it.

## SPECIAL EVENTS: BIG CORPORATE BUSINESS

Special events and news conferences constitute a forum with potential for causing immediate high-impact exposure with target audiences. It is the "big hit" that can help launch a public relations campaign or add spark to ongoing plans.

Special events and news conferences are probably the best means for introducing a new issue, product, or organization or rejuvenating an old one. The special event or news conference can accelerate the agenda-setting process.

Whereas the news conference is typically a meeting called exclusively for the media, usually at a convenient centralized location to make some type of announcement or examine an issue, the special event attempts to attract participation by target audiences as well as journalists.

Special events have become big investments for corporate America. Nearly 3,000 companies spend more than $1 billion annually on special events sponsorship. Special events are enjoying a tremendous thrust in popularity, brought on by the successful corporate tie-ins at the 1984 Olympics, Live Aid, and Hands Across America.[1]

Corporations are not the only entities sharing in the benefits of special events. Mayors are using them to win votes, chambers of commerce to increase tourism, downtown merchant associations to increase business, and cultural organizations to raise funds and to expose large groups of people to their artistic message.[2] Pepto-Bismol has its chili cook-offs, Kentucky Fried Chicken has its gospel music festivals, Pepsi has its rock concerts, Rolls Royce has polo, and the city of Chicago has the Chicago Blues Festival.[3] Messages from these events will reflect mutual benefits for both participants and sponsors.

Successful special events usually bring together civic, municipal, and corporate bodies. Attendance is jeopardized when there is no civic involvement. Without the support of local government, there can be no street closings, park permits, sanitation crews, or police. And corporate funding is usually necessary to put on a top quality event.[4]

While special events are a rapidly increasing specialty in marketing departments and advertising agencies, this book, as a public relations writing and media usage text, will focus on the publicity side of special events.

> With what other corporate-sponsored events are you familiar? Which ones have you attended?

## PUBLICITY AND SPECIAL EVENTS

Major events can draw millions of spectators and thousands of reporters. The Brooklyn Bridge Centennial celebration in 1983 attracted 2 million people and nearly 1,000 journalists and support staff. The 1984 Summer Olympic Games also drew millions of visitors, 8,200 select members of the news media, and 2 billion television viewers.[5,6]

Interestingly, the U.S. Olympic Committee could not generate much enthusiasm from the national media for the Olympics held in Los Angeles until it launched one of the premier special events in public relations history: the eighty-two-day, 9,100-mile Olympic Torch Relay. Once the relay kicked off, the XXIII Olympiad became the most talked-about event in the United States. It remained on top of the public agenda through, and for weeks after, the "final burst of pyrotechnics" and was enjoyed by the largest television audience in history.[7]

In fact, the Olympics overcame a tremendous amount of negative exposure that had haunted it from the start. According to John Hansen, Los Angeles Olympic Organizing Committee public relations director:

> Years and even weeks before the games, news stories filled with all the bad things that could happen in Los Angeles during the Olympics were carried locally, nationally and internationally. The Soviet press hammered the hardest but media everywhere took on the issue.[8]

In the end, however, thanks to aggressive planning and execution, and some good fortune, the many predicted negatives—traffic problems, poor air quality, a crime wave—did not materialize. The planning became a model for future cities hosting the games. Los Angeles received extensive accolades for a job well done and became a prime example of how government and business can effectively work together toward common goals.

When Colonial Williamsburg hosted the Summit of Industrialized Nations in 1983, its leaders also had to address a number of risks when they made their action plans to increase local attendance and conference business. "There were probably more foreign dignitaries in this country than have ever been here before, except maybe for John Kennedy's funeral or the U.N.," said Al Louer, director of the press bureau. "The security plan was one of the most complicated in recent history. With the amount of publicity the conference would generate, if something went wrong public awareness might be of 'Williamsburg, the site of this horrendous disaster of a conference,' " said Louer.[9]

Their solution? "Literally nothing was left to chance," said Norm Beatty, Colonial Williamsburg vice president of media and government relations.[10]

These two examples represent some of the more glamorous special events, but events of every shape and size need ingenuity and detailed planning for success. Whereas organizers of major events have many anxieties, they have little trouble attracting attention. They are legitimate newsmakers. On the other hand, those charged with generating interest for building dedications and grand openings pray that a sufficient number of reporters attend to meet publicity objectives.

When Scripps Memorial Hospitals dedicated the Whittier Institute for Diabetes and Endocrinology in San Diego, it could have easily opted for a dignitary cutting a ribbon at the facility's grand opening. Instead, diabetic children provided a touching time capsule burial of the symbols of their disease (a vial of insulin, an empty syringe, a food exchange list) as a visual demonstration of what the facility could mean to the worldwide future of children with diabetes.

Think of a potential special event for the following situations: (1) a local landing strip expanding to become a municipal airport and (2) reorganization of a county zoo to house animals by continent instead of by species.

## THE NEWS CONFERENCE

Presidents of the United States are criticized for not having enough news conferences; public relations practitioners are frequently berated because they have too many. The difference between the two, of course, is that journalists want words from the president and that is not necessarily the case for the public relations practitioner.

The news conference is an opportunity to enhance an issue's importance with the media and ultimately the target audience. Collectively, newspapers, magazines, radio, and television are invited to one efficient convenient centralized site to face a chief executive officer making a major announcement that will affect the community, or interview an out-of-town scientist visiting a local hospital to share new research findings.

Unfortunately, the journalistic community is deluged with news conferences, many of which do not have the substance to warrant elevating them to this level of importance.

Public relations sages suggest that a news conference is not warranted if you can get the same impact with other techniques, such as one-on-one interviews with key reporters. The benefits of a worthy news conference, however, are plentiful. A news conference supports the immediacy criterion of news. It is an event. Consequently, chances of wire service coverage are increased significantly and competitive pressures can force reporters to deliver stories.

In the one-hour time span it takes to make a brief presentation (30 minutes plus a question period), you can plant the seed of an idea, which, if successful, can burst onto the public agenda with a barrage of stories in print and broadcast media, followed by a second round of local stories, followed by yet a third round of reporter-initiated articles, followed by coverage in the major magazines, followed by. . . . If a message is packaged effectively, it stays intact for the ride.

The American Society for Bone and Mineral Research's public affairs committee planned a Key Result Area to raise research funds to fight osteoporosis, a relatively unknown disease in 1980. The public relations plan was designed to make osteoporosis an important issue, to put it on the public agenda. A news conference was planned for the society's annual meeting in 1981 to kick off this Key Result Area. Research was presented by the country's leading bone and mineral scientists positioning osteoporosis as a disease as crucial to women as cancer or heart disease. The country's first prevention guidelines were introduced.

For two years after the news conference, the group's primary spokesperson received weekly calls from reporters worldwide. Tens of thousands of news stories appeared in a publicity mushroom that had its origin at that initial news conference. In 1984, the National Institutes of Health, a federal government agency that recommends public health policy and funds research, included osteoporosis in a series of scientific consensus conferences on important health issues, joining cancer, obesity, and heart disease. In 1985, the Osteoporosis Foundation was funded with approximately $1 million earmarked for education and research.

News conferences are not always that rosy. They are expensive and typically significantly risky. Even if you have a good news hook, you can always get passed over by a better one. The authors have had such experiences a number of times, including a health-related news conference the day the *Challenger* spacecraft exploded.

It takes only one conference with no journalist attending to demonstrate the risks involved.

### Media Availability

A compromise option is called the "media availability." What this means is that the practitioner trying to generate publicity for conventions, professional meetings, special events, or media tours can specify a period of time when spokespersons are available to talk to the media. Spokespersons are put on alert that they should be ready to be interrupted (from the meeting or event) between the hours of 10 and 11 A.M. in case reporters drop by and want an interview. If several reporters show up, then a news conference is held. If one or two arrive, then individual interviews are organized. If no one comes, then spokespersons go about business as usual.

Experience demonstrates that reporters appreciate the courtesy of making individuals available for interview during a certain period of time. Executives and public relations professionals are also freed of potential embarrassment in the event of a fast-breaking competing story in another part of town. And there is a time-saving factor as well because you are not forced to scramble around town to as many interviews as you would be otherwise.

Preparation on the part of the practitioner is the same for both the news conference and media availability. The level of anxiety, however, for both professional and participant is significantly lowered when using the media availability.

> Describe under what conditions a special event or a news conference would best achieve an organization's outcomes, and why?

## PLANNING THE SPECIAL EVENT/ NEWS CONFERENCE

Both the media event and the news conference are means of moving toward long-term end result objectives. It takes more than just one news story or event to move an audience to adopt a new attitude or behavior, but a successful media event can start the ball rolling.

Public relations professionals who consistently orchestrate successful special events depend on carefully detailed action plans with tasks, responsibilities, and timetables spelled out on paper. Special events can seem awesome if not broken down into manageable components. Carefully laid out action plan documents, like those described in Chapter 2, help to minimize such anxieties. Planning documents and frequent progress-against-plan meetings provide the practitioner with a detailed road map—tasks to be achieved, by whom, and when. This helps to avoid letting important tasks fall through the cracks (See Figure 8–1.)

### Start with the Message/Media Outline

The message/media outline questions should begin discussion at pre-event strategy sessions. Answers to the message/media outline questions should be documented in writing following pre-event meetings so all planning team members are working from the same set of expectations.

As you will remember, the message/media outline questions are

What is our communications outcome?

Who are our target audiences?

What are the needs/concerns/interests that individual target audience members share regarding our product, organization or issue?

What is the message(s)?

What are the most effective channels for reaching these individuals?

Who will be the most believable spokespersons?

What forum will be most effective for raising an audience need, concern, or interest and for offering our product, issue, or organization as a solution.

### Expand Outline for Visual Impact

Wally McGuire, of McGuire & Barnes, takes the process a step farther. McGuire, one of the country's leading media events experts, says that the intended visual impact of your message should also be carefully thought out during media event planning. He adds these additional questions:

What visual picture do you want the audience to remember from the event?

What headline or photo do you want to appear in the print media?

What picture do you want the television viewer to remember?

"People don't remember words as much as they remember pictures or visual concepts," said McGuire. "The electorate could not be expected to remember what Bobby Kennedy said when he mourned Martin Luther King's death in Pittsburgh but they could be expected to remember the picture of Kennedy reaching out to the crowds of Black Americans with empathy."[11]

Betty Ford served as a spokesperson for the dedication of a chemical dependency center at Scripps Memorial Hospitals for that very reason. She is not only widely recognized as the wife of a former president but as one who overcame chemical dependency and since then has dedicated her life to helping those suffering from alcohol and drug abuse.

McGuire cites the 1984 Columbus Day Parade in New York City, the day after a presidential debate as an example of prime media message positioning. "We wanted to demonstrate that the debate had instilled renewed support for the Mondale-Ferraro ticket," McGuire said. New energy, new life in what was a troubled campaign to that point was the visual concept McGuire planned to project to the American electorate through the news media.

Ten thousand signs and 20,000 balloons were placed in the crowds and reporters were *not* left to their own resources for covering the event. "A flat-bed truck was provided

KRA Place scientists' concern for increased use of vitamin/mineral supplements among U.S. women on the public agenda

OBJECTIVE By Dec. 31, increase concern for use of supplements among U.S. women by 20 percent

STRATEGY Conduct May 5 Washington D.C. conference

| ACTION STEPS | WHO RESPONSIBLE | SCHEDULED COMPLETION DATE | ACTUAL COMPLETION DATE | REMARKS (e.g., new opportunities or problems uncovered; key contacts discovered) |
|---|---|---|---|---|
| 1. Develop message and research potential angles/speakers | SL/KT | Dec. 1 | | |
| 2. Confirm dates/site/ logistical arrangements | GG | Dec. 1 | | |
| 3. Confirm co-sponsors | KT | Jan. 15 | | |
| 4. Confirm scientific panel | KT/SL | Jan. 15 | | |
| 5. Conduct conference call to confirm role of each panel member/ messages | KT/SL | Feb. 1 | | |
| 6. Complete news angles | KT/BM/GG | March 1 | | |
| 7. Develop graphic concept of message | AT | March 1 | | |
| 8. Set up travel arrangements for staff/speakers | GG | March 1 | | |
| 9. Call reporter "friends" to determine date conflicts/interest | GG/BM | Dec. 15 | | |
| 10. Call wires for potential advance | GG/BM | April 15 | | |
| 11. Call Post for potential advance | GG/BM | April 15 | | |
| 12. Update media lists | GG/BM | March 1 | | |
| 13. Send query letters to national broadcast news talk shows | GG/BM | March 15 | | |
| 14. Supervise printing of materials (press kits, letterhead stationery/news releases, envelopes, invitations | GG | March 1 | | |
| 15. Complete interviews with panelists | GG/BM | Feb. 15 | | |
| 16. Prepare monthly client progress reports | GG | 1st of each month | | |
| 17. Complete news release bios/photos on each speaker | GG/BM | April 1 | | |
| 18. Complete story for wire placement | KT | April 1 | | |
| 19. Obtain client/panel approval of materials | KT | April 15 | | |

**FIGURE 8–1**

KRA Place scientists' concern for increased use of vitamin/mineral supplements among U.S. women on the public agenda

OBJECTIVE By Dec. 31, increase concern for use of supplements among U.S. women by 20 percent

STRATEGY Conduct May 5 Washington D.C. conference

| ACTION STEPS | WHO RESPONSIBLE | SCHEDULED COMPLETION DATE | ACTUAL COMPLETION DATE | REMARKS (e.g., new opportunities or problems uncovered; key contacts discovered) |
|---|---|---|---|---|
| 20. Write and distribute media memos | GG/BM | April 20 | | |
| 21. Complete speaker graphic (charts, etc.) | AT | April 25 | | |
| 22. Begin telephone follow-up employing back-up media list for those uninterested | GG/BM | April 25 | | |
| 23. Complete conference logistics/staff assignments schedule | GG | April 25 | | |
| 24. Complete compilation of press kits | GG | April 25 | | |
| 25. Develop list of potential questions/answers | KT | May 1 | | |
| 26. Arrive in Washington | GG/BM | April 28 | | |
| 27. Meet with site staff | GG/BM | April 29 | | |
| 28. Complete media calls/personal meetings | GG/BM | May 5 | | |
| 29. Confirm conference on AP/UPI calendar | GG/BM | May 4/5 | | |
| 30. Arrive in Washington | KT/SL | May 3 | | |
| 31. Conduct speaker briefings to confirm schedule, messages and potential questions/answers from reporters | KT | May 4 | | |
| 32. Call radios for interest in phone interviews | GG/BM | May 4 | | |
| 33. Conduct staff meeting to run through news conference | KT/SL/GG/BM | May 4 | | |
| 34. Conduct news conference | KT/TEAM | May 5 | | |
| 35. Complete post-conference media calls | GG/BM | May 5 | | |
| 36. Man contact telephone number for incoming calls | BM | May 5 | | |
| 37. Messenger/hand deliver press kits to key no-shows | GG/BM | May 5 | | |
| 38. Prepare final coverage report for client | GG | Aug. 1 | | |

**FIGURE 8–1 (continued)**

for members of the news media and it preceded the candidates, Walter Mondale and Geraldine Ferraro, and New York Governor Mario Cuomo on foot," McGuire said. The newspaper headlines/photos and television coverage throughout the United States echoed his message. A good example came from the *Sacramento Bee*: "The Day After: Democrats Galvanized. NY Groundswell for Mondale. Debate Altered Reagan Image."

Interestingly, the parade grand marshall was the incumbent vice president, George Bush. Bush was virtually overlooked in event coverage.

> What benefits do you see in planning the visual opportunity versus waiting for it to happen spontaneously?

### Local Events Take the Same Thinking

Though the same thought process applies to media events large and small, a more frequent challenge for professionals is the opening of a new facility beyond having local dignitaries shovel dirt for the ground breaking or cut the big red ribbon.

Though community newspapers may occasionally publish the "shovel" ground breaking or "ribbon-cutting" photograph, it often takes more novelty for consistent success in publicity placements at sophisticated major metropolitan newspapers. Broadcast media are even more particular, as noted in Chapter 6. Novelty, in fact, heightens audience attention and motivation, especially when audience members expect a traditional or trite experience.

### Do Visuals Raise an Audience Need/Concern/Interest?

An equally important consideration to meeting media needs should be developing content to satisfy target audience needs/concerns/interests. Will those you want to reach—customers, donors, public officials—be attracted to the shovel or ribbon-cutting photograph? Is this picture enough to transfer your message to the real-life needs/concerns/interests shared by the target audience?

This is not to undermine such photographs as end results in themselves. Sometimes generating personal publicity for the boss or a major donor is important. If so, such a strategy should be identified when plans are laid.

### A Case in Point

It might be useful here to illustrate the use of the message/media outline in special event or news conference planning.

Assume you have been retained by the Bank of Brannan, a rapidly growing community bank in a prosperous area of the Florida Keys. With such rapid growth, bank officers have purchased a new bank site, and construction of a larger facility is in the works. They are concerned because such a move may jeopardize what research shows to be a primary point of difference between the Bank of Brannan and its larger competitors. The bank is perceived as having a "homey" personality with easy access to top management. This is viewed as a genuine strength in contrast to large, impersonal institution-type banks.

The move is six months away, but bank officers want to get started helping customers begin the mental transition to the new facility about three months before the move, culminating with a celebration-type special event.

Their fiscal objective is to move into the new facility without losing their growth momentum. Consequently, their objective is to increase the net number of customers by 20 percent the quarter following the move. In other words, to achieve this objective, any customers lost as a result of the move will have to be replaced with new ones.

As you and your staff begin to organize your thinking, you turn to the message/media outline. It is completed as follows:

***Communications Outcome.*** To increase the customer base following the move.

***Target Audiences.*** Existing and potential upper-scale customers.

***Audience Need/Concern/Interest.*** Special individual attention to banking needs by top management.

Friendly, intimate atmosphere
Easy access to top management
Unfamiliar with new location

***Message.*** Bank is moving to new location.

***Communications Channel.*** Special events/publicity generated.

***Spokespersons.*** Bank president and executive vice president.

***Message Packaging.***

NEED/CONCERN/INTEREST: Special attention to banking needs and easy access to top management will continue when the Bank of Brannan moves to its new location.

SOLUTION: Join us in a series of celebrations and see for yourself.

BENEFITS: Continued personalized consultative banking with new features like automatic teller machines, safe deposit boxes, more cashiers, less standing in line.

CONSEQUENCE: If banking relationship is discontinued, you will lose the relationship with the individuals running the bank.

MENTAL IMAGERY: The new location is across the street from the Blake Theater, the only movie house in the neighborhood.

With this as a base, public relations staff brainstormed the following scenario of special events. Keep in mind that the special event was only part of the transition plan. There were also advertising, direct-mail, and in-bank promotions.

1. Two construction milestone "hard-hat" receptions for community leaders, one at the halfway completion point and another the day the vault is installed.
2. A champagne reception for community leaders at the Blake Theater, with hard-hat walking tours of the almost completed facility, and ongoing showings of a new film in each of the five theater screens.
3. A week-long series of receptions, beginning on Monday, the week before opening, for various community groups, bank board of directors and friends, and customers.
4. A Sunday parade (school bands, clowns, children's groups) starting at the bank's existing location through town to the new facility, led by an antique armored car driven by the president and executive vice president with the oldest customer riding "shot-gun," and bank staff dressed in cowboy guard gear walking alongside.

A "summer in winter" festival on the grounds of the new facility following the parade with 10-cent hot dogs and cola, Dixieland music, hot air balloon rides, free bank visors, hourly drawing for a month of free movies at the Blake Theater, walking tours of the bank, and a finale drawing for free use of an automated teller card for five minutes. The charge would be to provide an old-time small town festival to reinforce the bank's "friendly" personality and primary point of difference. Local community groups would be solicited to set up food and game booths as fund raisers.

> How do you think the bank demonstrated points of difference between itself and its larger competitors by staging these events?

## ACTION PLANS/BUDGET

Once decisions have been made on the message/media outline, it is time to turn to logistical plans. Action plans similar to those described in Chapter 2 should be drawn to confirm staff responsibilities and deadlines for obtaining an event budget, date, site, event participants, invited guests, and the mass media.

### Developing a Budget

Special events can range in cost, including professional time, from a few thousand dollars to several thousands to millions of dollars. The public relations budget for the grand opening of the California State Lottery was approximately $1 million. While a local news conference might be pulled together on a shoestring, a national news conference can easily cost between $50,000 and $75,000.

Budgets should be carefully determined as action plans are developed. A line item budget that details where dollars are spent should be estimated with a 10 percent plus or minus contingency. The budget is only a projected (albeit carefully) estimate of costs.

Like anything else, developing a line item budget takes a good deal of research. It is much better to budget high than low. Practitioners tend to underbudget both hours and out-of-pocket expenses. This can be a serious offense. A far more uncomfortable position is to come in over budget than to come in below projections.

So what do you include in your line item budget?

For a news conference, standard charges include rentals of conference sites (hotel rooms, press clubs), audiovisual equipment ("press patch" or single microphone for several broadcasters and additional electrical support for television), and temporary telephone lines for direct dialing in and out. (Hotels charge exorbitant rates per phone call.)

Graphics and printing are a "big ticket" expense item. This can include original art for a news conference logo, stationery, envelopes, and site signage—podium sign, banner, directionals. Honoraria are often paid to presenters and, as such, must be budgeted. Photocopying involved with the development of press kits costs money and should be budgeted.

Long distance telephone charges (for media and spokespersons), travel, and lodging for out-of-town presenters can be significant costs. We do not want to forget postage and messenger service line items either. Hundreds of query letters and press kits are mailed to journalists in the development of a major news conference. Messenger services are necessary for delivering news releases and press kits to those who may have forgotten receiving them.

Last, but not least, charge for professional time. Even if you do not employ the services of an outside public relations firm, the time spent by internal staff should be projected with hourly rates attached (as described in Chapter 2). It is ridiculous to project cost for paper clips while suggesting by omission that professional time is worth nothing.

When a media or special event is planned, there are even more costs. Entertainment, refreshments, and city or county services all constitute expense items.

How do you determine projected cost for each of these items? Some guess but the risks of underbudgeting are too high. Prudent professionals call venders and get estimates of cost for each line item. Venders should follow up with written estimates.

Figure 8–2 shows an actual line item budget for a news conference; while Figure 8–3 shows an actual line item budget for a local media event.

> If you were a member of the planning team for a special event taking place at a newly constructed art center, what items would you include in the budget?

### Dates

Dates should be selected and checked against conflicts with target audiences, participants, and potential news media attendees from six months to a year before the event. Keep in mind for news conferences that days early in the week like Monday and Tuesday are the slowest news days working up to Friday, which is usually the heaviest day.

If, for example, your local Economic De-

ANNUAL NEWS CONFERENCE
ESTIMATED BUDGET

| | |
|---|---|
| <u>Program Development</u> | |
| Campaign (logo) identification development | $ 1,500 |
| News angle,message development | 9,500 |
| Printing (press kit covers, news release letterhead, correspondence letterhead) | 3,500 |
| Graphics (signs) | 500 |
| <u>Ambassador workshop, ADA meeting</u> | |
| Room rental, | 500 |
| Development of localized materials (including research, writing of fill-in-the-blank news releases query letters) | 3,500 |
| Travel/hotel/meals for agency personnel | 1,500 |
| Attend meeting, conduct workshop | 3,000 |
| Office expenses | 500 |
| <u>News Conference</u> | |
| Travel/hotel/meals for speakers/agency personnel | 16,000 |
| Speaker honoraria | 2,000 |
| Speaker dinner/briefing | 1,000 |
| Development of news angles, press kit materials, news releases, media queries and telephone follow-up | 21,000 |
| Evaluation | 2,500 |
| Out-of-pocket expenses (long distance telephone, xerox, postage, messengers) | 3,500 |
| | $ 70,000 |

**FIGURE 8–2**

Final Budget
October 1, 1985

**NST ESTIMATED SAN DIEGO LOTTERY EXPENSES**

Extravaganza Estimated Expense

| | |
|---|---|
| Three school buses | $ 630 |
| One Double Decker Bus | 216 |
| Event Insurance Rider | 500 |
| Bands/Musical Groups | 1,000 |
| Entertainers -- stiltwalker, mimes, clowns, jugglers | 1,250 |
| Photographer | 300 |
| Hudson and Bauer | 300 |
| Bear | 1,000 |
| Stage props & flowers | 2,500 |
| Jet Ski and Stuntman | 200 |
| Parking | 300 |
| Sound | 800 |
| Staging, media platform & electrical | 2,000 |
| Walkie-talkie's | 150 |
| Podium & press patch | 200 |
| Piano | 330 |
| Security | 1,500 |
| Medical | 500 |
| Chairs, tables & theater chain | 300 |
| Fire extinguishers | 100 |
| Banner & podium cover | 600 |

**FIGURE 8–3**

| | |
|---|---|
| Labor | 900 |
| Clean-up | 650 |
| Kiosks | 300 |
| PA system | 150 |
| Lottery ticket mounting | 200 |
| Lottery ticket display | 500 |
| Balloonatiks (500 balloons at Horton Plaza) | 116 |
| Production services | 1,000 |
| Contingency | 1,000 |
| NST Travel/Los Angeles, Sacramento, Imperial Valley | 500 |
| Out of Pocket--long distance telephone, overnight mails, courier, copying, postage | 800 |
| NST Fee | 25,000 |
| TOTAL ESTIMATE | $45,792.00 |

**FIGURE 8–3 (continued)**

velopment Corporation has selected potential dates for its annual news conference for financial writers, staff then begin checking for potential conflicts. Calendars are checked for holidays or religious celebrations. Reporters are called to ensure clear dates. Major meetings that could have an effect on potential speakers are also explored.

### Site

The proposed site is also an important variable. Hotels often book six months to a year or more in advance. Typically, two options for dates are secured with an event site before calls are made to potential speakers. Though the sites of most events are selected for target audience/media convenience, a retreat or special site can be used to lure attendees and participants. In fact, some local press clubs can be the preferred site for a quickly assembled news conference or interview.

Sites for special events have additional requirements: government permits and liability insurance.

The site selected must work with all logistics to make a media event successful. If you are working with a hotel, its management and staff must be clear on what you want. Too often the communication between those putting on an event and those expected to carry out the basic site logistics remains vague until the eve or day of the event. Personal visits should be made to the site and agreements with site staff clearly spelled out in writing. If contracts are negotiated, legal advice should be sought.

Basic logistical needs to consider for the news media include press rooms with direct telephone lines, typewriters, paper, and refreshments. A press patch and a sufficient number of electrical outlets are necessary for television stations. Logistical details should not be left until the last minute; some details, such as telephone or computer installation, can require several weeks' advance notice.

The question should continue to be: How can this site best contribute to the visual picture you want to project to the audience both directly and through the media?

McGuire, who orchestrated the Olympic Torch Run for the U.S. Olympic Committee and its sponsor, American Telephone and Telegraph Co., drove every foot of possible torch routes six times. Revisions were made daily to get the right kind of scenic backdrop for the runners who would carry the lighted torch from coast to coast.

"You shouldn't do a special event until first visualizing it through the eyes of a camera," said McGuire. "Our communications outcome was to raise a spirit of pride in the U.S. prior to the Olympic Games. If that runner was carrying the torch without scenery depicting 'America as a backdrop,' we would not have taken full advantage of the opportunity."

Olympic Torch Run sites that first week included the United Nations in New York City, Mystic Seaport in Connecticut, historic Boston, small-town America, West Point, Philadelphia, and Annapolis. Daily themes were established to draw in something for all Americans—from the big city to the seaport, to U.S. history, to the small town, to West Point, to Annapolis, to a blind man re-creating the run from the movie *Rocky* in Philadelphia.

Flat-bed media trucks, with broadcast outlets, preceded the runner and positioned reporters to best capture the visual outcomes McGuire had planned on his earlier dry runs. Television crews and print photographers were allowed to shoot only from the truck or the side of the road.

The point is this: An event site, whether it be the roads of America, a hotel conference room, the local press club, a shopping center, or a convention hall, can be developed to support the message and visual outcomes. Even a standard hotel meeting room can support such outcomes with the right kind of graphic treatment, especially with banners, an easel board highlighting the message, and podium and hallway signage.

> Think about the town in which you live. What scenic visuals could you create if you were using this town as a backdrop for the Olympic Torch Run?

## PRESENTERS

Once options for dates and a site are selected, then choose who will participate in the special event. Develop lists of potential presenters based on knowledge of the subject area and ability to present information effectively. The ability to communicate with an audience is crucial. If the speaker cannot get through to the audience, everyone's time is wasted. Some practitioners take this asset so seriously that they will not book a presenter without two endorsements from colleagues who have directly witnessed the presenter in action.

Presenters should be contacted three to six months before an event: some require even more lead time. Those most desired should be contacted first. If budget permits, presenters should be offered assistance with audiovisual materials: slides, charts, easel pads. Graphics, for example, communicate a technical message to a lay audience. Graphics also emphasize the visual message you want delivered. Add the benefit of helping the more technical presenter speak from effective slides. There is nothing more discouraging to an audience than having a complex subject presented with complex or unreadable slides. Chapter 10 deals more thoroughly with audiovisual materials.

Also important at this time is to agree with presenters on

a. Specific dates when biographies, 8 × 10 photographs, and abstracts will be sent to you
b. Honoraria amounts (if necessary)
c. Specific subject objectives and content
d. Time commitment expected
e. Length of presentation
f. Equipment needs
g. Graphic needs
h. News release interview date
i. Rehearsal dates

> What date, site, and presenters would be most appropriate for the Bank of Brannan's move to a new facility? How might you graphically support the visual message you want to project? What agreements are needed from the presenters?

The roles of those participating in the special event should be very clear, spelled out in the initial telephone conference and developed further in writing and, if possible, in person. This helps the participant to contemplate how a presentation can best support event outcomes. Speaker briefings should be held to explain outcomes and lay the groundwork for participants when they arrive for the event. Rehearsals are also a good idea that help ensure successful communications outcomes. So is developing potential questions and answers for presenters.

As explained in Chapter 7, presenters or spokespersons are experts in their fields; you are the communications expert. It is very easy to be intimidated by the kind of individuals you may consider as presenters . . . but do not be.

> What would you say to a potential expert speaker to get him or her to agree to participate in a rehearsal prior to the presentation?

## TARGET AUDIENCE/MEDIA LISTS

Preparation of lists of target audiences and media is next. Trade associations, professional societies, or community groups often provide their membership lists for a fee. One can also get this information from membership rosters. Media lists are developed according to target audiences from media source books, such as *Bacon's Publicity Checker*. However, names should be confirmed by telephone for accuracy.

## GENERATING ATTENDANCE

Nothing can be more nerve-wracking than conducting a special event or news conference with minimal or, what is worse, *no* attendance. You have flown in the corporate head from New York City expecting to see several hundred potential customers at your event, or you have an eminent scientist from the Mayo Clinic waiting for the flood of reporters to come walking through the door to hear about "earth-shattering research" and two, one, or no reporters attend.

### Attendees

We will address special event attendees and reporters separately here. First the attendees: Mail invitations six weeks in advance for any event. A second follow-up mailing, two to three weeks later, is often a good strategy. Publicity and, if you have the budget, advertising in media reaching those targeted for attendance also can be a good idea. Professional or trade periodicals, for example, often carry event calendars, a good way of alerting an audience to a coming event. Frequently, however, publication lead time requires notifying editors several months in advance of the event.

Not-for-profit groups can write and place public service announcements for radio and television and brief announcement releases for print media. Radio stations often sponsor community calendars to publicize such events. For-profit groups can sometimes take advantage of those outlets if the event is a public service, such as a health screening or educational seminar presented in the public interest and offered free or at nominal cost to consumers.

### Out-of-Town News Media

If the event is out of town or will take reporters away from the office for a full day or more, give reporters several weeks' written notice followed up by telephone queries of their attendance plans two weeks after sending the invitation. You will still have those who say, "I don't think that far in advance, get back to me the day before the event." However, you will cover your bases with those who appreciate the advance notice. The Dairy Council of California sends annual news conference invitations to newspaper food editors and writers, complete with comprehensive news slants and reply cards, six weeks before the event.

One area of controversy is whether or not journalists should be offered reimbursement for travel expenses for out-of-town events. The journalism community has come down hard on reporters and media representatives accepting gratuities. Most major metropolitan newspapers have policies against "freebies"; some medium-sized newspapers do too. However, many smaller newspapers are prohibited from covering such events if expenses are not reimbursed by the host. To offer to reimburse expenses is a sensitive issue. Disney World was chastised by journalists for offering to host expenses for its anniversary celebration. The decision regarding expense reimbursement is a delicate one that should be made on a case-by-case basis.

> How do you feel about offering reimbursement to media participants? Why?

### Local Media

For the standard news conference or in-town event, media memos should be mailed a week prior to the event and, even then, broadcast assignment editors rarely take it seriously until the day of the conference (or the day before). Newspaper city editors act the same way. However, specialty editors tend to appreciate the advance notice.

Local and national wire services provide daily budgets of local news events. Get your event placed on the budget of each wire service. This is particularly important for radio and television news and the city desk of newspapers. Simply send each wire service a media memo asking to be placed on the daily budget for the day of your event. Follow up early on the morning of the event to make sure it is there. If not, ask if it can be added.

### Writing the Media Memo

Writing the media memo inviting reporters to a special event or news conference resembles writing the query letter described in Chapter 6. Longtime publicity veteran Valerie Lemke says that the media memo—not the news release—is the most valuable form of written communications with newspaper editors and reporters, and radio-television news and assignment editors. "While the news release can provide space in the media it is usually treated as filler," said Lemke. "It is the news conference interview with a reporter or on-air conversation with a talk show host that provides the biggest 'editorial splash' and opportunity to move individuals to an intended action or behavior."[12]

The media memo piques interest in the event or news conference. A mental picture is painted for those who make decisions regarding who gets in the newspaper or on a broadcast news or talk show. It is one page, hard-hitting and matter-of-fact.

Successful media memos have common characteristics. First, they get your attention with a hard-hitting paragraph about why your event should be covered. Second, they read fast (short words and sentences). Third, they are contained in one or two pages. And fourth, they are sent to the right person.

The media memo for a New York City media availability began with the following paragraph: "New research from Massachusetts Institute of Technology (MIT) disproves widespread speculation that cooking and processing fish destroys beneficial omega-3 fatty acids, thought to prevent heart disease." Two additional paragraphs briefly described the study and the available spokespersons, and logistics were presented at the bottom of the page. (See Figure 8–4.)

In another media memo, for a Sail America Foundation news conference, the lead was as follows: "Dennis Conner, skipper of Stars & Stripes '87, the United States contender for the America's Cup, will be available to answer media questions at a final press conference Friday, Aug. 22, prior to his Sunday departure for Australia." Three additional brief descriptive paragraphs and logistical information were listed at the bottom. (See Figure 8–5.)

### Telephone Follow-Up

Although reporters frequently bemoan follow-up telephone calls, few practitioners can afford to omit them. You really never know whether a reporter will attend, regardless of what is promised on the telephone. Gained by the call, however, is the opportunity to pitch the story in person. Reporters and editors receive volumes of mail, and a practitioner can never make the assumption that because a letter was sent, it was read. In fact, about one-third of the follow-up calls are met with, "I didn't get anything on it. Tell me what it's about." It also will give you the opportunity to evaluate your angle. If you perceive from responses during the calls that your angle will not succeed, be flexible enough to create alternate approaches using the same message with a different angle.

> What do you say to a fellow staff member who believes that simply a media memo or a few calls are enough to get reporters to your news conference?

The Omega 3 Connection

# NEWS

Bumble Bee Seafoods, Inc.
P.O. Box 23508
San Diego, CA 92123
(619) 560-0404

Contact: Valerie Lemke or
Gretchen Griswold
(212) 883-1234
July 25 - 29
or (619) 296-0605
After July 30

MEDIA ADVISORY

New research from Massachusetts Institute of Technology (MIT) disproves widespread speculation that cooking and processing fish destroys beneficial omega-3 fatty acids, thought to prevent heart disease.

The MIT Sea Grant program tested five of the most commonly consumed fish to measure levels of omega-3 fatty acids, including canned tuna and breaded fish filets. The results point to inexpensive and more practical alternatives to fish oil capsules.

The MIT officer in charge of this study will be available to discuss the findings. Also available will be a UCLA lipid researcher who can sift through the health claims and outline the best omega-3 sources. Visuals provided.

EVENT: Presentation of MIT findings of Omega 3 levels of commonly consumed cooked fish

WHERE/WHEN: Monday, July 27, 1987, 10 a.m. to 11 a.m.
Room 1428, Grand Hyatt Hotel
Park Avenue at Grand Central Station

PARTICIPANTS: Arthur Clifton, project director
MIT Sea Grant Program

Judith Ashley, M.S.P.H., R.D., research associate
UCLA School of Medicine

# # #

Courtesy of Bumble Bee Seafoods

**FIGURE 8–4**

SAIL AMERICA
AMERICA'S CUP CHALLENGE '87
Sail America Foundation for International Understanding

(August 18, 1986)

Contact: Becky Russell
Valerie Lemke
(619) 296-0605

Media Memo

Dennis Conner, skipper of Stars & Stripes '87, the United States contender for the America's Cup, will be available to answer media questions at a final press conference Friday, Aug. 22, prior to his Sunday departure for Australia.

The conference is slated for noon at the San Diego Yacht Club.

The formation of the America's Cup in San Diego Committee to spearhead continuing fundraising efforts for the American crew also will be announced at the conference.

A public send-off for Conner will be held Saturday, Aug. 23 beginning at noon in Horton Plaza.

| | |
|---|---|
| Event: | Dennis Conner Final Press Conference |
| Date: | Friday, Aug. 22 |
| Time: | Noon |
| Location: | San Diego Yacht Club<br>1011 Anchorage Lane |
| Participants: | Dennis Conner<br>Skipper<br>Stars & Stripes '87<br><br>Malin Burnham<br>President<br>Sail America Foundation |

###

401 West "A" Street, Suite 615, San Diego, California USA 92101
(619) 262-1987 TELEX 257265 SAIL UR
FAX (619) 531-0160

Courtesy of Sail America Foundation

**FIGURE 8–5**

## PREPARING THE PRESS KIT

What goes in the press kit? Whatever it takes to make the case for the news hook and message in a digestable way for reporters. This means some spoon-feeding with background papers written for easy understanding, fact sheets to back up the message, news releases packaging the message to support the message/media outline, reprints of professional journals supporting your point of view, biographies and photographs of spokespersons, and artwork to help the message be visualized.

A GTE Sprint press kit for telecommunications and political writers in key states targeted for legislative public relations campaigns, following the deregulation of AT&T, included

- □ A background paper describing the history of telecommunications leading to deregulation.
- □ An objective situational analysis of every priority issue with potential for introduction as state legislation, including who traditionally supported the issue, who opposed it, and quotes from third parties representing both sides. This was followed by GTE Sprint's position on the issue.
- □ Outlines for editorials supporting the GTE Sprint point of view.
- □ A background paper describing the strengths and pitfalls of deregulation in other industries.
- □ Appropriate fill-in-the-blank news releases for use by lobbyists in key states.

A press kit for a Bumble Bee Seafoods series of media availabilities in key metropolitan markets included

- □ Reprints from the *New England Journal of Medicine* on the growing significance of the preventive effects of omega-3 fatty acids on heart disease.
- □ Reprint of an article from *FDA Consumer* describing a study of Greenland men who suffered significantly fewer incidents of heart disease because of their consumption of fish.
- □ An in-depth, easily understood background paper describing the state of research on omega-3 fatty acids.
- □ A dietary fat glossary of terms.
- □ Reports of comparison research by a private research firm and the Massachusetts Institute of Technology Sea Grant Program showing the omega-3 fatty acid content of the most commonly eaten foods.
- □ A news release from the Massachusetts Institute of Technology describing an additional research project demonstrating canned tuna to be among the highest sources of omega-3 fatty acids.
- □ Comparison charts of the omega-3 fatty acid content of the most commonly consumed fish.
- □ Cost comparison charts of the most commonly consumed fish.
- □ A series of sidebar news releases on regional tuna consumption, tuna sales, types of tuna, and consumption of fish oil capsules.
- □ A background paper on the history of Bumble Bee Seafoods.
- □ A background paper on how tuna is caught.
- □ A pamphlet Bumble Bee offered free to consumers.
- □ Omega-3-rich recipes.
- □ Food photographs featuring the richest sources of omega-3 fatty acids.
- □ Biographies and photographs of two university spokespersons appearing at the news availabilities.

Press kits are dispersed to reporters attending a news conference or media event. Material is packaged to meet the message/media outline. Press kits are also sent to those reporters who do not attend the event. Frequently, particularly in magazines, items appear from press kits delivered following an event.

Figure 8–6 demonstrates one press kit.

> Suppose your college athletic department was funded by a federal agency to conduct a physical fitness screening study for students. What would you put in a press kit organized for local media?

Courtesy of Bumble Bee Seafoods

**FIGURE 8–6**

### Graphics

Exclusive graphic treatment can add importance to an event. An event logo or title graphically represented visually supports the public relations message. Stationery, news release paper, notepads, invitations, signage, podium identification, banners hanging behind the presenter—all can add perceptions of importance to an event and contribute to making an event unique. Graphics should also be designed to project the intended message. Large easel cards should be created to tout key messages. Never use white placards because of the glare from the television lights; use colors like beige or light grey.

### Facilitating Message Coverage

Developing the news angles, piquing the interest of the media through the media memo, positioning the message in press kit news releases, backgrounders, and fact sheets and incorporating the message/media outline facilitate media coverage, help reporters project the message with target audiences while getting the best story possible.

Those who successfully orchestrate special events also make sure the media are logistically positioned to bring about planned message communications. When the Columbus Day Parade was organized the day after the 1984 presidential debate between President Reagan and challenger Walter Mondale, reporters could have just been invited to attend the parade and see the new, energized Mondale. Instead, however, a flat-bed truck for the media was positioned directly ahead of Mondale. The crowd was equipped with the right tools, thousands of signs and balloons. The special event was designed to support a visual outcome.

When McGuire traveled the Torch Run route over and over again, he organized routes around his visual outcome for the Torch Run, emotional patriotism. When he was faced with talking-head dignitaries who would light the torch to begin the run in New York City, he dramatized these talking heads by placing them in front of the United Nations building with two children from every country as backdrops. In every instance, a tremendous amount of thought and time was given to "looking through the eyes of a reporter and camera." If you want the media audience to get the message, then the reporter must get it first.

The orchestrator of any special event, from a health fair to a trade show to a press conference to a ground-breaking, can incorporate visualization and facilitate media coverage in support of planned messages—both visual and written.

When U.S. WEST introduced a cellular telephone system at a news conference, it constructed an electronic light board demonstrating the new technology. Such thinking separates the effective special event from that which is ordinary or uninteresting to the media or, more importantly, uninteresting to the audiences targeted for influence.

### Contingency Plans

Contingency or what-if plans are those that result from careful thought to every conceivable mishap that could occur on the day of the event. For special events this can mean anything from crisis plans to contingencies for inclement weather. A rodeo should be ready for animal rights protests; a grand prix car race should be prepared for every possible incident that could cause bodily harm to viewers.

For a news conference, it means written plans for what to do in the event of limited attendance by the media, or if your opposition in a controversy decides to disrupt your conference. At the very least, practitioners should prepare and rehearse answering a list of potential questions (with potential answers) for spokespersons, particularly the sensitive ones. One should assume that the most difficult and embarrassing question will be asked, so prepare for it. Figure 8–7 is a written contingency plan for a Washington, D.C., news conference organized for the American Dietetic Association.

April 29, 1986

To: NST STAFF
From: Kerry Tucker
Re: May 5 Contingency Plan

What if we hold a news conference May 5 and no one (or some one shows):

1. Conduct informal one-on-ones with moderator/ADA president and reporter(s) attending.

2. Kerry, Bev & Gretch huddle to agree on best telephone pitch to woo media and get message across. Bev to alert pre-determined messenger service for immediate distribution of press kits where needed.

3. Think through additional angle, and write and place new story if necessary.

4. Bev to call wires to make sure meeting was on the budgets of national and local wires. If it didn't make budget, we have a stronger reason for calling media for phoners and on-site interviews. At the same time, Bev pitches wire reporter of phone interview with moderator and/or ADA president. **The Message: Consume food before supplements; scientists concerned about long-term use of supplements.**

5. Gretch prioritizes radios and calls, in order of priority for phoners, grabs one panel member, if moderator and ADA president are tied up, and utilizes phone in press room. Provides speaker with 30-second pre-written message. **The Message: Consume food before supplements; scientists concerned about long-term use of supplements.**

6. Bev prioritizes television news operations and begins calls from press room to book moderator and ADA president for in-studio or visual interviews (thought through before conference, including potential sites) either today or a future date. **The Message: Consume food before supplements; scientists concerned about long-term use of supplements.**

7. Kerry grabs one panel member, but preferably the moderator or the ADA president -- whomever Gretch is not using -- and ushers he or she to phones for phoners to prioritized list of newspaper reporters. The other option is future interview dates for moderator and ADA president. **The Message: Consume food before supplements; scientists concerened about long-term use of supplements.**

8. Bev, Gretch & Kerry (if necessary) usher speakers to interviews.

FIGURE 8–7

> If you planned a news conference and prepared spokespersons for an all-out interrogation by reporters, but only two showed up, what would you do to save the situation?

## THE DAY(S) OF THE EVENT

The day has come for the big news conference or special event. Final details cloud your mind. Will the speakers arrive on time? Will there be time for last-minute briefings? Is there a need for one more rehearsal? Will the facility be set up as it should? Never assume that the staff of a facility knows what you want. Will the public address system work? Which reporters who have confirmed attendance will not show? Are contingency plans ready if reporters do not come? Has everything been done to help the media get the message that we want projected? Have we briefed our own photographers?

Probably the most important rule of any special event is: *Take nothing for granted.*

### Written Detailed Assignments Necessary

A last-minute detailed staff meeting should be held the day before the event and the first thing on the day of the event. Each staff person needs a detailed schedule of events, down to the minute, with assignments carefully laid out to ensure that all tasks have someone accountable for their success. At this staff meeting each individual briefs the entire team on his or her area of responsibility, leaving no area untouched. For example, a staff person must see that the room is set up as planned and equipment is in place. Audiovisuals and microphones should be tested an hour before the program begins. Another staff person should be responsible for last-minute media calls. Someone else should see that speakers are at the right place an hour before presentation time. Even if every detail is the job of one person, a written schedule of events should guide the workload, including every task to be accomplished, no matter how small. See Figure 8–8 for a sample of written action plans and assignment sheets.

### What to Do if Coverage Is Minimal

When coverage at a news conference is minimal, that is no reason to throw in the towel. It is time, however, to launch those contingency plans you have in your back pocket. These plans typically include at least four strategies:

1. A news release prewritten in the past tense, wire service style, as though you were covering the event for a newspaper. A lead in a contingency release written for a Bumble Bee Seafoods media availability reads as follows:

   > New York, NY (July 27) . . . You can get more omega-3 fatty acids, thought to protect against heart disease, in a can of white tuna than from the same amount of the five most commonly consumed fish, according to a study released here today.

   The contingency release should be hand-planted at local wire services and key media at your first notion that the conference could be a bomb or a key reporter is not present. A practitioner should follow up on the telephone within an hour of delivery offering a telephone or on-site interview.
2. Query radio stations, wire services, and newspapers for telephone interviews and television stations and magazines (and any others) for on-site interviews.
3. Begin distribution of press kits to key media with contingency release attached to the outside.
4. Have staff standing by the telephone that was noted on the release for incoming calls.

A large dental insurer wanted a fluoridation program it was offering to schools introduced at a press conference in the late 1970s. Dental scientists from the federal government, and American Dental Association officials were flown in from around the country. Rehearsals were made that day with everyone assembled at a hotel at the appointed

ASSIGNMENT SHEET

May 4 - 5

NEWS CONFERENCE

WASHINGTON, D.C.

**Tuesday, April 29**

10:15 a.m. Gretch and Bev meet at Salt Lake City airport, fly to Washington, D.C.

4:55 p.m. Gretch and Bev arrive in D.C., take cab to Shoreham Hotel.

5:30 Check into hotel, confirm rooms for other staff, panel members and task force. Cancel unneeded rooms and transfer into individual names.

Make sure hotel staff sends all "Pills" mail and phone calls to our suite. Make sure instructions are left for all staff shifts.

5:45 Call into Tucker, Long, Larry and Bill for update. (2:45 p.m., West Coast time)

6:00 Gretch and Bev prep for Wednesday meetings.

* * *

11:00 a.m Tucker and Long meet with Heber. Make sure all press kits, table tents, banners and any other graphics are on their way to hotel.

Tucker completes Sunday program and contingency (what if...) plans.

* Tucker/Long completes potential media questions and answers, panel summary statements (for Heber) and Heber/Owens outlines. Meet with Heber and pick up visuals.

* Tucker starts Al on visuals.

**FIGURE 8–8**

Schedule Page 2

**Wednesday, April 30**

Tasks for Gretch and Bev for the day include (with time as yet undetermined):

* Handplant media memo to major magazine, newspaper and wire service bureaus

* Meet with audio-visual staff of hotel to confirm the recording of Sunday night meeting

* Contact Jeanne Clark (Washington Dairy Council) for briefing lunch that day.

* Visit National Press Club and survey for further logistical planning. Confirm recording of conference with NPC engineer. Confirm refreshments for a.m.

* Confirm photographer (Fred Sweets, Washington Post) Determine if meeting is appropriate (Gretch)

* Confirm messenger service

* Begin follow-up calls
    1. FDA Reporters
    2. Health and Medical writers
    3. Food Press (In order of priority. If one uninterested, move to the next priority)

* Set up meeting with Jim Green, FDA PIO. In meeting, discuss best way to get message to MDs. Do they work with medical trades?

* Contact Chuck Woolsey (Gretch's network contact)

* Contact Bill Pieronnett (Gretch's Bates contact)

* Check in with Tucker, Long, Larry and Bill

**Thursday, May 1**

Tasks for Gretch and Bev for the day (with times as yet undetermined):

* Attend any meetings set up on Wednesday.

* Obtain "pills" visuals and write script for Heber to accompany demonstration

* Continue follow-up calls, resend memo where necessary (hand deliver where necessary)

**FIGURE 8–8 (continued)**

Schedule, Page Three

* Send two-page news release to BusinessWire to be carried on feature wire early Monday a.m. to attention of food editors (Gretch)
* Work with The New Leaf (hotel restaurant) to arrange Sunday night dinner for all persons involved (25 people)
* Determine local site to reproduce tapes after Sunday and Monday meetings.
* Develop questions and possible responses for speakers, with consideration given to questions asked during media calls.
* Survey catering selection and place order for appetizers and wine for Sunday at 7 p.m.
* Check in with Tucker, Long, Larry and Bill.

**Friday, May 2**

Tasks for Gretch and Bev for the day (with times as yet undetermined):

* Attend any meetings set up Wednesday or Thursday
* Continue follow-up calls, resend or hand deliver where necessary
* Make best effort to get on the budgets (skeds) for AP City Wire (833-5366), UPI City Wire (628-6621) and D.C. News (885-4249)
* Contact Jeannie Lessem of UPI, New York, if necessary
* Check in with Tucker, Long, Larry and Bill
* Leave notes with registration desk with Sunday meeting suite number and time. (Speakers, 3 p.m. including Charles Marshall. Other participants, 4 p.m.)

**Saturday, May 3**

9:00 a.m. Gretch and Bev relax; but continue to think about responses to potential "what if" scenarios, and additional media follow up if needed.

1:06 p.m. Charles Marshall arrives

FIGURE 8–8 (continued)

Schedule, page four

8:55 Tucker and Long arrive, check-in.

Later Evening: Tucker, Long, Gretch and Bev meet for drink, update.

**Sunday, May 4**

10:00 a.m. Staff meeting. Tie together all loose ends including confirmation of A/V arrangements and refreshments for evening meeting. Press kits are stuffed with additional materials. (To include reaction form, toxicity chart, ADA brochure)

10:02 Jim Marshall arrives in D.C.

12:00 p.m. Gretch confirms evening meal reservation

Tucker, Long meets with Dairy folks for briefing. Poses potential questions on dairy issue and rehearses answers.

2:00 Audio/visual sets up suite for recording.

2:30 Robert Heaney arrives in D.C.

3:00 Speakers, Long, Tucker and Bev meet in suite for briefing. Tucker hands out honorarium checks.

Victor Herbert checks into hotel.

4:00 Remainder of participants arrive for briefing.

6:00 Gretch checks on the New Leaf reservations, set up

7:00 Refreshments brought in (wine, beer, cheese)

8:15 Bev leads group to restaurant for dinner.

**Monday, May 5**

7:30 a.m. Staff meeting, suite

8:00 Gretch, Bev handplant wires with two-page release and press kit.

9:00 Speaker briefing, suite with catered continental breakfast

FIGURE 8–8 (continued)

Schedule, page five

| | |
|---|---|
| | Gretch to NPC to confirm and check on arrangments |
| | Bev make last-minute follow-up calls from NPC |
| 10:00 | Group takes cabs and/or rental cars to NPC |
| 10:15 | Bev situated to greet media. Gretch situated to direct media to NPC Newsroom. |
| 10:30 | Owen calls meeting to order, makes why we're here/ADA plans presentation. Owen introduces Heber who summarizes panel presentation, cites case studies, utilizes visuals and calls on MDs to begin reporting harm to FDA. Forbes explains reporting process. Heber opens group to questions and answers. |
| 11:00 | Bev and Gretch prioritize media no-shows and wrangle speakers after question and answer period slows down. Arrange for phoners, in-office media visits for speakers available to stay. |
| | Continue follow-up; hand deliver press kits where necessary. |
| 5:00 p.m. | Staff meets to determine if additional follow-up required. |

**Tuesday, May 6**

| | |
|---|---|
| 9:00 a.m. | Staff meeting, suite, to tie up loose ends and direct additional follow-up. Make Chicago (meeting with Phil White) and\or New York (media placements) arrangements if necessary. |
| | Continue follow-up. Hand deliver press kits where necessary. If speakers remain, continue phoner pitch. |
| 3:00 p.m. | Begin to check-out, settle accounts. |
| 5:00 | Depart D.C. for respective homes. Reset watches. |

**FIGURE 8–8 (continued)**

TO: Ron Kole, Sharon Levandovich

FROM: Kerry Tucker

RE: 12th Annual Press Conference Analysis

DATE: September 21, 1982

Sixty-three stories in 41 newspapers reached into more than 7 million California households from our 12th Annual Nutrition Press Conference. Of these, 28 (21 from McCarron and the rest from White and Beno) dealt with the need for more calcium in the diet. Fourteen stories carried four food group endorsements. An added plus were the 10 stories dealing with the affect of cutbacks on school lunch programs, including the special milk program -- a critical issue for the dairy industry.

Coverage on the importance of calcium in the diet almost doubled over last year's 16 stories. Four food group coverage was down slightly from last year's 16 stories. However, we think, that hitting at two critical issues facing the dairy industry--controversies over salt and school lunch -- more than made up the difference. It's our recommendation to continue providing forums for issues critical to the industry.

To put this year's coverage into perspective:

| Year | Papers Publishing Stories | Number of Stories | Impact Millions | Four Food Group Endorsements |
|---|---|---|---|---|
| 1982 | 41 | 63 | 7.1 | 14 |
| 1981 | 33 | 57 | 6.9 | 16 |
| 1980 | 24 | 47 | 5.9 | 22 |
| 1979 | 24 | 51 | 4.6 | 15 |
| 1978 | 26 | 51 | 5.5 | 24 |
| 1977 | 28 | 58 | | |
| 1976 | 24 | 64 | | |
| 1975 | 17 | 23 | | |
| 1974 | 19 | 32 | | |
| 1973 | 23 | 17 | | |
| 1972 | 9 | 14 | | |
| 1971 | 17 | 10 | | |

The following are our four press conference objectives and with one exception, we did very well with each:

1. Generate news for sound nutrition information backed by scientific evidence.

FIGURE 8–9

2. To reinforce credibility among homemakers for the four food groups as a method for balancing family foods.

3. To obtain at least one story in each newspaper represented at the conference.

4. To reinforce Dairy Council's position as a liaison between the scientific community, the news media and the consumer.

As far as we can see, two newspapers did not carry a story: The Ontario Daily Report and the Oceanside Blade-Tribune. As far as value is concerned the Chico Enterprise-Record story was virtually worthless. The Eureka Times-Standard piece wasn't much better.

The fact that Ontario, Oceanside and Chico carry our news releases (6, 18 and 10 respectively last year) probably justifies inviting them again next year. The Eureka Times-Standard, however, only carried one news release last year.

Heather Verville's problem appears to be her unfamiliarity with nutrition, judging from the following comment on her evaluation form:

"Speaking just for myself, a writer who enjoys covering nutrition and related topics yet who is not a full-time food writer, I found some of the material too technical. I realize this technical info is meaningful to some writers, yet I think even if I understood it, it would go over the heads of my readers."

There were others who had problems with the information being technical but most got through it in the small group interviews. We appear to be still pleasing the major metro newspaper reporters. The Los Angeles Times published three stories -- which has only occurred once before. The following comments are also worth noting:

"This was an unusually strong group of speakers. Very impressive and plenty of good information and story leads."

Marge Rice, San Diego Evening Tribune (two stories)

"Great topics this year. The entire program is so helpful and informative."

Jan Townsend, McClatchy Newspapers (four stories)

Our patience with McCarron paid off as he was far and away the most popular speaker and produced the most coverage of any speaker. His message also had the most benefit to the dairy industry. White

**FIGURE 8–9 (continued)**

and Derelian were given the next best marks in terms of presentation (from the evaluation sheets) and the rest were rated considerably lower. However, the White-Derelian team fell behind Calloway/Seltzer and Beno in the number of news stories. (Please see attached breakdown.) Though Seltzer was the biggest disappointment to us, it appears the Saltman/Scully team was the biggest disappointment to the reporters if those turning in evaluation forms are indicative of all the reporters who attended.

A surprizing number of the reporters who filled out evaluation forms say they would like to attend a nutrition education workshop. We're not sure whether they were just trying to be polite or they didn't know what we meant by a workshop or whether there is legitimate interest. Regardless, we should follow up, if we haven't already, with Shirley Boody, Heather Verville, Marge Gross, Verne Palmer, Jan Townsend, Barbara Burklo, Marge Rice, Janet Parker, Jan Molen, Pam Mattox, Carol Fowler, Mary Jane Scarcello and Rita Moran.

Too much food was again voiced as a complaint from reporters -- this time from four reporters. Evidently, a few of them got together and discussed it because the following recommendation showed up on two evaluation sheets: Skip the Thursday night reception and appetizers and have dinner early -- about 7 p.m.

There were some internal problems which appear to have frequented both this and last year's conference. The problems can be summarized by five words: poor utilization of hotel staff.

Some examples:

* Some editors were told they had to pay for their rooms at the front desk

* Some editors were given the wrong rooms

* Press kits which were scheduled to arrive in reporters rooms at noon didn't arrive in some cases until 6 p.m. or later

* Crown Room was holding dinner reservations for 35 Wednesday night and nobody came...

* Nutrition break for Friday was not scheduled for the right time and the hotel staff was not alerted until the break time...the punch arrived very late.

Other areas of discomfort included:

* The engineer failing to record Wednesday's proceeding

**FIGURE 8–9 (continued)**

* Inadequate instructions to engineer and, as a result, Saltman's slides weren't ready to go when he was

* Beno's slides and Seltzer's talk

* Tucker's rudeness to Beno about her slides/presentation

* Too much information in too short a period of time for speakers; every one was rushed to meet our schedules

Despite our internal problems, it was a good conference. In our opinion one of the best, in terms of content. In fact, for the first time, we heard that there was "almost too much news to cover."

This, to us, is the greatest of compliments.

**FIGURE 8–9 (continued)**

time. Not one reporter walked through the door.

Needless to say, it seemed like a lifetime passed for the public relations staff during that first half-hour wait for reporters. However, contingency plans were put into action immediately. Telephone interviews were secured for both radio and wire services. Media placements were arranged in five major markets during the three days following. In the end, the company received more coverage than it might have from the news conference alone. What first appeared to be a disaster was saved through the implementation of contingency or what-if-no-one-shows-up plans, which should be considered prior to conducting any news conference.

## EVALUATION

There are many ways of evaluating a special event. The first and foremost is whether or not strategies agreed upon in pre-planning sessions were utilized and objectives achieved. If not, why not? Were calendars and schedules followed and deadlines met?

Written evaluation forms may be provided to those attending. How did you do? How do you candidly feel about the event? What were the strengths and weaknesses? Where were the surprises?

One very important duty remains and that is your frank, written evaluation of the event, comparing performance against objectives and action plans. Outline strengths and weaknesses. Such an evaluation can be invaluable in planning the next special event, improving upon the weaknesses and taking full advantage of the strengths.

Evaluations should be written in a *formative* style, that is, for purposes of using the recommendations and suggestions in planning the next event or conference. Therefore, the summary report should specify what worked so it can be repeated and what did not work so it can be avoided. (See Figure 8–9.)

Appreciate the value of good planning and written plans but be flexible to opportunities as they arise. Once the event message concept is firm in the minds of event staff, encourage them to stay alert to new and better ways to project the message.

Your most important consideration should be the picture the audience will take home from the event. What headline or visual will best support that picture? Logistical checklists and written strategy have their place, but the end result is the effect your communication had on the audience. Did they remember the message? Did they believe it? Will they act on it?

## SUMMARY

- ☐ The special event or news conference is an effective means for launching an issue onto the public agenda.
- ☐ The message/media outline combines with detailed logistics plans to successfully orchestrate a special event or news conference that best supports public relations objectives.
- ☐ The most consistently successful use of visual opportunities is carefully planned, not spontaneous.
- ☐ Budgeting events demands careful investigation of costs and development of a detailed line item budget.
- ☐ The media memo is the tool used to generate special event and news conference coverage.
- ☐ Contingency planning guards against being unprepared for most unexpected crises.

## EXERCISES

1. Suppose you were retained by a hotel chain to reopen a historic hotel in your community that was due to be completely refurbished and open for business in six months. The public relations plan calls for creating awareness for the opening of the facility with potential customers.
   Develop the following:
   - ☐ Message/media outline
   - ☐ Action plan documents with dates/sites/presenters
   - ☐ Project budget
   - ☐ Presenter preparation

- □ Graphics
- □ Generating attendance
- □ Media memo
- □ What-if-no-one-shows-up plan
- □ List of materials necessary for the press kit
- □ How you will facilitate media coverage
- □ Schedule of events
- □ Evaluation

2. A large group of brand-new multicity 24-hour first-aid clinics have asked you which would be better for them: To try to have "a bunch" of announcement news conferences, one in each city, or to have their physicians placed on television to discuss first aid and their clinics. What would you discuss and advise them to do?

## REFERENCES


1. Robert Selwitz, "Special Impact with Special Events," *Marketing Communications* (May 1987), 58.
2. Lesa Ukman, "Special Events," *Advertising Age*, April 18, 1983, p. M-29.
3. Lesa Ukman, "What Works and What Doesn't," *Adweek*, Special Event Marketing 1986, June 17, 1986, p. 8.
4. Ukman, "Special Events," p. M-31.
5. John A. Fransen, "Public Relations Capture the Gold," *Public Relations Journal* (September 1984), 14.
6. Ibid.
7. Ibid.
8. Ibid.
9. Al Louer, *PR Reporter*, July 25, 1983, p. 1.
10. Ibid.
11. Wally McGuire, Personal Communication, Feb 1986.
12. Valerie Lemke, Personal Communication, June 1985.


## CASE STUDY

### The Problem

In the late 1970s, Scripps Memorial Hospitals began toying with a new concept: a community health education facility, off the hospital grounds, which would be dedicated to preventing the very illness that brought patients to the hospital. By mid-1980, a site at a nearby shopping mall was donated and plans for operating "The Well Being" were in the works. The hospital public relations team was called in to help design and orchestrate a grand opening to introduce this new concept to the community.

### Situational Analysis

The Well Being was founded on the assumption that Americans would continue their new quest for a healthier lifestyle. This being the case, Scripps Memorial Hospitals faced a tremendous opportunity to foster strong community relationships with healthy individuals before they were faced with hospital decisions. Two registered nurses would staff the facility during 9 A.M. to 5 P.M. workday hours with support as needed from hospital staff. Targeted publics included women because of their household influence on health-care decisions and senior citizens because their hospital needs were more immediate. A community survey revealed the health topics of highest interest, and ongoing classes in exercise, nutrition, weight reduction, pre- and post-natal care, and smoking cessation were planned at nominal cost to the consumer. Health screenings for conditions such as blood pressure and certain forms of cancer were organized. And presentations by hospital staff on timely medical issues were planned.

The Well Being was not without problems:

1. People were unfamiliar with the concept of a "wellness" store and had no idea what to expect.
2. The Well Being staff was concerned that because the center was sponsored by a major medical facility, the consumer might not perceive the facility as a center dedicated to wellness.
3. The location in the shopping center was in a remote lower level corner, immediately

adjacent to a for-profit exercise and fitness center.

Public relations Key Result Areas included generating awareness for the facility and its services among target audiences and keeping classes filled.

Develop a message/media outline(s) and a comprehensive yet tight-budgeted grand opening action plan supporting the two Key Result Areas, including objective(s), strategies, and action plan documents.

# CHAPTER 9

# Employee Communications

*IN THIS CHAPTER*

Employee communications programs can make relationships between the employer and the work force more effective if top management is willing to consider the employee need to be kept candidly informed about future plans and involved where a difference can be made in carrying them out. An effective program is not a panacea for problems, but with a genuine effort, it can help spot them early and hit them head-on at their most manageable time.

Too often top management thinks that the answer to improving relationships is to create an organization newspaper or hold a company picnic. Practitioners also are frequently driven to produce professional communications vehicles without adequate attention to the end results desired by their employers and the needs/concerns/interests of their employee constituencies. There is no relationship between the cost of a medium and its effectiveness. A monthly rap session or mimeographed bulletin can be just as successful as an expensive video news show.

Six steps are offered to develop or revitalize employee relations programs:

1. Assess organizational structure/identify audience segments
2. Secure written purpose/policies from top management
3. Develop plans
4. Develop message/media outline
5. Implement communications
6. Evaluate

While this chapter addresses an analysis of the strengths and weaknesses of employee media and offers media mix selection criteria and the message/media outline to implement the plan, the priority is on employee communications programs aimed at effective relationships that mutually benefit both the employer and employee.

## *CHAPTER OBJECTIVES*

The reader will be able to

1. Discuss how mutual benefit is employed in an effective employee communications program.
2. Outline each of the steps necessary to set up an employee communications program with the best odds for establishing an effective relationship between management and employees.
3. List the strengths and limitations of common employee techniques and criteria for making media mix selections.
4. Explain the importance of feedback mechanisms to an effective employee communications program.
5. Write a story for a company newspaper using the message/media outline.

## THE OUTCOME: EFFECTIVE RELATIONSHIPS

Developing and maintaining an effective relationship between employees and management should be the planned result of any employee communications program. Employee newspapers, newsletters, video programs, electronic mail, and face-to-face or computer-to-computer communications are only a sample of the means used to achieve this end result. Each and every technique should be carefully planned to enhance two-way communications between management and employees. Special attention should be paid to feedback mechanisms that seek out employee input.

### Meeting the Employer's Needs

A positive work environment has been associated in the literature with less absenteeism, less turnover, fewer accidents, less product waste, improved teamwork, and an internal constituency capable of supporting external public relations programs.

"The communicator is not going to design wide-scale systems for improving productivity." says Louis C. Williams, Jr., a former chairman of the International Association of Business Communicators (IABC). "But he or she can assure that the message of why productivity must be improved is communicated in ways that will assure it will be improved."[1]

Productivity improvement does not necessarily mean working harder, but it does mean working smarter. The practitioner must know and understand the issues that affect how employees feel about their jobs and why. Communications should appeal to emotions and minds to help bring about changes to improve the environment.[2]

An effective employee communications system can provide a framework for establishing positive relationships between management and its employees. It is not a panacea for problems, but it does help hit them head-on and act as a warning system to detect problems early, when they are most manageable.

The ideal organizational relationship is characterized by seven conditions:

1. Confidence and trust between employer and employees
2. Candid information flowing freely up, down, and sideways
3. Satisfying status and participation for each person
4. Continuity of work without strife
5. Healthful surroundings
6. Success for the enterprise
7. Optimism about the future.[3]

### Meeting Employee Needs

What employees want most from internal communications systems is to be kept informed about organization plans for the future, job advancement opportunities, job-related how-to information, and productivity improvement. So says a series of studies of Canadian and U.S. employees conducted by

IABC and Towers, Perrin, Forster and Crosby (TPFC). Human interest stories and personal news—historically the mainstay of employee publications—fall at the bottom of their interest level.[4] Employees also want a flow of candid and accurate information. According to these same studies, less than one-half think they are getting the straight scoop from employee communications vehicles, and two out of three say that official communications do not tell the full story.[5]

The surveys showed that employees would like more organizational news from the mouths of top executives. In fact, the most critical factor in job satisfaction, according to research conducted by Goodman and Ruch, is employee perception of top management. It is more important than salary, fringe benefits, job training, co-worker relations, and company policies and procedures.[6]

Employees are increasingly critical of their opportunity to provide input to upward levels of management. The fact is, listening seriously to employees is a relatively new phenomenon for most organizations. Sharing information with employees has traditionally followed the "need-to-know" philosophy—share only enough information to enable an employee to do his or her job. Listening to and sharing information with employees has not traditionally been taken seriously primarily because of its questionable effect on profits. But this is changing.

"Managers are beginning to understand that we do not have control over an employee's work commitment and productivity," says J. Bruce McCristal, director of worldwide employee communications for General Motors. According to McCristal, employees work at maximum levels, if we:

- Treat them with dignity and respect
- Share with them the plans, objectives, and problems of the business
- Involve them in the decision making and problem solving
- Recognize their membership on the team.[7]

The kind of attention that McCristal describes is not necessarily typical. To be successful, such an approach must have the blessing of top management: Corporate leaders must be convinced of the benefits of being candid and open about the direction of the enterprise. Being willing to let employees in on the competitive scenario is not always comfortable for executives. Many are more comfortable carrying company information close to the vest. Some fear leaks to competitors. Others use information to wield internal power and influence. To these, practitioners must be able to clearly demonstrate that benefits outweigh risks.

When two-way communication or a feedback system is initiated, top management must be prepared to consider seriously the input of its employees. To ask for input and not include it in the planning data base is worse than not asking for it at all.

"At a minimum, people in an organization should know where their organization is headed, why it has chosen to go that way, and what their personal role in the mission is to be," says Irving Shapiro, former Du Pont board chairman.

"Their feelings about these three matters must be solicited and considered. They must have the opportunity to contribute to policy formulation, even though the eventual final decisions still rest with management. But their sense of participation and support is vital."[8]

> Think of a work experience you have had. What employee communication took place? Was it successful or unsuccessful from your perspective as an employee? Do you think it was successful or unsuccessful from management's point of view? Why?

### Setting Up the Employee Communications Program

The authors advocate six steps in the development of a new or revitalization of an existing employee communications program:

1. Assess the organizational structure/audience segments.
2. Secure purpose/policies in writing from top management.
3. Develop plans.
4. Develop message/media outline.
5. Implement communications.
6. Evaluate.

### *Step 1: Assess Organizational Structure/ Audiences*

The structure and environment of an organization should be analyzed prior to establishing employee communications action plans. Two types of management systems seem to be prevalent in the United States. Although there are always exceptions and sometimes hybrids of the two styles:

1. The *open system* is composed of top managers who tend to be more comfortable with change. More opportunity exists here for establishing two-way communications between management and employees. Top managers speak candidly with employees and listen with the intention of responding to employee feedback.
2. The *closed system* is composed of a top management team more comfortable with top-down communications. Change is more difficult for these managers. They tend to want employees to adapt to their styles rather than negotiating and working with employees.

Research from James Grunig of the University of Maryland also categorizes organizational structures into two styles:

1. Highly structured environments with top-down management styles (similar to closed system)
2. Less structured environments with a minimum of top-down management styles (similar to open system)[9]

Identifying the type of organizational structure will help identify an acceptable system of employee communication. Within each of these structures, publics or segments of the employee population with similar needs/concerns/interests beyond simply sharing the work site can be identified.

A study of management and nonmanagement employees at two highly structured utility companies identified three publics in one organization and four in another, each with its own characteristics:

1. Management in both groups—most receptive of all groups to employee media, particularly hard news rather than propaganda.
2. Older, lower-level employees in both groups—do not care much about communications but like people news.
3. The dissatisfied, younger employees in one group—do not care much about communications but like people news.

The second organization share the first two publics but separated its younger employees into two separate categories:

a. More educated younger employees not happy with their organizational involvement but use company media to evaluate their future.
b. The less educated, younger employees dislike their work and the company and do not have much interest in the company or employee media.[10]

Three less structured organizations also identified segmented publics in another Grunig study:

1. Professional specialists—scientists, engineers, and researchers who passively process research information in the company media and spend little time using formal media.
2. Administrators—they too process rather than seek out information in company media.
3. Less educated support personnel—active seekers of employee information while processing research information.
4. Noninvolved public—care little about their work or the company.[11]

The more a practitioner can escape the notion that there is a "general public" in any public relations arena, the better. All organizations have segments of the employee population that can be clustered by needs/concerns/interests. Research can help carve out these segments for more effective communication. Such audience segmentation, based on common needs/concerns/interests, relates more to communications planning than simply the fact that employees share a work site. Consequently, employee communications can more easily transfer messages to real-life experiences and increase the probability for a more productive work environment through communications.

If the younger, more educated employees and management publics are interested in corporate goals and objectives, then their communications should be designed to answer that need. If the older, less educated employee is interested in the traditional esprit de corps information, such as employee activities and people news, then their needs should be met as well.

Though the trend in large organizations is toward tailoring media to the needs/concerns/interests of specific audiences, smaller companies are not always blessed with budgets adequate to fund separate media for separate audience segments. One option is to define content ratios for existing media. The front page of a company newspaper, for example, addresses the needs/concerns/interests of as many audiences as possible. The inside pages can carry sections tailored to specific audience segments. You can complement these ongoing publications with simple, inexpensive newsletters. Another option is to design face-to-face programs to satisfy each audience segment.

An initial needs assessment can help identify management philosophy and point to the communications program most suitable to the organization. Such an assessment can also identify segments of the employee population who share common needs/concerns/interests. Management, employees, and existing communications programs should be investigated prior to the development of an employee communications system. Top management and employees alike should be surveyed to determine answers to at least three groups of questions:

1. What does top management want from employee communications? Is it willing to be candid with employees about the direction of the company? How candid? Is it willing to share the good news and the bad? Is employee feedback encouraged? Does a formal system for collecting employee feedback exist? If so, how is the feedback used? Is it valued? If not, why not?

2. What are the employee population segments who share common needs/concerns/interests? What does each segment know about the company and its management? What doesn't each segment know? What misconceptions are held? How is information about the company received? What do employees think about the information they receive and the way they receive it? About what do they most/least want to know?

3. What are the current strengths and weaknesses of the employee communications system? Is it meeting the needs of management and employees? How can strengths be maximized and weaknesses be eliminated or minimized?

The result should be a clear picture of what senior management wants to say to employees, what employees want to hear and know, and how effectively the organization is communicating to meet those needs.[12]

Practitioners should call on professional researchers to conduct the investigation and help with the interpretation of findings. The role of the practitioner here is to formulate research objectives with the researcher and add interpretation to findings. An appropriate research methodology for a needs assessment may include three stages:

***1. Intensive Interviews with Senior Management.*** A series of one-on-one interviews is conducted with members of senior management, including the chief executive officer, chief operating officer, all other senior officers, and anyone else who can initiate or enforce corporate policy. The charge is to determine the corporate culture at the senior management level, their concerns, and the messages they see as key to winning employee understanding and support.

***2. A Survey of Employees.*** One-on-one interviews with an employee sample are ideal but can be expensive. Telephone interviews are also effective and can provide opportunities for probing for more information, but this method can be expensive too. Printed surveys with well-structured questions, either mailed to the home or filled out at the work site, can be effective if response is high enough. (See Figure 9–1.) Good response rates, 50 percent or better, with employee surveys are based on two factors:

a. An assurance of no negative repercussions from participation in the survey. An outside research firm reaffirms confidentiality.
b. A belief that participation in the survey will lead to change.

It is particularly important to test printed surveys. Response ratios are predictable. If 50 of 100 employees respond to a questionnaire, you can project that 500 of 1,000 employees will respond.

***3. A Review and Evaluation of Employee Communications Practice, Structure, and Materials.*** [13] The final research step is the review of existing organizational structure and communications vehicles, both formal and informal, to see how they compare and contrast to the expectations cited by senior management and employees. Such interpretation is completed by the professional research group with additional interpretation provided by the practitioner.

Such a needs assessment should identify or clarify

- Top management communications philosophies and goals in need of communications support
- Specific employee segments
- Needs/concerns/interests of each audience segment
- Data for the development of an information system that ensures that messages and information move efficiently in both directions.[14]

> Describe the benefits you see in conducting an employee needs assessment prior to launching an employee communications program or revitalizing an existing program.

### *Step 2: Secure Agreements on Purpose/Policies in Writing from Top Management*

Employee communications programs often include their own mission statement or written purpose as well as a set of written policy statements spelling out what the company expects from employee communications.

The needs assessment will provide the employee communications team with the realities of the organization. From that assessment, an employee communications mission similar to that found in Chapter 2 can be written: What needs does employee communications meet? For Whom? Where? How?

> General Motors combines both purpose and philosophy in its employee communications mission statement. The first half reads:
>
> "The mission of General Motors Corporation employee communications is to promote employee understanding of GM's worldwide business, GM's objectives and the individual's role in the corporation through continuing two-way communications systems. . . ."
>
> What needs does employee communications at GM meet? For whom? Where? How?

The GM statement in the box above continues with a philosophical description of how the purpose will be carried out:

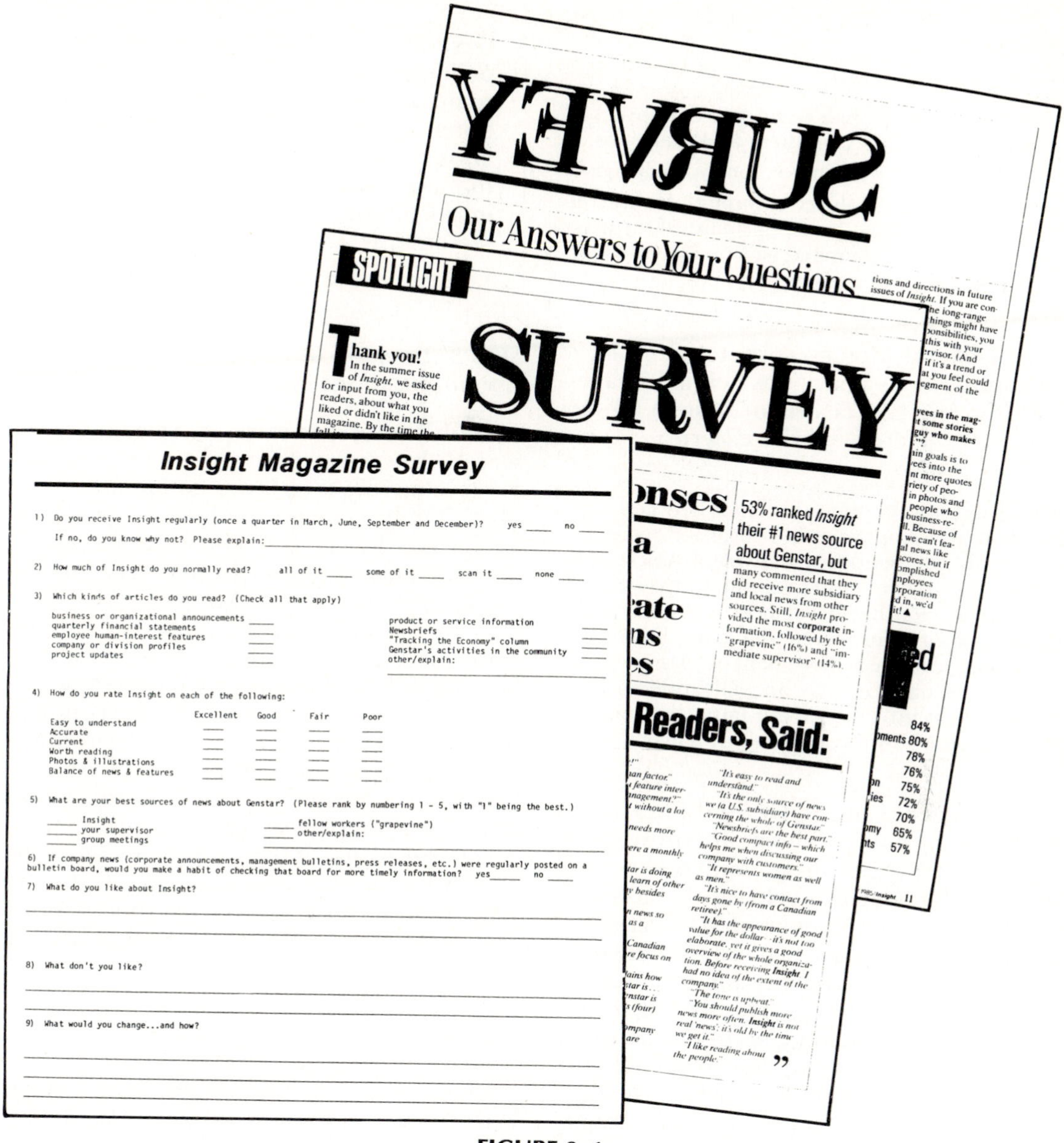


**Insight Magazine Survey**

1) Do you receive Insight regularly (once a quarter in March, June, September and December)? yes ____ no ____

If no, do you know why not? Please explain: ____

2) How much of Insight do you normally read? all of it ____ some of it ____ scan it ____ none ____

3) Which kinds of articles do you read? (Check all that apply)

business or organizational announcements ____
quarterly financial statements ____
employee human-interest features ____
company or division profiles ____
project updates ____
product or service information ____
Newsbriefs ____
"Tracking the Economy" column ____
Genstar's activities in the community ____
other/explain: ____

4) How do you rate Insight on each of the following:

| | Excellent | Good | Fair | Poor |
|---|---|---|---|---|
| Easy to understand | ____ | ____ | ____ | ____ |
| Accurate | ____ | ____ | ____ | ____ |
| Current | ____ | ____ | ____ | ____ |
| Worth reading | ____ | ____ | ____ | ____ |
| Photos & illustrations | ____ | ____ | ____ | ____ |
| Balance of news & features | ____ | ____ | ____ | ____ |

5) What are your best sources of news about Genstar? (Please rank by numbering 1 - 5, with "1" being the best.)

____ Insight
____ your supervisor
____ group meetings
____ fellow workers ("grapevine")
____ other/explain: ____

6) If company news (corporate announcements, management bulletins, press releases, etc.) were regularly posted on a bulletin board, would you make a habit of checking that board for more timely information? yes ____ no ____

7) What do you like about Insight?

8) What don't you like?

9) What would you change...and how?

**FIGURE 9–1**

In the interest of GM and its people, we will function as advocates of employee understanding by providing open, accurate and timely communication in a climate of mutual respect. To accomplish this mission, we will provide information, training, research guidelines, counsel and a means to measure specific communications action.[15]

Written policies and guidelines that spell out the needs/concerns/interests of both management and employees should also be developed. These policies or guidelines are in writing as a declaration from top management as well as a mandate for how internal communications will operate.

Some examples of policy statements might include

- □ We shall be the first to inform employees of information affecting them and their jobs.
- □ We shall tell the bad news along with the good.
- □ Clearance of employee communications content shall be the sole responsibility of the executive vice president and vice president of corporate communications.

At General Motors, corporate employee communications policy was defined in a letter from the GM chairman sent to all GM employees. Here is a brief excerpt:

> Effective two-way communications between management and employees is critical for success in our highly competitive worldwide business. The need for employee understanding, involvement and cooperation has never been greater—and a broad base of information about the business is fundamental to the achievement of all these goals. More than that, GM has an obligation to keep its employees informed about important matters that affect the business and their own livelihood.[16]

In another example, General Electric has the following policy with six supporting principles: "Over the years, employees have learned that they can rely on the accuracy of management statements, and this credibility is a valuable asset jealously guarded by all who bear responsibility for communication with employees."[17] The six GE principles include maintaining accuracy, avoiding exaggeration, separating facts from opinion, correcting misstatements quickly, avoiding inappropriate use of company informational materials, and clarifying the company interest in communicating on public issues.[18]

Statements of mission or purpose and policy for employee communications are best developed with top management as a participant. A rough draft of purpose and policy based on the needs assessment is a good starting point to receiving the commitments necessary from top management for an effective employee communications program.

> Describe how both the mission and policies described would help you manage an employee communications system. How would you go about getting agreements from top management on an employee communications purpose and policy statement?

### *Step 3: Develop the Employee Communications Plan*

With the first two steps providing a research data base, the practitioner is ready to develop the employee communications plan. (This process is fully described in Chapter 2.) Key Result Areas or goals are developed, and measurable objectives are outlined under each Key Result Area.

A Key Result Area that describes an outcome for improving employee morale would be followed by objectives for each employee audience segment. One objective might read: To increase awareness of corporate goals and objectives by 30 percent by December 31. Another might read: To reduce by 20 percent, employees who believe the statement: Feedback is not taken seriously at Richard James Co. by December 31. Action plans then spell out the tasks, responsibilities and completion dates for carrying out each objective.

### *Step 4: Develop Message/Media Outline*

Once plans are established, determine what it takes in both message and media to bring those plans to fruition. Simply put, messages describe what will achieve each objective; media selection indicates the means you will use to reach the intended audience. The message/media outline described earlier in this text for external audiences is also helpful in organizing communication for the employee audience.

The *communications outcome* is your link to the plan. That basic end result statement helps direct the development of the communication. Outcomes are simple end result statements reflecting Key Result Areas, such as improve teamwork, reduce employee turnover, cut absenteeism, or improve product efficiency.

*Clarification of audience* refers to segmenting the employee population. The employee needs assessment can be helpful in identifying employee segments that share commonality beyond working at the same site. One approach to segmentation is to cluster employees according to needs, concerns, or interests.

*Audience needs/concerns/interests* are identified by the needs assessment and by staying close to professional research such as the IABC study described earlier. Research, for example, may uncover a majority of employees interested in knowing more about future company direction, the views of top management, or concern that their feedback is not taken seriously. By addressing the priority needs, concerns, or interests of employees, you get the attention necessary for effective communications.

*Message statements* should be designed consistently to minimize what works against a positive work environment and to strengthen or accelerate what works in your favor. An employee needs assessment provides the best data base for identifying positive and negative forces in the work environment. If, for example, a large segment of the employee population does not feel the company takes employee feedback seriously (and in fact it does or wants to), then changing this attitude may be a priority objective. A message might read: Richard James Co. values employee feedback and incorporates it into company plans for the future.

Employee communications—feedback mechanisms, newsletter stories, one-on-one management briefings—can demonstrate the validity of this message statement by describing how employee feedback is gathered and used by top management. The message statement then is used, at least in concept, in each communication to employees.

Use of employee feedback can be incorporated into any number of company newspaper stories. Most issues can carry a story, photo, or illustration with a feedback slant. The statement itself can also be incorporated into each communication in a variety of ways. A story on corporate planning, for example, can carry a headline such as "Employees Have Input Into Top Management Planning Sessions." A story on a feedback mechanism can easily contain a quote from the chief executive officer on how and why the company supports and values employee feedback. A caption to a graphic illustration in the company newspaper can demonstrate the route taken from feedback to top management and back again.

A message statement, such as this one, is a part of an objective in the employee communications plan: To increase by 30 percent the number of employees who agree with the statement: Richard James Co. values employee feedback and incorporates it into its planning for the future by December 31.

Changes in how employees answer questions on pre- to postcampaign surveys validate program success or failure.

If employees do not believe they are kept well enough informed about the company's future, a message statement can be developed to make employees aware of one or two key corporate goals and objectives. Stories in the company newspaper can address progress compared to plans, issues with potential for affecting performance (e.g., energy costs, product waste, absenteeism, potential legislative or regulatory change, community pressures), and the role employees can take in accomplishing goals and objectives.

The GM mission statement makes message priorities easy to speculate. They could include:

1. Improve employee understanding of business problems and goals.
2. Increase employee involvement in problem solving and decision making.
3. Demonstrate cooperation among management, employees, unions, and other constituencies.
4. Improve the work environment for all employees.

Anheuser-Busch also focuses on providing employees with a clear understanding of company goals, how they are to be carried out, and the employee role in their accomplishment. Research also identified some additional employee needs, concerns, and interests: job security, government intervention, cost containment, and nurturing a family culture.[19] Employee communications at Southwest Bell Telephone also listens carefully to its employees, and following the deregulation of AT&T, Southwest Bell launched an education program to address divestiture-related employee needs, concerns, and interests.[20]

*Channels of communications* decisions are made only after message statements are developed. But this does not always happen. Too often employee communications planning starts first with the media. Messages are treated as casually as news stories. While that may be acceptable for a newspaper, the employee media mix has outcomes beyond journalism. The end result should be an effective management-employee relationship.

Employee media mix options may include a newspaper, magazine, magapaper (combination newspaper and magazine), newsletter(s), video news programming, annual report (print and video), bulletin boards, telephone hot lines, face-to-face and computer-to-computer communication, electronic mail, booklets, brochures, and more. Effective employee communications need not be this elaborate to be effective. The most important element is face-to-face, two-way communication. With that in place, a one-page mimeographed newsletter may be all that is needed for an effective media mix. The number of dollars spent is no indication of success in employee communications.

A brief overview of the strengths and weaknesses of some of the more popular employee media follows.

MAGAZINES: The strength of the company magazine is in its ability to examine and interpret thoroughly an employee issue with liberal use of copy, photographs, and illustrations. Consequently, its ease of readability and capacity to draw in the low-interest reader can work harder for each production dollar. The production quality of magazines also contributes to a longer life expectancy: Employees are not as likely to discard a magazine as quickly as they would a newspaper. Magazines are generally distributed monthly, bimonthly, or quarterly. Costs and production time are primary weaknesses. Little or no evidence suggests that the magazine is the most superior medium for moving employees to attitude and/or behavior change, though it may cost more. (See Figure 9–2.)

NEWSPAPERS. The typical employee newspaper provides the reader with a vehicle he or she is accustomed to: the daily or weekly newspaper. Though not as quality-slick as a magazine, the effective newspaper runs shorter, more timely articles, feature stories, and photographs at lower cost. Newspapers can also be produced quickly. The standard size is 8½″ × 11.″ (See Figure 9–3.)

MAGAPAPERS. The magapaper represents the employee communication industry's attempt to produce a newspaper/magazine hybrid. Though the quality of paper often remains less than that of a magazine, it is generally better than newsprint. Short articles combine with longer stories. Liberal use of photographs, illustrations, and white space eases reading. Distribution is similar to newspapers. The standard size is 8½″ × 17″ with a full-page feature photograph for a cover. (See Figure 9–4.)

NEWSLETTERS. Newsletters are one of the fastest-growing employee media, primarily because they can be computer produced simply at a very low cost and designed for specific segments of the employee population. Because it can be produced quickly, a newsletter can be newsier than most other media. The newsletter often supplements magazines, newspapers, and magapapers with varying distribution frequencies. The standard size is 8 ½″ × 11.″ (See Figure 9–5.)

Courtesy of Anheuser-Busch, GTE, and Bank of America

**FIGURE 9–2**

# DuPont News

Vol. 14 No. 9 October 1985

What is faster than *Du Pont News*, sent by computer, received in an 'electronic mailbox' and gives you a 5-minute digest of the latest company events? For answer, see back page.

**Posting 'News' at Moberly**

## Hazardous waste: Du Ponters make less

By Sara Garrison-Leo

If you make it, make less of it. This may seem to be a strange marching order in today's competitive atmosphere of increased productivity and higher product yields. But making less hazardous waste is the objective of Du Pont plants around the world as the company focuses on how it can better manage and even reduce chemical wastes.

Mobilizing the companywide effort is the Hazardous Wastes Advisory Committee, an arm of the corporate Manufacturing Committee. Four subcommittees are attached to the Advisory Committee, representing each department. The waste minimization subcommittee (with representatives from Agricultural Products, Materials and Logistics, Engineering and Chemicals and Pigments) is examining the amount of hazardous wastes produced at each site; establishing goals and cost-effective ways to implement them; and developing short- and long-term programs to guide Du Pont plant sites. A reevaluation of hazardous wastes practices, site-by-site, begins this fall.

According to Petrochemicals' Dick Cooper, vice chairman of the Hazardous Wastes Advisory Committee, Du Pont established a corporate policy

*Continued on page 3*

*As a vital first step to controlling wastes, Cape Fear plant employees instituted a carefully monitored system of labeling, storing and transporting waste in these red drums, prenumbered and issued only by the plant. Inspecting drums are senior engineer Bob De Haas (left), and hazardous waste handler Charlie Justice.*

*Listening intently to farm customers to meet their needs has been a hallmark of Du Pont field representatives. Next year, Agricultural Products' marketing force will have a good story to tell, too, as Du Pont prepares to launch the largest number of new crop protection products ever commercialized by a major corporation in a single year.*

## Woolard: Affirmative action continues momentum

*Vice Chairman Edgar S. Woolard Jr., who headed the corporate Affirmative Action Committee (AAC) for the last 17 months, looks at recent accomplishments and future pathways of the committee.*

**Du Pont News:** What is the most significant happening in affirmative action now?

**Edgar S. Woolard Jr.:** I believe that overall, we are making good progress despite ERO, the depressed business climate, and shifting government policies.

We made a significant step forward recently with the formation of two new AAC study groups composed largely of women and minorities to examine two important issues — child care and communications. We sought employee input and we got it. We recently reviewed the results of some fine work by these panels.

**Du Pont News:** Can you give specifics?

**Woolard:** I'd be pleased to. First, let's discuss child care. The group surveyed employees at four Wilmington area sites and found, as we suspected, that we had pushed an employee "hot button."

Although less than 2% had an interest or preference for company-sponsored, on-site child care, many want Du Pont to help promote community-based programs. (See companion article.) More than 25% of all Wilmington area employees use some form of child care, and about 70% of all employees with children under 13 use some form of child care outside the home.

The study group recommended that the company demonstrate community leadership regarding child care issues in the corporate headquarters area by working to upgrade state regulations and to improve the quality and availability of child care services. Also recommended was the creation of a community-based agency that could assist parents with finding needed child care services. There has already been progress in both areas. As one example of community leadership, Dale Wolf (group vice president in Agricultural Products), who was the group's adviser, was named by the governor of Delaware to a new State Commission on Work and the Family. The company also contributed $35,000 in seed money to start up a new child care resource and referral service of the Delaware United Way.

What we have learned from this project may be applicable to sites outside of the headquarters area, and we intend to make the group's findings available.

Second, the communications study group, with Nick Pappas (group vice president, Polymer Products) as its adviser, made recommendations that gave us a candid review and frank perceptions of affirmative action progress and problems. They deal not only with communications and the perceptions that employees have, but also with upward mobility, mentoring, training, counseling and the role of the Affirmative Action Committee itself. We are actively considering all of the recommendations and, in fact, will be implementing some training and upward mobility recommendations near-term.

**Du Pont News:** What is the company's overall track record on affirmative action?

**Woolard:** Since 1975 we have in-

*Continued on page 2*

*"Equal opportunity is good business practice as well as good social policy."*

Edgar S. Woolard Jr.

1

Courtesy of DuPont

**FIGURE 9–3**

*A Breath of Fresh Air:*

## Rainier Adopts Smoking Policy

The health hazards of cigarette smoke have led Rainier to adopt a policy that affects the one aspect of our work place that we all share: the air that we breathe.

The new smoking policy, which will make Rainier a smoke-free environment in September 1986, is being implemented out of concern for employees' health and comfort.

According to John Mangels, president, the policy reflects the company's concern for the overall health of all employees, both smokers and non-smokers. "We are committed to ensuring a healthy and comfortable environment for all," he said.

"We realize that this policy could cause a hardship for some smokers," said Don Summers, head of the Personnel Division. "However, the negative effect of cigarette smoke cannot be ignored. Rainier owes its employees the best work environment possible."

The smoking policy will be im-

*Continued on page 2*


# VENTURE

**September 1985**

**For the people of Rainier Bancorporation**

*The company's new smoking policy will improve the air quality at Rainier and ensure that employees work in a healthy, comfortable environment.*

Photos by Preston Spencer

Courtesy of Ranier Corporation

**FIGURE 9–4**

# Management Report

Southwestern Bell Telephone

Volume 42, Number 50
December 17, 1985

## FCC adopts lifeline guidelines to provide greater assistance

The FCC has adopted a Federal-State Joint Board recommendation for broader lifeline assistance measures to help low-income households afford telephone service.

Under the plan, the commission proposes waiving the $2 subscriber line charge, which will become effective June 1, 1986, provided each state matches the reduction by a

## Statue restoration donations reach $25,000 matching limit

Contributions to the Stat of Liberty

Volume 4
Issue #1 1985

# Management PERSPECTIVE

## A-B approaches computers, oh so deliberately

Frank notes that over the past three years, 118 projects have been approved as pa pany's Off

In addition, the company is testing the use of personal computers at the vice presidential level in one subsidiary, developing applications for use in various department functions, such as project control, budgeting, follow-up monitoring and other business-related functions.

Yet another facet of the Office Effectiveness Program is a loan program, wherel

# Management Newsletter

## New Automated Loan Appr Service for Dealers Tested

BankAmerica Payment Services and Glob sumer Markets together are testing an au loan approval service for automobile deal new service, being tested at two auto deale the San Jose area, provides approve/decl sions within two minutes on contracts to automobiles. These contracts are sent by co the bank.

"Using computer equipment they alread their offices, dealers call a bank telephon and establish on-line connections with approval service," explains Steve Yotter, Information Services. "To receive a decisi keys into pre-formatted computer screens us the contract information. We then resp approve, decline, or review message."

When the new service processes a con lows the same steps as the current manu scores the application, obtains a cr report if the application meets the mi ing requirement, checks the credit re the contract for consistency, and searc tive credit information.

In some cases, the creditworthiness of will be borderline. When that oc receive a message that the contract i ated manually. Financial service offic automatically when a review is ne most instances, they can make an a decision within minutes.

Two advantages of the new service can use equipment they already hav have to fill out paper loan applicati financial service officers at the Sa Consumer Loan Center have on-l contract information entered by d credit reports on the applicants. Us

Bank of Ameri

# PARDON OUR DUST

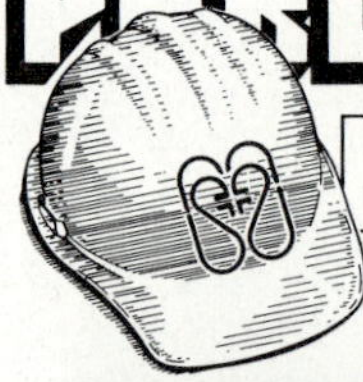

## A Construction Update published for employees of Scripps Memorial Hospital, La Jolla

NOVEMBER, 1985

*Progress continues on the expansion of Radiation Oncology. When it is completed, the new Mericos Eye Institute will be built on top of it.*

## EXPANSION, RENOVATION UNDERSCORES COMMITMENT TO HIGHEST QUALITY CARE

After seven years of careful planning, our La Jolla campus expansion and renovation now begins. Over the next four years, the blueprints and architect's renderings will be turned into reality.

The results will make us proud.

We willhave a new, expanded main lobby, emergency room, outpatient surgery center, and a new wing for operating rooms and critical care units. Also planned is a new health education facility.

Already under construction is the expanded Radiation Oncology building, and above it, will be new quarters for the Mericos Eye Institute. When that construction is completednext year, Radiation Oncology will feature the most advanced equipment in San Diego County. Its high-energy linear accelerator will dramatically

(cont. on p. 4)

## FROM MARTIN BUSER, ADMINISTRATOR

These are exciting times at Scripps Memorial Hospital. We are beginning a major renovation and expansion of our campus that will allow us to remain one of the finest facilities in the country.

When the dust settles we will be working in an environment especially created for us to continue providing the highest quality medical care available.

Hand-in-hand with your expertise, the improvements to our hospital will enable us to expand our excellent 60-year tradition of service.

Each of you are most important as we launch ourselves into health care of the 1990s. That is why your needs, your likes and dislikes, your comfort and well being in the work place are important factors in our expansion planning.

I think you will be delighted by the ongoing results and benefits of this construction. Each phase of construction is planned to keep inconvenience temporary and to an absolute minimum.

To keep you informed on the latest progress, we have created this special newsletter. It will be issued on an as-needed basis. Each issue will feature a campus map that shows you where construction is taking place and what it means. It is designed to keep you fully informed on expansion.

A most important part of future issues will be a question and answer section. Any question you may have on any phase of expansion is most welcome.

In order to get your question and its answer in the next issue, you may call any of the staff in Hospital Administration at Extension 6100. Tell them your question and they will forward it to me for an answer. You may also write your question down on paper and send it via interoffice mail. Send it to "Construction Update" and route it to Hospital Administration. I will review your questions with our engineers and consultants and give you a complete answer in a following issue.

I invite you to also share any expansion information with hospital patients and their families. Feel free to give them a copy of the newsletter and share the exciting things that are happening on our campus.

Thanks for your support as we begin a new era at Scripps Memorial Hospital.

Courtesy of Scripps Memorial Hospitals, Bank of America, Anheuser-Busch, and Southwestern Bell Telephone

**FIGURE 9–5**

According to IABC, 31.5 percent of organizational publications are magazines, 12.5 percent are newspapers, 8.5 percent are magapapers, and 39.5 percent are newsletters.[21]

AUDIOVISUALS. Corporate video is a growing employee media choice. Research shows it to be particularly effective at reaching younger employee audiences who grew up watching television. Both sight and sound contribute to its ability for high-impact communications and for transferring organization news into real-life scenarios for employees. Corporate video uses include regular newsmagazine shows (weekly, biweekly, monthly), annual reports, and teleconferencing. The primary weakness is expense. To be credible, employee video productions must be comparable in quality to commercial television productions. This takes sophisticated equipment and personnel trained in broadcast technology. Another potential weakness is that those involved tend to get caught up in the technology, often at the expense of the message.

TELEPHONE HOT LINES. This medium can complement regular media with daily news recordings into which employees can dial. They can also provide feedback to employees seeking company answers to questions. Constant promotion is required because the employee receives no information unless he or she recognizes the telephone as a communication device.

BULLETIN BOARDS. Among the most often used company media are bulletin boards. Information can be disseminated within minutes; and when careful thought is given to its physical appearance, content, and location, the bulletin board will be widely seen and read. Progressive employee communicators treat bulletin board programs with the same serious planning as publications and corporate video. Content and design support the message/media outline.

FACE-TO-FACE COMMUNICATIONS. Face-to-face communications is now recognized as the most effective and most desired employee communications tool. Increasingly, employee publics are calling for more interaction with supervisors and decision makers. According to the IABC and TPF&C surveys cited earlier, most employees want to hear more organization news directly from top executives, though nine out of ten still prefer their immediate supervisor as their primary information source. The top sources are, in order of preference, immediate supervisors, group meetings, and top executives.[22]

Face-to-face communications systems are a growing phenomenon among progressive companies. Informal meetings, group lunches or breakfasts, group rap sessions with corporate officers, or question and answer sessions with supervisors are among the most frequently used vehicles.

> Briefly, in your own mind, describe the purpose and use for each of the following: bulletin boards, telephone hot lines, face-to-face communications.

## CHOOSING THE MOST EFFECTIVE MEDIA MIX

So how do you choose the most effective media mix?

The employee needs assessment will again give you a data base for what is and is not working. You will find out which employees read the company newspaper, who read it cover to cover, who passively digest it by skimming headlines, subheads, photos/illustrations, and captions, and who do not read it at all.

### Needs of Public

Certain channels may be more effective than others at reaching specific employee population segments. If younger employees are more receptive to messages received from video news programming or face-to-face communications, then these techniques should be considered in the employee communications media mix. If older employees are more receptive to internal newspapers, then they too should be considered in the media mix.

### Cost/Budget

Cost also enters the decision-making process. A great truth in internal communications is that there is no relation between the cost of a medium and its effectiveness.[23] An important point to remember: A mimeographed bulletin or monthly rap session between supervisors and workers can be just as successful as an expensive video news programming system. It can also bomb if it meets no real-life needs/concerns/interests of employee population segments. Traditionally, practitioners put too much emphasis on technique. Communications techniques should not evolve on their own but, rather, should stem from careful thought, analysis, and planning for the best means of delivering the content.

Like the budgeting process described in Chapter 8, an annual line item cost estimate should be written for each strategy used to carry out an employee relations objective. Line items for an employee newspaper, for example, might include research, concept development, layout, writing (time plus expenses), photography, graphic illustration, printing, and distribution. Included in all line item budgets should be a 10 percent plus or minus contingency clause in the event costs change. Calls to the proper venders will help establish realistic costs.

### Timing

Timing is also a criterion. If a manufacturing plant is issuing employee layoff slips in four hours, you cannot wait for next week's company newspaper to explain the situation to employees. The situation demands immediate action. Face-to-face briefings from supervisors are usually best for issuing immediate news. Face-to-face communication can often avoid the obstacles a communicator has in obtaining authorization for *written* materials. If immediate authorizations can be obtained, then a one-page instant-printed newsletter or bulletin or a spot on a daily telephone hot line are good supplements to the face-to-face vehicles.

### Matching Message to Medium

Suitability of the message to the medium sometimes comes into play as a criterion for media mix selection. An annual report or news program on video can often be more effective than printed words in a newspaper in helping individuals picture corporate leaders as human beings or seeing for themselves how a change in the work situation affects them personally. There are also instances where print is a better fit. Briefing employees on a proposed city ordinance that could affect company performance, for example, might be better placed in the company newspaper where employees can read it thoroughly at their leisure or keep as reference in the event of questions and answers from neighbors and friends.

### Feedback Mechanisms

Feedback mechanisms should also be a consideration for selecting the employee media mix. Another word of caution: If an organization asks employees for their input on productivity improvement or absenteeism, it should take that input seriously.

For employee communications to be two-way, formal feedback mechanisms must be in place. Practically speaking, feedback mechanisms add interest, credibility, and acceptance to the media mix. Response to feedback must be fast and honest and must protect the source from harm.

"People want to know that they're important and that the work they do is valuable," says Ray G. Foltz, TPF&C vice president. However, according to the IABC/TPF&C survey, less than one-half of U.S. and Canadian employees think that employers act on their ideas.[24]

Foltz believes that upward communication should mean more than simply giving employees a chance to comment on subjects or issues about which they would like to hear. "It also means openly seeking their opinions and giving them the opportunity to comment on or question anything related to the organization and their jobs. . . . They [employees] believe that the people who do the work are the ones most likely to know how to improve their operations."[25]

Feedback, according to Roger Feather, is at the very heart of human, sophisticated management systems. It is also at the heart of the new demands of persons in the workplace and society, in general. "That demand is for individuals to be heard and to be recognized," says Feather.[26]

Feedback programs can be formal or informal. Examples of formal programs are climate surveys, readership surveys, confidential response mechanisms for airing questions, problems, and opinions, open forums where employees can receive answers to questions (face-to-face communications), advisory committees, and ombudsmen. On the other hand, any communicator can do his or her own minisurveys, set up publication letters to the editor, establish listening posts or individuals within the organization who know what is going on, tune in the grapevine, or set up suggestion systems or telephone information systems. (See Figure 9–6.)

Face-to-face communications is the best feedback mechanism, but a very difficult one. Not all executives or supervisors are comfortable with their interpersonal communication skills, especially when responding to criticism. There are not always answers to employee questions. Executives and supervisors should be provided with training in communication skills to develop their ability to successfully communicate with employees.

Selecting the spokesperson can also be a strategy for minimizing restraining forces. The IABC research indicates that employees want to hear more from chief executive officers. Immediate supervisors are also viewed as highly credible sources. And one should not forget about outside experts and employees themselves. The key questions are: Who has the expertise? Who is the most believable?

Raising an audience need, concern, or interest and offering the organization as a solution is the last step—prior to communicating to employees. Specific message statements can position the organization as a solution to an employee need, concern, or interest. If employees are concerned about feedback mechanisms, then the organization can demonstrate both its value for employee input and how it incorporates feedback into the planning process.

If employees are interested in knowing the future of the company and how it affects them, then campaigns can be designed to demonstrate how they can best support the company in achieving those goals and objectives (e.g., less absenteeism, less product waste, improved teamwork).

The consequences of not acting on appeals to improve the work situation can be addressed as well as helping employees think through how to do their part to improve the situation.

The key here, as in all communication, is in involving employees in decisions that affect them.

Employee communication is a primary element in providing employees with involvement opportunities for the benefit of both the employee and the employer.

> Imagine yourself an employee of a large corporation. From your own preferences, which medium or combination would you find most informative and useful?

### *Step 5: Implementation of Message/Media*

Now it is time to develop the message vehicles to communicate the priority messages identified.

#### Get Professional Design Help

The design of the selected vehicle—be it a newsletter, newspaper, or video news show—should be developed by profession-

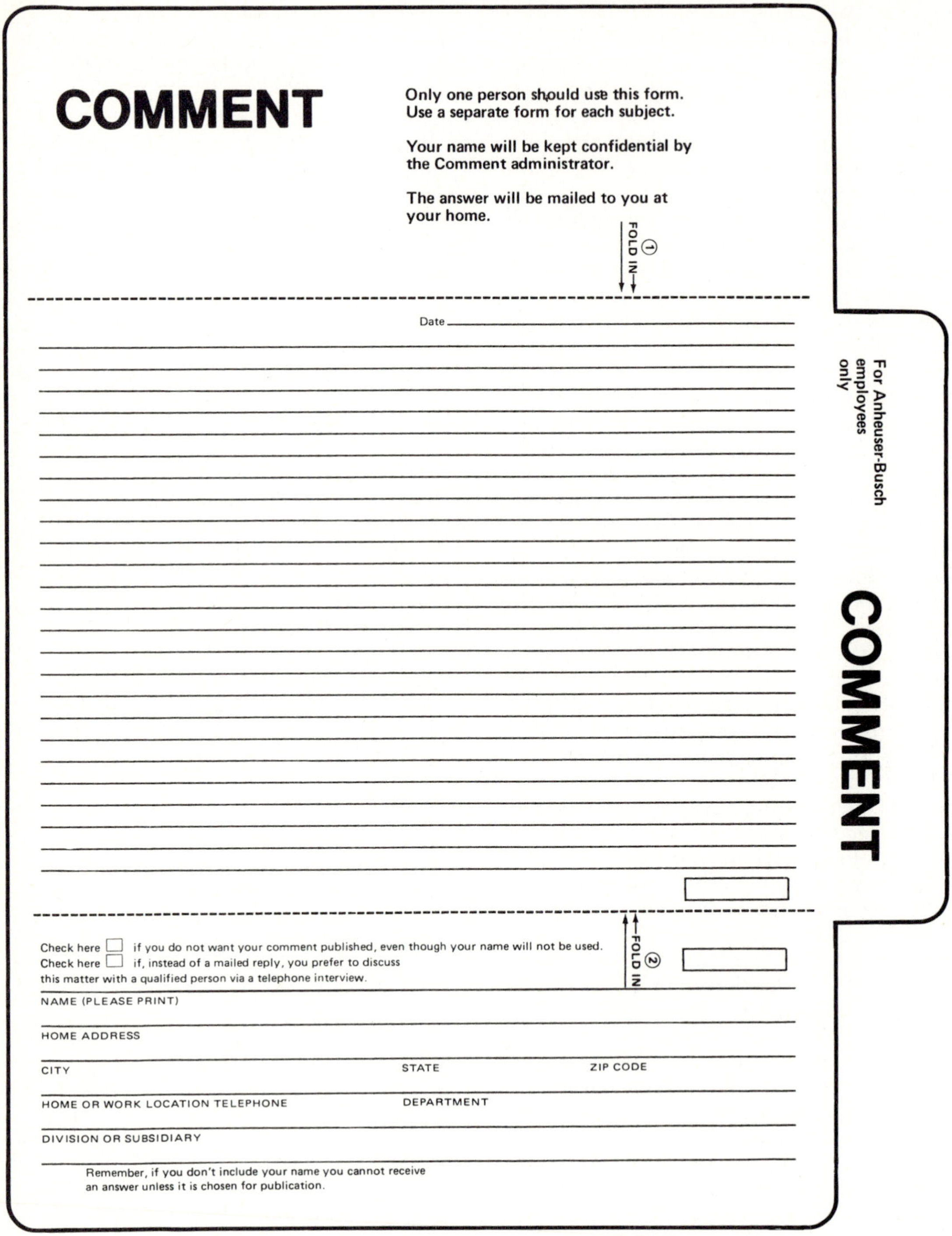

COMMENT

Only one person should use this form.
Use a separate form for each subject.

Your name will be kept confidential by the Comment administrator.

The answer will be mailed to you at your home.

① FOLD IN

Date ______

② FOLD IN

Check here ☐ if you do not want your comment published, even though your name will not be used.
Check here ☐ if, instead of a mailed reply, you prefer to discuss this matter with a qualified person via a telephone interview.

NAME (PLEASE PRINT)

HOME ADDRESS

CITY STATE ZIP CODE

HOME OR WORK LOCATION TELEPHONE DEPARTMENT

DIVISION OR SUBSIDIARY

Remember, if you don't include your name you cannot receive an answer unless it is chosen for publication.

For Anheuser-Busch employees only

COMMENT

**FIGURE 9–6**

als. Few practitioners carry credentials in professional graphic design or television production. Program design, or packaging, is crucial to drawing the audience into the medium. Even the simplest newsletter should enjoy professional design so that it can compete with all the other information sources an employee sees and hears in everyday life.

Graphic artists should be called in to discuss how the medium will achieve the planned objectives. The size of the publication and columns, type style, use of photographs and illustrations, masthead design, and how short and long stories are graphically treated for readability are among the recommendations a graphic designer can make to draw the reader's attention.

Have a graphic artist design each issue of the publication if possible. Printing companies often employ artists who provide this service. Graphic illustrators are also found in public relations and advertising firms and as private consultants.

Even a budget-strapped employee communications program should seek out professional design help for the first issue. Cost can be amortized over a year's worth of monthly newsletters, for example, making cost appear more reasonable. A designer not only can develop a layout for the first issue but can also provide a number of layout options for future issues and design guidelines for the editor to follow. The use of a professional to assist in design and production is especially true for audiovisual presentations.

Some firms generate graphics for all types of communication tools using in-house computer hardware and software. Professional help should nonetheless be called in to design the format so that the graphics does not overshadow the message just because it is so easily created.

### Identifying Content

With the format of the medium designed, the practitioner can turn to the development of communications or stories to deliver the priority messages identified.

Management can be surveyed annually to determine publication or video news ideas for communicating the priority messages identified. These ideas can be incorporated at a team brainstorm session held to collect content for six months' or a year's worth of communication. But these ideas must be coupled with the needs/concerns/interests of the employee population.

The message/media scenario bears repeating:

If management wants a more productive work environment, then it should package its communication to satisfy employee interests, employee needs, and employee concerns. If one employee population segment is interested in the future direction of the company, then a company newspaper story can capitalize on that interest with a story on company goals and objectives and position the company to satisfy that interest. If an organization needs to conserve energy, then this same audience can be brought into the situation with a story demonstrating the role energy conservation plays in the achievement of company goals and objectives.

A message/audience matrix can be helpful in developing program content. With messages across the top of the matrix and employee audiences listed along the left-hand side, story ideas and techniques can be matched with message and audience. (See Figure 9–7.)

### Information Sources

The next step is to develop a list of company information sources. To develop a story on a segment of the strategic plan, who do you call to get further interpretation of the intent of an objective? If your plan calls for a number of stories to support an employee safety objective, who is your best source of information? How about energy conservation? Cost control? Affirmative action?

Senior decision makers in these areas are your best resources. Develop a list, recruit their participation either directly or by delegation, and get them involved in your program. Use them as story idea generators.

| PRIORITY MESSAGES → | COMPANY GOALS/ OBJECTIVES | PUBLIC ISSUES AFFECTING COMPANY | JOB ENVIRONMENT | EMPLOYEE ACTIVITIES | PEOPLE NEWS | EMPLOYEE FEEDBACK |
|---|---|---|---|---|---|---|
| STORY IDEAS → | Spot News: CEO Announces 3rd Quarter Results<br><br>Update: Energy conservation campaign | Spot News: City Council to Annex Parking Lot<br><br>How will Proposition 8 affect you? The Company? | Features: Where to go for Benefit Information<br><br>"That's my Job" employee profile | Photo Essay: Families enjoy Company Picnic | Jones Elected President of Downtown Rotary | Spot News: "Employee Ask" Columns<br><br>Employee input aired at top management planning meeting |
| EMPLOYEE AUDIENCE SEGMENTS ↓ | | | | | | |
| Management | X | X | X | X | X | X |
| Older, lower-level employees | | | X | X | X | X |
| More educated, lower-level employees | X | X | X | X | | X |
| Dissatisfied younger employees | | | X | X | | X |

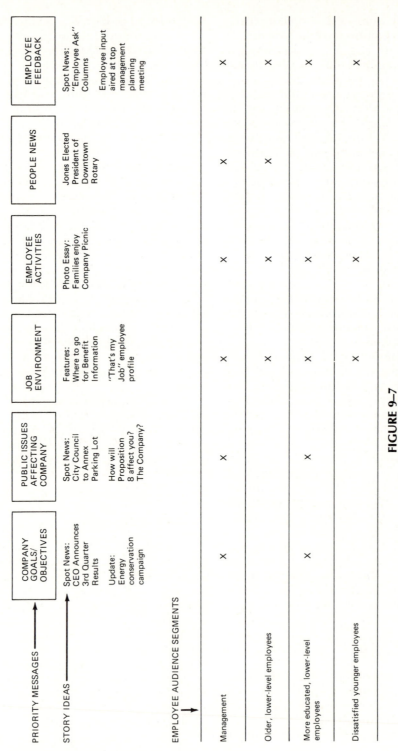

**FIGURE 9–7**
**Audience/Message Matrix**

For example, you might ask "Is there anything new or unusual you are doing to demonstrate how employees can conserve energy?" "Are there some individuals who are successfully doing what you would like other employees to do?" Resources also can be used as sounding boards for story ideas to best desseminate their expertise across the employee population. You might ask, "Would this idea interpret the objective accurately? If not, what is needed to make it work?"

Many employee communicators recruit a network of correspondents similar to newspaper or wire service correspondents in various departments or locations throughout a company.

### Utilize Message/Media Outline

The message/media outline described in Chapter 3 can be helpful in planning an employee media story. Before sitting down to write a company media story, ask yourself

1. *What is my communications outcome?* What do you want your audience to do with the information? Do you want them to be more motivated by goals and objectives? Do you want them to take some action to conserve energy? A simple end result statement here can help you organize a story that will work the hardest to bring about the desired action.
2. *Who is my target audience?* What employee segment are you writing for? Is it an issue that crosses employee segment lines? Which segments can do the most to achieve your communications outcome?
3. *What are the needs/concerns/interests of that audience?* If an employee segment(s) is concerned with an issue as basic as keeping their jobs, then a story that demonstrates an increase in new company contracts next month can set the company up to minimize that concern.
4. *What is the message?* Every communication should be planned around a specific message statement. Goals and objectives, feedback programs, should have specific messages designed for retention by the employee.
5. *What channels of communication should I use?* Should it be the company newspaper? Telephone hot line? Management newsletter? Supervisor face to face? A combination of these?
6. *Who is the most believable spokesperson?* Should it be top management? A supervisor? An executive with special expertise? An employee demonstrating success with the outcome?
7. *How can I raise an audience need/concern/interest and offer the company as a means to meet that need, minimize that concern, or satisfy that interest?* The subquestions are as follows:
   a. Does the communication raise an audience need, concern, or interest? Can the audience members easily put themselves into the situation? Can you paint a real-life scenario with words or visuals?
   b. Is your organization offered as a solution in a clear and concise manner? Are the benefits to the solution clearly presented? Can the receiver jot down in one sentence "What's in it for me?" Is it believable? Did you use the most believable spokesperson?
   c. Are the consequences of leaving the need, concern, or interest unresolved clearly presented?
   d. Have you helped the individual members of the target audience mentally rehearse the action you would like them to take?

   If, for example, an employee group wants more input into the direction the company is moving, then a company can meet that need with a story on a new employee feedback program: the benefits of participating, the consequences of not participating, and the "how-to-participate" steps can be clearly laid out with copy and photos or illustrations.

The message/media outline starts story development; it helps you organize the process to best achieve employee communications objectives. Next come researching and writing the story.

### Research and Writing

Research comes in at least two forms: perusing existing materials (like plans and reports on the subject) and interviewing senior decision makers and employees. Studying existing materials should, along with the message/media outline, provide you with the questions needed for the interview. Develop a list of questions before calling your interviewee. Use them as an outline in the interview but stay alert for additional outcomes or items to humanize the story. Share your expectations with your source. See if he or she might have some ideas on how best to achieve them. Be sure you fully understand what the resource is telling you. The only stupid question is the one you do not ask.

Nolte and Wilcox offer a shopping list of potential story ideas for employee communications:

1. New or improved facilities
2. New or improved products
3. Changes in the organization
4. Sales results
5. Advertising campaigns
6. Organizational policies
7. Employee rules
8. Job openings
9. Opportunities for training
10. Organizational accomplishments
11. Employee benefits
12. Unfavorable news
13. Information about executives
14. History of organization
15. Awards to organization
16. General news affecting the organization
17. Sources of materials used
18. Use of products or services
19. Importance of organization to public
20. Editorials
21. Chief executive letters
22. Solicitations to charitable organizations
23. Sponsored activities and events[27]

When it comes to writing your story, the rules of journalism and the message/media outline described in previous chapters prevail. The rules of journalism will keep the story lively and interesting. The message/media outline will work best to deliver your message.

### Utilize Visuals to Expand Message

Employee communicators should be on the lookout for visuals to support outcomes and raise audience needs, concerns, or interests. As far as photographs, the rules of photojournalism and the message/media outline apply. The photo should be a story in itself. Photos should be edited by "cropping," or cutting out extraneous material that does not contribute to the photo message. The message supports the organization in meeting need, minimizing concern, or satisfying interest.

Your employee needs assessment should help you determine if your audience is an active seeker or passive consumer of information. The passive consumer tends to skim your publication. Use of headlines, subheads, photos and photo captions, and graphic illustrations helps deliver messages to such a consumer.

We may differ here from journalism style, which tends to use the above to draw the reader into the story. True, we would like to attract the reader, but more important is to see that he or she gets the message we are communicating. Consequently, headlines, subheads, captions, and photos/illustrations can be used to help the passive consumer get the message without ever reading the story. If the story is on energy conservation, the reader learns key points in the headline, subheads, photos, and captions.

### *Step 6: Evaluation*

Research, or the employee needs assessment, conducted at the beginning of the employee communications program can serve as a measurement baseline. Goals and objectives can be measured against it. Message awareness, retention, and acceptance objectives can be evaluated, as can attitude and behavioral results. An employee needs assessment should be conducted at least biannually, with media effectiveness surveys at least once a year in the form of readership, viewership, or use studies.

## SUMMARY

- ☐ Effective, well-planned employee communications programs result in more productive relationships between management and employees.

- Effective employee communications programs share common commitments from top management to inform employees about plans for the future and how they fit in.
- Communicators should know what senior management wants to say, what employees want to know, and the effectiveness of existing employee communications programs.
- Employee populations can be segmented by needs/concerns/interests.
- Formal feedback systems provide employees with input and involvement in organizational decision making.
- There is no relationship between program costs and its effectiveness in employee communications.

## EXERCISES

1. Because your company has never had an employee communications program before, no one is quite sure what the demographics of the employee population is, or how informal communications happen now. How would you go about obtaining this information?
2. If the top management of your firm is reluctant to do one-on-one employee communications, make a list of and prioritize three or four alternative media channels you might use. What criteria did you use in your selection?
3. Your company has an effective employee feedback system in place. Since not all employee input is reflected in company decisions, how would you handle employees who question the value of their input?
4. For almost a year, the glossy, upscale expensive magazine produced to enhance employee morale has been met with little or no interest. What might be done either to improve the magazine or replace it with a more effective employee communication system?
5. Your company is about to be purchased by a large conglomerate. The employees do not know of the impending sale.
   a. What might be the agreed-upon message statements that top management communicates to employees?
   b. Write a news story for the employee newspaper including the message statements.

## REFERENCES


1. Louis Williams, Jr., "Trends and Issues: Challenges Ahead," in *Inside Organizational Communication,* 2nd ed., ed. Carol Reuss and Donn Silvis (New York: Longman, 1985), p. 339.
2. Ibid.
3. Scott M. Cutlip, Allen H. Center, and Glen M. Broom, *Effective Public Relations*, 6th ed. (Englewood Cliffs, NJ: Prentice-Hall, 1985), p. 315.
4. Karen Rosenberg, "What Employees Think of Communication: 1984 Update," *Communication World*, 2, no. 5 (May 1985), 50.
5. Ibid.
6. Ronald Goodman and Richard Ruch, "The Role of Research in Internal Communications," *Public Relations Journal*, 37, no. 2 (July 1982), 14.
7. Bruce J. McCristal, "Working from the Inside Out—Improving Employee Communications," *IABC World Conference* (Montreal, Quebec), June 14, 1984, p. 4.
8. Irving Shapiro, in J. Paul Blake, "Creative Approaches to Institutional Internal Relations," *Public Relations Journal*, 39, no. 3 (March 1983), 24.
9. James E. Grunig and Todd Hunt, *Managing Public Relations* (New York: Holt, Rinehart & Winston, 1984), p. 247.
10. Ibid., pp. 255–256.
11. Ibid., pp. 256–257.
12. Myron Emanuel, "Auditing Communication Practices," in *Inside Organizational Communication*, 2nd ed., ed. Carol Reuss and Donn Silvis (New York: Longman, 1985), p. 50.
13. Ibid., pp. 50–53.
14. Ibid., p. 49.
15. McCristal, "Inside Out," p. 8.
16. Ibid.
17. Thomas A. Ruddell, "Chartering the Communication Function," in *Inside Organizational Communication*, 2nd ed., ed. Carol Reuss and Donn Silvis (New York: Longman, 1985), p. 71.
18. Ibid.
19. Anheuser-Busch Companies, Corporate Communications Plan, June 28, 1985, p. 4.
20. Michael A. Kelne, for Southwestern Bell

Telephone, written communication, January 6, 1986.

21. Joan Kampe and Lyn Christenson, "Publications: What's in the Package," in *Inside Organizational Communication*, 2nd ed., ed. Carol Reuss and Donn Silvis (New York: Longman, 1985), pp. 130–131.
22. Rosenberg, "What Employees Think," p. 49.
23. Carl Lewis, "How to Make Internal Communications Work," *Public Relations Journal*, 36 (February 1980), 14.
24. Roy G. Foltz, "Communication in Contemporary Organizations," in *Inside Organizational Communication*, 2nd ed., ed. Carol Reuss and Donn Silvis (New York: Longman, 1985), p. 10.
25. Ibid.
26. Roger Feather, "Feedback for Evaluation and Information," in *Inside Organizational Communication*, 2nd ed., ed. Carol Reuss and Donn Silvis (New York: Longman, 1985), p. 315.
27. Lawrence E. Nolte and Dennis L. Wilcox, *Effective Publicity: How to Reach the Public* (New York: John Wiley, 1984), p. 315.

## CASE STUDY

### The Problem

The Ronald P. Kole Company is one of the largest commercial and residential insulation subcontractors in the United States. The organization has grown dramatically with development in the Southwest, and what was once a company with a "family" culture has become a highly structured enterprise. High interest rates have put the skids on the building industry, and Kole's business has decreased significantly. Employee morale has been negatively affected. Top management is concerned for the morale of its employees and the impact of low morale on company goals and objectives.

### Situational Analysis

The Kole Company has 200 employees and seven offices located in the Southwest. There has been no formal employee communications program to date. After meeting with top management, the following questions have been answered with regard to the mission of a proposed employee communications program:

What needs will an employee communications program meet?

**To improve understanding of Kole's goals and objectives and the individual's role in the company.**

For whom?

**Employees.**

Where?

**Company-wide.**

How?

**By informing employees of Kole's goals and objectives, strategy for achievement, cause and effect of recent low profits, Kole's projections for future, and involving employees in decisions affecting the company.**

A priority Key Result Area for Kole's top management team is to improve employee morale. Kole employees can be categorized into three audience groups that share common needs/concerns/interests:

1. Insulation installers (skilled labor)
2. Sales staff (sales)
3. Branch managers (middle management)

Assume that budget allows only face-to-face communications and two printed publications: a monthly newsletter and a quarterly report of corporate stability. From the information above and some assumptions of your own, develop the following:

- ☐ Employee communications mission statement
- ☐ Written employee communications policy statements
- ☐ Objectives and action plans
- ☐ Message/media outline
- ☐ Outline of stories to be covered for first newsletter
- ☐ Front page story announcing newsletter

# CHAPTER 10

# Writing the Presentation with Audiovisual Support

*IN THIS CHAPTER*

Preparing group presentations for dissemination of the planned public relations message is yet another of the tasks often assigned to the public relations practitioner.

The message/media outline forms a basis for selecting the appropriate words and materials contained in a well-designed presentation. Often the public relations staff member must utilize specialists in either speech writing or graphics.

The presenter requires sufficient training and rehearsal to bring to life the words written into the presentation. Not all orators have skills in delivery of spoken or audiovisual programs.

A good presentation will consider the additional needs for attracting the audience's attention by use of an awakening lead, novelty, involvement, and personal terms.

A good presentation tells a story with which the audience relates because their needs/concerns/interests have been addressed in the message communicated.

*CHAPTER OBJECTIVES*

The reader will be able to

1. Apply the message/media outline to prepare a presentation.
2. Describe presenter preparation requirements.
3. Apply specific criteria to decisions regarding use of audiovisual support material.
4. Organize a speakers' bureau.
5. Write a five-minute presentation.

## PRESENTATIONS COMBINE WRITING, TRAINING, AUDIOVISUAL

Writing presentations, like making presentations, is a skill that demands consideration of all components of the process presented in this text.

Presentations prepared by public relations personnel cover wide-ranging situations from planning workshops to board of directors briefings. Practitioners may find themselves outlining a brief welcome to be given by an administrator to visiting dignitaries, preparing a nervous employee to speak before a peer group, or reviewing an audiovisual program developed to convince local community groups to support a new county ordinance. In each case, the practitioner must remember that these oral communications differ from those that communicate in print.

Writing fluid prose represents only about half of the job. Coaching is also essential, particularly if the spokesperson has limited experience in group presentations. Overseeing the development of audio and/or visual message support materials finds itself in the purview of the public relations professional as well.

### Audience Most Important

As you progress through this chapter, think about how the steps in the message/media outline set up the audience to process information with the potential for causing change. These variables support success with members of an audience because they tap into the motivation and contemplation necessary to get your message through to the listener.

The fundamental route an individual member of the listening audience takes to changing behavior is to transfer the message to their own lives, attend to it, act on it, and, finally, reinforce that behavior with their own experience. If the message is packaged as a solution to a need/concern/interest of the audience, then each individual will attend more closely to the presenter and to the articulated message and proposed action.

Too often concerns about the method and form of delivery get in the way of satisfying the audience. The presenter, for example, is often asked by the public relations practitioner to open with a clever statement that means little to the overall point of the talk. Sometimes the writer is more concerned about the sophistication of the words than about the presentation of the message. If the audience-grabbing need/concern/interest components have been neglected by the writer or the presenter, then the chances of your message getting through to your audience are greatly diminished.

### Identify Objectives

The objectives for any public relations plan range from simple message awareness (level 2 impact) and acceptance (level 3 impact) to an individual adopting an attitude (level 4 impact) to implementation of an action contained in that message (level 5 impact). The same is true for preparation and delivery of a presentation. There are talks that do nothing more than occupy a space in time for listeners. In these cases, the presenter is there to make an audience feel good about him or her and, perhaps, about the enjoyment of the material presented. Presentations also cause individuals to literally rally around an issue both in spirit and person. Political activists often use these kinds of speeches, with carefully chosen words and actions created with behavioral expectations. Such a presenter would be disappointed if the audience only felt good about him or her or the topic. This sequential escalation from comprehension to behavioral objectives is found in both the education and psychological literature and recently in public relations.[1]

In another example of this contrast between objectives at differing levels, a presentation by a corporate financial officer might be to inform board members of current financial investment status. A presentation by a major stockholder, on the other hand, might be designed to convince other shareholders to vote one way or the other. In each case, the listener is required to respond to the information but, in the first example, comprehension is the objective, whereas in the latter case a specific behavior is intended, raising the level projected on the impact ladder (Chapter 2).

### Message/Media Outline

As with other public relations techniques, a specific communication outcome should be identified long before scheduling a presentation to deliver a specific message packaged to achieve that outcome. The writer should walk through the same message/media outline as presented in previous chapters:

1. What is the communications outcome?
2. Who is the audience?
3. What are their needs/concerns/interests?
4. Who is your spokesperson?
5. How will you raise a need, concern, or interest with your message packaged to meet that need, minimize that concern, satisfy that interest?

The most important consideration, of course, is formulating a presentation to raise the audience's interest as identified in the message/media outline and offering the campaign message as the solution. Included in that step is the identified action benefits, consequences of inaction, and a means for helping the audience think through the action you want it to take.

Nolte and Wilcox suggest four steps including thought-provoking questions under each for planning effective public oratory opportunities. These steps look remarkably like the steps outlined above.

1. Establish outcomes
   "What do I want as a result of this presentation?"
2. Analyze audience
   "How much do they have on the subject?"
   "How will they react to the recommendations: positive, negative, neutral—why?"
   "In what ways can my ideas and recommendations benefit the audience?"
   "What are some of the objections to be encountered and responses to them?"
   "What tone would be most effective? Serious? Technical? Lighthearted? Casual? Entertaining? Businesslike?"
3. Select main ideas and supporting material
   "What are the main ideas I want the audience to get?"
   "What materials will support those ideas?"
4. Organize the presentation
   "What is the opening? Benefits? Objections?"
   "What should be in the body? What are my key points? Supporting material?"
   "What action do I want the audience members to take?"[2]

Mulling over the concepts presented, the flow of information, and the audience interaction are essential if the presenter is to be supported with the appropriate and attention-sustaining words. The actual presentation phrases and words are best written from this type of planned framework.

> **How would you discuss the message/media outline in regard to presentation writing with a fellow public relations staff member assigned with you to prepare a presentation for a local community group on effective media relationships?**

### Using a Specialist

Most public relations departments do not include speech writers on staff. Frequently, a writer with skills in this area can be hired freelance to prepare necessary speeches or presentations. When this is the case, the practitioner must see to it that the message/media outline is clearly communicated and the writer is briefed on the style of the presenter.

More often than not, however, the public relations writer will put on his or her jack-of-all-trades hat and prepare a presentation for either a company insider or outside spokesperson. When this happens, it is best to be prepared with the necessary skills to manage the development of that program and to interact with the assigned presenters. Many public relations practitioners also find the preparation of the finished audio or visual product best done by specialists in arts and graphics design, especially if the presentation will be complex and multimessage/multimedia. The utilization of these skilled people again demands consultation and supervision by the professional public relations staff so that the final product(s) reflects the objectives contained in the plan.

## THE COMPONENTS OF A SUCCESSFUL ORAL PRESENTATION

### The Lead

Preparing a presentation has many of the same characteristics as broadcast writing. A presentation is not read (although copies supporting key concepts can be made available); it is heard and seen. Choice and placement of words are critically important. Like radio, the audience may need a few opening words to acclimate itself to the speaker. In fact, individuals may not be attending to the message until the third or fourth sentence. Consequently, the first few words should be used to draw attention or warm up the audience. It should not include the message. Messages are most often placed one-third of the way into a presentation and then repeated again at the conclusion.

A presentation lead, then, can be used to raise and substantiate an audience need/concern/interest. The message should be introduced as a solution to the need/concern/interest in the body of the speech along with the consequence of inaction. The conclusion can then demonstrate how the message meets all the audience needs to think and act and how individuals can think about incorporating that message into their real-life situations.

> Which of the leads in Figure 10–1 is best and why?

For example, if a CEO wishes a state-of-the-company presentation prepared, then the practitioner needs to examine which messages might be of interest or concern to the employees to whom the CEO is speaking. A lead that begins with a description of how added employee efforts improved profits during the preceding year rather than a lead that begins with the profit and loss statement will interest the listeners in the presentation early on.

> Think of lead statements you have heard when attending a group presentation. Which ones struck you as being especially awakening?

### Time

While writing for the news media often requires saying the most with the fewest words, presentations are not necessarily that restricted. The presenter is usually designated an allotted period of time in which to speak. He or she knows in advance that the information to be presented must be accomplished in a specified time period. Seminars and workshops most often give presenters an hour, though some are thirty minutes. With this specified time arrangement, the writer is given the opportunity to modulate the material so that listener interest and cognition are maintained throughout the key areas where message content and desired behavior are presented. The most pressing needs, in this case, are to help the presenter alternate the static with interactive modes of the message so that the talk can arouse and hold the interest of the individual audience member.

In addition to the timing of the speech itself, there is also the timeliness of a presentation. No member of the audience will be attending to the message or action if the subject is hackneyed or trivial. History can be interesting to some individuals, but most likely long historical narratives are *not* likely to arouse the audience to establish or strengthen an important message or concept.

### Humor

When a speaker is nervous, so are the listeners. In most cases the audience is just as anxious as the unnerved speaker about the outcome of a presentation. Everyone has anxieties about speaking before an audience, regardless of who he or she might be. The

#1

Fact..Dental disease is the most prevalent malady in this country. Nine of ten Americans are affected.

Fact..The last time the federal government checked, we Americans averaged 1.3 decayed teeth and 5.3 missing teeth.

Fact..One in three of us past the age of 29 have at least one denture.

Fact..One of every two of us has some degree of periodontal disease.

These facts certainly indicate that we're not as healthy as we could be, but we are improving in each generation. Dental disease is largely unnecessary. If you don't want it you can do something about it with very little effort and fairly minimal expense.

#2

People go where the jobs are. Each year nearly 20% of the nation's jobs are created by growth opportunities. With jobs must come housing, transporation, office buildings and public services. All of these need to be planned, financed and built. Without long-term planning, there may not be enough housing to meet the needs of a growing, changing society. Adequate and affordable housing is a key economic factor. Local regulations that severely limit or stop growth -- through high fees or moratoriums -- are controversial. Communities that use them believe they are creating a better future. But when cities reject reasonable growth, they also restrict the opportunities for jobs.

**FIGURE 10–1**

trick is to channel that anxiety in a positive direction. Humor is one way of relieving tension. When appropriate, humor reminds the audience members about the personable nature of the speaker.

Humor in a speech holds both attention and interest. And, in fact, use of humor tends to reduce the artificial space between the presenter and the audience member. Tension is relaxed and the message can be conveyed in an open environment.

Tarver asks three questions about humor in presentation writing and delivery:

1. Is it relevant to an idea contained in the presentation?
2. Is it in good taste?
3. Is the humor fresh?[3]

Perhaps the best advice on humor is that jokes, per se, are not normally the best avenue to take, for several reasons connected with Tarver's questions. First, you cannot guarantee the telling ability of the presenter. Second, a joke circulates quickly and is often "old hat" to the audience. Third, jokes are often too far removed from the content at hand and the teller is forced to try to bring the audience back to its needs/concerns/interests. In all cases, joke telling is not an adequate means to make spoken words memorable.

> Which of the 2 introductions in Figure 10–2 uses humor, i.e., a joke appropriately and why?

For instance, many speakers have a favorite tale to tell on one of their family members. They use that story at the beginning of the presentation in order to "warm up the audience" and let them know the speaker is human. However, that humorous anecdote might not work when the audience contains members who relate to the object in the story and find nothing funny about it.

> How would you tell a presenter *not* to use a joke or amusing story?

When humor is written into a speech, the presenter should be able to move smoothly through the words even if the humor falls flat or is misunderstood. Jokes and storytelling are best left to situations when the speaker is not trying to convey a significant message.

### Novelty

Another way of increasing audience attention and motivation is through the use of novelty, with words, alternating speech patterns, and audience interaction techniques such as questions.

Novelty is a good way to soften an audience not entirely enthusiastic about the prospect of your presentation. A novel query or piece of information can attract the audience early on. Community college students do not get too excited about nutrition lectures, so one professor created a slide depicting the food intake of a typical college student. The audience was then asked to compare what they ate that day with what they saw on the screen. From that novel introduction on, students were drawn into the subject because it related to their own lives and their immediate food selection experiences.

In another example, a member of a board of directors of a large engineering company was required to present some important but technical data on electronics to management personnel. Instead of beginning with a traditional approach that might have included definitions, diagrams, or other data, he initiated his presentation with an old-fashioned light switch from an old house. He then drew a comparison between that antiquated mechanical switch and the current condition of electronics. Each person in the room had handled a similar light switch thousands of times and had never thought of the connec-

#1

Thank you for the opportunity to speak to you tonight regarding the issue before us: controlling the pet population. Inspite of cartoonist Gary Larsen, who frequently shows life from the animal's viewpoint, we have to be concerned about the uncontrolled breeding of dogs and cats. One of Larsen's funniest cartoons shows a dog couple escorting a woman to the doctor: both dogs have their fingers crossed behind their backs and smiles on their faces.

At issue here is when it is proper to spay or neuter your pet...

#2

In coming to speak to you today I am reminded of a funny story my partner told me last night. Did you hear about the man who went to the psychiatrist with a frog on his head? The psychiatrist asked him "what can I do for you?" The frog answered: "Get this guy off my butt!"

I'm here to discuss with you the development of a chemical compound which alters the effect of cleaning on restored surfaces...

**FIGURE 10–2**

tion between the simplicity of that switch and the complexity of today's electronic technology in which the company was involved. He had everyone in the room attentive and listening from the beginning.

It should be clear that an audience requires more than a simple flow of words for effective communications. They need inspiration. They need relationships and pictures developed for them by the speaker. They need help connecting the data to their own real-life experience.

Novelty helps to change the expectations of the audience and brings individuals into the circle of the presentation, causing them to attend to the presentation by creating a difference between what they expected to hear and what is happening in front of them.

The use of metaphors, similes, and analogies adds just as much color and expression to presentations as it does for other forms of communication. Some of the greatest speechmakers are remembered because they provided listeners with such vivid pictures of their words that no one was able to forget the message even over great time spans. The listener, like the reader, needs to make that internal transfer by imagining the concept clearly and comparing it to some other familiar thing.

To ensure novelty, the key question is: How can this be made more unusual by changing words and phrases, actions, supporting material, or audience interaction? However, public relations counselor Mark Perlgut reminds us of one all-important point: "More important than rhetorical flourishes, more important than humor or quotations of Plato, is an original thought, analysis, perspective or solution."[4] In other words, novelty for novelty's sake offers little in transmitting the message or messages, the very reason for scheduling the presentation in the first place.

### Personalization

Personalizing the presentation is another method of enhancing the listener's cognitive processing of the message. Use of personal pronouns—you, me, I, he, she—will assist the audience to know the speaker is talking to and about them. One of the great advertising successes is Chrysler's use of chief executive Lee Iacocca. When Iacocca speaks, he is believable. He cares about you, the individual in the audience, and he is talking directly to you.

Messages written in personal terms bring the concept, and especially the desired behavioral action, within the scope of the listener's mind and life.

Personalization requires that the writer incorporate pronouns into the message. Instead of writing, "Now the company has the opportunity to excel in both computers and electronics," a better sentence is, "*We* are now able to offer *you* and others excellence in both computers and electronics." The message is the same, but the employment of personal pronouns makes the listener more a part of the discourse.

Personalization also makes the talker more likely to pay attention to his or her audience, because when a person uses pronouns and names, it helps strengthen the connection with the audience.

### Audience

When a presenter addresses an audience, it is important that individual members of the audience perceive the speaker talking directly to them. Unlike the element of "eavesdropping" that is so natural for television, the presenter should strive for the impression that he or she knows the needs/concerns/interests of those individuals and how best to satisfy them.

The computer expert who uses technical jargon regardless of the audience is a classic example of how *not* to give a talk. So is the scientist who attempts to explain the workings of disease to a lay audience from the same slides used to teach medical students. Public relations professionals should provide the appropriate audience research and work it into each phase of the presentation—that is, define the target audience well. In fact, appropriate anecdotes, scenarios, and analogies should all be woven into the copy throughout the presentation.

Advance people for presidential candidate Robert F. Kennedy took great efforts to introduce the candidate to the right type of individual to complement his talk. Kennedy would then work into his speech that individual and an appropriate anecdote that supported his message—for example, "And, Robin Schmidt has been on welfare all of her life. Her mother was on welfare as was her mother before her. When will people like Robin Schmidt be provided adequate employment and compensation?"

Though not all politicians are as adept as Kennedy, most begin addresses with salutations like "It is a pleasure to address the Association of Handicapped Artists this evening." After recognizing and identifying the specific group, the speaker then adds some positive comments about the organization. The audience must know that the speaker knows what makes them unique and that the presentation has been tailored to their needs.

When preparing speeches for mixed audiences, the well-planned speaker often identifies similarities between the groups as a means for unifying them in his support or the support of his message. It can be as simple as "We're all Democrats" or "We're all taxpayers." Black leader Jesse Jackson, who in 1984 was the first serious black candidate for president, called his followers the Rainbow Coalition to reinforce the similarities of the multitude of ethnic groups banding together in his support.

An audience interest is cultivated and a presenter's influence bolstered by knowing and expanding upon the characteristics of the audience.

> How does planning for an audience of astronomers differ from planning for an audience of space club enthusiasts?

### Putting the Presentation on Paper

Begin as with writing for other media: The message/media outline is the base. What do you want the audience members to do once they have been exposed to the presentation? Who makes up the audience gathered for the program? Of course, their needs/concerns/interests must be known in order to package the message(s) conveyed through the presentation. Write that message. It is usually the core of any presentation. Selecting channels refers to identifying priority presentation platforms that best reach the target audience (e.g., a presentation to the Downtown Kiwanis Club might be the best forum for reaching business leaders). Selection of the spokesperson is the final step before packaging the presentation to meet audience needs/concerns/interests. Criteria for spokespersons include subject expertise, presentation skills, and credibility.

The writer has an "ace in the hole" in preparing the presentation: the message/media outline. Suppose, for example, as a public relations practitioner, you are hired to prepare a presentation for the administrator of a drug and alcohol rehabilitation center. The target audience is employers, and you have scheduled a meeting of the local Chamber of Commerce to deliver the presentation. If you were to walk through the message/media outline as a means of organizing the presentation, it might look something like this:

COMMUNICATION OUTCOME. Improve utilization of the center by employers with drug- and alcohol-related employment problems.

AUDIENCE. Business leaders.

NEEDS/CONCERNS/INTERESTS. To reduce drug- and alcohol-related employment problems (such as absenteeism, low productivity, reduced health and safety of the work site).

MESSAGE(S).

1. Reduce absenteeism; improve productivity; increase safety and health by sending problem employees to the center.

2. The rehab center has complete packages designed for continuing job maintenance or in-residence services—whatever the employee requires.
3. Fees are competitive and we cater to the needs of business.

COMMUNICATIONS CHANNEL. Presentations before business leader groups.

SPOKESPERSON. Administrator of the Rehab Center.

### *Packaging for Needs/Concerns/Interests*

AUDIENCE NEED. Reduce drug- and alcohol-related employee problems.

SOLUTION. Enroll employees at a center in a job-maintenance or in-residence program. Programs are tailored to meet the needs of business at competitive fees.

CONSEQUENCES. Continued uncontrolled drug and alcohol abuse at the work site.

HELP THINK THROUGH ACTION. Complete a questionnaire to ascertain the problem at individual work sites; introduce intervention techniques; offer appropriate financial plans.

The message/media outline provides the writer a framework for organizing a presentation.

There are still pitfalls to guard against. One is a presentation philosophy that was once the cornerstone of speech writing: "Tell 'em what you're gonna tell em. Tell 'em. Then tell 'em what you told them." This is no longer an appropriate direction because audiences are more sophisticated and need greater diversity in approach. Now, more than ever, there is a need for the audience member to interact with the presenter and his or her message.

Another speech writing pitfall is the KISS system. This refers to the term, "*K*eep *I*t *S*imple, *S*tupid." Again, it might be adequate to present a very simple presentation if the message, audience, and speaker must interact simply. However, in the greatly expanded public speaking roles of many executives, a message might be too complex for such a system. While the presentation might be complex, it is still important to maintain two to three clear, concise points.

Still another cliché of equally unrealistic value is: "The words don't matter, only the way they are spoken." Once more, we must face the fact that competition in the marketplace has put all orators on notice that both thoughtful words and delivery are vital, truly a marriage in a successful presentation.

With the message/media outline and these appropriate warnings, a writer is armed with a conceptual basis for creating well-balanced, audience-involving presentations.

## Personal Style

The speaking characteristics of the presenter are the next considerations for the preparer. What are his or her delivery strengths? Weaknesses? Does he or she have any unique characteristics?

If you have created a presentation, for example, that requires simultaneous verbal and visual input but the presenter cannot compete with the intensity of the visual, then the order should be altered to deliver the verbal first with the visual to follow. That way the message builds to a higher level of drama and attention rather than leaving the speaker to compete with his or her own presentation. If the administrator in the example shows a slide depicting an employee injecting heroin in the company restroom, the administrator should remain silent because the visual message is more powerful than any words said.

Effective presentations take advantage of an individual's ability to perform and build on that ability with tone and style. Make plans to build on the strengths and minimize the weaknesses of the individual for whom the presentation is written.

A classic contrast of two successful speaking styles can be made between Presidents Eisenhower and Kennedy. Eisenhower offered the listener very little personalization and verbal imagery even though his words were precise and appropriate to the message.

Kennedy, on the other hand, offered the listener more opportunity for interaction with the message, especially his use of questions, humor, and sentence brevity.

### Coaching Presenters

Platform style differs from written style because so much depends on someone else's ability as a communicator. Therefore, the public relations practitioner should take responsibility for coaching those who will represent the organization in public arenas. Professional training should be organized for those who frequently carry organization messages to the public.

Rehearsals and candid assessments prior to the presentation should be scheduled by the public relations professional. Often, however, the only coaching a speaker receives is that provided by the practitioner immediately prior to a major presentation. When this happens, the writing itself carries a disproportionate load for creating listener impact.

Coaching presenters incorporates some of the same techniques as coaching spokespersons for interviews or special events:

Be active.
Be enthusiastic.
Be positive.
Be prepared.
Be relaxed.

To get potential performers to understand and implement these admonitions requires observing rehearsals, providing constructive criticism, and refining the prepared words and visuals as needed to ensure compatibility between the materials and the talker.

One cardinal rule: A presenter should never appear to have difficulty with the message, even though occasionally he or she may have trouble with a particular word or phrase. The message should be so well agreed upon and practiced that the presenter can comfortably get that message across no matter what his or her personal style.

> What can you envision taking place at a coaching session for four outside scientists hired by your organization to present your message to a regulatory board?

### Before the Presentation

Once the message/media outline has been fleshed out and you have sketched a presentation draft, it is time to meet with the intended presenter(s) to talk through the material and identify potential problems before the final draft is composed. Such a step should relieve the writer of additional worry later.

Seek input from the speaker. It is important that he or she accept your message/media outline. Make any necessary revisions and get agreements on content. This should be accomplished several weeks ahead of the presentation. If a meeting is not possible, then written material, clearly annotated and with adequate content, should be circulated for the presenter's review and comment.

The writer's primary job is to make certain the message and final action(s) are written in such a way that the presenter will have no trouble articulating them and the audience members will have no trouble identifying their personal attachment to the content.

The last obligation is to rehearse the presentation. Transfer of words from paper to voice is often the way to find glaring errors and omissions due to variability among speakers. The public relations professional cannot afford to wait until the presentation to find out that the speaker cannot pronounce the words as written.

Some academicians think formal speech training is essential for individuals called on frequently for presentations. The public relations department is responsible for finding professional speech trainers and scheduling trainings.

> How might you manage a potential presenter who insists on ad-libbing through much of the prepared material because he believes it is more "homespun" that way?

### Speaking Platforms

The public relations department is usually responsible for generating speaker platforms for corporate executives or third party spokespersons who support company positions on public issues.

The presentation should be considered as a channel of communications in the message/media outline. Specific platforms may be a priority for accomplishing objectives in a public relations plan. A presentation, for example, can be an excellent means for fulfilling a strategy to generate publicity.

For Delta Dental, interested in marketing a new dental insurance program, interactive programs were the primary vehicles for selling a new dental plan to dentists and insurance brokers. Following deregulation of the long distance telephone market, GTE Sprint sponsored a number of forums around the country in association with the League of Women Voters to help consumers understand changes occurring in long distance telephone service. In this case, the presentations were used as a forum to generate exposure in the news media reinforcing GTE Sprint as a company trying to help minimize confusion in the marketplace. Increased levels of awareness and credibility with target audiences were the objectives, not the speaking forums themselves.

An organization typically cannot afford to be everything to everybody. Speaking platforms should be carefully analyzed for how well they reinforce the public relations plan. If a priority target audience is the legal community, then it makes sense to target those platforms with the potential for reaching the largest number of leaders in that community. If a presentation at the local Lions Club does not reach a substantial number of lawyers, then it is not an appropriate forum, unless publicity can expand the impact of that Lions Club presentation into the legal community.

Once the communications outcomes, audiences, and their needs/concerns/interests have been spelled out, the practitioner can begin to investigate those placements that best meet the need of the plan. Priorities can then be set and a campaign begun to make speaker placements. The chamber of commerce was selected for the rehab center example because of the large group of local business leaders represented at meetings.

The process usually begins by developing lists of groups, setting priorities, writing to top priority groups, following up by telephoning, and scheduling presentations.

### Publicity Expands the Presentation

In every effort, the practitioner should try to expand the audience with publicity in the mass media and specialized publications. In most cases there are at least two opportunities for publicity. First is the release announcing the presentation. Second is publicity on what is said. This can be accomplished by reporters attending the presentation, interviews placed before or after, or planting a news release with the media. Such a release should be written in the past tense, as though covered by a reporter.

A complex presentation can take a great deal of time, effort, and dollars. Every effort should be made by the public relations professional to maximize those dollars through expanded exposure.

### Speakers' Bureau

Providing a pool of trained experts or willing speakers is often the function of the public relations professional. This often occurs when an organization foresees the need for continuous and diverse presentation demands. For example, the American Nurses

Association found several years ago that information about self-care in medicine needed communication to interested Americans all over the country. With those audience needs in mind, the nursing association formed a speakers' bureau and offered qualified nurses as speakers to community groups.

Organizing a speakers' bureau requires the following activities:

1. Selection of a key functionary who answers requests and schedules programs
2. Selection of a core group of interested and willing presenters
3. Training of the speakers in subject matter areas and presentation skills
4. Compilation of speaker data and event calendars, as necessary
5. Promotion campaign to potential target audiences
6. Evaluation by speakers about their programs and evaluation of usage by sponsoring organization

Successful speaker's bureaus are very time-intensive and expensive endeavors. They should operate from measurable objectives that are evaluated annually against cost.

## AUDIOVISUAL SUPPORT

### To Use or Not to Use

"Do we need graphic support?" asked Cynthia Carson, manager for a major food industry trade association. Carson was concluding a top management team meeting to plan a presentation seeking board approval for their largest budget in history.[5]

Commonly, decisions are made to do a slide show or videotape without carefully analyzing what graphic support materials should accomplish. Public relations professionals appear to enjoy rolling up their sleeves and creating a multimedia audiovisual presentation so much so that too often the cart comes before the horse. In too many meetings, techniques are discussed *before* presentation objectives. In fact, technique decisions are frequently made prior to determining what should be accomplished from a speech or presentation.

According to Nolte and Wilcox:

> Large amounts of money have been wasted on audio visual materials because someone leaped into production without considering the purpose to be served, the audience to be reached and the aid which could be most effective. Motion pictures are produced when a slide production would do the job. Slides are prepared when charts or an overhead projector would be better. Costs are overlooked and budgets wrecked because decisions are made without thinking about the need and values of various aids.[6]

The preparation of audiovisual support materials, printed charts, overhead transparencies, slides, filmstrips, motion pictures, and videotapes requires as much careful thought as any other public relations technique.

The first question should be similar to Carson's: Do you need it? What will be the result of adding audiovisual material to the presentation? Will you be more effective? Will message comprehension be improved? Will the opportunity for causing the audience to act be greater? Or will you be more effective speaking directly and personally to each and every member of the audience?

> **How is the speaker shown in Figure 10–3 assisted in conveying her ideas by the use of the chart?**

Newsom and Siegfried contend that the person presenting the material is the most critical influence on the impact that information can have on the audience:

> Direct interaction with an audience, either in a speech or slide presentation, brings out the best in most of us who really want to please others. Preparing materials especially for audiences is the key to pleasing them. But the person preparing the material must remember that although

FIGURE 10–3

the audience is the ultimate receiver of the information, the person presenting it is the most important.[7]

As an example, an organ donor procurement organization prepared a program for physicians on the importance of recommending to patients that they bequeath organs for transplantation. At the planning meeting many ideas were discussed, including the preparation of large colored maps containing various statistics on where organ donors are found, who they are, and so on. These visuals were to be used by an organ-donating woman who had been asked to speak.

Before long, the staff involved in the program planned to create four charts, three overhead transparencies, and several slides. However, before the materials reached the drawing board, the presenter suggested that instead, she, the organ donor, the organ receiver's wife, and the organ receiver himself be allowed to simply stand before the physicians and tell their stories. The audience responded most favorably and the procurement organization met its goals.

### Visuals to Assist Mental Imagery

We have seen throughout the text the importance of helping individuals create mental pictures that assist them in transferring messages to their real-life experiences. This is essential to helping audience members move through the outline presented. Audiovisual support can be important to creating mental pictures for the recipient. What is proposed here, however, is that the practitioner carefully scrutinize the additional benefit of charts, slides, motion pictures, and videotapes versus the cost of production. Obviously charts, easel pads, or the use of an overhead projector can be considerably less expensive than a slide presentation or videotape. Can they be as effective?

An interesting contrast comes from two groups at a health facility with the same goal: to persuade consumers utilizing the facility to make a decision on a form of birth control. Group A obtained a substantial financial grant and produced an elaborate booklet, poster, slide-audiotape program, and motion picture. Group B produced a four-page interactive pamphlet, with the help of a local graphic artist at greatly reduced cost. When an evaluation team validated the results of both programs, the pamphlet was highly successful at moving individuals to a selection while the more expensive program produced minimal results. The lesson here is to budget according to what you want to achieve, and that does not necessarily mean spending all the money you have to spend.

Carson successfully increased her group's annual budget in 1985–86 from $3 million to $4 million by convincing her twenty-five-member board of directors of the cost-benefit. She used graphic illustrations on easel boards to reinforce a well-rehearsed presentation. Only the key concepts necessary to tell her story were illustrated.

Nolte and Wilcox offer the following guidelines for choosing the audiovisual aid:

For a meeting of less than about 50 people, charts are probably most efficient. If the meeting is larger it may be necessary to use an overhead projector. If pictures are important it may be advisable to use slides. If the presentation is to be given many times and in scattered locations, the film strip is probably the choice. If movement and emotional reaction are important, a motion picture may be indicated.[8]

With the exception of a presenter writing key points on an easel pad or on an overhead projector, audiovisual materials should be left to professionals. Though many practitioners prepare their own slide presentations, and they can often be very good, a presenter risks his or her credibility with slides that appear anything less than professional. Hundreds of reference books are available describing correct visual preparation guidelines.

On the preparation of visuals, particularly slides, Hendricson says, "Because slide production is relatively easy and inexpensive, we often overlook the basic concepts of visual communications." He acknowledges that almost everyone tries to prepare his or her own slides, but "most do it quite badly." The most frequent problem is too much information on each slide. A rule of thumb Hendricson suggests is to hold the slide up to light at arm's length and try to read it. If you can't, you have too much on it.[9]

Public relations firms with art departments and specialized production studios can be invaluable in preparing professional support materials. And the advent of high-quality portable videotape recording equipment and computer-generated graphics increases the range of potential uses and reduces the cost of presentations.[10]

There are generally two ways to go about working with audiovisual specialists:

1. Write the presentation and call in the professional to discuss presentation objectives and the options for best delivering the message. Then let the professional go to work.
2. Organize a series of conferences before the presentation is written to share objectives, outlines, and the most effective way of making the presentation.[11]

Delta Dental developed three versions of a slide presentation to help market a new program to dentists, insurance brokers, and consumers. Professionals were called in for a series of conferences. During the first conference, objectives, the message/media outline, and a rough draft were shared. The audiovisual professionals were then set loose to fine-tune the copy and make it come alive visually. Following a number of revision meetings, the product was completed and proved highly successful in group presentations.

In another example, the director of an underprivileged children's camp wanted to enhance a fund-raising speech planned for the business community of a major city. He wanted to create an emotional response to the benefits of his camp. He could not afford to produce a motion picture, but he could afford to adapt existing slides of the children at camp into a simple slide show with an audiocassette of children explaining how the camp had changed their lives. In this instance, he could not expect *his* words to raise the kind of emotion that the faces and experiences of these children could. Consequently, his part of the presentation consisted of a brief introduction and a conclusion that emphasized the need to raise funds and how to make a contribution.

There is no magic formula for making cost-beneficial decisions for audiovisual support, but there are several important production steps that would probably receive agreement by most public relations professionals:

1. Think of the audience.
2. Say it simply.
3. Think visually.
4. Keep to the point.
5. Never forget the objective.[12]

## The Presentation

The day of the presentation has arrived. The speaker is well rehearsed, and the audiovisual support materials are ready to go.

You have even hired a sound engineer for insurance against slip-ups. Can you relax? Better not . . . many a good presentation has been sabotaged by the inability of personnel or equipment to perform up to par. Even sound engineers have been known to fall asleep and miss their cue or be momentarily baffled by equipment that they themselves operate daily. One can never make assumptions about equipment or human beings, particularly when your own job or credibility is on the line.

Rehearsal, the solid offense, is the best defense against mishaps. This means trying out or watching an engineer test all equipment necessary for a successful presentation, such as microphones, seating arrangements, projectors, easels, and speakers. Presenters and the public relations staff support should run through presentations one more time on-site. Often the vagaries of an unfamiliar location or a difficult audiovisual program can be spotted ahead of time and modifications written into the presenter's directions so that simple mishaps do not ruin an otherwise well-thought-out program.[13]

## SUMMARY

- □ Preparation of presentations affords an opportunity to communicate the organization's message or messages.
- □ The message/media outline serves as the foundation for including the desired components in the presentation.
- □ A well-thought-out presentation considers the lead, the audience and its ability to attend, and uses the allotted time judiciously.
- □ Presenters need coaching and rehearsal to ensure competence at delivering the intended message.
- □ Finding the platforms from which the spokespeople can present is part of the public relations function.
- □ Speakers' bureaus expand the outreach of the organization and the spread of the message.
- □ Use of audiovisual support must be made with understanding of its usefulness to increase the audience members' interest and acceptance of the message and enhance the likelihood of changed behavior.

## EXERCISES

1. Write an action plan for the development and implementation of a presentation.
2. Write a five-minute presentation on the subject of how to give a good speech.
3. Develop a news release based on the presentation in Figure 10–4 using the message/media outline.
4. Select several audiovisual support items such as slides for use with the presentation in Figure 10–4. What criteria did you use to select these items?
5. Write an action plan for the formation of a speakers' bureau.

## REFERENCES


1. James E. Grunig and Todd Hunt, *Managing Public Relations* (New York: Holt, Rinehart & Winston, 1984), p. 134.
2. Lawrence E. Nolte and Dennis L. Wilcox, *Effective Publicity: How to Reach the Public* (New York: John Wiley, 1984), p. 274.
3. Jerry Tarver, "How to Put 'Good' Humor in Your Next Speech," *Public Relations Journal*, 30 (February 1975).
4. Mark R. Perlgut, "Write a Speech for a CEO," *Public Relations Journal*, 42 (April 1986), 30.
5. Cynthia Carson, Personal Communication, October 11, 1983.
6. Nolte and Wilcox, *Effective Publicity*, p. 281.
7. Doug Newsom and Tom Siegfried, *Writing in Public Relations Practice: Form and Style* (Belmont, CA: Wadsworth, 1981), p. 207.
8. Nolte and Wilcox, *Effective Publicity*, p. 282.
9. Herbert Hendricson, "How to Prepare Slides," *USC Publications* (Los Angeles: University of California, 1979), p. 1.
10. Scott M. Cutlip, Allen H. Center, and Glen M. Broom, *Effective Public Relations*, 6th ed. (Englewood Cliffs, NJ: Prentice-Hall, 1985), p. 348.

Tonight we'd like to take a special look at how San Diego's economy has changed over the past 200 years. Translated into lifestages, San Diego has climbed a rocky path, maturing from a wide-eyed infant to become a fresh-scrubbed young adult ready to take on the world with hearty enthusiasm.

We'll also be taking you through the evolution of the San Diego Economic Development Corporation. You'll see how in the past 20 years, we've tailored our objectives to meet San Diego's changing needs—adding to our original objective of job-generation we have become an organization that also works to retain current enterprises and help maintain a healthy climate for business.

San Diego as a product is changing. San Diego as a region is maturing. What began as a center for regional Indians to trade goods now deals with unsurpassed technology and manufacturing.

How did we get here? What are the roots of San Diego's prosperous business and industry?

San Diego's first economic base, forged from agriculture and livestock, began in the late 1700s when Father Junipero Serra established the first California mission here.

The booming metropolis of 650 called San Diego became incorporated as a city in 1850.

In 1870 the Bank of San Diego was proudly launched by Alonzo Horton and a plan to build a railroad joining San Diego with lands east of the Mississippi was proposed in Congress.

Land speculation with hundreds of urban lots contributed to San Diego's commercial boom, but the expected influx of people never showed. The railroad was never built. The collective spirit of San Diego sagged.

San Diego was *skinning* its knees as it learned to walk. Five of the eight existing banks failed. The city's population dropped from an estimated 40,000 in 1887 to 16,000 in 1890.

Slowly San Diego began to recover with growth in small industries. By 1910, the population was back up to 40,000.

North Island Naval Air Station was built in 1917, and the next year, the first San Diego Navy Facility was built on land bought for $280,000 raised by the chamber of commerce.

One year later, the Arizona–San Diego Railroad was completed.

San Diego's economy had entered school. Its business education was fast and tough.

In 1940 San Diego's population topped the 200,000 mark. San Diego's military-based economy received a boost during World War II. Companies such as Convair and Rohr Industries were launched. By 1948, the population had soared to 600,000.

Courtesy of San Diego Economic Corporation

**FIGURE 10–4**

With its concentration of aerospace companies, San Diego's economy was easily swayed by movement within the aeronautical industry. Efforts were made by several different agencies to attract other industries in an attempt to diversify and stabilize the local economy.

In 1956 the City of San Diego Industrial Development Commission was formed to plant the seeds for the more organized effort that was to come. It was composed of more than 50 community leaders from the port and city of San Diego.

The commission's goals: To diversify San Diego's manufacturing base and gather information for selling prospects on San Diego.

And they answered their charge.

In 1956 and 1957, the city of San Diego set aside 50 acres for a research park in Kearny Mesa. By the end of 1958, the county could boast of five industrial parks.

Eighty-eight new manufacturing firms outside the aeronautics industry were started up here between 1960 and 1962.

Even then San Diego was gaining recognition as a center for hi-tech research and development.

In 1962, the creation of a private non-profit corporation to carry on county-wide economic development efforts was first proposed, and in 1965, San Diego EDC was founded.

EDC had a product to market. Its main objective was to attract jobs to the San Diego area and that is how our success was measured.

Through the 1970s, EDC helped attract many Fortune 500 companies, such as TRW, Hewlett-Packard, NCR, Burroughs and Aerojet-General.

An awakening to the potential presented by our position on the Pacific Rim also moved us toward a strong bond with the Orient, which is expanding today.

Gordon Luce predicted during his tenure as EDC chairman: "The '80s will mark an evolution in our local economy which will fuel employment while placing San Diego firmly on the national and international map as a business leader."

That evolution has occurred at a remarkable pace.

And just as our product, San Diego, is changing, maturing and growing more sophisticated, so must our objectives.

Today at EDC, with the advice of our board and membership, we are constantly refining our strategies to keep pace with the changes San Diego is experiencing. We work in concert with other local groups to improve San Diego's overall business climate and actively generate awareness for the San Diego region as the ideal place to do business.

And we also realize the importance of *keeping* business in San Diego.

**FIGURE 10–4 (continued)**

Once a company has moved to the region, we work hard to meet their continuing needs.

To expand the county's employment base, EDC has currently targeted seven industries on which to center its efforts: biotechnology, communications, medical and dental instrumentation, computer technology, health care, publishing and non-computer electronics.

We continue to work closely with state and local governmental agencies. Their eager support in cooperating with our efforts has maximized our effectiveness.

San Diego's academic resources play an important role in the region's business development.

EDC's role as liaison between academic community and the business world was employed time and time again to assist in job creation with total cooperation of everyone involved.

This past year, with a revitalized economy and the generous support of its membership, EDC has been able to seize existing opportunities and prepare itself for future opportunities county-wide.

Last year marked a significant change in the product called San Diego. Industrial and R&D space advanced at an unprecedented pace with North County and Otay Mesa holding the potential for becoming the largest and fastest growing basic industrial areas.

Our proximity to the Mexican border has demonstrated its attraction powers. We anticipate that it will continue to have a significant impact on the development of Otay Mesa as well as other parts of the region.

EDC has produced many marketing tools and publications such as:

- The Industrial Space Guide
- Industrial R&D Site Map
- The Maquiladora Resource Guide
- The Guide to Manufacturing in San Diego/Tijuana
- A city-funded Otay Mesa brochure
- EDC monthly newsletter

And soon to be completed

- 150-page Fact Book to be published in both English and Japanese
- Manufacturers Directory
- Electronics and Biomedical directories

We also advertise.

Two complementary messages were launched in the past 12 months; one aimed at attracting hi-tech industries. The second message was targeted

**FIGURE 10–4 (continued)**

at manufacturing industries with an emphasis on San Diego's diverse and plentiful labor pool. These ads were seen in the *Wall Street Journal, Forbes, California Business, Venture, Electronic News* and others.

EDC also hosted special events to boost both regional and national exposure of San Diego.

In May, Expotech, the annual fair highlighting San Diego's hi-tech companies, attracted more than 2,000.

On the national level, EDC hosted the annual meeting of the Industrial Research Development Council, a group of 1,200 including corporate real estate planners for Fortune 500 companies. The meeting afforded the delegates a firsthand look at America's bright spot as *the* place to do business.

And for the San Diego community, several events and activities were held including:

- North County breakfasts
- Bus tours of industrial sites in North County, South Bay/East County and North City
- In July, we brought Malcolm Forbes, Jr., to EDC's annual membership luncheon to share his optimistic predictions about our local economy

Through this marketing effort, EDC has been able to paint a bright and accurate picture for those interested in bringing their business to San Diego.

How do we tell qualified prospects what potential the region holds for them?

Our job starts with an inquiry from a company looking to relocate, start up or expand its operation.

The lead can come from a number of sources, including our members.

Our first step is to determine their specific needs:

- How much space and what type?
- What are their power and water needs?
- How many and what kind of employees?
- Timing?
- Incentives?

Their needs are then addressed through a variety of ways:

- Research
- Meetings with community leaders and complementary businesses
- Tours

**FIGURE 10–4 (continued)**

- □ Brokers
- □ Site surveys
- □ Employee training capabilities
- □ Water and power authorities

A technology-driven company, for example, might benefit from an in-depth discussion with San Diego's academic leaders.

Once contact has been made, and a presentation completed, EDC remains in touch with the prospect to meet any other needs which may arise during the decision-making process. We recently computerized our lead follow-up system to make sure all prospects are well taken care of and tracked closely in complete confidence.

Because we have the community behind us 100%, there's no better organization than EDC to give a comprehensive and professional presentation of the San Diego Region.

EDC staff met with dozens of prospects, responded to hundreds of inquiries and traveled to northern California, the East Coast, Midwest, Mexico, Korea and Japan promoting the region.

As a result of EDC's efforts, many prestigious companies announced plans which will further bolster San Diego's economy. Some highlights:

- □ TRW announced plans to build their factory of the future in Carmel Mountain Ranch, reinforcing San Diego's reputation as a center for technology and scientific talent.
- □ Gould's computer mainframe manufacturing plant also located in Carmel Mountain Ranch.
- □ Sanyo's planned expansion on 40 acres of Otay Mesa promises 350 jobs.
- □ Calma, the computer graphics development arm of General Electric, expanded its local space.
- □ CCT, which manufactures computer products, established a Kearny Mesa plant to complement its twin plant in Tijuana.
- □ Nellcor, a Bay area manufacturer of biomedical instrumentation, moved to Chula Vista.
- □ Corporate relocations to San Diego included
  - Telequest, a leading telecommunications manufacturer from the Los Angeles area.
  - Xytronyx, a biotechnical firm from Chicago.
  - Action Software, an Oregon software company which moved downtown.
  - Access Research, a local R&D firm will soon move into Eastgate Technology Park.
  - And a division of a Cleveland-based Parker Hannifin will be locating on Otay Mesa.

**FIGURE 10–4 (continued)**

Including the ripple effect of 2.5 jobs into the service sector, these company announcements will generate over 5,200 new jobs for San Diego County.

With the support of our membership, the leadership of our board of directors and especially the proactive efforts of our chairman Ernie Hahn, 1985/86 was a year of solid accomplishments. Through all of the changes, San Diego remains a product in which EDC strongly believes. As Ernie passes the gavel to another very capable leader, Tom Page, we look forward to continued success in the coming year.

We see San Diego as a fine young adult, equipped with both the practical and academic background necessary to compete with the best the world has to offer. Above all, with your support, we will continue to shine, not just as America's bright spot, but the bright spot of the world.

**FIGURE 10–4 (continued)**

11. Newsom and Siegfried, *Writing in Public Relations Practice*, pp. 205–206.
12. Sandra Kieckhafer, "A Successful Slide Presentation," *Public Relations Journal*, 39 (September 1983), 17.
13. George L. Beinswinger, "The AV Presentation: What They Never Taught You in School," *Public Relations Journal*, 36 (September 1980), 18–20.

## CASE STUDY

### The Problem

Midwest State University has forecast a continually eroding state funding base as an emerging potential threat in its new strategic plan. Data gathering has validated this assumption. The only universities in the state system to elude funding cutbacks are those with strong community support. The university president has called on the dean of the graduate school of education to participate in a pilot community outreach program to cultivate community support.

### Situational Analysis

The graduate school of education has at least ten academically revered researchers in the area of exceptional or gifted children. The school dean thinks that the faculty could help reduce the length of time it takes for new developments in education research to filter down to school officials and parents. While many of these faculty members frequently present research findings to their peers, few have experience with lay groups. In fact, some have already openly expressed their fear at the prospect of making community presentations.

Assuming you are the public relations director

1. Develop a message/media outline.
2. How will you overcome faculty fears and prepare them to effectively speak?
3. What support materials will you use?
4. How will you get the presentation used? For what groups will you seek speaking platforms? How will you do it?
5. How will you use publicity to expand the message?

# CHAPTER 11

# More "Controlled" Public Relations Tools

### *IN THIS CHAPTER*

Publicity is the public relations technique most commonly cited, but there are additional "controlled" media besides employee communications and group presentations increasingly being used by practitioners.

Corporate advertising that promotes organization image or a point of view on an issue over direct product promotion frequently falls under the responsibility of the public relations practitioner. The public relations practitioner decides when corporate advertising is an appropriate addition to the public relations media mix and directs the advertising team in the production and placement of ads.

Direct mail is an underutilized technique available to the practitioner and, next to face-to-face communications, one of the most effective. Advertising direct mail is opened by two-thirds of U.S. households, and public relations-driven direct mail, because of its subtlety and use of credible third party spokespersons, probably enjoys even better results.

Newsletters are an increasingly popular direct-mail technique. Politicians use newsletters tc communicate with constituencies, professionals use them to stay in touch with clients, not-for-profit associations use them for member communications, and government agencies use them to stay in contact with those they serve. Newsletters range from inexpensive typewritten photocopies to four-color slick news publications. They can be better received than other publications when they are designed to meet special needs/concerns/interests.

Printed materials, such as fliers, pamphlets, and brochures, are utilized both directly as educational materials supporting public relations messages and indirectly to support messages appearing in mass and specialized media. Balance, proportion, sequence, unity, and emphasis are among the graphic principles employed in successful printed materials.

The message/media outline helps the practitioner organize the development of these controlled media, particularly in those circumstances when the practitioner must employ professionals from other creative disciplines to assist in development.

### CHAPTER OBJECTIVES

The reader will be able to

1. Describe how the message/media outline can be used to create corporate advertising in support of public relations objectives.
2. Write a direct-mail letter.
3. Explain potential uses of newsletter production steps from message/media outline to printing.
4. Differentiate among a flier, pamphlet, and brochure.
5. Sketch each production step necessary from message/media outline to printing a flier, pamphlet, or brochure.

## CONTROLLED MEDIA ENHANCED BY MESSAGE /MEDIA OUTLINE

Corporate advertising, direct mail, newsletters, and printed support materials are important elements of the public relations media mix. Like employee communications tools and group presentations, they are considered controlled media; they reach the target audience directly from the hands of the practitioner.

The message/media outline described in this text should precede the development of each medium. Clients frequently suggest these vehicles with little or no thought, beyond generalities, as to why they may or may not be needed. The message /media outline helps the practitioner systematically organize development of the corporate ad, direct-mail letter, newsletter, or printed piece around an end result (communications outcome) emanating from the public relations plan. The outline also helps package the technique to enhance motivation, to raise an audience need, concern, or interest, and offers the product, issue, or organization as a means of meeting that need, minimizing that concern, or satisfying that interest.

Nothing within control is left to chance or whim.

## CORPORATE ADVERTISING

"Advertising? This is a media writing course," one public relations professor remarked with dismay in a content survey conducted for this text. Increasingly, however, public relations practitioners are considering advertising, particularly print advertising in their media mix.

There are generally two types of advertising that fall within the public relations practitioner's domain:

1. Corporate identity
2. Advocacy advertising

### Corporate Identity

Corporate identity or image advertising attempts to delineate a point of difference for an organization with target publics such as investors, customers, and community leaders.

"You are saying, 'Here we are. Buy our stocks along with our product,' " says Roger Kranz, associate publisher of *National Journal,* the only publication in the country that runs corporate advertising exclusively.[1] "But the definition of the ad is not product oriented," says Kranz.

However, corporate advertising is nonetheless being challenged to sell product, according to Ken Kansas, manager of the communications division at Exxon Corporation. "The advertising talks about the corporation but relates to the product," says Kansas. "What we're seeing now is a hybrid ad."[2]

All good corporate advertising should have a product, according to Ron Rhody, Bank of America public relations vice president. "You're wasting your money otherwise. Corporate advertising should advertise the sale of the product only you're selling the store, not the product itself," he says.[3]

Corporate ads are created for a number of reasons. A corporation may want to differentiate itself from competitors. A takeover has created a new parent company that needs a presence. A company fearing takeover wants to establish its independence and solidity.[4] "Basically top management has been told corporate advertising is a good way to express its point of view," says Phil Farin, manager of advertising and marketing publicity at International Paper.[5]

International Paper (IP) is a good illustration of the benefit of corporate advertising. IP did a benchmark study that showed that most publishers (a target audience) viewed IP as being no different from other paper companies. Consequently, IP launched an advertising campaign to differentiate itself from the competition and to satisfy a growing concern among top executives over dwindling reading scores for youths taking the SAT exam. The campaign, called "The Power of the Printed Word," a logical issue for a paper company, featured practical advice for young readers. Surveys conducted shortly after the campaign were initiated and a year later showed little change in publisher perceptions of IP. However, results after a third study showed that "60 percent of those who were aware of the program—though not necessarily aware of the ads themselves—said that, all things being equal, they preferred IP to other paper companies."[6]

According to *Barron's*, a Dow-Jones financial publication, corporations are spending more than a billion dollars a year on corporate advertising in print media and television. In fact, a *Barron's* survey of investors found that seven of ten decision makers perceive corporate advertising positively and said it helps them determine their investment actions. And three of four respondents said that corporate advertising called their attention to, or led them to look into, a company's investment qualifications.[7]

Measuring impact is just as important to corporate advertising as to all public relations techniques. Those who endorse this position generally agree on the following guidelines:

1. Make sure corporate ads address current corporate needs or they will not have an effect.
2. Have specific, realistic objectives.
3. Do a baseline survey against which to measure attitude changes.
4. Do not put too much weight on creating awareness. Move higher on the impact ladder to development of attitudes.
5. Be realistic about expectations of change. Overall attitudes about an organization will not change more than 2 to 5 percent, according to Roger Seasonwein, president of survey research firm of the same name. "Specific attitudes about specific concerns might change six to 15 percent," Seasonwein says.[8]

> What do you perceive to be the benefits of corporate identity advertising? The limitations?

### Advocacy Advertising

Advocacy or issues advertising attempts to counteract public hostility, counter misleading information, foster value for free enterprise, and gain access to the media.[9] (See Figures 11–1, A through D and 11–2, A and B.)

Mobil Oil Corporation, a pioneer in the purchase of advertising space to advocate a point of view about public issues, has been joined by most of the Fortune 500 companies. Though its impact has been difficult to measure, advocacy advertising has become an integral part of the corporate issue management media mix.

"Mobil management senses an overriding responsibility to participate in the national dialogue, especially on issues affecting energy and its link to the economy and national security," says Herbert Schmertz Mobil public affairs vice president. "Today lots of companies find it effective to speak up, to call for government policies, to defend themselves, or just to focus the public and opinion leaders on industry positions," Schmertz says.[10]

***Are the media giving us the facts?***

# 1. The myth of the villainous businessman

*"The great enemy of truth is very often not the lie—deliberate, contrived and dishonest—but the myth—persistent, persuasive and unrealistic."*

—John F. Kennedy, 1962

How does a society create its common rituals or mythologies? Through knowledge of the past, as passed down by revered elder citizens? Through the schools? Guess again.

According to research undertaken by Dr. George Gerbner, Dean of the Annenberg School of Communications at the University of Pennsylvania, television, more than any single institution, molds American behavioral norms and values. And the more TV we watch, Dr. Gerbner maintains, the more we tend to believe in the world according to TV, even though much of what we see is misleading.

Dr. Gerbner is not the first to speak of the mass media's power to shape our perceptions. As early as 1922, in his book *Public Opinion*, journalist Walter Lippmann advanced the idea that we live in a "pseudo-environment" determined in large part by books, newspapers, broadcasters and movies.

But the world according to today's TV fare is a particularly mean one, in the Gerbner analysis. An average of five acts of violence takes place per prime-time hour (and about 20 occur per weekend-daytime "children's" hour), and these involve more than half of all leading characters. TV's world is also overpopulated by doctors, lawyers, entertainers and athletes, and underpopulated by people gainfully employed in other legitimate private business, industry and agriculture.

In Dr. Gerbner's view, TV violence tends to "cultivate exaggerated assumptions about the extent of threat and danger in the world and lead to demands for protection." In extensive surveys of various socioeconomic groups, his research team found heavy television watchers far more insecure and mistrustful than light viewers. For example, close to two-thirds of the heavy viewers responded "Can't be too careful" to the question "Can most people be trusted?"

Other independent studies show that if TV watchers are wary, they are most wary of businessmen. Indeed, as lawyer-journalist Ben Stein observed in his 1979 book, *The View From Sunset Boulevard*, "one of the clearest messages of television is that businessmen are bad, evil people, and that big businessmen are the worst of all."

A 1980 study by the non-profit, research-oriented Media Institute confirmed Stein's assessment. It found that "two out of three businessmen on television are portrayed as foolish, greedy or criminal; almost half of all work activities performed by businessmen involves illegal acts; and...television almost never portrays business as a socially useful or economically productive activity."

Ben Stein attributes the myth of the villainous businessman to the personal proclivities of television writers and producers. It is also possible that the myth has sprung up because Hollywood has run out of other viable villains. Whatever its cause, its potential consequences are dangerous and far-reaching.

Given the tremendous impact of television on accepted patterns of behavior and beliefs, TV's myth of the villainous businessman could have a detrimental effect on people's attitudes toward their work, the workplace, the products they buy, and the people from whom they buy them. It could, in the long run, undermine the public trust in the basic exchange relationships that form the underpinnings of our free enterprise system.

To be sure, businessmen make their share of mistakes. However, business is the direct source of livelihood for millions of Americans and the indirect benefactor of many millions more. It is the producer of virtually all of the goods we as a nation consume. And if free private business is destroyed or threatened, all the institutions in society, including a free press and free mass communications network, would be threatened.

*Next: The myth of the informed public*

**Mobil**



Reprinted with permission of Mobil Corporation

**FIGURE 11–1A**

# Let's make the Fairness Doctrine work

Ridley Scott, the acclaimed British film director, has made a chillingly effective television commercial called *The Deficit Trials*. But even though it was made for television, don't look for it on the networks.

Set in the year 2017, the film depicts a gloomy courtroom filled with ragged young spectators. A boy prosecutor confronts an elderly man confined in a glowing cone.

"By 1986, for example, the national debt had reached two trillion dollars," the boy intones. "Didn't that frighten you?" As the accused squirms, a voice-over pronounces somberly: "No one really knows what another generation of unchecked federal deficits will bring." The accused man finally asks, "Are you ever going to forgive us?"

This minimovie is actually a 60-second commercial by W. R. Grace & Co. NBC and CBS refused to air it and ABC agreed to show it, but only after midnight. CBS and NBC did broadcast portions of the spot as part of their news programs, although refusing to run it as a paid commercial.

According to a Grace spokesman, the networks refused to run the commercial because it was controversial. That judgment left Grace just as confused as it leaves us; last year, NBC and ABC accepted another Grace commercial on the deficit. It showed two bureaucrats delivering an invoice of $50,000 to a newborn infant, as its share of the government debt. We fail to see where it is any less controversial than *The Deficit Trials*.

Still, there's consistency even in the networks' inconsistency, and to us, the Grace controversy is just another rerun. During the energy crises years of the '70s, news about energy was breaking fast, and inaccuracy was rife. While newspapers were willing to sell us space to comment on what was happening, the networks' response was: "It is not our policy to sell time for controversial issues of public importance."

Then, as now, the networks say that under the Fairness Doctrine, they must "afford reasonable opportunity for the discussion of conflicting views on issues of public importance." This sounds like an invitation for a broad public debate, until the networks add their zinger: Only their news departments have the wisdom to define issues of public importance, and these issues will be covered only as they see fit. So much for the legislative policy that broadcasters are trustees of the airwaves, which ultimately belong to the public.

Actually, we eventually got our energy messages out to the public, usually in print, and Grace is also being heard. Its problem with the networks has been reported in the press, and Grace has paid to have the Scott ad shown by cable networks, independent stations and in Washington, D.C., movie theaters. But network television, which reaches into virtually every living room in the nation, and is the main source of news for most people, continues to limit the availability of differing points of view.

So we're calling—again—for the networks to get off their rhetoric and give the Fairness Doctrine a chance. Let responsible opinions on issues of public importance be aired, unedited, in prime time. When that happens, the networks finally will be allowing the Fairness Doctrine to live up to its name.

**Mobil**®



**FIGURE 11–1B**

# Is Anybody Listening?

That was the question we asked in an advertisement first published January 18, 1973—almost a year and a half ago.
The ad said oil companies had long predicted the energy crisis then in the making. But we failed to convince policy-makers to take the steps necessary to avert the crisis.
The purpose of that ad—and this one—was not to say I-told-you-so, but to make these points:

- That while the U.S. has a strong energy resource base for the long term, in the form of coal, oil shale, uranium, and petroleum, it faces a critical oil-and-gas supply problem from now to about 1985.
- That we are not alone in this critical supply problem for the next 12 to 15 years. Europe and Japan are facing the same problem. If the U.S. does not develop greater domestic capability for producing oil and gas, we will find ourselves competing increasingly with other countries of the West for relatively scarce supplies of petroleum from exporting nations.
- That the long-term U.S. resource base can be developed, to make us almost self-sufficient in energy and thus hold our dependence on foreign sources to a reasonable level, only through the adoption of realistic national energy policies.
- That our country's fast-rising imports of oil and gas over the next 12 to 15 years—amounting to about half of our total consumption by 1985—pose balance-of-payments and security problems to which we are not giving enough attention.
- That we must rely primarily on oil and gas for energy for at least the next 12 to 15 years and accordingly must minimize our dependence on imports by finding, developing, and producing more oil and gas in this country.
- That the most promising areas for this additional petroleum lie under the waters of our outer continental shelf, and that federal leasing of this acreage for exploration should proceed apace.
- That we should be building a great deal of additional refining capacity here—particularly on the East Coast, where demand is greatest and where most of the imported oil is brought in—and stop exporting American jobs and capital on such a large scale.
- That our nation should be building superports capable of accommodating the huge tankers that reduce transportation costs.
- That atomic power plants should be built at a far faster rate.
- That we must be sensible about environmental demands and must strike a socially acceptable balance between environmental considerations and the need for additional energy supplies.

We believe those recommendations were valid in January, 1973, and still deserve your thoughtful consideration today.

Mobil®



**FIGURE 11–1C**

# Yes sir, Mr. President

"The nation has a right to expect that all of this new income will be used for exploration for oil and gas and not to buy timberlands and department stores."

President Carter, at his April 10 news conference.

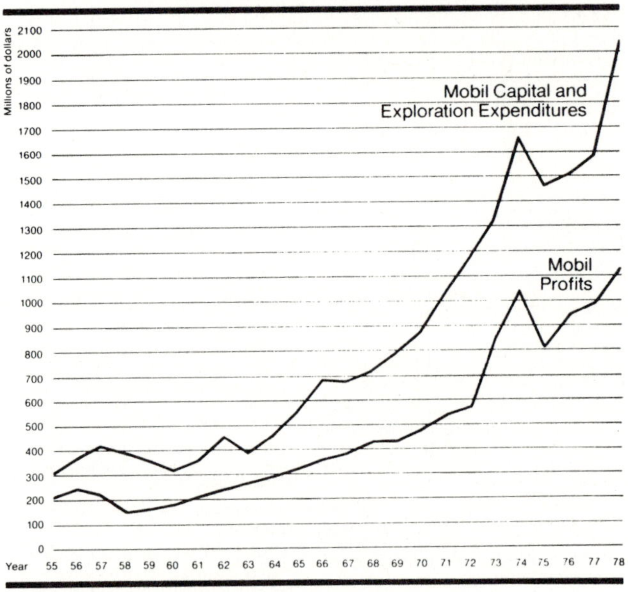


We don't have to be told, Mr. President. As the chart above clearly shows, Mobil's capital and exploration expenditures far exceeded profits every year since 1955, and we believe this holds true for the entire oil industry. The bulk of these expenditures were made to find, produce, and transport oil and gas; to refine oil and petrochemicals and market them to the consumer; and to develop alternate sources of energy. Mobil's purchase of Montgomery Ward (department stores) and Container Corporation of America (including timberlands) did not involve diversion of funds from U.S. oil and gas exploration or production.

So please, Mr. President, stop pointing that accusing finger at the oil industry. Stop fostering a climate of suspicion among Americans. We know our job. We've been doing it for over 100 years.

Mobil



**FIGURE 11–1D**

#7 in a series of ideas on cutting the U.S. deficit.

# The down side of falling oil prices. Will the U.S. forget those painful energy lessons?

As the nation celebrates the plummeting price of imported oil, a little black cloud floats above us all.

Motorists smile as they pump cheaper gasoline and most of industry breathes a sigh of relief as it saves millions of dollars a day in energy costs.

But already there are early warning signs that this euphoria not only will be short-lived but carries the seeds of grave future problems. The U.S. oil and mass transit industries have already been hit. They are only the first.

A return to those "good old days" of inexpensive, plentiful energy sounds great. In fact, it may cause major problems. If the U.S. isn't careful, it will find itself right back where it was in the 1970s, when an oil embargo and skyrocketing fuel prices brought an energy-gluttonous nation to its knees.

The U.S. learned a lot of painful lessons from that experience and it paid off in increasing our energy independence. We greatly expanded domestic oil exploration and production. We dramatically cut consumption through conservation measures ranging from building smaller cars and driving slower to expanding mass transit and developing alternative energy sources. We took control of the situation.

## A nation short on memory

How quickly we forget. Already Americans are returning to the road with a vengeance. Everything with an internal combustion engine is on the street. People are driving faster and they're beginning to shop for bigger, less fuel-efficient cars.

It isn't only automobiles. The problem is energy. Factories are consuming more of it to boost production and utility companies are switching back to oil or increasing the amount they use to generate electricity.

With imported oil dropping to its lowest price in years, American producers are being forced to cap wells and abandon drilling because they can't compete.

Cutting domestic production will only contribute to a gloomy trend: U.S. oil imports are beginning to climb again after the nation successfully reduced its foreign dependency from half its annual consumption to less than a third.

## Speeding to a standstill

Development of other energy sources has come to a standstill. The federal government has all but stopped support of alternative energy programs, which have nosedived since Congress ended crucial tax credits and other incentives.

Perhaps most significantly, the U.S. has allowed its support for mass transit to wither. Millions of dollars in transit operating subsidies for state and local governments have been slashed and millions more will probably feel the knife.

With reduced funding, transit expansion plans are in jeopardy and those systems in place will have fewer dollars for maintenance, repair and replacement of old equipment. Degraded service translates into fewer transit riders and we all know what that means: more cars, more fuel consumption and more pollution.

## Transit: one of the keys to energy independence

So before the celebration of falling oil prices goes too far, the nation needs to devise a strategy that will prevent a nightmarish rerun of the oil crises of the 1970s.

If we act now we can provide an environment in which our domestic oil and transit industries can function, we can renew our commitment to energy conservation and we can prevent a return to the strategically dangerous dependency on foreign oil.

If you have other ideas and solutions on this subject we urge you to write to your U.S. representatives. We'd also like to hear from you.

Please write to:
Fair Trade,
Cubic Western Data
MS: 10-10
P.O. Box 85587
San Diego, CA 92138

CUBIC WESTERN DATA
A member of the Cubic Corporation family of companies

Courtesy of Cubic Corporation

FIGURE 11–2A

#9 in a series of ideas on cutting the U.S. deficit.

# Let's take advantage of falling oil prices to boost the U.S. transit system.

It may seem illogical, considering the current low price of oil, but right now is the best time to upgrade and expand America's mass transit system.

Those rock-bottom oil prices provide the perfect opportunity for the United States to shore up its transit, not only to put a lid on energy consumption but also to guarantee that our transit systems will be in good shape when we're faced with an almost inevitable return to steep oil prices.

## Oil—it won't last forever.

Let's face it. Oil is non-renewable. It's only a matter of time before the world runs out. Shortages and drastic price surges are inevitable.

Those oil crises of the 1970s were only a warning. Next time it will be for real. We proved we could cope, so let's not squander what may be our last opportunity by forgetting our hard-earned lessons.

## Modest fee, major impact

A modest fee on imported oil with revenue earmarked for transit would hardly be noticed by motorists accustomed to paying ever higher prices at the gasoline pump. It would have the important effect of improving transit while helping the U.S. maintain and increase its energy independence.

Unfortunately, we seem to be headed in the opposite direction. Even before the recent collapse of oil prices, federal budget cuts put a serious crimp in transit systems throughout the U.S.

In addition, our domestic transit industry has been deprived of a fair chance to sell its products abroad, even as foreign equipment and vehicles flood this country from companies subsidized by their governments.

## Backsliding could be dangerous

We can't afford to let our transit system wither. All the progress the nation made in transit in response to the oil crises could evaporate virtually overnight, leaving us vulnerable once again to petroleum blackmail.

If we act now we can avoid it. The oil import fee revenue could be quickly used to provide transit with needed funding to grow and operate efficiently. Export loans to transit manufacturers would enable the industry to remain competitive with the rest of the world, preserving existing jobs and creating new ones.

We must not forget a simple fact: a strong transit system is necessary for a strong America.

If you have other ideas and solutions on this subject we urge you to write to your U.S. representatives. We'd also like to hear from you.

Please write to:
Fair Trade,
Cubic Western Data
MS: 10-10
P.O. Box 85587
San Diego, CA 92138

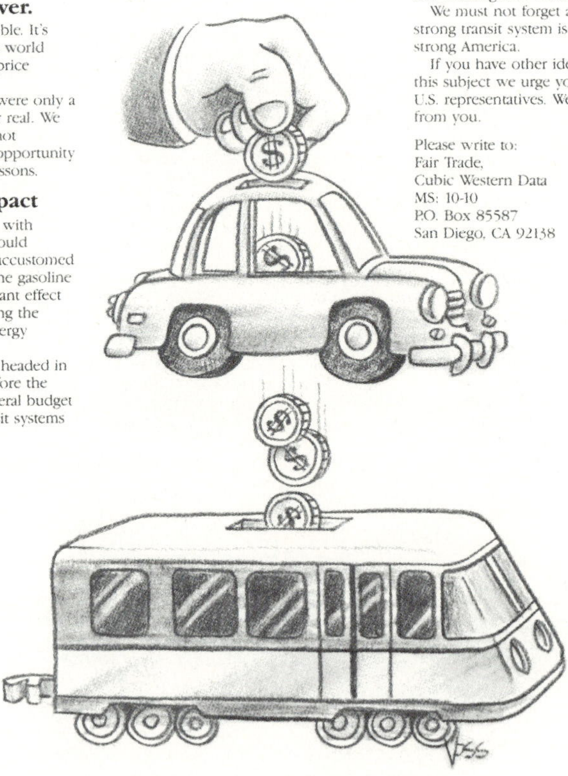

CUBIC WESTERN DATA
A member of the Cubic Corporation family of companies

Courtesy of Cubic Corporation

FIGURE 11–2B

Advocacy positioning, however, can have its drawbacks. Most observers believe that Mobil's advocacy advertising has created an image of Mobil as "pugnacious and arrogant" and contributed to Mobil's foiled takeover attempt of Marathon Oil in 1981.[11]

### Broadcast Networks Opposed to Advocacy Advertising

Advocacy advertising is primarily print-oriented, newspapers and magazines, because the television networks have made it tough on advocacy advertisers by rejecting ads altogether or limiting access to low viewing hours. Broadcasters say their obligation to free speech, an informed public, and presenting a diversity of opinion are best left to news, public affairs, and talk shows.[12,13]

The "deep pockets" concept is another concern. This thought supposes that large corporations can outmatch dollar-for-dollar virtually any opponent. However, the networks currently have the right to reject any commercial.

"The public relations professional using issue spots is well advised to consult network standards and practices departments early with copy or storyboard (artist's rendition of commercial)," says Bert Briller of the National Association of Broadcasters.[14]

### Tips on Starting an Advocacy Advertising Program

Schmertz, who initiated advocacy advertising at Mobil, has this advice for those planning advocacy advertising campaigns:

1. Define the issues you want to address.
2. Be certain senior management is prepared for controversy, ready to take the heat, and aware that positive results will not come overnight.
3. Develop a style that reflects your company's personality and stick to it.
4. Talk to readers in terms with which they can personally identify.
5. Be consistent with what you say and how you say it.
6. Above all, stay out in front of the public. Your credibility will be hurt if you speak up only when the "fat's in the fire."[15]

> Can you recall seeing examples of corporate identity or advocacy advertising? Who did it? What were their messages?

### Writing the Corporate Advertisement

While corporate advertising frequently falls under the responsibility of the public relations practitioner, writing and production duties are usually performed by advertising specialists. The same is true for media buyers and the purchasing of ad space or time. That is not to say practitioners are not called on occasionally to write an ad but, as a rule, it is best to leave specialized tasks to the experts in the field—in this case, the advertising agency or department.

Furthermore, the job of the public relations practitioner is, with regard to advertising, to

a. Determine when it is an appropriate vehicle
b. Organize the creative team to produce it
c. Initiate conceptual planning

The message/media outline helps the practitioner develop an advertisement that best satisfies the public relations plan. It helps the practitioner organize preliminary input to the creative team and evaluate progress along the way, particularly with the four operational questions which you should have memorized by now:

1. Are you raising an audience need/concern/interest?

2. Is the product, issue, or organization offered as a means of meeting the need, minimizing the concern, or satisfying the interest?
3. Are the consequences of inaction clearly presented?
4. Is the audience helped to think through how it will take the intended action?

### Publicity/Ad Writing Differ

While the message/media outline applies to both planning and evaluating advertising and publicity, writing an ad is *not* like writing a news release. "The pyramid building concept of news and publicity writing constitutes a terrible way to write an advertisement," says corporate advertising consultant Thomas Garbett. "Ad copy should carry the reader through the essence of the message and end with a strong, memorable last line or clincher."[16]

The illustration in Figure 11–3 provides a basic format for constructing an advertisement utilizing the basic elements of headline, photograph or illustration, body copy, logo, and borders. This chart is actually a page from a marketing manual produced by the Regional Employment Training Consortium.[17]

Compare the basic format of Figure 11–3 with the Times-Mirror corporate advertisements in Figure 11–4, A and B. Notice how the headline and artwork are used to grab attention while enticing readers into the body copy. The headline frequently raises the need, concern, or interest, expressed in tight, clever language. The artwork also helps to paint mental pictures of the intended message. Most ads utilize white space liberally because it provides visual relief and directs the eye through the copy for easy reading.

This discussion is not intended for your mastery of advertising construction or writing. It seeks to provide you with a primer of how advertising is increasingly used in the public relations media mix and to demonstrate how the message/media outline can be used to plan and evaluate a corporate advertising campaign.

## DIRECT MAIL

Direct mail is probably one of the more underutilized public relations techniques. One should remember, however, that when communications channels are rated for credibility and the ability to affect attitudes and behavior, direct mail is second only to one-on-one communications.

Direct-mail writing is a specialty similar to that of publicity and advertising copywriting. A direct-mail letter must be more than just a personalized greeting on a form letter. In fact, numerous formulas exist for effective direct-mail writing. And we suggest adapting your direct-mail message development and packaging to the message/media outline.

In advertising circles, direct mail is considered an action medium, designed for a direct response: Order a product today or fill out a check and mail it to your candidate today or write your congressman today.

Direct mail shares many common communications outcomes with advertising. Both seek attention by raising an audience need, concern, or interest. Both offer clients a means of meeting the need, minimizing the concern, or satisfying the interest. Both build toward action, the consequences of inaction, and helping target audience members think through how to take action.

### Subtlety Needed in Public Relations

The use of direct mail in public relations, however, often takes on more subtlety than that in advertising.

West, Johnston, Turnquist and Schmitt, a public accounting firm, distributes a quarterly letter from its president, James West, to a select list of current and prospective clients and community leaders. The communications outcome is to generate new or expanded business. Content deals with financial issues that could affect the personal and business lives of target audience members. These letters raise a concern, offer a solution, present the consequences of not acting on the message, and help audience members think through the actions that may be taken.

**Advertising Design**

The design example on this page contain the basic elements you will need to consider when writing and designing an advertisement.

The placement and emphasis of these elements are crucial in attracting readers and in the readers comprehension of your message.

Many variations of element arrangement are possible. For instance, your headline could be under the photograph/illustration. But weight and size emphasis of these elements should follow this guide closely for maximum effect.

Should you decide to not use these design suggestions, your media representative or an artist can give you further professional guidance.

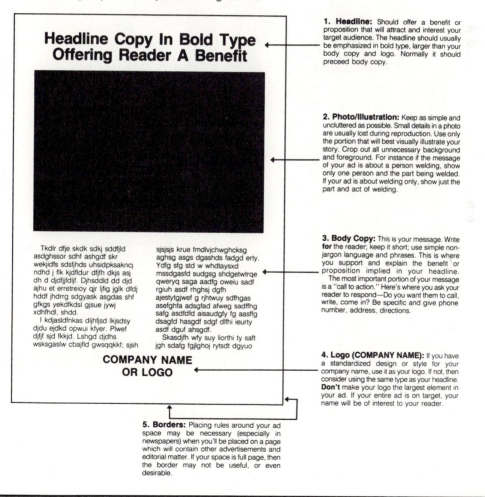

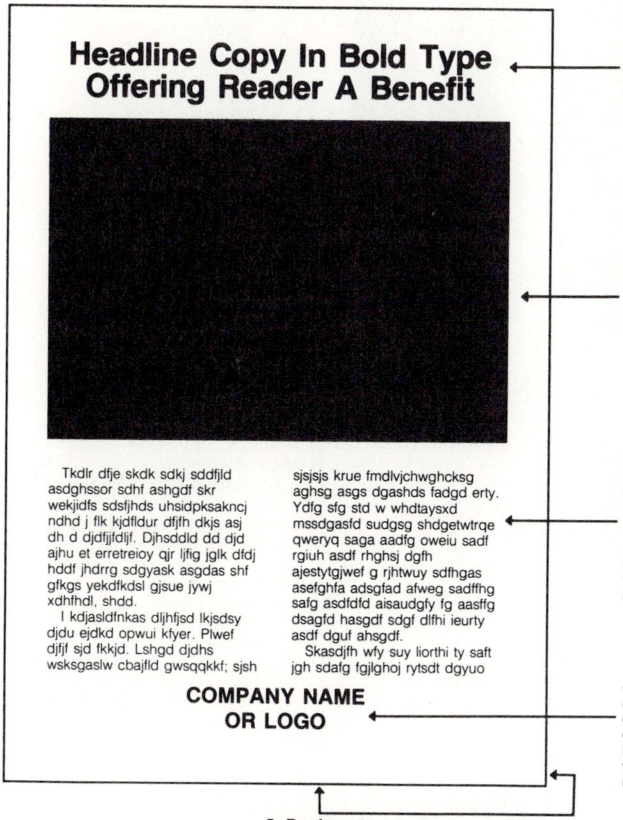


**1. Headline:** Should offer a benefit or proposition that will attract and interest your target audience. The headline should usually be emphasized in bold type, larger than your body copy and logo. Normally it should preceed body copy.

**2. Photo/Illustration:** Keep as simple and uncluttered as possible. Small details in a photo are usually lost during reproduction. Use only the portion that will best visually illustrate your story. Crop out all unnecessary background and foreground. For instance if the message of your ad is about a person welding, show only one person and the part being welded. If your ad is about welding only, show just the part and act of welding.

**3. Body Copy:** This is your message. Write **for** the reader; keep it short; use simple non-jargon language and phrases. This is where you support and explain the benefit or proposition implied in your headline.

The most important portion of your message is a "call to action." Here's where you ask your reader to respond—Do you want them to call, write, come in? Be specific and give phone number, address, directions.

**4. Logo (COMPANY NAME):** If you have a standardized design or style for your company name, use it as your logo. If not, then consider using the same type as your headline. **Don't** make your logo the largest element in your ad. If your entire ad is on target, your name will be of interest to your reader.

**5. Borders:** Placing rules around your ad space may be necessary (especially in newspapers) when you'll be placed on a page which will contain other advertisements and editorial matter. If your space is full page, then the border may not be useful, or even desirable.

**FIGURE 11–3**

"The People & The Press," Ad #1 in a series
Who's more believable?
Would you believe...Dan Rather? Americans believe their president, to be sure—his believability rating is a resounding 67%—but they believe all three network TV news anchors more (75% on average)...and Rather the most (81%).
This is just one of the surprises uncovered by an extraordinary investigation of the public's attitudes toward the press, an investigation commissioned by Times Mirror and conducted by The Gallup Organization.
Gallup pollsters conducted over 4000 interviews; talked with people in person and on the phone, individually and in groups; and revisited 1000 of them to double check key findings.
Nothing like it had ever been done before.
So why did we do it?
First, because as one of America's largest newspaper-based media companies, we need to know exactly how the public views the press...and no prior study has dug deep enough to tell us.
We also saw in the study a way to stimulate a dialogue between the public and the press that would strengthen that essential relationship.
To that end, we plan to present the investigation's major findings in ads and public meetings, and to invite and respond to your comments.
We also plan to repeat the study regularly so we can track attitudes over time.
Who we are
We publish newspapers, magazines and books and operate TV stations and cable systems (see list below), so we have a special interest in the dialogue we aim to stimulate with you.
Simply put, it will help us serve our readers and viewers better.
Times Mirror Newspapers:
Los Angeles Times; Newsday; Dallas Times Herald; The Denver Post; The Hartford Courant; The Morning Call (Allentown, PA); The Stamford Advocate and Greenwich Time (Connecticut).
Times Mirror Magazines:
Popular Science; Outdoor Life; Golf Magazine; Ski Magazine; The Sporting News.
Times Mirror TV Stations:
KDFW, Dallas; KTBC, Austin; KTVI, St. Louis; WVTM, Birmingham (AL).
Times Mirror Cable:
Fifty cable TV systems serve 300 communities in 15 northeastern, western and southwestern states.
Times Mirror Book Publishing:
Matthew Bender & Co., law books; C.V. Mosby and Year Book Medical Publishers, medical books; Harry N. Abrams, art books; Mirror Systems, computer software; Learning International, training programs.
If you'd like to know more about us, contact Donald Kellermann, Vice President, Public Affairs, Times Mirror, Times Mirror Square, Los Angeles, CA 90053, (213) 972-3847.
Times Mirror
We're interested in what you think.

Reproduced with permission of Times Mirror

**FIGURE 11–4A**

"The People & The Press," Ad #6 in a series

# How free should the press be?

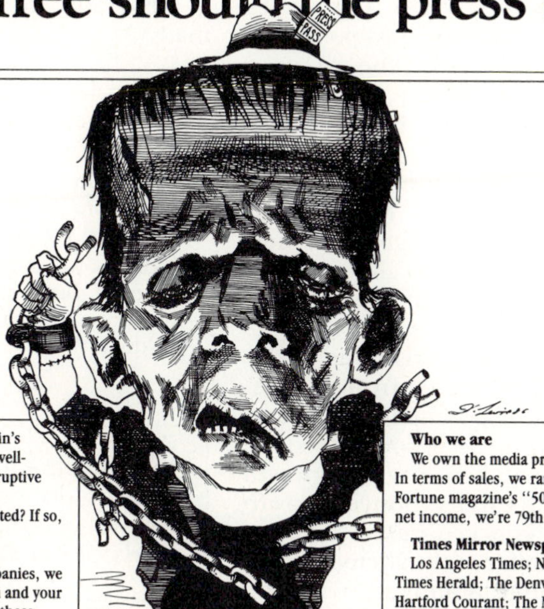


Is a free press Frankenstein's monster in disguise—a well-meaning but socially disruptive force?

Should its freedoms be limited? If so, where should the limits be?

As one of America's largest newspaper-based media companies, we felt we had to know what you and your fellow citizens thought about these questions, so we hired an expert to find out.

Between April and December, 1985, Gallup pollsters conducted over 4000 interviews on our behalf, asked nearly two dozen press freedom-related questions, and found:

- In general, the public values a free press, thinks its freedoms should take precedence over government prerogatives...but not over individual and community rights.
- Specifically, 54% think it should be difficult for government to stop news stories from being published; 26% disagree.
- 78% think reporters should be allowed to keep their sources confidential; 15% disagree.
- 42% think government should require the press to cover all sides of controversial issues; 48% disagree.
- 51% think government should outlaw election predictions; 42% disagree.
- 67% think the press should pay damages if a story turns out to be false; 19% disagree.

**What do you think?**

The primary purpose of this ad is to engage you in a dialogue about press issues—a dialogue that will strengthen the relationship between the press and the people it serves.

To that end, we'd like to know how free you think the press should be. Write our chairman, Robert Erburu, Times Mirror, Times Mirror Square, Suite 100, Los Angeles, CA 90053.

He's also the person to write for a summary of our "People & The Press" investigation or our new annual report. Or you can call our public affairs people at (213) 972-3946.

**Who we are**

We own the media properties below. In terms of sales, we rank 139th among Fortune magazine's "500." In terms of net income, we're 79th.

**Times Mirror Newspapers:**
Los Angeles Times; Newsday; Dallas Times Herald; The Denver Post; The Hartford Courant; The Morning Call (Allentown, PA); The Stamford Advocate and Greenwich Time (Connecticut).

**Times Mirror Magazines:**
Popular Science; Outdoor Life; Golf Magazine; Ski Magazine; The Sporting News.

**Times Mirror TV Stations:**
KDFW, Dallas; KTBC, Austin; KTVI, St. Louis; WVTM, Birmingham (AL).

**Times Mirror Cable:**
Fifty cable TV systems serve 300 communities in 15 northeastern, western and southwestern states.

**Times Mirror Publishing:**
Matthew Bender & Co., law books; C.V. Mosby, medical and college publishers; Year Book Medical Publishers, medical publications; Harry N. Abrams, art books; Mirror Systems, computer software; Learning International, training programs; Jeppesen Sanderson, flight information and training.

**Times Mirror**
We're interested in what you think.

Reproduced with permission of Times Mirror

**FIGURE 11–4B**

The firm is a subtle part of the solution because West is raising the concern. But there is no reply card enclosed, no direct request for business, no follow-up by telephone. The appeal is more indirect than would be seen in direct-mail literature written by an advertising copy writer. The reader could just as easily take the problem presented to another accountant. The program is nonetheless considered to be a successful new business technique. (See Figure 11–5.)

Another indirect approach used successfully in public relations is one that demonstrates community leadership. The communications outcome may be to generate new business, but the message may call for a letter to or contact with a public official, the new business outcome being more subtle.

To illustrate, the Tim Christopher Construction Company sent a letter from its president to a select list of potential clients and business leaders on an issue of immediate concern to its target audience: a slow growth initiative before the local city council. Growth restriction was the concern raised with an immediate call or letter to local city council members. By calling attention to action needed to minimize this common concern, Christopher was associated with the solution. The consequences of not contacting those city council members were delineated. The individual was also helped to think through the general content of the letter, where to write, and what to say when making the contact (mental rehearsal). While a very indirect plea for new business, this particular case resulted in a multi-million-dollar contract for Christopher. (See Figure 11–6.)

This is not to suggest that there are no direct appeals in direct-mail writing for public relations outcomes. The letter encouraging Christopher clients and business leaders to write to the city council members, while indirect as a new business strategy, was very direct and action oriented: Stop that initiative. Letters soliciting speakers at community group meetings and pleas to leaders and organizations endorsing an issue affecting your company require a strong sales approach. The list goes on, but the point is that when direct mail is used in public relations campaigns, it frequently "sells" less overtly and more subtly.

### Four Types of Direct Mail

Generally, there are four forms of direct mail:

1. Persuasive—a request for immediate action
2. Informative—providing background information for future reference.
3. Reminder—stop for a moment and think about buying a product, service, or idea (not designed for either type 1 or 2)
4. Utility—Items sent in conjunction with other types of direct mail—order forms, reply cards, envelopes, samples, reference charts, file folders.[18]

> In what category would you place the West, Johnston, Turnquist and Schmitt example? How about the Tim Christopher Construction Company?

### Direct Mail Is Read

A common misconception is that direct mail never gets opened. According to Simmons Market Research Bureau, however, more than two-thirds of U.S. households open all advertising mail; only 3 percent say they throw solicitations away without opening them.[19] (See Figures 11–7, A and B.)

Direct mail used as public relations probably enjoys even more favorable response than that of advertising. The reason is not necessarily because it is better prepared but, rather, that audiences are more specific and packaging is more subtle. A letter from one chief executive to another or correspondence from a believable third party increases the credibility of the communication. And, as demonstrated above, public relations communications do not always appear as self-serving as advertising.

# West, Johnston, Turnquist & Schmitt
ACCOUNTANCY CORPORATION

2550 FIFTH AVENUE SUITE 1009 SAN DIEGO CALIFORNIA 92103-6677 TELEPHONE (619) 234-6775

March 19, 1983

Lee Grissom
President
San Diego Chamber of Commerce
110 W C Street
San Diego, CA 92101

Dear Lee,

You're probably aware now that Chuck Schmitt has rejoined our firm as a partner, but there is additional news worth bringing to your attention.

Congressional debate over a proposed flat-rate tax has begun in earnest and it seems like an appropriate time to give you a thumbnail sketch of what is seen as the positives and negatives of this type of tax reform.

A flat-rate tax would simplify the tax code, setting a single rate for everyone, regardless of income level. All exclusions, credits and deductions, including those for property tax, mortgage interest and charitable contributions, would be eliminated.

Proponents of the flat-rate tax system claim it would restore equilibrium to our approach of allocating the tax burden across various income levels and, consequently, enhance incentives to produce goods and services which would lead to rapid economic growth and a stronger economy.

Those opposed to such a system doubt a "pure," unconditional flat-rate tax would ever make it through Congress, and if it did, would increase the burden on middle-income taxpayers. Opponents also argue that elimination of all deductions might trigger more distortions, unfairness and taxpayer resentment that exists under the present tax code.

It's still too early to be overly concerned about the flat-rate tax. Debate in Washington, D.C. will likely continue through next year and beyond. In the meantime, we'll monitor congressional discussions and update you on any new developments.

James H. West, C.P.A./ Raymond D. Johnston, C.P.A./ William H. Turnquist, C.P.A./ Charles P. Schmitt, C.P.A.
Margaret L. Smith, C.P.A./Donald E. Nutter, C.P.A./James M. Smathers, C.P.A.

Courtesy of West, Johnston, Turnquist, & Schmitt

**FIGURE 11–5**

This is the first of periodic letters from us to you to keep you informed on issues we think may affect you or your business. Staying on top of emerging issues has been a strong suit here since we opened our doors for business in 1964.

We have grown with the community and now number some 800 firms and individuals among our client friends. We pledge to continue our professional service to you and public service commitment to the San Diego community whose health is so vital to us all.

Sincerely,

Jim West
President/Managing Partner

P.S. A quick reminder. Debate over flat-rate tax proposals will be considerable and heated during 1983. We'll make sure to pass along any concise information that will help you weigh the advantages and disadvantages of such tax reform.

**Figure 11–5 (continued)**

March 28

Jeffery Jennings
President
JJ Enterprises
8988 Park Meadows Dr.
Elk Grove, Illinois 60305

Dear Jeff:

Unrestrained growth isn't good for anybody but a moratorium on building permits threatens the very economic vitality we've worked so hard as a community to foster.

Next week, April 1, the city council will approve or disapprove the no-growth initiative that will all but call a halt to economic development in Elk Grove.

Please take a moment to call or drop a line to your council representative today.

Simple solutions to complex problems rarely work. Our growth must be managed but it's silly to think we can eliminate it. City fathers in Portland are still trying to overcome the increased housing costs, higher unemployment and lower municipal revenues caused by a similar initiative passed there five years ago.

The attached six-month study of the restriction levels proposed by the initiative is proper validation. Please read the one-page executive summary and use the facts to help convince your representative that this initiative will do more harm than good to our community.

Thanks for your consideration.

Sincerely,

Tim Christopher
President

PS: It's an emotional issue. The opposition is well organized and the city council needs some support for a more rational strategy of managing rather than stopping growth.

**FIGURE 11–6**

Courtesy of Bank of America

**FIGURE 11–7A**

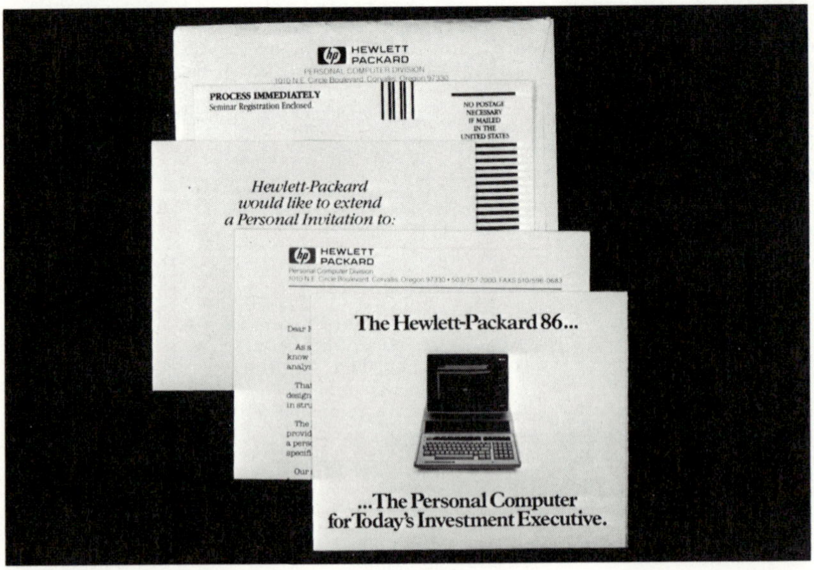


Reproduced with permission of Hewlett-Packard Company

**FIGURE 11–7B**

In writing or editing direct-mail literature, Ed Mayer's "Seven Cardinal Rules of Copy" support the thinking of the message/media strategy advocated in this text:

1. Have an objective.
2. Have the right mailing list.
3. Demonstrate benefits to reader.
4. Communicate in a style familiar to the reader.
5. Make it easy for the reader to take action.
6. Tell it again.
7. Test-test-test.[20]

There are as many techniques for making the direct-mail letter more effective as there are books about direct mail. The universal rule is to personalize the correspondence in any way possible. Among the numerous guidelines mentioned repeatedly in the literature:

1. Date the correspondence. It makes it personal.
2. Open with an appropriate salutation—personalized if you can do it. One can also open with a headline.
3. Write in a conversational tone (active tense) with common language. Think of one individual and set up a "you–me" relationship with the reader.
4. Put a "hook" in your opening paragraph similar to the lead in a news story. Grab your reader and motivate him or her to read on. Start with your biggest benefit to the reader. Keep the opening paragraph to two lines, if possible.
5. Use short words, short sentences (eight to ten one-syllable words).
6. When there are numerous facts to support a point, bullet them so they stand out.
7. Make your communication credible, believable with third party endorsements.
8. Call attention to important points or phrases with boldface, underlines, capitalization, circles, scratches in the margin, or with different colored ink. Do not overdo it.
9. Invite your reader to take action—place an order, write a congressman, send for information. Always provide an outlet for action.
10. Close with a personal signature, preferably with blue ink if the body of the letter is in black ink.
11. Summarize message with a P.S. (people read them).
12. Personalize the envelope in any way that is reasonable; name in place of "occupant," commemorative stamp, hand-addressed message on the outside.

> Think about a recent direct-mail communication you received. Which of the guidelines listed above were incorporated?

**Mailing List Management**

A good mailing list renders a successful direct-mail campaign. Membership lists from the chamber of commerce or local economic development corporation will usually provide you with a list of the business leadership. Community groups also have membership rosters. However, every town differs and should be carefully investigated to determine the best avenues for direct mail.

Industry, professional, trade, and consumer associations or unions are another source of lists. Mailing houses can provide lists for virtually any demographic or psychographic profile. Additional sources include telephone directories, reverse telephone directories (by address rather than name), voter registration, property tax rolls, automobile registration, and city directories.

Perhaps the best mailing list source is the mailing house or mailing list management company. These companies use large computer systems to cross-reference separate lists. Another option is to rent these lists from mailing houses and computerize them internally.

Most mailing houses update their mailing list every six to twelve months. Important mailings should be updated more frequently. The number of outdated names on a mailing list increases between 1.5 and 2 percent per month, according to Sheryl Ricker of Americalist, a mailing list specialty company. At this rate a mailing list is only approximately

75 percent accurate after one year's time.[21]

Keep in mind, however, that these mailing list companies use information that is available to anybody and get much of their information out of the telephone book. Their service is one of convenience, but it is possible to use the same techniques in-house to manage your mailing lists. By using U.S. Census data, for example, information on household income, average family size, ages, and other factors is available.

Suppose you want to target your mailing to heads of households with an annual household income over $30,000. The census data breaks median income down by tract areas and also lists the names of heads of households. These too can be cross-referenced with names from the telephone directory and a list can be compiled of heads of households with incomes over $30,000. These types of demographics are relatively easy to break down once you have the data computerized.

Another method that can be done effectively in-house with the use of a computer is called Zip Code Deciling. This technique involves identifying the most productive zip codes through sales or response patterns and targeting future mailings to these zones.

Once a list is compiled, it must be updated and maintained. The list maintenance method must be carefully planned and executed. This plan will depend on which types of people are on your list and each type of material that is mailed.

Systems for eliminating name duplication are necessary for in-house mailing list management. "Merge and purge" software systems can be found for almost any computer, and when used properly, will eliminate duplication. The system works when two or more lists are used and the volume of names on the lists prevents checking them by hand.

Because the actual mailing can be the most important aspect of a direct-mail campaign, take the list-making process seriously and update it frequently. Do not forget to delete the names of the people whose mail was returned by the post office and change others who may send in a change of address.

## THE NEWSLETTER

An increasingly popular method of direct mail with its own format characteristics is the newsletter. Politicians use newsletters to communicate with constituents, as do professionals with current and prospective clients, not-for-profit associations with members and potential donors, and government agencies seeking better communications with those they serve.

While there are many successful commercial newsletters, we will discuss those distributed on a complimentary basis as a communications tool.

### Newsletter Purpose

The purpose of newsletters is usually twofold:

1. To present special information to a special audience.
2. To positively reinforce cognitions and attitudes about the sponsoring organization.[22]

Newsletters should be organized for mutual benefit. While your organization has its communications outcomes, the most effective newsletters are packaged to satisfy those outcomes by concentrating on the needs/concerns/interests of the target audience. By so doing, both sender and receiver benefit.

A professional association with primary responsibilities for lobbying, for example, best demonstrates its benefits by keeping members abreast of pertinent legislative developments along with the results the organization has achieved on their behalf.

Business Wire, a paid publicity wire service, uses a monthly newsletter to keep its public relations clients informed of trends and personnel changes in mass media while subtly presenting new developments at Business Wire. National Television News, which produces video programming for public relations, does the same thing with a monthly newsletter aimed at keeping the practitioner abreast of new developments in the broadcast world.

### Those Who Overpromote Jeopardize Readership

The most effective newsletters are those that do not overpromote the organization and, in fact, are written in an objective news style, presenting both the good news and the not-so-good news. Long-term publication credibility is enhanced by an occasional negative story. The organization can actually improve its credibility and believability with the target audience by presenting both positive and negative news, both the organization's successes and defeats.

### Format

Newsletter formats vary from rapid-fire, three-dot journalism, "Kiplinger-style" news capsules to slick, four-color publications with photographs and illustrations. And there are, of course, those in between.

Figure 11–8 illustrates this diversity with a news capsule type of newsletter produced by the San Diego Economic Development Corporation for industrial site selectors, a newspaper-style newsletter by Scripps Memorial Hospitals for potential users of hospital facilities, and a four-color newsletter produced by the San Diego Private Industry Council for potential employers of workers trained by the federal government.

The standard size is four pages, but pages can be easily added without upsetting design. Enclosures are also common. Most newsletters are at least typeset, though many are typewriter script or computer-generated. It is important to remember that the more an individual wants the information you provide, the more he or she will do to get it. While most of us wish we were in that position, in most instances, format should be designed for easy reading.

Format is also a reflection of the sponsor. Whereas it may be proper positioning for a charitable not-for-profit association to look prudent as it communicates with its members for donations or volunteer time, a prestigious law firm might be better packaged more upscale.

#### Maximizing Use of Graphic Elements

Use of messages in headlines, subheads, photographs, and photo captions can be useful in getting the attention of the more passive reader.

The *Dairy Council of California News*, illustrated in Figure 11–9, is distributed bimonthly to 3,000 dairy farmers and 200 dairy processing companies. Research shows that while the readers say they peruse the publication from cover to cover, they are more apt to skim it than read it carefully. Consequently, each story is told twice: once comprehensively in the body copy and again using the main points in the story headlines, subheads, photos, and photo captions. While newspapers use these graphic elements to draw the reader into the story, the Dairy Council uses them to both create interest and disseminate the critical elements of each article.

#### Planning the Newsletter

Planning the issues of a newsletter should start with the message/media outline. A number of priority message concepts should be identified to support the communications outcome.

The *Dairy Council of California News* communications outcome is to maintain a supportive funding constituency. Newsletter stories are planned around four first priority messages that must be supported somehow in each issue. There are also second and third priority messages, each of which must appear in one-fourth of the issues. Graphic elements are designed to support the message concepts rather than the story or photograph itself. Each issue is designed for both the more thorough reader and the "light" reader.

Once a year the management team is organized to brainstorm story ideas for each message concept. The newsletter then organizes a bimonthly story matrix, illustrated in Figure 11–10.

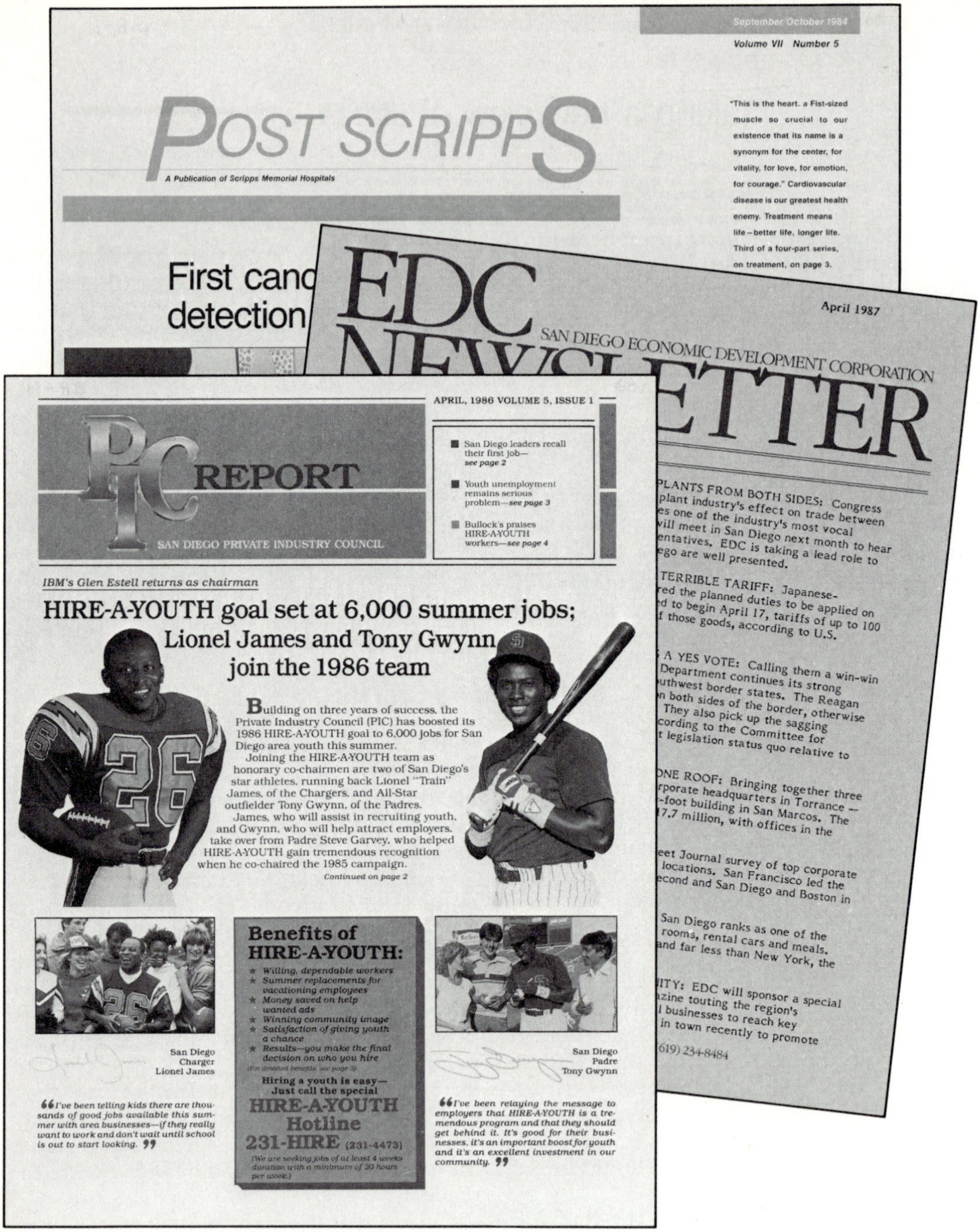


Courtesy of Scripps Memorial Hospitals, San Diego Private Industry Council, and San Diego Economic Development Corporation

**FIGURE 11–8**

Dairy Council of California

# NEWS

**In This Issue:**

- Trends Task Force Monitors Fat, Cancer Link
- DCC's Nutrition Education Program Makes 10-Year-Old Menu Planners
- Clover-Stornetta's Benedetti Joins DCC Board

*Developing Lifelong Values for Milk Through Nutrition Education: Mar.-Apr. 1987*

*Taking the Pressure Off Animal Fats*

## Scientists Tell Journalists & RDs: Balance Fats & Nutrients

*Los Angeles*—Consumers are shifting to lowfat dairy and meat products, key nutrient sources, but any benefit realized may be undermined by dramatic increases in use of vegetable and salad oils, a scientific panel told reporters and dietitians in February.

"People don't realize that salad and cooking oils are 100 percent fat despite cholesterol-free claims," said David Heber, M.D., Ph.D., chief of clinical nutrition at UCLA medical school.

Obesity, cancer and heart disease are linked to consumption of too much dietary fat.

Heber chaired a conference on dietary fat for registered dietitians and journalists, sponsored by Dairy Council and the California Dietetic Association. (CDA).

**Don't Go Overboard on Any One Fat**

The primary conference message was that consumers should not go overboard on any one fat but balance intake between saturated, polyunsaturated and monounsaturated fats. An equally important message was maintaining nutrient balance with the four food groups (milk, meat, vegetables and fruits, breads and cereals).

**Use of Cooking Oils Doubled Since '50s**

According to Heber, use of salad and cooking oils has more than doubled since the late 1950s and increased 15-fold since the early 1900s. Combined salad and cooking oil and shortening make up nearly 75 percent of the "fats and oils" group of fats in the American diet today.

**Animal Fats Decreased 20%**

Animal fats, on the other hand, have dropped in the diet from 78 percent to 58 percent since the late 1950s.

"Consumers are doing fine moving to lowfat dairy selections and lean meats, it's time now to look at other sources," Heber said.

In addition to vegetable oils, Heber said fat is hidden in foods such as doughnuts, potato chips, pies, cakes, crackers and packaged foods.

According to DCC Manager Cynthia Carson, the conference is part of a campaign to help health professionals and consumers interpret cut-back-on-fat recommendations to include milk and dairy foods.

"We picked up a concern in the health community over a trend toward increased use of vegetable and salad oils and saw it as a strategy to bring perspective to the fat issue," said Carson.

**Reduce Fats, Oils, Extras First**

"The conference hit the heart of our message," she said. "Consumers who want to cut back on fat should look first at extra foods, including fats, oils and foods with hidden fats.

*(Continued on page 4)*

*'Consumers are doing fine moving to lowfat dairy selections and lean meats, it's time now to look at other sources,' said David Heber, M.D., Ph.D., chief of clinical nutrition at UCLA medical school.*

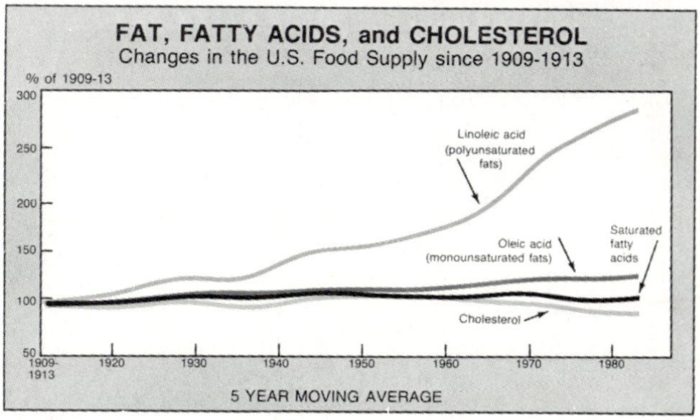


Courtesy of Dairy Council of California

**FIGURE 11–9**

CONCEPTS

First Priority

a. Program effect on target publics' consumption
b. Competitive niche: our business is behavior change vs. general nutrition education
c. Calcium/supplements/fat
d. Dairy food choices

Second Priority

e. 50% increase in impact
f. DCC leadership on a national scope

Third Priority

g. Importance of planning to future threats/opportunities
h. Quality of board members

| | JAN/FEB | MARCH/APRIL | MAY/JUNE | JULY/AUG | SEPT/OCT |
|---|---|---|---|---|---|
| FEATURE | a: Report of 5th grade program testing<br>c: Supplements press conference: program | | | | |
| BOX ITEM | b/f: Shortridge article in SNE Journal: Nowlin/Shortridge article in JNE | | | | |
| PHOTO | h: New board members | | | | |
| PHOTO ESSAY | a: Photos of Corona teenagers drinking milk/eating dairy foods | | | | |
| PROFILE | h: DeBos, new board chairman | | | | |
| HEADLINE | All concepts listed | | | | |
| TESTIMONIAL TEACHERS | b/d: Teenage program in Corona schools | | | | |
| INDUSTRY LEADER TESTIMONIAL | | | | | |
| GRAPH | a: Fifth grade test results | | | | |

**FIGURE 11–10**
**DCC Newsletter Content**

### Preparation of the Newsletter

News for the external newsletter is gathered in the same fashion as that described in Chapter 9 for employee communications. Photos and artwork are generated to expand priority messages.

Newsletter design should be developed by a commercial artist. The commercial artist can recommend the best design and format for the positioning you want to project and the messages you have to deliver. This expertise is most valuable in making masthead, column size, art, and typeface work the hardest to support the public relations message. If budget does not allow you to employ a commercial artist for every issue, retain one for the first issue and have a number of format variations drawn for future issues.

Once stories and headlines are written, photographs taken, and captions attached, the practitioner sketches a rough dummy (where you want each story and photo to go page by page) to share with the commercial artist or printer. Give the artist flexibility in strengthening the messages you want to deliver with each story. This process usually becomes more informal as the artist learns your basic likes and dislikes, and vice versa. The graphic artist sends out the copy for typesetting, photographs are sized, and a more precise, final dummy is prepared for your review. Now is the time for adjustments. Changes made later will be more expensive. Once you proof the final dummy for graphic adjustments and typographical errors, the final dummy is revised accordingly and sent to the printer who produces a proof from the print film or "blue line." You get one last chance to review it before printing. With the final approval, the newsletter is printed.

Newsletter distribution decisions are the same as those for any direct mailing. Lists can be drawn internally or through an outside mailing house.

## FLIERS/PAMPHLETS/BROCHURES

Fliers, pamphlets, and brochures are frequently used as support materials in public relations campaigns. A flier may be used to announce a community meeting; a pamphlet may be offered as additional information to write for in a news story; a brochure describing a company's capabilities might be used to enchance a legal firm's new business development.

Careful thought to the last step of the message/media outline or how a printed piece will be communicated or distributed is an important but frequently ignored step, according to graphic designer Al Townsend. Townsend asks five questions pertinent to the development of printed materials:

1. Will the piece be presented one on one with a member of the target audience?
2. Will it be distributed in a display rack with hundreds of other printed materials?
3. Will it be distributed as a point-of-purchase item?
4. Will it be picked up at a trade show booth?
5. Will it be distributed by mail?[23]

Answers to these questions assist the commercial artist in producing material with the greatest probability for a successful exchange of message between the sender and receiver.

### The Flier

Fliers are the simplest form of printed communications. Messages in fliers should be very basic, with little written or illustrated explanation. A flier might announce a special event or a speaker at next month's publicity club meeting. (See Figure 11–11.)

Flier design should move briefly through each stage of the message/media outline. Headlines are frequently used to raise an audience need, concern, or interest. The product, issue, or organization is offered as a solution in the headline, body copy, or logo. The consequences of inaction can often be implied in the headline; and mental rehearsal can be as simple as helping an individual with directions to get to an event or a voting site. The content of the flier should be clear, concise, and to the point.

A typical flier consists of a single 8½″ × 11″ sheet with one or both sides utilized.

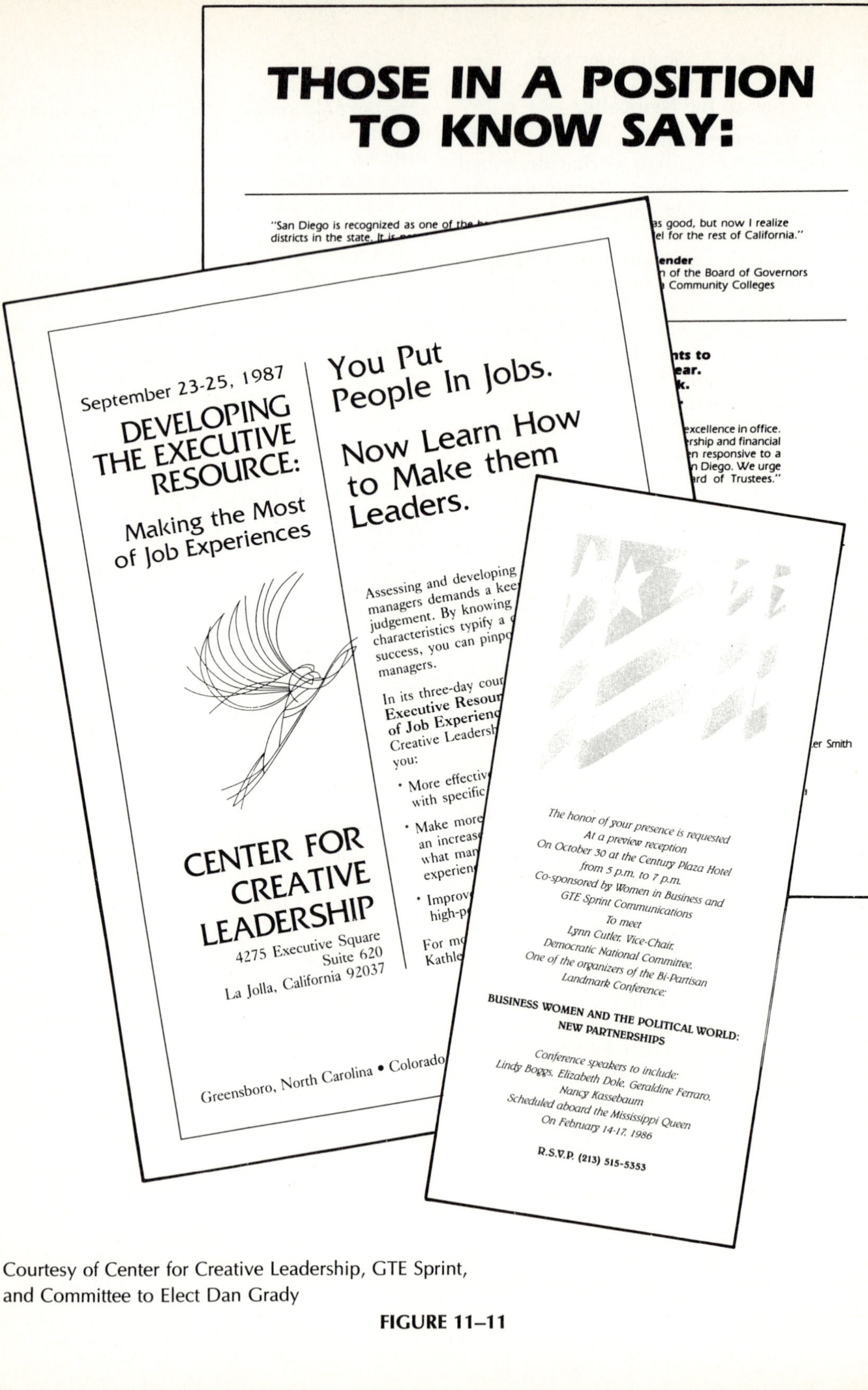

THOSE IN A POSITION TO KNOW SAY:
"San Diego is recognized as one of the
districts in the state.
s good, but now I realize
el for the rest of California."
of the Board of Governors
Community Colleges
excellence in office.
rsship and financial
n responsive to a
Diego. We urge
rd of Trustees."
September 23-25, 1987
DEVELOPING THE EXECUTIVE RESOURCE:
Making the Most of Job Experiences
You Put People In Jobs.
Now Learn How to Make them Leaders.
Assessing and developing
managers demands a kee
judgement. By knowing
characteristics typify a
success, you can pinpo
managers.
In its three-day cour
Executive Resour
of Job Experienc
Creative Leadersh
you:
CENTER FOR CREATIVE LEADERSHIP
4275 Executive Square
Suite 620
La Jolla, California 92037
Greensboro, North Carolina • Colorado
The honor of your presence is requested
At a preview reception
On October 30 at the Century Plaza Hotel
from 5 p.m. to 7 p.m.
Co-sponsored by Women in Business and
GTE Sprint Communications
To meet
Lynn Cutler, Vice-Chair,
Democratic National Committee,
One of the organizers of the Bi-Partisan
Landmark Conference:
BUSINESS WOMEN AND THE POLITICAL WORLD:
NEW PARTNERSHIPS
Conference speakers to include:
Lindy Boggs, Elizabeth Dole, Geraldine Ferraro,
Nancy Kassebaum
Scheduled aboard the Mississippi Queen
On February 14-17, 1986
R.S.V.P. (213) 515-5353


Courtesy of Center for Creative Leadership, GTE Sprint, and Committee to Elect Dan Grady

**FIGURE 11–11**

As a practical matter, if both sides are used, never assume that the reader will turn the flier over.

A public accounting firm is sponsoring a forum to help professionals take advantage of new tax law changes. The communications outcome is to generate new business. The public relations staff wants to produce an announcement flier to be mailed to potential clients.

What headline would raise a need, concern, or interest among potential account clients? How would you position the firm as a solution? How would you present consequences for not attending the forum? How would you help the reader think through the steps necessary to attend the event?

### Pamphlets

Like fliers, pamphlets may also consist of a single sheet of paper. The difference is that the one sheet of paper is folded into panel sections, either horizontally, vertically, or both. Each panel then represents an opportunity to separate content into manageable proportions and build it for reader retention.

The front panel frequently contains the headline, illustration, and some body copy. A headline lures the reader into the pamphlet, raising an audience need, concern, or interest. Each subsequent panel can be used to take the reader through the application steps of the message /media outline. The pamphlet design enables the writer to help the reader move to action with step-by-step directives. Pamphlets might also contain formats with which the reader can interact, for example, questions or answer blanks. (See Figure 11–12.)

Pamphlets are ideal formats for direct mail. A simple one- or two-fold can often be self-mailed with one panel devoted to the address. As with any printed matter designed for distribution by mail, check with your postmaster to be sure the planned design satisfies postal regulations.

To illustrate, the communications outcome for a Regional Employment Training Consortium (RETC) pamphlet is to sell employers on hiring RETC-trained low-income workers. The pamphlet headline describes the tax benefits (audience need) of hiring RETC-trained employees. Pamphlet panels are categorized by additional benefits for hiring RETC employees. The pamphlet leads the reader to the action he or she must take to realize the tax advantage. Distribution is to a carefully selected list of potential employers. The personalized direct-mail letter utilizes a personalized envelope as well. The pamphlet also responds to program inquiries, handouts at exhibits, or any number of uses.

### Brochure

The brochure is a step up in size from the pamphlet. Typically, a brochure has eight pages, or more, in four-page increments. It is bound by stitching, staples, glue, or other mechanism. (See Figure 11–13.)

The brochure should be reserved for more detailed and complex messages. Its size allows for expanded development of theme,

Try collecting samples of public relations fliers, pamphlets, and brochures. Check them closely. Do they raise an audience need, concern, or interest? Do they offer the product, issue, or organization as a means of meeting the need, minimizing the concern, or satisfying the interest? Are the consequences of inaction clearly presented? Do they help the reader think through how he or she can adopt the intended behavior in a real-life situation?

Describe situations where you would use a flier, pamphlet, or brochure.

Courtesy of West, Johnston, Turnquist & Schmitt, Ron Metz, and San Diego Private Industry Council

**FIGURE 11–12**

design, and multiple illustrations. Paper stock and color enhance the perceived importance of the piece.

West, Johnston, Turnquist and Schmitt produces a brochure as an annual report describing the firm's professional capabilities. The annual report is merely a packaging tool with financial material only generally presented. The true intent shows clients and prospective clients what the company accomplishes and how the reader can take advantage of new or expanded services.

This brochure is part of a Key Result Area to generate new business through existing and prospective clients. Thus, the communications outcome, outlined in the message/media outline, is to generate new client business. The financial needs, concerns, or interests of the audience are presented with elaborate graphics, and West, Johnston, Turnquist and Schmitt is effectively positioned as a solution. Distribution lists include clients, a carefully selected list of prospective clients, and key community and business leaders.

### Basic Design Principles

Placement and emphasis of graphic elements (i.e., headlines, photos, even the size and weight of the paper) can attract reader-

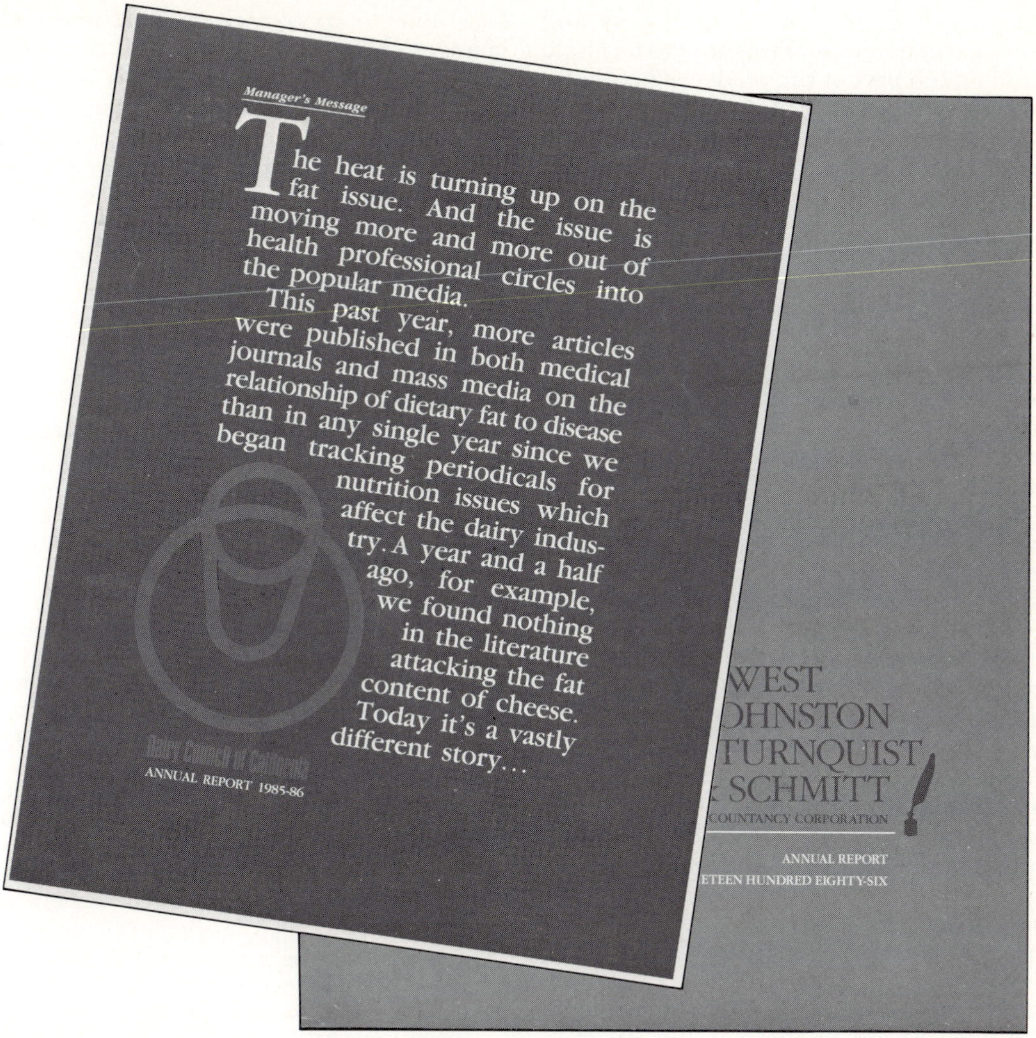


Courtesy of West, Johnston & Schmitt, and Dairy Council of California

**FIGURE 11–13**

ship and improve comprehension of the printed piece. A few basic principles can be applied to decisions on how graphic elements should be organized for a printed flier, pamphlet, or brochure:

1. The arrangement should have balance between headlines, artwork, body copy, logo, and white space.
2. The space should be divided into proportions pleasing to the eye.
3. A directional pattern (for the eye) should be evident.
4. A feeling of unity should prevail; avoid clutter.
5. One element, headline or artwork, should dominate all others.

These principles can be considered a design checklist that reads: balance, proportion, sequence, unity, and emphasis. All of these design principles work together to produce the most effective flier, pamphlet, or brochure. Headline, artwork, body copy, and white space should work together to facilitate action on the part of the reader. The reader should have a clear picture, through words and illustration, about the action he or she can take to achieve the benefits presented and avoid the consequences, however subtle, of inaction.

### Seek Professional Counsel

The most effective printed materials are those designed by a professional graphic designer or commercial artist. The practitioner must clearly communicate the elements of the message /media outline and provide best-guess judgment about where each element fits. Success or failure, to a large degree, depends on how effectively you communicate with production professionals. Past experience demonstrates that if you find a good commercial artist, printer, or artist/printer team, hold on to him or her. Such people are a valuable commodity worth any reasonable difference in competitive price.

Communication with graphic professionals is best accomplished by sketching a rough dummy with headlines, illustration/photo locations and approximate sizes, and body copy with every intention of creating balance, proportion, sequence, unity, and emphasis. All elements and the company name, address, and telephone number are typewritten on a separate page(s). A copy of the company logo and any photos you want incorporated into the printed piece round out the package of materials needed to share with your graphic artist or printer.

Note: When translating an English publication into another language, a material development specialist in foreign-language production is necessary because language differences can be major.

When you and your designer or printer agree on the content of the piece, placement of the graphic elements, and size and style of type, you are ready for printing. Your printer will assemble all of the elements on art boards for your first review; this is the best time to correct errors and make any changes. The second review will be a proof of the printing film or blue line. If your flier, pamphlet, or brochure uses several colors, you may request a color key that shows the elements in the colors as they will be printed. This proof is your last opportunity to make corrections or revisions before printing. Check for errors before returning to the printer for project completion.

## SUMMARY

- The message/media outline helps the practitioner systematically organize development of the corporate ad, direct-mail letter, newsletter, or other printed materials to best support the public relations plan.
- Two types of advertising can fall under the responsibility of public relations: corporate identity and advocacy. Corporate identity advertising aims at establishing an organizational image, and advocacy advertising directs a point of view at key opinion leaders on public issues that affect the corporation.
- Direct mail is one of the most effective but underutilized public relations techniques. While two-thirds of Americans read advertising direct mail, this ratio is enhanced in public relations because of increased subtlety and credibility.
- The effective use of newsletters by public relations practitioners balances the target audience's desire to be kept abreast of special needs/concerns/interests with information supporting communications outcomes. Most effective newsletters do not overpromote but present an objective, real-life view for credibility.
- Fliers, pamphlets, and brochures are utilized as educational materials and public relations support materials, from the simple announcement flier to a folded educational pamphlet to a more elaborate brochure describing an organization's capabilities.
- Printed materials should have graphic balance among all style and graphic elements. Graphics specialists are important to the success of printed materials and presentation of the message/media outline.

## EXERCISES

1. Prepare a list of pros and cons on both corporate identity and advocacy advertising that you would use in discussing these two techniques with fellow public relations students.
2. Assume you have called two advertising agency account executives into your office to discuss starting a corporate identity campaign. How would you explain the use of the message/media outline?
3. Assume you have been hired by your university extension to write a direct-mail letter to students aimed at increasing summer school enrollment. Develop a message/media outline and write the letter. How will you obtain a distribution list? How will you distribute the letter?
4. What printed material format would be most appropriate to promote summer school enrollment? Write the copy and develop a rough layout for a meeting with your commerical artist or printer.
5. In one of your first tasks as a new public relations staff person for United Way, your boss has asked you to evaluate all existing printed materials. To what questions will you seek answers?
6. Prepare a production schedule for the development of a newsletter for United Way donors.

## REFERENCES


1. Herbert Swartz, "Clout," *Public Relations Journal* (December 1986), 26.
2. Michael Winkleman, "Corporate Advertising," *Public Relations Journal* (December 1985), 22.
3. Ibid.
4. Ibid.
5. Ibid.
6. Michael Winkleman, "Workshop," *Public Relations Journal* (December 1985), 39.
7. Pat Botwinick, "The Image of Corporate Image," *Public Relations Journal*, 40 (November 1984), 28.
8. Roger Seasonwein, "Workshop," *Public Relations Journal* (December 1985), 38–39.
9. James E. Grunig and Todd Hunt, *Managing Public Relations* (New York: Holt, Rinehart & Winston, 1984), p. 517.
10. Special Report No. 1989, "Conversation with Herbert Schnertz on Advocacy Advertising," *PR News*, December 10, 1984.
11. Philip Maher, "Network TV Warms Up to Issue Advertisers," *Industrial Marketing* (August 1982), 39.
12. Bert Briller, "The Issue of Issue Ads," *Public Relations Journal* (October 1986), 32.
13. Ibid., 31.
14. Briller, op cit.
15. Special Report No. 1989.
16. Thomas F. Garett, "Two Worlds of Corporate Advertising," *Public Relations Journal*, 40 (November 1984), 28.
17. Tim D. Mullennix, ed., *Tools for Marketing* (San Diego: Regional Employment Training Consortium, 1986).
18. Richard S. Hodgson, *The Dartnell Direct Mail and Mail Order Handbook* (Chicago: Dartnell, 1980), p. 101.
19. Freeman Gosden, "Adweek Marketing Idea Showcase," unpublished workshop, Los Angeles, October 1984.
20. Len Strazewski, "Special Report," *Advertising Age*, March 7, 1985, p. 16.
21. Sheryl Ricker, Americalist, personal communication, July 29, 1987.
22. Grunig and Hunt, *Managing Public Relations* p. 455.
23. Al Townsend, personal communication, March 18, 1986.


## CASE STUDY

### The Problem

Local businessman Ryan Wallace is running for his fourth term on the Community College Board of Trustees. The faculty at one of the four community colleges in the district has aggressively campaigned to unseat all incumbents.

### Situational Analysis

During Wallace's tenure, part of which he served as chairman of the board, the community college district has experienced steady growth and an increase in academic quality. Wallace has a national reputation as a leader in the fight against illiteracy, and he recently organized a key seminar on the subject for the annual conference of the National Association of Community College Trustees. He is supported by leaders in the community and in education circles.

Students strongly support the quality of education offered at district colleges as demonstrated by the results of a poll taken by the three incumbents running for office:

- Ninety-three percent believe the district academic offering is excellent.
- Ninety-two percent rate the quality of vocational training high.
- Ninety-five percent say if they had it to do over again, they would attend a district college.

Wallace's opponent is a retired college professor. He is heavily supported by the faculty, particularly those at one campus faced with dwindling student census and severe fiscal problems. Trustees have put pressure on campus administration to "clean up its act." Animosity runs high between the troubled campus and district administration. In fact, the faculty senate there accused district trustees of poor management of the campus and unanimously expressed a vote of no confidence toward the board. Faculty district-wide has stalled collective bargaining in the hope of increased salaries though district salaries are above the national average. Wallace's opponent is using faculty unrest as a campaign issue.

Wallace has called you in for public relations counsel. He is concerned that the controversy could affect the outcome of the election, three weeks away.

Upon some investigation, you find that the heaviest concentration of voters are 30 to 44 years old and evenly distributed between gender and political affiliation. You know that you can purchase mailing lists by zip code of those registered to vote, those who have voted in prior elections, and those households with more than one voter. You also know that the biweekly newspaper in Wallace's area is highly read.

You recommend two large advertisements one week prior to the election and one direct-mail piece to those who have voted in prior elections (under the assumption that people don't get too excited about district college races). Wallace has given you the go-ahead.

1. Develop a message/media outline.
2. Sketch out a rough advertising concept, using the message/media outline as a guide, for a meeting with an art director.
3. Develop a direct-mail letter.
4. Develop copy for a direct-mail pamphlet to go with the letter, and sketch out a rough layout to go over with your printer.

# Index

## C



## D

## E



## F

## G



## H



## I

## J



## K



## L



## M

## N

## O

## P

## Q



## R

## S

## T



## U

## V



## W



## Y



## Z